# The Best Book of PFS: First Choice®

# The Best Book of

Joseph B. Wikert

## SAMS

*A Division of Macmillan, Inc.*

*11711 North College, Suite 141, Carmel, IN 46032 USA*

International Standard Book Number: 0-672-22663-4
Library of Congress Catalog Card Number: 90-70779

Publishing Director: *Richard Swadley*
Development Editor: *Richard Swadley*
Manuscript Editors: *Amy Perry, Lisa Bucki*
Production Coordinator: *J. Stephen Noe*
Cover Design: *DGS&D Advertising, Inc.*
Cover Photography: *Cassell Productions, Inc.*
Illustrator: *T. R. Emrick*
Production Assistance: *Wm. D. Basham, Claudia Bell,*
*Jill Bomaster, Sally Copenhaver, Travia Davis, T. R. Emrick,*
*Denny Hager, Tami Hughes, Bill Hurley, Cindy L. Phipps,*
*Louise Shinault, Bruce Steed, Mary Beth Wakefield*
Indexer: *Joelynn Gifford*
Technical Reviewer: *C. Herbert Feltner*

*Printed in the United States of America*

*To my mother- and father-in-law, Janet and Joe Craig. Thanks for all your support and words of wisdom over the years.*

# Overview

# Contents

## 12 Utilities 391

# Introduction

## What Is First Choice?

First Choice is a multipurpose, integrated software program that lets you perform five different types of tasks. For example, if you need to do any of the following, then PFS: First Choice may just be the tool for you:

- Write a significant number of letters, memos, reports, or papers.
- Keep track of numerous files and/or records of related information.
- Manipulate a large quantity of numbers and prepare financial reports, including graphs.
- Create presentation-quality graphs—and even slides.
- Use a computer to communicate with an electronic bulletin board such as CompuServe, or to send and receive files to another person's computer.

In industry terminology, each of these tasks is a specific *software application*. With First Choice, these applications are all rolled into one single integrated package rather than being available in five separate programs.

The beauty of First Choice is its flexibility and its ease of use. All the applications can stand on their own, or they can work together, sharing information created with one application and integrating it into another. You can easily switch from one application to another, using a set of commands and menus common to each. This feature is what makes the First Choice *environment* (the program as a whole and the way a user interacts with it) so easy to master. You are not required to reinvent the wheel every time you start working in one of the five applications.

Since its introduction, First Choice has progressed through several improvements and refinements to offer the user more benefits and features. This book focuses on the latest version of the program, Version 3.02.

# Five Applications in One!

If you have any experience with computers, you will recognize at a glance the power of the features offered by First Choice. Users new to computers will soon fall in love with the ease of use and flexibility of each application. Specifically, the applications offered by First Choice include the following:

- Word Processing
- Database Management
- Electronic Spreadsheet
- Graphs, Charts, and Slides
- Communications

The best feature of First Choice is that all the applications work together. When used individually, each enables you to complete a number of tasks satisfactorily. When used together, they will organize your work and automate your business or personal needs, thus becoming a tremendous boon to productivity. For example, you can add a word processing document to part of a spreadsheet and print it out, or move a spreadsheet report to a data file, or merge two data files together to make a larger one. First Choice does all these without your having to make any compromises. To get an overview of the entire program, let's review these five applications and the ways in which they can make you more productive.

## Word Processing

Home users and hobbyists, students and teachers, as well all business people, have a use for word processing. Using a word processor can simplify the writing of letters, memos, reports, articles, term papers, books, etc. Obviously, all of these tasks can be completed with a typewriter or even paper and pen; however, a word processor has a big advantage over the other two options. It allows you to display your words on a screen, change them, and move them around until you are satisfied—before you print those words out on paper. In addition, you can even store your words on a disk for future use.

First Choice's word processor includes a 75,000-word spelling checker, a 5,000-word personal dictionary, and a 20,000-word thesaurus to help you polish your writing. It is even easy to perform mail-merge (print customized form letters) using the features of the word processor.

Word processing not only offers greater flexibility and ease of use for the wordsmith, it also increases productivity. This is the real reason computers and word processing are so popular.

## Database Management

First Choice's database management function is sometimes referred to as the *file manager*. The typical analogy made when discussing a file system is to the card index. You remember those, don't you? A set of 3-inch by 5-inch cards, usually arranged alphabetically, which contain information such as names, addresses, telephone numbers, etc. Your card index may be secured with a large rubber band, or neatly placed in its own card file. Another filing system is the phone book. However, these filing systems are limited in their use because they can only be referenced in one manner, typically by recalling the last name. Suppose you can remember someone's street address but not his or her last name; or perhaps you know that the information you want is accessible either through the individual's occupation or social security number, but you can't remember which. Because a database manager enables you to find information in variety of ways, you can find what you need through whatever data you do happen to have about that person.

You create your own *forms* (layout and content for your "file cards") and set them up to be cross-referenced however you want. You design the form the same way that you might design your index card deck or file folder. You store the related information electronically within the specified form onto the hard disk or diskette. Once the form is designed and the information is stored, you can sort lists of information, print it out, or add, delete, and retrieve it without remembering particulars such as whether George's last name was Smith or whether he recently left IBM to start his own company in Delaware.

## Electronic Spreadsheet

By definition, the spreadsheet is an electronic matrix of rows and columns containing data and formulas used for mathematical manipulation and decision-making purposes. Seem complicated? It isn't. A spreadsheet is a tremendous aid in setting up accounting applications, such as an income statement or a balance sheet. Even better, suppose you want to play "what if" and change just a single value within the statement to see the impact on the bottom line of a financial report? A spreadsheet can quickly recalculate any scenario you desire and save valuable time because you don't have to redo the affected rows and columns manually.

As a bonus, the First Choice spreadsheet even offers compatibility with Lotus 1-2-3, the industry leader in standalone spreadsheet software. The spreadsheet is one of the most commonly used business applications today. (It also is the application that popularized the microcomputer.)

## Graphs and Slides

It is often desirable to add that "something extra" to a presentation. Using First Choice's graph feature, you can easily produce graphs of various types—choosing one of several typical graph types, or a text chart. If you wish you can create graphs and charts from scratch, or you can use the data imported from First Choice's spreadsheet. First Choice's flexibility also allows you to *preview* your graphs or charts (view them on-screen) before you print them out on paper.

## Communications

First Choice also offers electronic communications. The ability to link computers in different locations and move information between them is becoming an increasingly important need in computing today. With this feature you can easily communicate or "talk" with other computers via a phone line and a computer hardware device called a *modem*. You will be able to link up with electronic mail services and information services (such as MCI Mail and CompuServe) as well as with electronic bulletin boards operated by individuals for information sharing and chit-chat. You can even do electronic shopping and banking.

# Who This Book Is For

This book is designed for anyone who performs several different kinds of business tasks routinely—whether as part of a large company or alone in a small business. This includes just about everyone in today's business world. Many home users and hobbyists also will find that First Choice meets most computing needs at a reasonable cost. *The Best Book of PFS: First Choice* is intended to meet their computing needs also.

No knowledge of computers or prior experience with First Choice is required in order to use this book. It is designed to teach you how to use all of First Choice's application tools productively without knowing all the technical details of the computer itself. Of course, if you pick up a little computer literacy along the way, you can add this new-found knowledge to your own memory banks. We call it "computerese."

# Features of This Book

This book is designed to simplify the process of mastering First Choice. I have included several features that will help beginners as well as more experienced users find information quickly. These include:

- step-by-step numbered instructions for creating sample letters, spreadsheets, graphs, and databases—instructions that allow you to work at your computer and at your own pace
- real-world examples that you can modify to meet your own needs
- chapter summaries to help you remember the key concepts and techniques discussed
- margin notes that provide tips, hints, reminders, and summaries of key points.
- Quick Guides inside the covers to provide a handy reference to First Choice speed keys and keywords

## Conventions Used in This Book

To use this book properly, you should be aware of the following conventions:

1. Text that you are to type at the keyboard is printed in special computer type, like this: Type `Dear Mr. Smith:` and then press Enter.

Sometimes what you are to type will be set off from the paragraph, like this:

`I will soon learn to master First Choice.`

When you see that kind of typeface, enter the text exactly as shown, including any spaces and special characters.

2. Options, field names, and messages found on the screen are printed in boldface. Some examples: Select option 1, **Create a document**. Type 555-1234 in the **Phone Number** field. Notice the **16% full** message.

3. If you are to press two or more keys in combination (that is, hold down the first key while pressing the second), such keypresses will be separated by a hyphen (-). However, don't type the hyphen. For example, Ctrl-Shift-Del means hold down both the Control and Shift key while pressing the Delete key.

4. File names are printed in uppercase, for example, LETTER.DOC.

## Acknowledgments

I would like to express my appreciation to Wendy Grubow of Software Publishing Corporation, who provided me with up-to-date versions of PFS: First Choice. Thanks also to the application programmers and other development personnel at Software Publishing Corporation who created this easy-to-use integrated package. Finally, thanks to my wife Kelly and my children Sarah and Craig—this book would never have been completed without your help and understanding.

## Trademarks

All terms mentioned in this book that are known to be trademarks or service marks are listed below. In addition, terms suspected of being trademarks or service marks have been appropriately capitalized. SAMS cannot attest to the accuracy of this information. Use of a term in this book should not be regarded as affecting the validity of any trademark or service mark.

CompuServe is a registered trademark of H&R Block, Inc.

dBASE IV is a trademark of Ashton-Tate Corporation.

Lotus and 1-2-3 are registered trademarks of Lotus Development Corporation.

MCI-Mail is a trademark of MCI Corporation.

MS-DOS, Microsoft Excel, and Microsoft Word are registered trademarks of Microsoft Corporation.

PFS and First Choice are registered trademarks and First Publisher, Professional File, Professional Write, and Harvard Graphics are trademarks of Software Publishing Corporation.

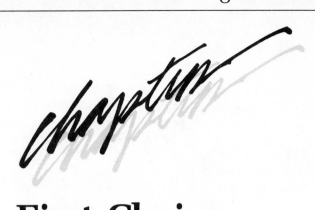

# First Choice Fundamentals

### In This Chapter:

- Quick Start To First Choice
- The Main Menu
- The Directory Assistant
- The First Choice Screen
- First Choice Menus
- Using Pull-Down Menus
- Getting Help
- Exiting First Choice

This chapter introduces you to the First Choice software, including a sneak peak at all the components that this rich software program offers. You will receive a tour of First Choice's Main menu as well as learn how to navigate in and out of the integrated programs and use specific menus with either the keyboard or a mouse. You will also discover how to use First Choice's help feature for those inevitable times when you get into trouble, and how to exit the program properly. We begin our quest by learning how to start First Choice from either a hard disk or a two-disk drive system.

# Quick Start to First Choice

*Back up your original*
*First Choice disks.*
When you start First Choice, you are transferring control of the computer to First Choice from DOS (Disk Operating System). How you start First Choice depends on your computer's configuration, that is, whether or not your computer has a hard drive or two floppy (or microfloppy) disk drives. Before you start First Choice, make a complete set of backups of your original First Choice disks and be sure First Choice is properly installed on your hard disk or floppy disk system. (If necessary, refer to Appendix A.)

## From a Hard Disk

After First Choice has been copied to the CHOICE directory (or the directory name you specified), follow these steps to start the program:

1. If necessary, turn on the computer and respond to the date and time *prompts* (angle brackets) as they appear. Press Enter after each time you respond. Soon, C> (the C prompt) appears. *Note:* Your hard disk drive may show D, E, or F instead of C in the *default* prompt (prompt that automatically appears unless you change it to something different).

   *Note:* You can accept the current date and time as set by the computer's internal clock by simply pressing Enter in response to each prompt. If you wish to enter a different date, type it in numerical form—that is, omit the day of the week and use the hyphen between numbers. (For example, December 1, 1990 becomes 12-01-90.) Then press Enter. Similarly, the time uses the computer's 24-hour system clock, so if you are entering a different time you must add 12 to the hours from 1:00 PM to 12:00 midnight. (For example, if you want 1:45 AM, type 1:45; for 4:45 in the afternoon, type 16:45.) Then press Enter.

2. Now, change to the directory where you installed the First Choice files (the CHOICE directory). Use the DOS change directory command (cd\) to specify the directory. Type

        cd\choice

   and then press Enter. If you called your directory something other than choice, type that name instead. (If you are already in that directory and you do this, no harm done—nothing will change.)

3. Type first and press Enter. Soon the First Choice Main menu appears on your screen, as shown in Figure 1-1.

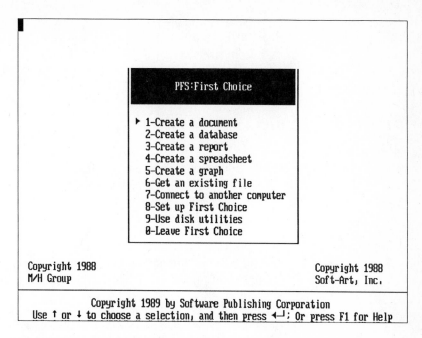

```
                    PFS:First Choice

              ▶ 1-Create a document
                2-Create a database
                3-Create a report
                4-Create a spreadsheet
                5-Create a graph
                6-Get an existing file
                7-Connect to another computer
                8-Set up First Choice
                9-Use disk utilities
                0-Leave First Choice

  Copyright 1988                        Copyright 1988
  M/H Group                             Soft-Art, Inc.

        Copyright 1989 by Software Publishing Corporation
   Use ↑ or ↓ to choose a selection, and then press ←┘; Or press F1 for Help
```

**Figure 1-1.** The First Choice Main menu offers several options.

## From a Two-Drive System

Start First Choice from a two-drive system using the following steps:

1. Insert the DOS diskette into drive A and then turn on the computer. (Remember to close the drive latch if needed.) Respond to the date and time prompts as they appear. Press Enter after each response.

2. The A> prompt should appear on your screen. If the B> prompt appears, make A the current drive by typing **A:** and pressing Enter.

3. Remove the DOS diskette from drive A and replace it with the disk labeled PROGRAM 1 for 5-1/4 inch drive systems, or for 3-1/2 inch drive systems, the disk labeled PROGRAM 1 and DICTIONARY DISK.

4. Insert a blank formatted disk into drive B. This is the drive you will use for the disks containing your files. (You will learn how to store files in the next chapter.)

5. Type **first** and press Enter. Soon, the First Choice Main menu appears, as shown in Figure 1-1.

*3*

*Note:* If you are working with a two-drive system instead of a hard disk, at times First Choice will direct you to remove the PROGRAM 1 disk from drive A and insert a different disk in order to complete specific tasks.

# The Main Menu

*You'll see the Main menu at the beginning and end of each work session.*

Every First Choice work session begins with the Main menu. Every time you start or leave an application, you will be returned to the Main menu. Let's examine the choices listed there.

The first five choices include all five parts of the First Choice program. Each of these five choices involves creating a new file for one of the applications: document, database, report, spreadsheet, or graph. These are the command options that you must use in order to start the application for the first time. Therefore, as you begin to learn each separate application, these are the commands you will use. If you wish to retrieve a file created in a previous work session, use the sixth choice, **Get an existing file**. This method is discussed in the next section.

The **Connect to another computer** command, option 7, starts the program for communicating with other computers. In Chapter 13, you will learn about using this feature. In order to use this option, you must also choose option 8, **Set up First Choice** (which is discussed in detail in Appendix A). Among other things, the setup option helps you install a modem for talking to other computers. Another, more common setup requirement is that of your printer—a must in order to print information created with First Choice.

The **Use disk utilities** option, 9, is handy for working with disks and files without ever leaving First Choice. For example, tasks generally completed at the DOS level, such as formatting and copying disks or erasing files, can be easily accomplished with this option.

And finally, the last item on the Main menu—**Leave First Choice**—is used for exiting First Choice and returning to DOS.

*To select an item, high-light it and press Enter; or point and double-click the mouse.*

To select an item from the Main menu, highlight the command name by pressing the arrow keys and then press Enter. If you have a mouse, you can also position the mouse unit pointer (the flashing rectangular box) on the command name and rapidly press the left mouse button twice, or *double-click*. The use of the keyboard and the mouse are explained in more detail later in this chapter.

# The Directory Assistant

*You can start an application by going into a file.*

The way you actually start a First Choice application is either by retrieving an existing file or creating a new one. If you choose to retrieve an existing file, you select the **Get an existing file** option from the Main menu. Choosing this command produces the Directory Assistant screen, which is shown in Figure 1-2.

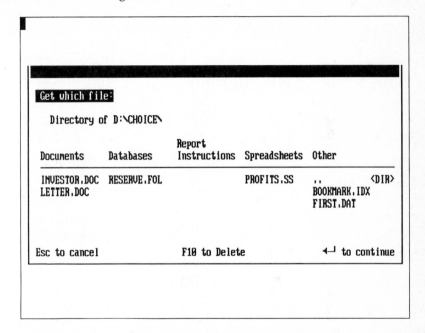

**Figure 1-2.** The Directory Assistant screen lists files available for you to work with.

The Directory Assistant lists all the files created in First Choice. This screen lists the files in columns according to the type of application in which they were created (**Documents, Databases, Report Instructions, Spreadsheets**, and **Other**, which lists graphs and other files that don't fit into any of the other columns). These file "types" are also identified by the type of file name extension (three letters following the period in a file name). All documents created with the word processor have the .DOC extension, databases have the .FOL extension, spreadsheets use the .SS extension, and graphs have the .GRA extension. As you progress through this book, you will learn more about all of the different file types and their extensions.

*First Choice includes some sample files with the program when it is shipped.*

When you access the Directory Assistant for the first time, you will notice that First Choice provides several sample files for your use, including two word processing or document files, INVESTOR.DOC and LETTER.DOC, as well as a spreadsheet file named PROFITS.SS. Not all file types appear the first time you access the Directory Assistant. For example, there is no .GRA file listed in the Directory Assistant because such a file has not yet been created. Later, after you have been working with First Choice for a while, the names and number of the files listed in the Directory Assistant will depend upon the type and number of files you have created during your previous work sessions.

# The First Choice Screen

The basic First Choice screen appears whenever you choose the **Get an existing file** command and use the Directory Assistant. It also appears when you begin an application by creating a new file, which you do by selecting one of the Main menu's "Create" command options. The exact appearance of the First Choice screen depends upon which type of application file that you create. For example, if you open a brand new word processing file with **Create a document**, then your screen looks like Figure 1-3. Figure 1-4 shows the First Choice screen of a new spreadsheet.

Although the elements of the First Choice screen vary from application to application, four key elements remain the same so that learning is easier. Each screen contains the following items:

- menu bar
- status line
- work area
- message line

None of these elements appears when you print your file; they are just there for your convenience and use.

## The Menu Bar

Running across the top of the screen is the area commonly referred to as the *menu bar*, from which you use either the keyboard or the mouse to

Flashing cursor                                                          Mouse cursor

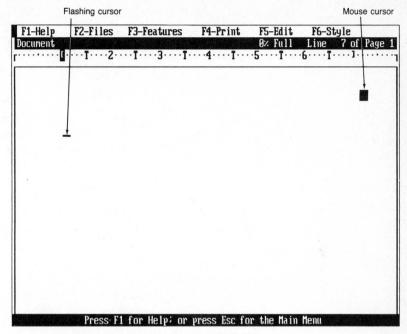

**Figure 1-3.** The empty word processing screen.

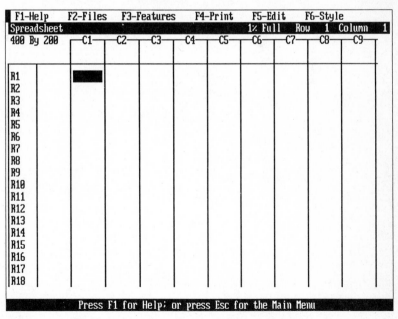

**Figure 1-4.** The empty spreadsheet screen.

pull down a list of available commands (the list is called a *pull-down menu*). The menu bar lists the same six menu items for all applications:

- Help
- Files
- Features
- Print
- Edit
- Style

Below each menu item itself is a separate list of commands that appears when you select that menu item. Although these commands vary slightly depending on the application, the basic consistency among many of them will help you master all the individual applications quickly.

To view the commands below a particular menu, select that option, using either the keyboard or a mouse (if you have one installed with your computer). With the keyboard, simply press the function key that appears next to the menu item in the menu bar. For example, to view the list of commands in the Files menu, press the F2 function key. If you do indeed have a mouse, you can open a menu by positioning the mouse unit pointer directly over the desired menu item and pressing the left mouse button once.

## The Cursor

*If you have a mouse, don't confuse the mouse pointer and the cursor. The cursor is smaller.*

One key element found on each First Choice screen is the *cursor*. The cursor shows you where what you type will appear on your screen (the *current location* or *current position*, in computerese). The way it looks depends upon which application you are using. If you are using the word processor, the database, or the communications application, the cursor appears initially as a blinking underscore. During a work session in any of these applications, the cursor may take on the shape of a flashing box (for example, when you type or delete text or when you press the Insert key to indicate insert mode in the word processor). In the spreadsheet and graphics applications, the cursor appears as a highlighted block that fills a particular cell (single section of a grid on the screen). The point to remember is that since the cursor "points" to the current position on the screen, any character that you type will appear at that location.

*The cursor actually points to the current location on*

If you have a mouse installed with your computer, you will notice that a second "pointer" appears on your screen. This pointer appears as

*the screen, while the mouse pointer simply shows the location of the mouse.*

a flashing rectangle and is called the *mouse pointer*. The movements of the mouse pointer reflect the movements you make with your desktop mouse. The pointer shows you the current position of the mouse itself—that is, where the cursor will appear if you click on the desktop mouse. Shortly, you will learn more about using the mouse with First Choice.

## The Status Line

*The Status Line tells the file name, the percentage of file space used, and the current position of the cursor.*

Located just below the menu bar is another handy feature consistently present in all First Choice Screens—the *status line*. This line provides you with useful information about your current application. For example, a new document file displays the word **Document** in the status line within the upper left-hand corner (see Figure 1-3). This indicates simply that you are using the word processor. (It would read **Spreadsheet** or **Graph** if you were using the spreadsheet or graphics application, respectively.)

The status line also tells you what percentage of the file space has been used as well as the current position of the cursor on the screen. As shown in the document screen in Figure 1-3, the status line in the word processing application shows **0% full** and **Line 7 Page 1** if you haven't entered any text just yet (First Choice automatically leaves six lines for the top margin). As Figure 1-4 shows, in the spreadsheet, the status line in a new file shows the words **Row 1 Column 1** at the top right. As you will see in Chapter 2, the status line changes as you enter new text on a second line or a new page.

## The Work Area

The work area is the largest area of the screen and is where you input information or data. The work area's exact characteristics depend upon which application you are using, and you will learn these as we progress throughout this book. For now, let's simply focus on the general features of the various First Choice work areas.

The work area of the *word processor* is relatively blank the first time you start a new document file. In the next chapter, you will learn to use this area to enter, edit, and change the appearance of text and print the result. In the *database*, the work area initially appears empty as well. The database work area is used to position the fields (places on the screen where you want each type of data—for instance, date of birth—to go). The *spreadsheet* work area shows a spreadsheet with rows and columns marked off, but with no headings or other information.

The *graphics* application presents a graph "form" that you will use to enter data and the labels for the graph. Finally, the *communications* application work area looks very similar to the word processor work area. You will use the communications work area to capture and manipulate information that you receive from another computer.

## The Message Line

*Use the message line as an additional resource when working through a task or application.*

At the bottom of the screen is another type of status line. This book refers to this line as the *message line*. The message line provides you with special information as needed about your current situation, such as which key to press to get help or how to escape to the Main menu.

# The First Choice Menus

Now that you are familiar with the basic First Choice screen, let's review the standard menus of the First Choice applications. Keep in mind that the wording of the commands below each menu varies from application to application but that the basic function of each command remains the same. The menus found on the word processing application are simple and representative of the others, so let's look at those.

## The Help Feature

*Press F1 for help related to where you are at the moment.*

At the far left of the menu bar is the Help feature, or F1 key. Unlike the other residents of the menu bar, the Help feature is not really a menu. Rather, it is a *context-sensitive* help function. This means that when you press the F1 key, the content of the help screen that appears relates to the operation you are trying to perform. For example, suppose you need more information about saving a new document to a diskette. Position the cursor on the command **Save a copy of this document** (which is found on the Files menu), and then press F1. First Choice displays a help screen that provides additional information about saving the document, as shown in Figure 1-5.

Many help screens contain more information than can be shown in a single screen. To remedy this problem, a message at the bottom of the screen will tell you to press the Page Down key (PgDn) to see a second screen (use PgUp to return to the previous screen). To exit the help screen, simply press the Esc key.

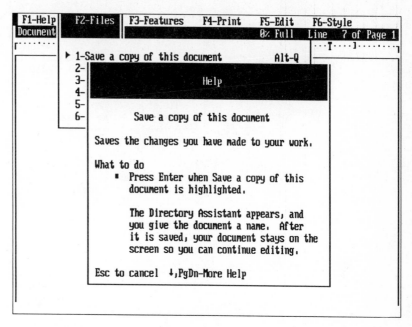

**Figure 1-5.** The Help feature provides context-sensitive help.

## The Files Menu

Named appropriately, the Files menu is what to select when you wish to work with files as units (rather than, for instance, changing the data in a file). For example, choose the Files menu (by pressing F2) when you want to store a document or a portion of a document to your diskette or hard disk. If you wish to retrieve an existing file already stored on your disk, then the Files menu is your choice. The Files menu also lists options for merging the contents of two documents, saving the file that appears on your screen in a different format, accessing the disk utilities feature, and making the current file the default one for that application. Figure 1-6 shows how the open File menu looks in an open word processing application.

## The Features Menu

The Features menu is the only menu that is very specific to the application that you are running currently. Press F3 to view a number of spe-

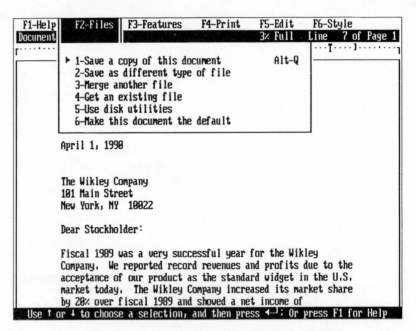

| F1-Help | F2-Files | F3-Features | F4-Print | F5-Edit | F6-Style |
|---------|----------|-------------|----------|---------|----------|

Document                                                    3% Full   Line   7 of Page 1

▶ 1-Save a copy of this document                Alt-Q
  2-Save as different type of file
  3-Merge another file
  4-Get an existing file
  5-Use disk utilities
  6-Make this document the default

April 1, 1990


The Wikley Company
101 Main Street
New York, NY 10022

Dear Stockholder:

Fiscal 1989 was a very successful year for the Wikley
Company. We reported record revenues and profits due to the
acceptance of our product as the standard widget in the U.S.
market today. The Wikley Company increased its market share
by 20% over fiscal 1989 and showed a net income of

Use ↑ or ↓ to choose a selection, and then press ◄─┘; Or press F1 for Help

**Figure 1-6.** The File menu with the word processor active.

cial tools specific to the current application. For example, in the word
processor (see Figure 1-7) you will find the commands to set margins
and tabs, search and replace text, use the spelling checker and thesaurus, set and modify rulers, and use the First Choice calculator.

Special commands are found on the Features menu as well. One
such option is the *bookmark* feature. The bookmark is the tool that you
use to mark your place for reference. This option is useful when moving
from one document to another or from one application to another (for
example, spreadsheet to word processor).


## The Print Menu

Choose the Print menu (F4) when you are ready to print the result of
your work. As shown in Figure 1-8, the word processor version of the
Print menu gives you the choice of printing the current document in its
entirety, or only a portion of it. You can also use this option to print
form letters and mailing labels, and to print or display slides from the
current document.

In other applications you find that the Print menu is limited in its
command options. However, in those and in word processing, once you
do elect to use one of the print commands, you will need to make addi-

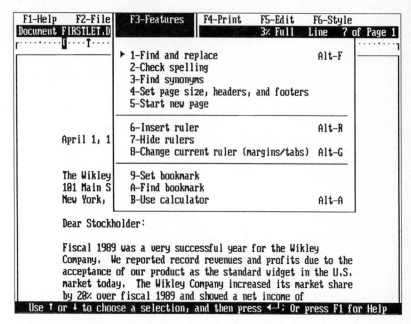

**Figure 1-7.** The Features menu with the word processor active.

tional choices, such as the placement of print, the quality of print, and the number of copies to print. You will learn about these as well as additional print selections as we progress through the chapters dedicated to the individual applications themselves.

## The Edit Menu

The contents of the Edit menu (accessible by pressing F5) also changes slightly from application to application. Like all menus, the basic function of the Edit menu remains the same—to change information that you entered previously. In the word processor, you will use the Edit menu to add, delete, or modify text (see Figure 1-9). The Edit menu makes use of a special feature in First Choice called the "clipboard." The clipboard is a temporary holding place in memory that allows you to cut, copy, and paste text into your documents. You will learn a great deal more about the clipboard and how it functions in the next chapter.

## The Style Menu

*Dress up your work with the offerings of the Style menu.*

Everything should have a little style, and the Style menu is your means for doing this. Not every application offers as many style selections as the word processor (the spreadsheet only offers two, for example). Press

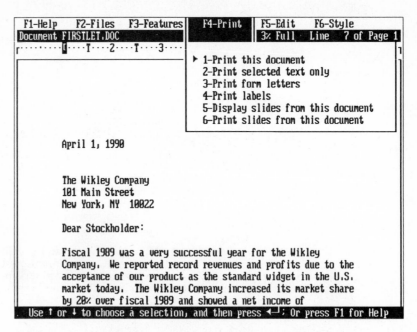

**Figure 1-8.** The Print menu when the word processor is active.

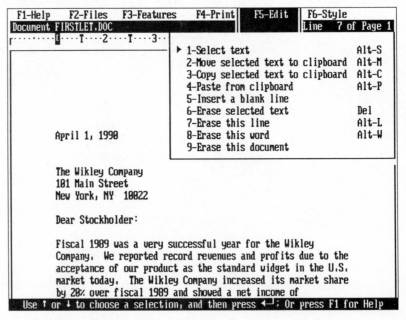

**Figure 1-9.** The Edit menu when the word processor is active.

F6 and you will see a list of options for really dressing up your documents, as shown in Figure 1-10. You can add boldface, underline, or italics to your text with the Style menu. You can even create superscript and subscript characters. Select from single or double spaced text, or change the font of slides easily and quickly with the Style menu.

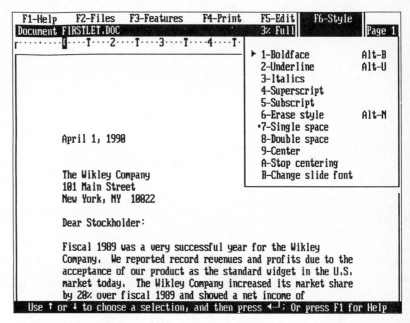

**Figure 1-10.** The Style menu when the word processor is active.

# Using the Keyboard

If you have ever used a typewriter (or even if you haven't), then using the keyboard will come naturally to you. It is important that you understand how the computer keyboard works in First Choice. Although the type of keyboard that you have may vary, all keyboards offer three general areas of keys: the typewriter keys, the function keys, and the cursor movement keys. Figures 1-11 and 1-12 depict two different keyboards featuring these basic keys.

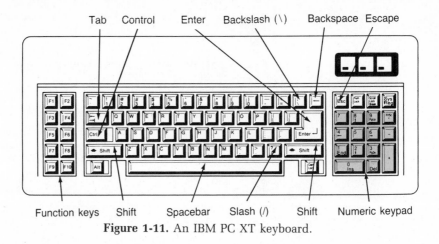

Tab   Control   Enter   Backslash (\)   Backspace   Escape

Function keys   Shift   Spacebar   Slash (/)   Shift   Numeric keypad

**Figure 1-11.** An IBM PC XT keyboard.

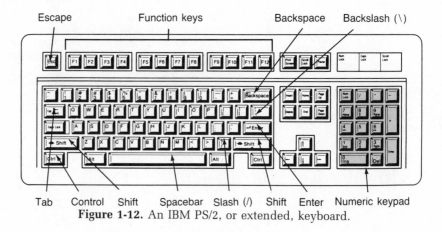

Escape   Function keys   Backspace   Backslash (\)

Tab   Control   Shift   Spacebar   Slash (/)   Shift   Enter   Numeric keypad

**Figure 1-12.** An IBM PS/2, or extended, keyboard.

# The Typewriter Keys

The typewriter keys include a subset of keys called the alphanumeric keys. The alphanumeric keys are located in the center of the keyboard and are identified by letters of the alphabet, numbers, and special characters. To enter a character, simply press the appropriate key on the keyboard.

In addition to the alphanumeric keys are the standard typing keys, including: spacebar, Tab, Shift, Caps Lock, and backspace.

These keys work much the same way as they do on a standard typewriter. For example, if you hold down the Shift key while pressing a letter key, then the letter appears on your screen in uppercase (or lowercase if Caps Lock is activated). If you press the Caps Lock key to activate the Caps Lock mode, then all the letters that you type appear in uppercase. Caps Lock only affects the letters of the alphabet, and not the special symbols, such as the asterisk. As a result, to type a special symbol, you must hold down the Shift key while you press the symbol key.

The most commonly used key of all is that of the Enter key. Identified as Return or with the ⏎ symbol on many keyboards, the Enter key tells the computer that you are finished with a command and are trying to communicate with it. In many applications, such as the word processor, pressing the Enter key moves the cursor like a carriage return and place it at the beginning of the next line.

*The Alt key is used in shortcut key combinations.*

One additional key that deserves special mention is the Alt key. Pressing the Alt key in combination with another key is a shortcut or "speed key" method for choosing a command or performing an action. For example, you can press Alt-B to apply boldface to text or Alt-Q to accomplish a quick save while working in the word processor. We will explore the speed key methods as we progress through each application, but if you want to see them now, turn to the Quick Guide on the inside front cover, which lists all the speed key combinations for quick reference.

## The Function Keys

Depending upon your keyboard, you will find a group of keys labeled from F1 to F12. These keys are referred to as the *function keys*. In First Choice, these keys are used frequently. F1 through F6 are used to open each one of the corresponding menus that appear on the menu bar at the top of your screen. The remaining function keys are used to perform a specific action that depends upon the application. For example, pressing F10 in the database application will start a search of the database or display the next record.

## The Cursor Movement Keys

The section on the right side of your keyboard features the cursor movement keys, and generally includes an area called the numeric keypad. Among other keys, the numeric keypad includes four arrow keys, plus the Home key, the End key, and a Page Up (PgUp) and a Page Down (PgDn) key. Basically, these keys are used to move your cursor around to different areas on your screen. For example, the left arrow moves your cursor one space to the left while the right arrow moves your cursor one space to the right. Pressing the Home key moves the cursor to the beginning of the line or row. Some keys pressed in combination with the Ctrl key move the cursor even faster. For example, pressing Ctrl-Home moves the cursor to the beginning of the file (often the upper left-hand portion of the screen).

Pressing the Home or End key twice in succession moves the cursor to the top or bottom of the screen respectively. Pressing the key three times in succession moves the cursor either to the top or the bottom of the file.

The movement of the cursor is generally consistent from one application to another within First Choice. Keep in mind that when you are using a numeric keypad, the Num Lock key must be turned off. If the Num Lock key is pressed, then the Num Lock mode is activated and any keypress on the numeric keypad will produce the designated number on your screen instead of moving the cursor. Table 1-1 lists all the movements of the cursor from the numeric keypad.

*Note:* A key not on the numeric keypad that is used to move the cursor is the Tab key. In the word processor, pressing Tab will move the cursor to the next tab stop. In the spreadsheet, pressing Tab will move the cursor to the next cell. See Table 1-1 for more cursor movements using the Tab key.

**Table 1-1.** Moving the Cursor with the Numeric Keypad.

| What You Press | Where the Cursor Moves |
|---|---|
| Left Arrow | Left one character |
| Right Arrow | Right one character |
| Up Arrow | Up one character |
| Down Arrow | Down one character |
| Ctrl-Left Arrow | Left one word |
| Ctrl-Right Arrow | Right one word |
| PgUp | Up one full screen |
| PgDn | Down one full screen |
| Ctrl-PgUp | To the top of the current column |
| Ctrl-PgDn | To the bottom of the current column |
| Home | To the beginning of a line or row |
| Ctrl-Home | To the beginning of the file |

| What You Press | Where the Cursor Moves |
|----------------|------------------------|
| End | To the end of the line or row |
| Ctrl-End | To the end of the file |
| Tab | Right to the next tab stop |
| Shift-Tab | Left to the previous tab stop (or previous cell or field) |
| Ctrl-Tab | To the previous cell or field |

# Using the Mouse

*Unless told otherwise, use the left mouse button.*

If your system comes equipped with a mouse, you will find it simple to use when working with First Choice. The mouse can increase your productivity by eliminating unnecessary keystrokes. A rectangular block, or mouse cursor, moves in directions corresponding to the way you roll your mouse around on your desktop. The mouse allows you to make selections from the screen by positioning the mouse cursor on a specific menu or command to highlight it, and then clicking, or pressing the left mouse button. Your mouse may be equipped with one, two, or three buttons. Unless told otherwise, use the left mouse button.

The mouse requires a flat surface such that you can move the mouse freely in approximately six inches in all directions. The movement of the mouse cursor corresponds to the movement of the small rubber ball on the bottom of the mouse. If you have trouble positioning the mouse pointer on the screen because the free surface is limited, lift the unit to another surface area. The position of the mouse cursor will not be changed until the ball is further displaced.

Using the mouse requires a little patience at first. Soon, however, you find that using a mouse is a natural extension of the way you work—basically, pointing and choosing. The following is a summary of the basic mouse operations:

*The small triangle also will appear next to a selected command.*

- *Moving the mouse cursor.* Use the screen as the reference point for the mouse cursor. Remember, the mouse can be lifted and put down again, allowing free movement of the unit.
- *Pointing.* When pointing the mouse pointer at an object, position the cursor directly over that object. For example, when selecting a command from a menu, position the mouse cursor directly

over the command name itself. You will know the command is selected because it will appear highlighted within the menu.

- *Dragging.* This operation is typically used for selecting text or cells. For example, position the mouse cursor at the beginning of the text or cells that you wish to select, press the mouse button, and—without releasing it—move the mouse unit to drag or change the location of the mouse cursor and thus highlight the text or cells. When you release the mouse button, the high-lighted text (or cells) remain highlighted and your selection has been defined.

- *Clicking.* Pressing the mouse button once is called *clicking.* Besides clicking to select menu items, you can use clicking to select a new location for the mouse cursor or to open a menu. For example, if you point at a specific menu name and click the left mouse button, the menu opens and stays open. Click outside the menu to close the menu.

- *Double-clicking.* Similar to clicking. The mouse button is rap-idly pressed and released twice. This is sometimes used to select and activate a choice in a single sequence or operation.

You will find that both the mouse and keyboard come in handy for using all the features of First Choice to their full power. The beauty of First Choice is that you can use either method, or a combi-nation of both, for accessing menus and choosing commands. The sections that follow use both methods. Try them both, and then decide what's best for you.

# Using Pull-Down Menus

This section briefly discusses the important features of First Choice menus. Specifically, we review how to open and close a menu, how to activate a menu command within a menu list, how to move from one menu to another, and how to exit a menu. All of these actions can be completed using either the keyboard or a mouse.

## Opening and Closing Menus

The simplest way to open any specific menu item is to press the corresponding function key. For example, if you wish to display the contents of the Files menu, press the F2 key once and release. A pull-down window appears to display its contents and remains open until you close it. If you have a mouse installed with your computer system, you can open a menu by simply moving the mouse cursor directly over the menu name and clicking the left mouse button.

*Repeatedly pressing the Esc key eventually takes you to the Main menu.*

To close the window, you have three options: simply press the same function key a second time, press the Esc key, or if you have a mouse, position the mouse cursor outside the open menu and click the mouse button once. If you press a function key to open a menu, pressing the Esc key will cancel the previous command and return you to where you were before the function key was pressed.

## Choosing a Menu Command

First Choice provides several options for selecting commands from a menu. One option is to use the up- and down-arrow keys to move the highlight to the desired command location. Highlighted text appears in reverse video (or background color if you have a color monitor) and is also marked with a blackened (or colored) right triangle. Then press Enter to choose that command. If the highlighting is already on the desired choice—and it usually is because the first option is usually the most frequently used— simply press Enter once. If you have a mouse, move the mouse cursor directly over the command to highlight it, and then click the mouse button.

A fast method for choosing a command is to simply type the number that precedes the desired command. Using this short cut method prevents the need to press the Enter key.

The last option for choosing commands is only available with some command options. This feature is the *speed key* option. Pressing any available speed key combination also eliminates the need to press the Enter key. For example, pressing Alt-L erases a selected line of text in the word processor application, while pressing Alt-B applies the boldface format to the same text. The latter option is faster than first opening the Style menu and then moving down to find the boldface option.

## Moving from One Menu to Another

Moving from one menu to another is easy with First Choice. During a work session you might open a pull-down menu by selecting the appropriate function key, complete your work, and close the menu by pressing the same function key again. If you wish to open a different menu instead, you can either close the first menu by pressing the function key a second time, or better yet, simply press a different function key that corresponds to a new window. First Choice will automatically close the first menu and open the second menu that corresponds to the specific function key.

As a handy resource, you can also use the Tab key to step through a cycle of open menus on the menu bar, moving left to right, closing and opening the respective menus with each successive key-press. Of course, for the Tab key to be used in this fashion, the menu bar must first be activated by opening any one of the menus.

# Getting Help

Many programs today offer a help feature, and First Choice is no exception. The First Choice help utility is designed to provide assistance with any action that you are currently performing. This context-sensitive type of help feature doesn't require that you know exactly what you're doing, you need only to know that you need additional information in order to complete a given task. When you need help with a specific situation you find yourself in, simply press the Help key, or F1. When you want information about a specific menu or command, first highlight that option and then press F1. Don't press Enter or click the mouse button once the option is selected; simply press F1 to display one of First Choice's help screens.

# Exiting First Choice

When you are ready to exit First Choice, return to the Main menu by pressing the Esc key several times until the Main menu appears on your screen. From the Main menu, press the 0 key or highlight the **Leave First Choice** command and then press Enter, or click the left mouse button. In the next chapter you will learn how to save your first file before exiting the word processor application. If you don't save the existing file before you attempt to execute the Leave First Choice command, First Choice will warn you to do so as a safeguard. Once you exit First Choice, you will be returned to the DOS prompt.

*Exit First Choice before turning off your computer.*

Do not simply turn off your computer without exiting First Choice properly. If you do, you will bypass the reminder about saving your current file and risk losing some valuable information that you wished to save. In general, it's simply poor practice not to exit First Choice through the Leave First Choice command.

# Summary

- You learned to start First Choice from a hard disk: type cd\ followed *immediately* by either choice or the appropriate directory, to change to the directory where the First Choice files are installed, and press Enter. Type first and press Enter. The First Choice program should appear on your screen.

- To start First Choice from a two-drive system, first load DOS and then insert the PROGRAM 1 disk into drive A. Type first and press Enter to load First Choice.

- You were introduced to the First Choice Main menu and how to use the Directory Assistant to retrieve an existing file.

- You learned about all the primary parts of a standard First Choice opening screen: the menu bar, the status line, the work area, the message line, and the cursor.

- You learned that there is essentially one standard menu for all the First Choice applications. The wording of the commands within each menu varies from one application to another, but the basic functions remain the same.

- You were introduced to some of the basics of First Choice, including the keyboard, the pull-down menus, and the mouse, and you learned how to choose a command with either a mouse or the keyboard.

- Finally, you learned how to get help if you need it and how to properly exit First Choice.

# Introduction to Word Processing

**In this chapter:**

- Starting the Word Processor
- Entering Text
- Correcting Typos
- Moving Around the Screen
- Inserting Blank Lines and New Paragraphs
- Typing Your First Letter
- Saving Your Document
- Printing Your Document
- Summary

Word processing is the most commonly used application today. If you ever have a need to create a letter, memo, report, or the like, then a word processor is your road to increased productivity. The reason is simple. Word processing allows you to make corrections, deletions, and modifications to your text without worrying about correcting misspellings and poorly written phrases when you are first writing. The beauty of word processing is that it allows you to concentrate on the creativity of the writing itself. Revising a draft is simple. Instead of trying to get it right the first time and/or wasting valuable time in retyping a letter, you can use all of the features of a word processor to revisit your work and modify it to improve the quality of writing.

In this chapter you'll be introduced to the basics of using the First Choice word processor. You'll learn how to enter text, move around the screen, and make corrections to simple typing errors. Then, you'll learn how to create, save, and print your first letter.

We begin by reintroducing the word processor screen. If you haven't yet installed First Choice, refer to Appendix A.

# Starting the Word Processor

Like all applications, you start the word processor from the Main menu. If the Main menu doesn't appear on your screen and the program is loaded, press the Esc key several times until it does. Once the Main menu appears, you have a decision to make in regard to how to start the word processor. You can elect to begin by opening a brand new *document file*, or you can retrieve one that already exists. (In First Choice, anything that you create is called a *file*, which is the basic storage unit on a disk or hard disk, and a file created with the word processor is referred to as a *document*.)

*First Choice provides some sample document files.*

Thus, to start the word processor from the Main menu, make either of the following selections:

**1-Create a document**. This starts a new document file.

**6-Get an existing file**. This accesses the Directory Assistant screen so that you can retrieve a document file that already exists.

Let's assume that you haven't created any new documents just yet and don't want to use a pre-supplied document. So press 1, or highlight the command with the arrow keys and press Enter, or move the mouse directly over the command and click the mouse button. Soon, the word processor screen appears, as shown in Figure 2-1.

# The Word Processor Screen

Once the word processor screen appears, you will notice several elements and their location immediately. As introduced in the last chapter, the blinking cursor appears in the upper left-hand portion of the screen.

## The Status Line and Menu Bar

The exact position is identified by the information line or *status line* that appears just below the menu bar. Specifically, the information indi-

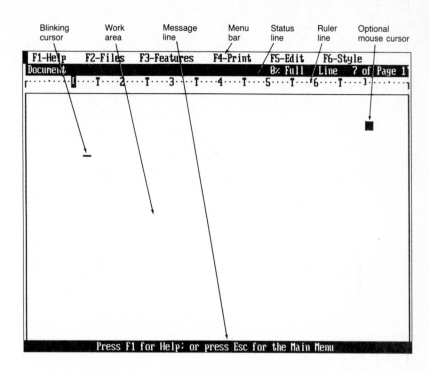

**Figure 2-1.** The blank word processor screen.

cates that the cursor is located at line 7 on the first page and that 0 per cent of the document space has been used. First Choice begins on line 7 instead of line 1 since a top margin of 6 lines is provided automatically, or as a *default*, in computer terms. Of course, if the information line doesn't read **Document** on the far left side, then you're not in the word processor.

*One document will hold about 20 single-spaced pages.*

The total amount of memory available for a word processor document is approximately 20,000 characters, or roughly 20 single-spaced pages. If your document will exceed this amount, divide it into more than one document.

At the top of the screen resides the menu bar. As explained in Chapter 1, the menu bar includes the following menus: Help, Files, Features, Print, Edit, and Style. At the bottom of the screen are two reminders—to use the context-sensitive Help function (press F1) if you get into trouble or simply need additional information, and to press the Esc key if you need to return to the Main menu.

## The Ruler Line

Finally, you'll find another row of information displayed on the screen, called the *ruler line*. The ruler line is the third line down from the top of the screen and includes column numbers, tab settings, margin settings, and the cursor position as expressed by a specific column. Column numbers on the ruler line are identified by periods and numbers in the following manner: The leftmost column is column 1 and the rightmost column is column 80. Each period represents a single column. The column numbers that you see on the ruler line are in increments of tens. In other words, the first period is column 1 and the column identified by the numeral 1 is actually column 10.

As you move the text cursor by typing text or using any of the cursor movement keys, you will notice that the cursor position is represented on the ruler line by a solid box. This cursor position corresponds to the movement of the cursor on the word processor "work area" and represents its exact column location.

Tab settings on the ruler line are identified by the letter T. As you can see from Figure 2-1, First Choice has set several default tab stops for you. The margin settings are initially set by First Choice at columns 10 and 70 and are identified by the square brackets ([ and ]) for left and right margin respectively.

If you opened an existing file by mistake and you really wanted to open a new document file (or vice versa), press Esc to return to the Main menu and then choose the appropriate command option.

# Entering Text

Entering text on a word processor should be simple—and it is. You don't need to worry about how your text looks now. If you make a typing mistake, you can easily fix it later. If you have ever used a typewriter, you will find the function and layout of a computer keyboard to be very similar. Yet, as you begin to master First Choice and use the keyboard, you will soon discover that a typewriter doesn't offer nearly the same amount of flexibility as the computer keyboard.

To begin our lesson on entering text, type the following paragraph exactly as it appears. Before you start though, there are two don'ts.

1. *Don't* worry about any typos that you might enter. (I have intentionally added a couple myself to be corrected in the next section.)
2. *Don't* press Enter as you reach the end of a line. If you accidentally press Enter, before you type anything else, press the backspace key once and begin to type again.

## Automatic Word Wrap

*Don't press Enter unless
you want to start a new
paragraph.*

First Choice offers a feature called *automatic word wrap*. As you type text and you reach the end of the line, First Choice recognizes the default right margin setting (at column 70) and then automatically wraps text to the next line. If a word is going to be incomplete when the end of the line is reached, then First Choice won't break the word into two parts, but rather it will move down to the next line and type the whole word there. Thus, the word wrap feature acts like an automatic carriage return on a typewriter. You don't need to press the Enter key unless you intend to start a new paragraph.

For an exercise and to get familiar with your keyboard, type the following: (*Note:* Your screen may hold more words on a single line than appears here. Just keep typing until the entire paragraph is complete.)

```
The forecast for saless in 1990 appears to be good despite a
decline in the market for the past year. Our positive forecast is
due to the introduction of the super dooper micro chip that will
drive the new line of products. This, coupled with the moderniza-
tion of the Mobile, Alabama plant, means production should be at
full capacity by the end of the second quarter.
```

As you entered the text above, did you notice the status and ruler lines changed some values as the cursor moved across the screen? You should have noticed the word wrap feature as well. Let's now take the next step and correct any typos that you may have entered as well as the ones that we inserted intentionally. To accomplish this though, you must first review how to move the cursor around your screen.

# Correcting Typos

As you enter text, you will likely make some typing mistakes. Before you can learn about making corrections, you need to have a clear understanding of how to get to the part that needs correcting.

## Moving Around the Screen

In Chapter 1, you learned how to move the cursor around your screen using the direction keys (the arrow keys) as well as the remaining cursor control keys located on the numeric keypad area of the keyboard. If you have a mouse installed with your system, you can move the text cursor by first moving the mouse cursor to the desired position on the screen and then clicking the mouse button. The importance of moving the cursor soon becomes apparent when you discover a typo in your text. To correct the typo, you must be able to move the cursor to that location on your screen.

*Check the Num Lock key if you see unwanted numbers on-screen when you try to move the cursor.*

If you press the arrow keys on the numeric keypad and you see numbers appear on the screen, that means the keyboard is currently in Num Lock mode. To remedy this, press the Num Lock key to toggle it off, and thus switch the numeric keypad to its other function as a cursor control pad.

## Methods of Correcting

In order to correct mistakes, you can use one of several methods:

1. Press the backspace key repeatedly until all the text is erased, type the correction, and then retype the remaining text all over again.

2. Move the cursor to the location just past the error, press the backspace key as necessary to erase the error, and then type the correction.

3. Move the cursor to the location just in front of the error, press the Del key as necessary to delete the error, and then type the correction.

4. Move the cursor to highlight or "select" the incorrect text, press the Del key to erase the text, and then type the correction. This method, including how to select text, is discussed in greater detail in the next chapter.

For most simple errors, you can use one of the first three methods to delete any unwanted text in your documents. To illustrate, let's correct the sample text that we entered previously. The first error occurs in line 1, where the word **sales** is misspelled as **saless**:

The forecast for saless in 1990 appears to be good

To correct this typo, do this:

1. From line 1, move the cursor to the blank character position just past the second **s** in the word **saless**.

2. Press the key labeled **Ins** (Insert) to change the keyboard to *insert mode*. Insert mode means that the computer will put any typed character at the location of the cursor, as opposed to overtyping, or

replacing, the character the cursor is on. When you press the Ins key, the cursor itself changes from a blinking underscore to a blinking box. We will discuss the insert mode in more detail shortly.

3. Press the backspace key once. The offending **s** is removed as the cursor moves one space to the left. Notice that First Choice moved over the existing text that follows the cursor by one space to the left as well.

Now to alter the sample text again, let's review the portion of sample text that reads as follows:

```
forecast is due to the introduction of the super dooper micro
```

Let's remove the word **dooper** at the beginning of the fourth line. To make this change, do this:

1. Once again, move the cursor to the desired location using the arrow keys or the mouse. In this case, position the cursor so that it highlights the first letter (**d**) in the word dooper.

2. If you haven't pressed Ins since our last correction, the keyboard should still be in insert mode. If it isn't, press the Ins key to toggle the keyboard into insert mode (the cursor will change to a blinking box instead of an underscore).

3. Press the Del or Delete key seven times. Each time you press Del, a highlighted character is removed from line three. The seventh key-press removes the extra character space and the text appears properly aligned. Figure 2-2 depicts the corrected text.

*Note:* The lines in your paragraph may end at different points than the lines shown in this book. This is nothing to worry about.

## Insert Mode versus Typeover Mode

In our last exercise on correcting errors, you were introduced to the word processor's *insert mode*. Insert mode is used for editing text and is easily identified by the shape of the cursor. When the word processor is in insert mode, the cursor appears as a blinking box instead of an underscore. The underscore indicates that the word processor is in the second of two possible modes, the *typeover mode*. In typeover mode, any new text that you type erases any existing text that appears after the cursor. In contrast, in insert mode, as new text is entered, any existing text that

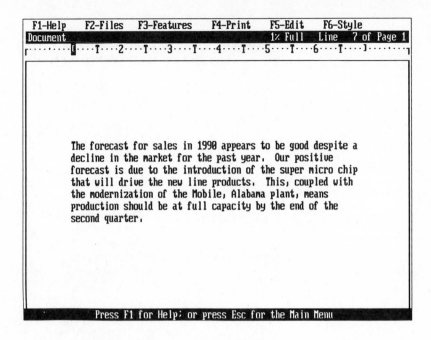

**Figure 2-2.** Sample corrected text.

follows the cursor location is moved to the right and down the document page to make room for the new text.

*Toggle to insert mode upon entering the word processor.*

You will find that the insert mode is the mode of choice for working with the word processor. Insert mode simply makes it easier to add new text, or to delete old text, and still retain the proper spacing of characters with that text. Unfortunately, when you first start the word processor, the keyboard is set in typeover mode by default. To toggle between typeover and insert mode, you need to press the Ins key.

# Inserting Blank Lines and New Paragraphs

*To add blank lines with the Enter key, you must always be in the insert mode. In typeover mode, pressing Enter simply moves the cursor.*

You can easily add blank lines between existing lines of text by using the Enter key. To do this, first switch to insert mode. Next, position the cursor either at the end or the beginning of a line. Then, press Enter once. The cursor moves to the beginning of a new line leaving a blank line inserted between the existing lines. If you placed the cursor at the end of a line, and you change your mind about adding the blank line, simply press the Delete key to remove the blank line. If you first placed the cursor at the beginning of a line prior to pressing Enter, press the backspace key repeatedly instead to remove the blank line.

*In Chapter 3, you will learn how to insert a blank line using item 5 on the Edit menu.*

Each time you press the Enter key, you are actually inserting a *paragraph break* into your document. For example, if you wish to break a single paragraph into two paragraphs, simply position the cursor where the break is to occur, and then press the Enter key once. Pressing the Enter key inserts what is called a *hard return* into the text, indicating to First Choice that you wish to start a new paragraph. The hard return itself is a special character that provides First Choice with the instruction to start a new paragraph and move the cursor to the beginning of the next line. When you use the Delete key to rejoin two paragraphs that you previously split, you are actually removing the invisible hard return character (along with possible trailing blanks) that separates them.

# Typing Your First Letter

*To clear your screen quickly, choose option 9 from the Edit menu.*

The best method of learning how to create letters in First Choice is practice, practice, practice. To start, clear any previous text from your screen. You can clear your screen either by using the backspace key to slowly erase one character at a time, or by using a quicker method with the Edit menu. Open the Edit menu with the mouse or press F5. At the Edit menu, click with the mouse on option 9, *Erase this document*, or select option 9 and then press Enter. First Choice provides a reminder to save the current working document, but resist doing so and simply press Enter again.

First Choice presents you with an empty screen with the cursor positioned in column 1 of line 7. You are now ready to type your first letter. The default settings for margins and the like will do just fine for now. We will make a few editing and formatting changes later. Complete the following steps:

1. Type the date and then press Enter three times. Pressing Enter the first time places the cursor at the beginning of the next line. Pressing Enter the second and third time inserts two blank lines. Type:

   ```
   April 1, 1990
   ```

2. Type the return address as follows. You will need to press Enter after each line of the address since we want each line to begin on a new line. If you make a mistake, you can use the backspace key to correct it. Type:

   ```
   The Wikley Company
   101 Main Street
   New York, NY 10022
   ```

3. Once again, press the Enter key following the last line of the address. However, only press the Enter key twice in order to insert a single blank line between the address and the salutation that follows next.

4. Type the customary salutation as follows:

    `Dear Stockholder:`

    and then press Enter twice to insert a blank line.

5. Your address and salutation is now set. Let's now type the body of the letter, which contains three paragraphs. Remember, the automatic word wrap feature eliminates the need to press Enter as you reach the end of the screen, unless you wish to start a new paragraph. Automatic word wrap does not break words at the end of a line and drops down to the next line as you continue to type. Type the first paragraph as follows: (Once again, your screen may hold more words on a single line than appears here.)

    `Fiscal 1989 was a very successful year for the Wikley Company. We reported record revenues and profits due to the acceptance of our product as the standard widget in the U.S. market today. The Wikley Company increased its market share by 20% over fiscal 1989 and showed an increase of $1,500,000 in net income.`

6. Press the Enter key twice to insert one blank line and to start a new paragraph. Type the second paragraph as follows:

    `At the time when the U.S. widget market was being saturated by our competitors, Wikley Company used innovative designs to expand our universe of customers. The new Super2 Plus widget was especially found to have broad appeal to the new widget customer. Its general use in both production and R&D helped spawn a new generation of widget consumption.`

7. Press Enter twice to start a new paragraph and to insert a blank line between paragraphs. Type the final or third paragraph as follows:

    `While we are committed to servicing our customer base of installed widgets, the Wikley Company is positioned for strong growth in the future. Our market research team is listening, and, more importantly, responding to customer requests for improvements in widget design. In fiscal 1990, we will introduce a brand new line of gotchas in response to this unique market opportunity. As always, our gifted leadership, innovative R&D, and strong marketing department will insure future success.`

8. Press Enter three times to insert two blank lines and then type the closing of the letter. Remember to press Enter enough times to leave as many blank lines as needed to write the closing signature. Type:

```
Sincerely,



Kelly Wikley
President and Chief Executive Officer
```

Congratulations! You have just typed your first letter. Although you can't see the entire document on your screen at one time, you can use the arrow keys to *scroll* the screen's contents (move the text up or down). The entire letter will look similar to Figure 2-3 when printed. Before you learn to print your letter, however, you first should learn to save your work, as discussed in the next section.

```
April 1, 1990

The Wikley Company
101 Main Street
New York, NY  10022

Dear Stockholder:

Fiscal 1989 was a very successful year for the Wikley
Company.  We reported record revenues and profits due to the
acceptance of our product as the standard widget in the U.S.
market today.  The Wikley Company increased its market share
by 20% over fiscal 1989 and showed a net income of
$1,500,000.

At the time when the U.S widget market was being saturated
by our competitors, Wikley Company used innovative designs to
expand our universe of customers.  The new Super2 Plus widget
was especially found to have broad appeal to the new widget
customer.  Its general use in both production and R&D helped
spawn a new generation of widget consumption.

While we are committed to servicing our customer base of
installed widgets, the Wikley Company is positioned for
strong growth in the future.  Our market research team is
listening, and more importantly responding to customer
requests for improvements in widget design.  In fiscal
1990, we will introduce a brand new line of gotchas in
response to this unique market opportunity.  As always, our
gifted leadership, innovative R&D, and strong marketing
department will insure future success.

Sincerely,


Kelly Wikley
President and Chief Executive Officer
```

**Figure 2-3.** What your first letter will look like when printed.

# Saving Documents

Saving your documents may be the single most important task that you must do while working with a word processor. It's not as important as the creative act of writing the letter itself, but it's a close second. If you fail to save your documents, then you will lose all your work when you leave First Choice and turn the computer off.

A crucial tip: as you work at your computer, it's a good idea to save a copy of your work every 15 minutes or so. This precaution allows you to retrieve your work from storage on the disk in case of accidental erasure due to a power failure in your computer. Saving your work every 15 minutes means that you only risk losing 15 minutes of work. The frequency at which you save your documents depends upon how much time you are willing to spend reentering your work.

## Providing a Disk

Before you begin the process of saving your letter, if you haven't yet determined whether your computer system is configured (set up) with a hard disk, do so, and if you don't know the number of disk drives, find out. If your computer has a hard disk and you decide to save your files on floppies instead of on your hard disk, insert a blank formatted disk into either drive A or drive B. (For how to format a blank disk, refer to your DOS manual.) If your system has two disk drives and no hard disk, then insert the blank formatted disk into drive B (the First Choice program disk resides in drive A). Now you're ready to save your letter.

## Steps for Saving Your Letter for the First Time

Let's now complete the steps required to save our first letter. Basically, this involves using the First Choice Directory Assistant and providing your letter with a descriptive file name, such as **FIRSTLET**. Complete these steps:

### Step 1: The Files Menu

Open the Files menu with the mouse or press F2.

## Step 2: The Directory Assistant

From the open menu, select the first option, which is entitled **Save a copy of this document**. Soon, the screen displays the Directory Assistant, as shown in Figure 2-4. Your screen may look different to some extent depending upon which files are stored on your disk and whether or not your system has a hard disk.

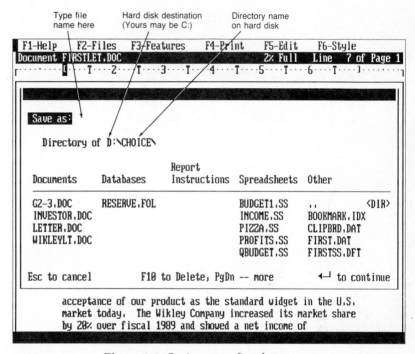

**Figure 2-4.** Saving your first letter.

## Step 3: The Drive and Directory

*A directory is a partition of space on your disk that generally contains similar types of files.*

You will note that the Directory Assistant screen includes several important pieces of information. For example, it lists the *directory* you are in—in this case, choice—as well as the current disk drive. (This is generally, A, B, C, D, etc.; **A** usually means the default drive located on the left side of the computer's system unit, **B** refers to the right disk drive, and **C** (or **D**, etc.) is generally the hard drive.) The Directory Assistant also lists all the files in that directory.

Depending upon your computer's configuration, do the following:

*Two Floppy Drives.* If your system uses two floppy drives instead of a hard disk, check to see whether the directory is identified with a **B**. If not, type **B:** and press Enter so that the B drive will be the active drive when you save the document. (*Note:* the active drive must contain a formatted blank disk when you actually perform the save operation.) Then move the cursor back up to the **Save as** field.

*Hard Disk Drive.* If you have a hard disk, check to see whether the screen lists the directory and subdirectory you want to save the file to. You can save your document file either to one of the floppy disk drives (A: or B:) or to the hard drive itself. You can also specify a subdirectory (you need to have already created this subdirectory in DOS). For example, to save your letter to a subdirectory named LETTERS, immediately following the backslash type the name of the subdirectory. The result will look something like this:

    C:\CHOICE\LETTERS

Then move the cursor back up to the **Save as** field.

## Step 4: The Document Name

At the **Save as** prompt, type the name you want to give to the document. It's best to choose a descriptive name so that later you can easily recall what's in it. (If you had previously saved this document, the file name would already appear at the location of the **Save as** prompt.) Here are some rules that your name must follow.

- The length of the file name cannot exceed eight characters but it may contain fewer.
- A file name's first character must always be a letter.
- The name may contain numbers and the following non-alphanumeric characters (starting at the top left corner of the keyboard):

    ~ ! @ # $ % ^ & ( ) _ - { } '
- If you choose an illegal character or type too many characters, First Choice will warn you. It will not let you enter an illegal file name.
- You can enter the file name in either upper- or lowercase characters. First Choice will later adjust your file names to all uppercase.

- Finally, you don't have to type the file name extension identifying this file as a document. First Choice will add the .DOC designation for you.

For our example, type

`FIRSTLET`

Then press Enter.

### Step 5: The Saving Message

Next, the **Saving** message appears. Also, the light on the disk drive (which is probably red if you have a two-floppy machine) comes on, indicating that First Choice is saving your file as FIRSTLET.DOC. Don't try to open the drive or remove the diskette while the light is on. When the Saving message disappears and the disk drive light goes off, the saving process is complete.

# Printing Your Document

The next step is to print your first letter. In Chapter 3, we will review all the details on printing documents. To get your feet wet, complete the following steps:

1. Be sure the printer is ready. Is it properly connected to your computer system, turned on with the *on-line* light on, and is the printer paper in position and ready for printing? (The on-line light indicates to the computer that the printer is ready to accept instructions to begin the printing process. If your printer has such a light, and most do, the printer won't begin to print until it is on.)

2. Open the Print menu with the mouse or press F4.

3. Choose the first option, **Print this document**, either using the mouse to click on 1, or pressing 1, or leaving 1 highlighted and simply pressing Enter. Next you see the Print Options menu, as shown in Figure 2-5.

4. The Print Options menu provides you with the opportunity to change several standard printing options, including the quality of the printing, the number of copies to be printed, and the place where printing should begin. In Chapter 3 we will explore all

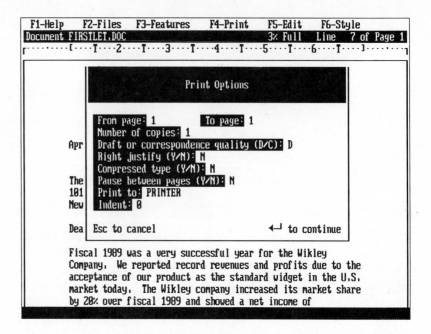

**Figure 2-5.** The Print Options menu.

these print options in detail. Before you decide whether to accept all the default values, you need to know the differences between draft and correspondence quality. Draft quality is listed as the default *printing mode* and is the fastest of the two options. However, the quality of the printing is also generally poor. If you wish to change this one option, press the Tab key to highlight the print quality area and type C.

5. To begin printing the current working copy with the standard print options in place, simply press Enter.

At this point, the printer should begin to print your first letter until completed. If the printer doesn't respond, then you should check two items first:

1. Check to see that your printer is properly connected (to the correct port on the back of your computer) and the cables are secure. If the printer is not properly connected, the screen displays a message to indicate that it tried to communicate with the printer but that the printer was not ready.

2. Check the on-line switch. It should be in its ready or on mode. If the screen indicates that printing has begun, and the printer is inoperative, turning the on-line switch from off to on should start the printer.

# Summary

- You learned how to start the word processor application, and took a tour of all the elements of the word processor screen.

- You learned how to enter text, move around the screen, and make simple corrections to that text. Specifically, you were introduced to the use of the backspace and Delete keys and the differences between typeover mode and insert mode.

- You learned how to insert blank lines and to create new paragraphs.

- Finally, you learned the basics for creating, saving, and printing your first letter.

# More Word Processing with First Choice

**In this chapter:**

- Editing Documents
- Using the Spell Checker and the Thesaurus
- Formatting Documents
- Using Bookmarks in Long Documents
- Saving Documents
- Printing Documents
- Summary

This chapter takes up where Chapter 2 leaves off and discusses more advanced word processing features. It teaches you all of the First Choice editing and formatting tools, including some of the more advanced features such as finding and replacing text. You will learn to retrieve existing documents, change them, and then save them again as new files. You will learn how to use First Choice's formatting tools to set margins, line spacing, and page length. You will also learn how to set indents and tabs and to set page numbers using headers or footers. The chapter also covers using bookmarks, checking spelling, and finding synonyms for a word. Finally, a review of all of the printing features wraps up your tour of the word processor.

# Editing Documents

The ability to edit your work is the attribute unique to word processing that gives it such a powerful edge over the common typewriter. Editing is a more flexible and less formal process than saving or printing. To master First Choice's word processor, you must first master all the editing tools. In this section, we will explore all the editing tools at your disposal.

## Retrieving an Existing File from Storage

Before you can make changes to a document that has been saved previously, you must first retrieve that file from storage on the disk. In other words, any file that is stored on a disk must first be brought into *active memory* on your screen as the current working copy. One point to keep in mind—when you retrieve a copy of a file from a disk, that file replaces any existing document that currently appears on your screen.

*First Choice warns you if you haven't saved changes to a document that you are about to take off the screen.*

As a helpful reminder, First Choice will provide a message to you indicating whether or not you have made any changes to the document since the last time that you saved the document. This feature provides you with one last chance to save the current working document before retrieving a new existing document.

To retrieve an existing document, do this:

1. From the Main menu, select item 6, **Get an existing file**. The Directory Assistant appears and lists all the files currently stored on the hard disk (or data disk—see note below).

2. Move the highlight to the file that you wish to retrieve with either the mouse or the arrow keys, and then press the Enter key. Once First Choice retrieves the document from the file, it is placed in memory as the current working document.

*or*

Type the name of the file at the **Get which file** prompt and then press Enter. You must type the entire name, including the extension, .DOC. If you enter the wrong file name, First Choice will let you know. If you wish to retrieve a file from a subdirectory on your hard disk, type in the name of the subdirectory, a backslash (\), and then the name of the file prior to pressing Enter.

*The original document remains intact while stored on the disk.*

When you retrieve a file from a disk, only a copy of that file is retrieved. The original file remains safely on your disk until you delete it or change it.

*Note:* If you stored your file on a floppy disk, you can substitute the following directions:

1. Retrieve existing files by first inserting the data disk into the B drive. Then, type **B:** and press Enter. The Directory Assistant appears as before; however, it now shows the files stored on the data disk instead of the hard disk.

2. Select the desired file and then choose Enter to retrieve that file from the data disk.

At this point, you are ready to begin reviewing the tools available to edit your document.

## Using the Edit Menu

You have learned many simple keystrokes for correcting typing mistakes, including the use of the backspace key, the Delete key, and the Insert key. (To use these keys, first position the cursor with the direction or arrow keys, and then press the corresponding Delete or Backspace key to remove a character, or use the Insert mode to add new characters.) While you can get by with these, the simplest tools, for maximum efficiency you need to use *all* of the available tools. In the sections that follow, you will learn how to use the additional commands on the Edit menu.

*Press F5 to display the contents of the Edit menu and a listing of the speed key combinations.*

Specifically, you will learn alternate methods for selecting text, block editing, inserting lines, and deleting text. As shown in Figure 3-1, many of the command options in the Edit menu have *speed key* combinations that can be executed in lieu of either the mouse or the keys to select a command from the menu.

## Selecting Text

To understand how to use many of the commands on the Edit menu, you must consider the editing procedure as a two-step process. First you select the text that you wish to change in some way (such as delete or move) and then you choose a command from the Edit menu to carry out, or execute, the change. You can select a single character, a single line, a paragraph, a block of text, or an entire document. With the help

Speed key
combinations

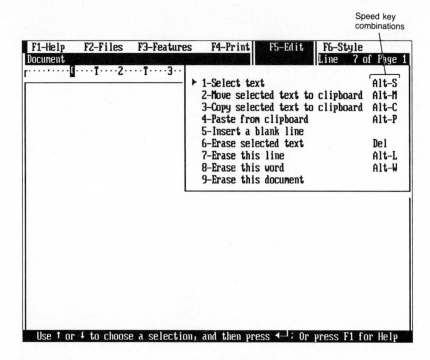

**Figure 3-1.** The Edit menu offers several editing command options.

of a special feature called the Clipboard, you can even select and then move entire blocks of text in and out of a single document or from one document to another.

When you select text, you are actually *defining* the text, that is, telling First Choice what parts of the text to act on. Selected text appears as an area of text that is highlighted in white letters on a black background (color monitors will highlight the text in the color that you select). For short and simple typing corrections, you probably won't need to select text first, just use the Backspace or Delete keys. Generally, you will select a text block consisting of more than one word, or even several paragraphs, in order to perform editing operations that will affect areas beyond the area of the correction, or even the entire document. This type of editing involves the use of the Clipboard and is called *block editing*. We will discuss block editing in the next section. For now let's learn the two primary methods for selecting text—with a mouse or with the keyboard:

### With a Mouse

With a mouse, you can select text by completing the following steps:

1. First, position the mouse cursor in front of the text that you wish to select.
2. Press the left mouse button and hold it down while dragging the mouse across the text to highlight it.
3. When you have highlighted all the text that you wish to select, release the mouse button.

If you change your mind about the text you selected with the mouse, you can "deselect" the text by simply clicking with the mouse anywhere on the document area.

### With the Keyboard

With the keyboard, complete the following steps:

1. Position the cursor in front of the text that you wish to select.
2. Open the Edit menu by pressing F5.
3. Choose item 1, **Select text**, or simply press Enter. Choosing **Select text** anchors the cursor and changes it to a "highlight mode" cursor. (You can also use the speed key combination by pressing Alt-S.)
4. Press the direction or arrow keys in the direction that you wish to expand the highlight, and select what you wish.

*Alt-H selects the line of text where the cursor is currently positioned.*

Once you have selected text using either method above, you can change your mind and deselect the text by choosing the **Unselect text** command from the Edit menu, or by pressing the Esc key, or by clicking once with a mouse.

Once you have selected text, the Select text command changes to **Unselect text** and acts as a toggle between the two command options.

## Moving Text

A fact sometimes overlooked is that writers often change their minds. Your first draft of a document need not be your last. You can use a wide number of methods to change, add, or delete text. It is sometimes an improvement of your prose to simply move entire blocks of text around, rearranging paragraphs, or deleting them entirely. In this section, we will discuss one of several methods of block editing—specifically, moving text.

Another term for block editing is "cut and paste." In this procedure, you first select an area of text that you wish to move. Next, you remove or "cut" the text from the document. Finally, you reposition the cursor and then "paste" the designated text back into the document in its new location. Cutting and pasting blocks of text provides you with a new advanced editing tool.

*The Clipboard has a limited amount of space for holding text.*

When selected text is cut from a working document, it is moved to a temporary holding place in RAM (Random Access Memory), where it remains intact either until new text is cut, moved, or copied again, or until you leave First Choice and turn off the computer. The Clipboard has a limited amount of space for holding text. If the area that you with to cut, copy, or move is too large, First Choice will alert you. In this situation, simply move the desired text in successive stages until all the text is moved.

*Several of the speed key combinations are a convenient alternative to the Edit menu's **Cut and Paste** command.*

First Choice allows you to move text in order to reorganize the structure of your overall document. You can move any amount of text that you wish, from a single character to several paragraphs. You can move text from one location in your document to another, or even from one document to another document.

To illustrate, use the following steps to move text within a document. First, retrieve the sample letter named FIRSTLET.DOC that you created in Chapter 2.

1. The first step to moving text is always the same. You must select the text that you wish to move. You can use any of the selection methods discussed earlier in this chapter. For our example, select the second paragraph that begins, "At the time," as shown in Figure 3-2.

2. Open the Edit menu by pressing F5 (or click it open with the mouse) and then choose item 2, **Move selected text to clipboard**. Of course, you can also use the speed key, Alt-M, to move the selected text. Once you choose this command, the selected text will be removed from your document, as shown in Figure 3-3, and placed on the Clipboard. (*Note:* You can't see the Clipboard, but rest easy, it does exist as a temporary holding place in RAM).

3. The next step is to position the cursor where you want the selected text to appear. You can use the arrow keys or the mouse to position the cursor. For practice, let's move the cursor to the beginning of the line just past the last paragraph in our sample letter. *Note:* You may wish to press Enter once to add a blank line for proper spacing before going on to step 4.

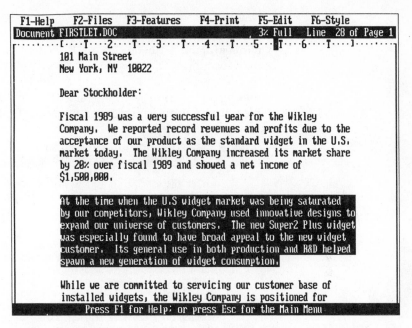

**Figure 3-2.** The first step is to select the text that you wish to move.

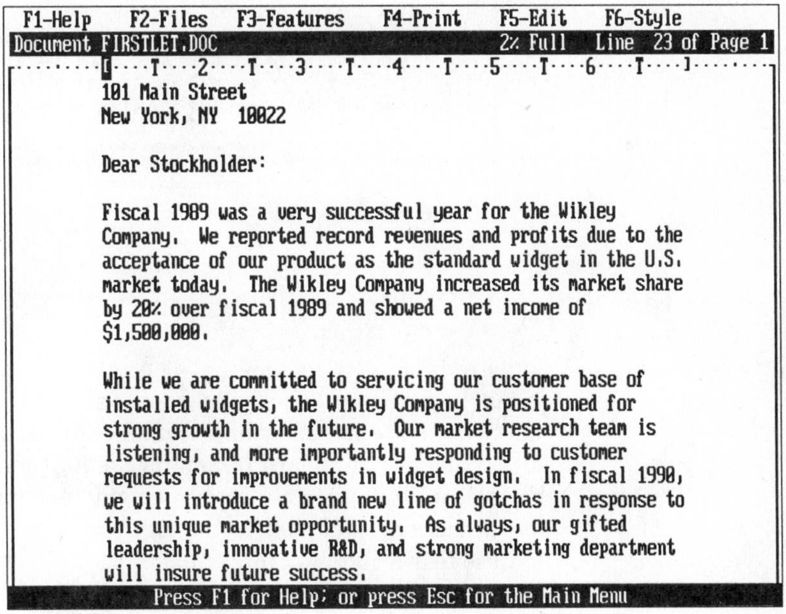

**Figure 3-3.** The selected text disappears from your document with the Move option.

4. Now, open the Edit menu a second time by pressing F5 or using the mouse. From the list of commands, select **Paste from clipboard**. First Choice moves the text from the Clipboard to its new location at the position of the cursor. (If necessary, the text that appears around the moved block of text is automatically reformatted within your document.) Figure 3-4 shows that our second and third paragraphs have been flip-flopped.

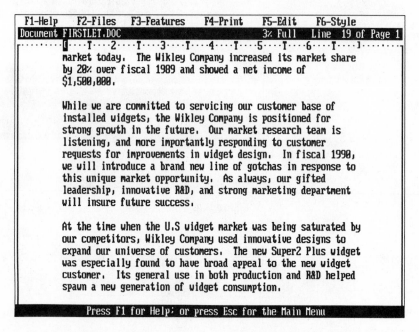

**Figure 3-4.** Pasting the selected block of text into its new location.

## Copying Text

Copying is similar to moving. The one difference is that moving text erases the text from its original location, and copying text merely duplicates the text, leaving the original text intact. Choosing the **Copy selected text to clipboard** option on the Edit menu places a duplicate of the selected text into the Clipboard, where it remains until a new selection is moved or copied to the Clipboard. In your work you probably will use this feature to copy a text block from the current working document, open a new document, and then move the text block to the new document. The following steps explain this procedure.

*To copy selected text quickly, simply highlight the text and press Alt-C.*

1. Select the text that you wish to copy.

2. Open the Edit menu by pressing F5 or click it open with the mouse.

3. Choose **Copy selected text to clipboard**.

4. The next step depends on where you want to place the copied text. If you simply wish to copy to another position within the same document, move the cursor to that location. If you wish to copy the text to a new document, then press Esc to exit the current working document. Remember, First Choice will remind you that you haven't saved any of the changes made during the current work session (Save them if you wish to do so). From the Main menu, choose **Create a new document**.

5. Position the cursor where you want the copied text to appear.

*You can also use Alt-P to paste.*

6. Open the Edit menu again and choose **Paste from clipboard**. The text is copied from the Clipboard to the location of the cursor.

## Inserting Lines

*You must be in insert mode for Enter to add blank lines.*

You have learned that you can add blank lines to text simply by positioning the cursor at the end or the beginning of a line in *insert mode* and pressing the Enter key. To break a single paragraph into two paragraphs, press Ins to get into Insert mode, position the cursor for the break, and then press Enter. Press it twice to insert a blank line between paragraphs.

You can also add a blank line between paragraphs by using the appropriate command from the Edit menu. To do this, complete the following steps:

1. Position the cursor at the beginning of a line, at the point where you wish the new blank line to appear. For example, in Figure 3-2, if for some reason there had been no blank line between the paragraph beginning "While" and the paragraph beginning "At the time," you could put the cursor on the W of "While" to insert one.

2. Open the Edit menu by pressing F5, or click with the mouse.

3. Choose item 5, **Insert a blank line**. The blank line will be inserted.

## Erasing Text

Because all writers make mistakes, and most change their minds, you'll need some tools for changing text as well as for removing it altogether.

To this end, the Edit menu provides four options for erasing text:

- Erase selected text
- Erase this line
- Erase this word
- Erase this document

No matter which of the options above you are using, you always begin by highlighting and selecting the block of text that you wish to erase. The location of the cursor tells First Choice where to remove text from your document. To erase a block of text, simply follow these steps:

1. Highlight the block of text that you wish to erase, employing any of the previous selection methods using the mouse or the keyboard.
2. Open the Edit menu (press F5 or use the mouse) and choose the desired option.

*or*

1. Press the speed key combinations as a shortcut. For example, you can first highlight the text and then press the Delete or Backspace key to erase the selected block. Also, Alt-L erases a selected line and Alt-W erases a selected word.

*Tip:* When you erase text with the Edit menu commands or the Delete and Backspace keys, the text is lost without any recourse. However, if you use the **Move selected text to clipboard** command, you can erase the text and still have it stored temporarily on the clipboard. This method safeguards you if you change your mind about removing text, or what is more likely, if you accidentally remove the wrong text. To retrieve that text, simply paste it back from the clipboard. (Remember, the text that you move to the clipboard will remain there only until another move or copy command is executed or until you leave First Choice and turn off the computer.)

## Searching and Replacing Text

*Find and replace is extremely useful.*

The last of the editing tools is not found on the Editing menu, but on the Features menu. Press F3 or use your mouse to open this menu and find one of the most powerful editing tools, the **Find and replace** option. Suppose that you have just completed a long document, and you have discovered that you need to change the name of a report which you refer to somewhere in that document. Instead of using the arrow keys to scroll the document manually line by line, you can use the **Find and replace** command to quickly search for its name. This option finds any word or phrase that you specify. Further, if you wish to change every occurrence of a word or phrase, either manually or automatically, the Find and replace feature will do that too.

The Find and replace option is also handy for simply jumping to a location in your document as specified by a word or phrase in the **Find what** box.

Before you try your hand at performing a Find and replace operation, keep the following points in mind:

- First Choice doesn't actually search for words in the sense that we think of them; it searches for a series of characters or codes strung together in a sequence that matches a sequence you have specified. However, First Choice does ignore whether the word or phrase that you are looking for is in uppercase or lowercase, as well as the style of typeface (that is, bold, italic, etc). For example, if you are looking for the word Christmas, First Choice will find *christmas*, CHRISTMAS, and chrISTmas.

- Since to First Choice many character strings appear alike, a search for a given word or phrase may produce undesirable results. For example, searching for the word *it* produces every occurrence of the exact character string IT (excluding spaces before, after, and multiple spaces between words) as well as any character string that includes the same letter sequence in a larger string, such as *item* or *summit*. Therefore, during a find and replace procedure, you may wish to use the manual option (M) instead of the automatic option (A) so that you don't replace a phrase that you didn't intend to.

- First Choice always begins the search at the location of the cursor and continues to the end of the document. So, in order to search the entire document, you need to move your cursor to the beginning of the document before you begin your search.

Finally, you can use the **Find and replace** command to find every occurrence of a word or phrase and replace it, or you can simply use this command to find the particular occurrences of a string without replacing it. This latter option is handy for moving the cursor to various locations of your document quickly.

*Alt-F is the speed key combination for Find and replace.*

To use the **Find and replace** command, complete the following steps (For practice, let's change the name of the *Wikley Company* in your first sample letter to *TEMPS-R-US*):

1. Move the cursor to the beginning of your document by pressing Ctrl-Home. Remember, the search procedure always begins at the location of the cursor.

2. Use the mouse or press F3 to open the Features menu. Select **Find and replace** from the Features menu. You can also open the menu and choose this command in one easy step with the speed key combination of Alt-F. The Find and replace display appears, as shown in Figure 3-5.

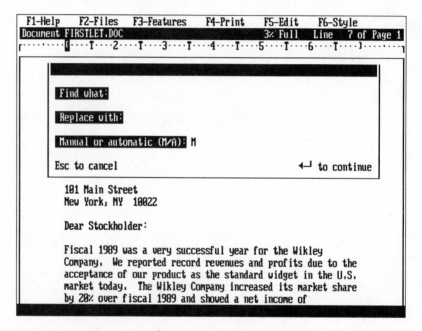

**Figure 3-5.** The Find and replace display.

3. At the **Find what** prompt, type the word or string that you wish to search for. For our example, type:

   Wikley Company

4. Next, press Tab to move to the **Replace with** prompt. You can use the Tab, Shift-Tab, Up Arrow and Down Arrow keys to move from one item to another within the Find and replace display.

5. At the **Replace with** prompt, type the name of the word or string that you wish to replace the existing text with. If you don't wish to replace the text, you can leave this area blank and First Choice will simply find all occurrences of the word listed in the **Find what** line. For our example, type:

   TEMPS-R-US

6. Now, select whether you want the Find and replace procedure to be automatic or manual. If you choose automatic (by typing **A** at the third line of the display), then First Choice changes every occurrence of the **Find what** line (Wikley Company) with the **Replace with** line (TEMPS-R-US) automatically without confirmation from you. If you enter **M**, then First Choice prompts you to verify each replacement before its made. For our example, choose the automatic option.

7. Press Enter to begin the Find and replace operation. First Choice finds all occurrences of the character string and completes the replacement automatically. After all the replacements have been made, a screen appears giving the number of replacements that were made and telling you to press Enter to continue.

# Using the Spell Checker and the Thesaurus

Humans tend to make mistakes and to forget things such as how to spell a word correctly. Fortunately, First Choice provides an ally to help us—the spelling checker.

A spell checker is a utility program that helps you find and correct typing mistakes within your documents. It also reminds you of spellings that you have forgotten. The spelling checker is a type of electronic dictionary. It consists of a built-in, main dictionary containing 75,000 words. You can add 20,000 new or unusual words by creating a *Personal* dictionary.

*The spell checker—your friendly neighborhood proofreader.*

The spelling checker in effect looks over your shoulder and proofreads your documents. It does this by examining the words in your document and comparing them to the words in the built-in dictionary and any personal dictionary that you may create. Specifically, a spell check looks for any of the following:

- **Incorrect spellings**. Basically, any word that doesn't appear in the built-in main dictionary or a personal dictionary. Examples might be "dicitionary" and "buisness."

- **Repeated words**. Any word that appears twice in a row (for example, "in the the middle").

- **Incorrect capitalization**. The spell check finds any word that appears to have an incorrect case such as "CHristmas", "tHe", and "IBm."

- **Incorrect punctuation of numbers**. Often, the culprit is a comma, such as "10,00.00" instead of "1,000.00."

# How to Use the Spell Checker

*On a two-drive system, make sure the Dictionary disk is in drive B before you begin the spell check.*

Before you begin to use the spell checker, be sure that it is properly installed on your computer system. The installation of the spell checker, of course, depends upon which type of system that you are using. If you have a hard disk, then you will have installed the spell checker in the same directory as the rest of the First Choice programs. If you have system with two disk drives, you must insert the disk labeled **Dictionary** into drive B of your computer.

The spell checker always begins its work at the location of the cursor. If you wish to spell check the entire document, you must move the cursor to the beginning of the document (press Ctrl-Home to move it there quickly). When you start the spell check process (via the Check spelling command on the Features menu), First Choice examines each word in your document and compares it to the entries in the dictionaries (built-in and personal, if any). When the spell check finds a word that it doesn't recognize, it stops and highlights that word. The spell checker produces an ''error'' menu screen that gives you three options:

1. You can accept the word as it appears. First Choice may think its a misspelling when in fact it's not (for example, many names of people or of companies).
2. You can add the word to a personal dictionary. Once again, you can add up to 20,000 words to prevent First Choice from ''thinking'' they are misspellings.
3. You can correct the word. Either type a new word or erase the misspelling altogether.

The spell checker even helps you further in the process of correcting misspellings. If First Choice stops during a spell check and highlights a word that it doesn't recognize, it usually lists suggested alternatives for the word from its dictionary. If you wish to replace the highlighted word with one of First Choice's suggestions, simply highlight the suggested word and press Enter or press the number next to the suggested word.

To use the spell checker, complete the following steps:

1. Position the cursor where you want the spell check to begin. Most of the time, you will want to move it to the beginning of the document. You can do this quickly by pressing Ctrl-Home.
2. Open the Features menu with the mouse or press F3.

3. Choose the **Check spelling** command. First Choice will begin to spell check your document. At the bottom of your screen, you will see the word "Checking" while the words in your document flash by in the accompanying space. If the spell check turns up a word that doesn't match the built-in dictionary or the personal dictionary, the spell checker will stop and the word will appear highlighted within the body of the document. It is likely that First Choice will assemble a list of possible substitutes to replace the unknown word, as Figure 3-6 shows. (Note: The "error" box displayed by the First Choice spell checker will vary depending upon the type of error found. For example, some spell check boxes might be labeled "Misspelled word" while another might be "Irregular capitalization.")

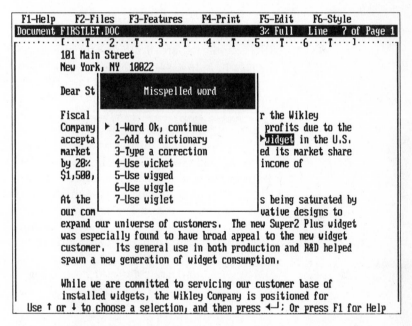

**Figure 3-6.** The Spell Checker provides several replacement words to choose from.

4. You have the following options:

- Choose item 1 and accept the word as it is.
- Choose item 2 and add the word to a personal dictionary.
- Choose item 3 and type a correction before continuing the spell check.

- Choose to replace the highlighted word from one of the suggestions provided by First Choice. As you can see in Figure 3-6, First Choice provided these alternative spellings for the word "widget": "wicket," "wigged," "wiggle," and "wiglet."

5. The spell check continues until the end of document is reached. Repeat step 4 for as many times as necessary. If you wish to stop the spell check at any time, simply press the Esc key.

The spell check is great for misspellings, but it won't find and interpret incorrect semantics (meanings). For example, it won't alert you too the to misspellings in this sentence.

## Creating a Personal Dictionary

All dictionaries are limited, and the built-in main dictionary is no exception. Many words flagged by the built-in dictionary as incorrect, are in fact, spelled correctly. Some of these words may be common to your profession, such as standard abbreviations that you use frequently. Other terms may simply be words not stored in the built-in dictionary. At any rate, First Choice will stop and identify these words as unknown during a routine spell check, which can be an annoyance, indeed. To remedy this problem, you can use the **Add to dictionary** option, which is found on every spell check box.

You can create several personal dictionaries that contain up to 5,000 words (assuming the amount of memory of your computer is sufficient). You build your personal dictionary by choosing the **Add to dictionary** option each time an unknown word is highlighted during a spell check, or by opening the personal dictionary from the First Choice Directory Assistant and modifying it as you would any other existing file—that is, by adding and deleting words and then saving the file. The name of the personal dictionary file is PERSONAL.FC and is listed in the Other category in the Directory Assistant. If you choose to open the file and edit its contents, be sure to save the changes before closing the file.

*Here's how to use a personal dictionary in a spell check.*

Although you can actually create more than one personal dictionary, First Choice will use only one during the spell check, and it is the one named PERSONAL.FC. If you wish to create more than one personal dictionary, create a new document file and save all the words in that file just as you would any standard document file. Give it a unique name, such as DICT1, DICT2, BUSDIC, etc. When you wish to use it during a spell check, perform a nifty trick as follows: use the disk utilities module to first change the name of the current

PERSONAL.FC file to something else, and then rename the dictionary that you wish to use to PERSONAL.FC. (For more information on using the disk utilities module, see Chapter 14.)

*Note:* The PERSONAL.FC file is located in the First Choice directory. If you are located in some other directory or subdirectory, type the correct hard disk drive, a backslash, and then `CHOICE` at the **Get which file** prompt in the Directory Assistant (for example, type `C:\CHOICE`). Pressing Enter should list the personal dictionary file in the Other category.

## Using the Thesaurus

*Use the thesaurus to add variety to your vocabulary.*

Another handy helper is the First Choice 20,000-word thesaurus. When you wish to find another word for a word used over and over in a document, use the built-in thesaurus to find a synonym. Further, once you have used the thesaurus to find a group of synonyms, you can find additional synonyms for any word within the first group of synonyms!

You can use the thesaurus in one of two ways. First, you can select a specific word from your document and then choose to look up a synonym for that word with the **Find synonyms** command from the Features menu. Second, you can simply choose the **Find synonyms** command at any time (the cursor must be on some word, or a space following a desired word) and type the word you want a synonym for at the Synonym prompt. Then press F10 to see a display of all the possible synonyms like the one shown in Figure 3-7. If First Choice doesn't find any synonyms, it displays the message **No synonyms found**.

Let's review the steps necessary to find a synonym for a specific word within a our sample letter. For example, let's choose the word *innovative*.

1. Move the cursor to any position on the word *innovative*. You don't have to highlight the entire word.

2. Open the Features menu and choose the **Find synonyms** command. Soon, the thesaurus displays the list of possible synonyms, as shown in Figure 3-7. If more synonyms are found than will fit on a single screen, use the PgDn and PgUp keys to view the entire list of synonyms.

3. You now have three choices:

   ● Select a word from the list of synonyms using the cursor keys or the mouse; then press Enter to substitute that word into your document (for the word innovative).

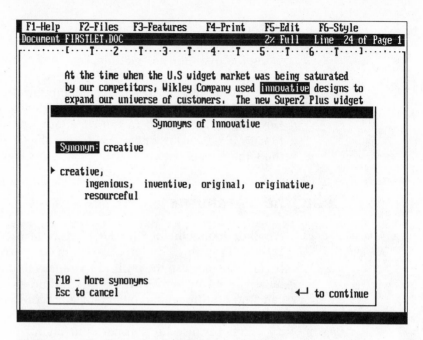

**Figure 3-7.** The First Choice thesaurus shows a list of synonyms to choose from.

*You can progress through a chain of synonyms until you find that "just-right" word.*

- Exit from the thesaurus by pressing the Esc key.
- Highlight a word from the group of synonyms listed and press F10 to find a new group of synonyms for that word in turn. You can continue this process until no more synonyms are listed.

For our example, choose the first option by selecting **inventive** and then pressing Enter. First Choice replaces "innovative" with "inventive" within your working document.

# Formatting Documents

You have now learned how to enter text, to correct errors, and to change your text using all of First Choice's editing tools. The next step is to learn how to *format*, or design the appearance of, your document. A good design can make your document communicate more effectively, just as an unattractive one can be off-putting. Not all documents should use the same format. For example, a basic business letter will look significantly different from a monthly sales report or a formal business plan.

In the sections that follow, you will review all of the formatting tools that help you change a document's appearance, including:

- text styles: boldface, underlining, italicizing, superscripting, centering
- spacing: single, double, etc.
- justification: left, right, full and centered
- setting margins: left, right, top and bottom
- indentation: setting different types of indents for different kinds of paragraphs
- headers and footers: putting text at the top or bottom of the document page
- setting tabs: changing, adding, or deleting tab stops

Most of the formatting options above are available through the Style menu, the Features menu, and the First Choice *ruler*. Let's begin our tour of these options by adding a little style to your text.

## Adding Text Enhancements

*Press F6 for a list of type styles.*

In this section, you will learn how to make your text stand out using several different *style* options from, appropriately, the Style menu. Pressing F6 lists all of the style options that affect the typography (appearance of the letters), as well as the options necessary for changing the location of particular bits of your text. We will review the latter in the next section. For now, let's look at some general aspects of the following typographic styles:

- Boldface
- Underline
- Italics
- Superscript
- Subscript

You can apply each of the above styles to existing text, or you can in effect turn on a particular style so that as soon as you begin a new paragraph all subsequent text will appear in that style, until you change it again. You will find it is sometimes desirable to boldface, underline, or italicize a word to emphasize a point. If you have one of the dot matrix printers on which italics look fuzzy, you may wish to stay with bold and underline. Of course, on a laser printer, the styles always look great.

Before we review the steps for changing the style of text, let's review some important cautions and guidelines:

- All styles will appear in either boldface or different intensities of highlighting (including different colors). However, some styles may not look on your screen the way they will when printed, so that it's not immediately obvious on-screen what style a given letter or word is in. If you need to find out which style has been applied to a given bit of text, you can do one of two things. You can move the cursor to any character with a particular style, and then press F6 to open the Style menu. The style(s) assigned to that particular character will be preceded by a bullet. Or, you can position the cursor on the particular character and then read the status line located at the top of the document. The abbreviated name for the style will appear on the status line.

- You can apply more than one style to a character at a time. For example, you can both boldface and underline a word. You can't however, apply both superscript and subscript to a character.

- To delete a style, select the text that has the style and choose the **Erase style** option from the Style menu. Or use the speed key combination, Alt-N.

The following are the steps for changing the style of an existing block of text to boldface. You can use the same set of steps to apply any of the styles found on the Style menu.

1. Select the block of text that you wish to boldface. For practice, let's select the date from our sample letter. To do this, move the cursor to the first letter of the block that you wish to select—in this case, the letter **A** in "April." Use the Alt-S speed key or use **Select text** from the Edit menu and the cursor keys (or click and drag with the mouse) to expand your selection.

2. Open the Style menu by pressing F6 or clicking with the mouse. Choose item 1, **Boldface**, and press Enter. You can also complete this step quickly by simply pressing Alt-B.

3. Turn off the selection by pressing Esc, or use the Alt-S speed key to deselect the block. The date should appear boldfaced on your screen. The text remains highlighted to allow you to select another style if desired.

*Note:* You can add a style to existing text, or turn on a particular type of style before you begin to type a new paragraph. In the paragraph approach to styling, all new text will appear in the style selected until you turn off the style. To turn off a style option, select **Erase style** from the Style Menu or press Alt-N.

## Centering Text

In First Choice it is easy to center new text as you type it, or to center a block of existing text. This feature is handy for centering a return address in a letter, a headline, a table, etc. To center new text as you type, do this:

1. Position the cursor on the line where you wish to begin centering your text.
2. Open the *Style* menu with the mouse or press F6.
3. Select the **Center** command and press Enter.

As you type new text, the text will be centered automatically between the existing margins. To stop centering text, choose the **Stop centering** command from the Style menu. *Important:* if you change the margin settings (discussed shortly), you will need to recenter your text.

If you wish to center a block of existing text, the steps are just as easy as centering new text:

1. Select the block of text that you wish to center.
2. Open the Style menu and choose **Center**.

That's all there is to it.

## Setting Line Spacing

The First Choice word processor offers both single spacing and double spacing. By default, the word processor is in single space mode. You change from single spacing to double spacing (and vice versa) by using the **Double space** option from the Style menu. You can, of course, mix both single and double spacing within the same document. If you haven't typed any text, choose your spacing from the Style menu and all new text will appear with the kind of spacing selected.

*Both line spacing commands act as toggles.*

Once you choose double spacing, you can easily switch back to single spacing by choosing item 7, **Single space**, from the Style menu. Thus, the double spacing and single spacing commands act as toggles.

If you wish to change the line spacing of existing text, simply select the text first (press the speed key Alt-S for quick selection), and then choose the desired spacing option. All text selected (from the point that you first begin to highlight the text to the line where the cursor is located) will change to the new spacing. Keep in mind that, because line spacing affects the whole line, the entire line where the cursor resides will change to the new spacing selected—even if only a portion of it is highlighted.

One last note on spacing: If you highlight text and then change its spacing, remember that only the highlighted text through the last line where the cursor resides will change its spacing. Any existing text that followed the highlighted text will retain its original spacing. If, however, you insert text into a paragraph or within a block where you changed the spacing of text, then the new text will appear with the same spacing format as the text around it.

To change the spacing of an entire document from single to double spacing, first select the document (press Ctrl-Home and then Alt-S, followed by Ctrl-End), and then choose Double spacing from the Style menu.

## Setting Justification

*You will learn how to change the margins themselves a little later in this chapter.*

Most word processing documents are formatted with left-aligned justification, which is also called "flush left." The First Choice screen automatically displays your document with the text flush left and the right side of the document jagged or a little uneven. You do have the option of full justification (where both the left and right margins appear as even, or "justified"). Full justification means that each line will print approximately the same length. (This paragraph is printed with full justification.) The word processor accomplishes this task by inserting irregular spaces within a text line—an effect that is sometimes a little distracting depending upon the number of words on the line itself. Full justification in written material produced by individuals in the home and workplace (rather than by typesetting machines) has been possible only since the advent of sophisticated typewriters and of word processors.

To use full justification, you simply make the right margin justified, since the left margin is already justified. The only way to accomplish this task is by using the Print menu just before you print your document. Specifically, turn on the **Right justify** option (move the cursor to the appropriate option and type Y) from the Print menu. Upon pressing Enter, the document will print with full justification. First Choice doesn't employ a strong right text justifier so don't be alarmed if the document seems to change either very little or not at all.

Whether you use left justification or full justification is a matter of preference and style. Many writers believe that left justification is more natural and readable. Many formal documents such as contracts use full justification, which some people consider more modern-looking. The choice is yours.

# Using Rulers

*The ruler settings are in tenths of inches.*

The First Choice *ruler* is the third line from the top of the screen. The ruler is used to set margins, indents, and tabs. Measured in tenths of inches, it also depicts the current location of the cursor on a "ruler scale" as well as visually representing the key page layout controls. For example, the margins are shown on the ruler with the bracket characters [ for left margin and ] for the right margin. Tab settings are identified with the capital letter T; indents are identified with the > symbol. Of course, neither the ruler nor its contents will print when your document is printed. Its purpose is to simply help you format your documents efficiently.

First Choice lets you use any number of rulers. You can use the single default ruler to set margins, indents, and tab settings for the entire document, or you can insert additional rulers where you want to modify those same settings. In other words, you can use the rulers to format each paragraph (or group of paragraphs) on an individual basis. All the text that appears following a ruler is affected by the settings of that ruler. If you wish to change any format setting, simply insert a new ruler, change its settings, and all the subsequent text will adhere to the new settings.

Before you learn how to change margins, tab settings, or indents with a ruler, let's review the mechanics of working with the ruler as a whole. Specifically, you will learn how to insert, prepare to change, hide, and delete a new ruler.

## Inserting New Rulers

To insert a new ruler, you use the appropriate command from the Features menu. To do this, complete the following steps:

1. Position the cursor where you want the new ruler to appear.

2. Press the speed key Alt-R, or open the Features menu by pressing F3 and then choose the **Insert ruler** command. Press Enter and the ruler will be inserted above the current cursor position.

Once a ruler is inserted into your document, it will take on the format characteristics of the previous ruler. If no previous rulers exist, then the new ruler will use the settings that appear on the default ruler at the top of the screen.

## Changing Ruler Settings

You can move to the ruler to change the settings by selecting Change current ruler (the current ruler is the closest ruler above where you are) from the Features menu or by using the speed key Alt-G. You can also change any ruler by simply moving the cursor in the usual way to a specific ruler and making the desired change right on it. After you use any of these methods the cursor moves to the previous ruler to allow you to modify it.

Of course, a change you make to the ruler will also change the format of any subsequent text that you enter as new text. As for existing text following a changed ruler, if you changed all the settings—margin, tab, and indent—only its margins will be affected; tabs and indents won't be.

## Hiding and Erasing Rulers

Rulers hidden from view via the **Hide rulers** command reappear whenever you choose **Show rulers** or insert a new ruler.

Soon you will master the use of rulers—so much so, that at some point you may wish to remove them from your screen to be able to look at your document without the ruler cluttering up its appearance. To do this, select the **Hide rulers** option from the Features menu. The rulers won't be lost, only temporarily hidden from sight. To view the rulers again, simply choose the **Show rulers** option from the same Features menu.

Sometimes you may wish to remove a particular ruler altogether. To do this, simply position the cursor anywhere on it and then choose **Erase this ruler** from the Edit menu. You can also use the speed key option Alt-L. Once a ruler is removed, all text that previously followed that ruler will now conform to the settings of the nearest ruler above the text.

# Setting Left and Right Margins

Now that you know how to manage and navigate the rulers themselves, let's learn how to change their settings. When you first look at a written document, one of the first things you notice is the placement of the information on the page. Is the document neat? Are the paragraphs properly aligned? Is the material attractive, and most importantly—readable? The ruler settings enable you to control these aspects of appearance.

One option that you can use to customize your document's overall appearance is that of setting the left and right margins. The size of the margins will determine how much white space appears around the body of your text. The margins that you choose can vary and should be dependent upon the type of document that you are creating. For example, the standard business letter looks well defined with the standard 1-inch left and right margins, while a birthday announcement may require more white space, and thus, larger margins.

*The right margin is measured from the left edge of the paper—really!*

The default settings for your margins are depicted on the ruler at 10 for the left margin and 70 for the right margin; these settings produce a 61-character line. For a standard 8-1/2 inch by 11-inch page, the left margin setting produces the common 1 inch while the right margin is a little wider than 1 inch. To get a 1-inch right margin, a setting of 74 would be about right. The maximum length of a single character line is 250, starting with a left margin of 1 and a right setting of 250.

*Note:* The First Choice screen is only 74 characters wide. If you create a wider document (such as when you turn an 8-1/2 by 11 sheet 90 degrees), a part of the document will not appear on the screen. The cursor will still be visible, however.

Once you determine that you wish to change the settings of your margins from the default settings, complete the following steps:

1. Move the cursor to first ruler of your document (the ruler at the top of the screen).

2. Move the cursor to the position (column) on the ruler where you want the left margin to begin and then press {. Remember, the default left margin is at 10. Typing { moves the left margin marker.

3. Next, move the cursor to the position or column on the ruler where you want the right margin to align. The default setting was at 70. Press } to set the right margin.

4. Press Enter to move the cursor to the first blank line following the ruler.

You can use the preceding steps to change the margins of a new document or an existing document. You can even change the margins of a paragraph or paragraphs that follow the first ruler by inserting a new ruler and applying the new margin settings. Remember, though, any text that follows a ruler on which you have adjusted the margins will format automatically to adhere to the new margin settings.

## Setting Top and Bottom Margins and Page Length

You can control how much text is printed on a single page by setting the top and bottom margins as well as the page length. First Choice presets the top and bottom margins at 6 lines each. A standard page length (on 8-1/2 inch by 11-inch paper) is about 66 lines. Thus, changing the number of lines in the top and bottom margins changes the amount of white space on a page. Keep in mind that the average document uses 1-inch top and bottom margins, and this just happens to be the same length as 6 blank lines. The maximum setting for top and bottom margins is 17.

To change the top and bottom margins, you use the **Set page size, headers, and footers** option from the Features menu as follows:

1. Open the Features menu by pressing F3.

2. Choose **Set page size, headers, and footers**, and the appropriate screen appears as shown in Figure 3-8.

3. Use the Tab key to move to either the **Top margin** or **Bottom margin** setting. *Note:* This screen depicts all the current margin settings. You can use these steps in lieu of the ruler to change the left and right margins as well.

4. Type the value for the margin setting as desired. For example, if you wish to replace the Top margin value of 6 with 15, type **15**.

5. When all your margins are set as you wish, press the Enter key, close the menu, and return to the main document screen.

Unlike changing the left and right margin on a ruler in the middle of a document, changing the top and bottom margin on the Page Size, Headers, and Footers menu will affect the entire document. When you save your document, the new top and bottom margin settings for that document will be saved as well. When you exit the current working document and create a new document, the default margin and ruler settings are returned. The only time this does not happen is if you choose the **Make this document the default** option

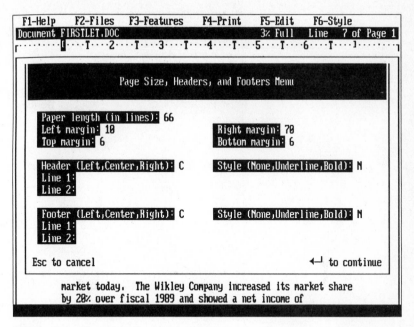

**Figure 3-8.** Changing the top and bottom margins and page length.

from the Files menu. Choosing this command will save all current ruler settings as the default settings for all new documents as well.

## Setting Indentation

The space that exists between the left margin and the first line of a paragraph is called an indent. Many writers use such an indent, typically five spaces, to begin each new paragraph. Like many formatting options, using an indent is a matter of preference. Indentation is also useful when you want to set off a single paragraph (such as a long quotation) within a body of text in order to bring attention to that paragraph. Figure 3-9 shows how using an indent emphasizes a paragraph.

To set an indent in First Choice, complete the following steps:

1. Either move the cursor to the ruler that controls the text that you wish to indent and select **Change current ruler** from the Features menu

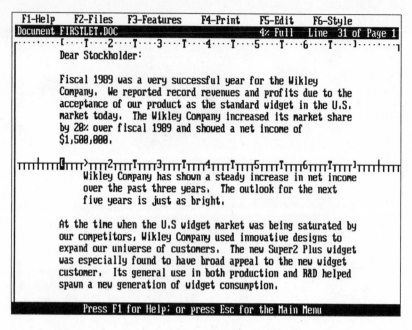

**Figure 3-9.** Use an indent to emphasize a paragraph of text.

*or* press speed key Alt-G

*or* move the cursor to the place in the document where you want the indent to occur and insert a new ruler by pressing the speed key Alt-R.

2. Move the cursor *on the ruler* to the place or column that you wish the indent to occur.

3. Type I or >. Pressing either key will insert the indent symbol, >, on the ruler.

4. Move the cursor off the ruler by pressing Enter or using the arrow keys.

*To make your screen easier to read, use item 7 from the Features menu to toggle between hiding and showing the rulers.*

After setting an indent, any new text that you add will be controlled by the indent format. However, any existing text will *not* be affected. If you wish to remove the indent from the ruler, simply press Alt-I and the indent marker will be erased from the ruler. However, this won't undo the indentation of existing text either. To change the indentation of existing text, turn on Insert mode, position the cursor in front of each line of indented text, and then use the Backspace or Delete key to remove the unwanted space.

*Alt-I removes the indent marker.*

## Setting Tabs

An easy method for setting a first-line indentation for every new paragraph is to simply press the Tab key. You can set regular tab stops, which are similar to that of a standard typewriter, across your page. Thus, pressing the Tab key repeatedly will move the cursor quickly at predetermined intervals. First Choice provides several default tab settings (every five columns, which is about every half inch) for you. These are identified by the letter T on the ruler at the top of the screen.

*To remove an existing tab, put the cursor on the ruler at the T and press the spacebar.*

Change, add, or delete tab settings by completing the following steps:

1. Move the cursor to the ruler where you wish to modify the tab settings and choose the **Change current ruler** option from the Features menu (or press Alt-G).

   *or*

   move the cursor to the position in the text where you wish to insert a tab stop and insert a new ruler with Alt-R.

2. Position the cursor *on the ruler* where you want to insert a tab stop (or delete a tab stop).

3. Press T to insert a tab stop (or press the spacebar to remove an existing tab stop.)

4. Repeat steps 2 and 3 for as many tab stops that you wish to add (or remove).

Once you have set your tabs, move the cursor off the ruler by press Enter or using the arrow keys. Press the Tab key to move to your new tab locations and enter new text as desired. If you remove a tab setting, keep in mind that any previous text that was formatted by a tab setting (such as columns of text) is not affected by removing those tabs.

## Creating Headers and Footers

This section discusses the formatting option that create headers and footers. (A header is running text that appears at the top of every document page and a footer is text that appears at the bottom of each page.) You can use headers or footers in almost any type of document, from books and research papers to letters; in fact, most documents today use headers or footers. Generally, a header or footer provides identifying information about the document, such as the title, the company name, or the date the document was created. Headers and footers typically include automatically generated page numbers. Headers and footers are not necessary, but I recommend them as quite useful and practical.

For practice, let's review our sample document named FIRST-LET.DOC. Use the first set of steps to add a simple header to this document, and then complete the second set of steps to add a footer.

To add a header:

1. If necessary, retrieve the document named FIRSTLET.DOC and make it the current working document.

2. Open the Features menu by clicking with the mouse or press F3.

3. Select the option, **Set page size, headers, and footers** to display the appropriate screen (see Figure 3-8).

4. Press the Tab key to move the cursor to the line **Header (Left, Center, Right)**. Specify where you want the information in the header to appear in terms of which margin you want it to be in (L means left margin, C—center text, R—right margin). For our example, type R.

5. Press Tab to move the cursor to the header Style position. Type B so that your header will be boldfaced.

6. Press Tab again to move the cursor to space where you are to enter the first line of the header. Next, type the text for the header. The text may be as long as the width of the screen. For readability, don't enter too much information. For our example, type:

   `Wikley Company--Quarterly Report`

7. Press Enter to return to the working document. The header will appear on your document, as shown in Figure 3-10.

*Create page numbers in First Choice by including \*1\* in a header or footer.*

Creating a footer is a similar process to that of creating a header. With your FIRSTLET.DOC still the current working document, complete these steps to add an automatic page number within a footer:

1. Be sure that the working document is indeed the document to which you wish to add a footer. In this case, the document, FIRSTLET.DOC, is the correct one.

2. Open the Features menu again by pressing F3 or using the mouse.

3. Choose **Set page size, headers, and footers**.

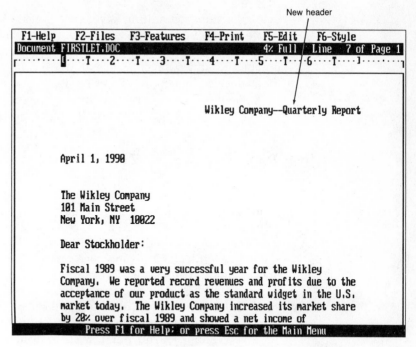

New header

| F1-Help | F2-Files | F3-Features | F4-Print | F5-Edit | F6-Style |

Document FIRSTLET.DOC                                    4% Full    Line    7 of Page 1

Wikley Company--Quarterly Report

April 1, 1990

The Wikley Company
101 Main Street
New York, NY  10022

Dear Stockholder:

Fiscal 1989 was a very successful year for the Wikley
Company.  We reported record revenues and profits due to the
acceptance of our product as the standard widget in the U.S.
market today.  The Wikley Company increased its market share
by 20% over fiscal 1989 and showed a net income of

Press F1 for Help; or press Esc for the Main Menu

**Figure 3-10.** The FIRSTLET document with header.

4. Press the Tab key until you arrive at the line **Footer (Left, Center, Right)**. Since we want to accept the default C or center selection, press Tab again to move to the footer Style option and type **B**. These two selections will center and boldface our footer information.

5. Press Tab to move to Line 1 of the footer information line. The next step is to tell First Choice to add automatic page numbers to every page of this document. To begin with page 1, type:

   *1*

   Note that only the page numbers will appear at the bottom of the page. The enclosing asterisks are necessary for obtaining automatic pagination.

6. Press Enter to return to the working document. The footer will appear on your screen with the number 1 centered and in bold type at the bottom of the page.

Once you have created a header and/or a footer, it's just as easy to delete or change them. Simply return to the **Page size, headers, and footers** screen and change the information on any of the lines using the standard editing keys. To remove a header or footer, simply delete all the information on the respective information line.

*Nifty, huh?*

*Note:* If you wish to create a document with automatic page numbering and a cover page without a number, simply enter ∗0∗ in the header or footer line. Entering a negative number will leave more than one page blank before pagination begins. For example, type ∗-2∗ to leave 3 blank pages at the start of a document.

## Setting Page Breaks

When you have filled up a page, First Choice will automatically start a new page for you. First Choice indicates a new page by presenting a solid double line across the entire screen. As you move the cursor from one page to another, you will notice that the information on the status line indicates the new page number as well as the line number of the cursor. You can easily see the effect of new pages by pressing the PgDn and PgUp keys. If you placed any headers or footers into your document, you will notice that these elements are automatically placed at the top or bottom of the new pages as well.

Now suppose you don't wish to wait until the entire page is filled with text before First Choice automatically begins a new page. At any point in your document you can easily instruct First Choice to begin printing on the next page (this is called forcing a page break). To do this, first position the cursor on the line *above* where the new page is to begin and then choose the **Start new page** command from the Features menu. First Choice inserts a special command, **∗NEW PAGE∗**, into your document on a separate line. It will appear on your screen but it will not print.

*Type ∗N∗ on a blank line to force a new page.*

As a shortcut to the **Start new page** command, you also have the option of typing ∗NEW PAGE∗ or simply ∗N∗ at the beginning of a new line where you wish to insert a page break. Keep in mind that this command must be on a separate line and no other text may be contained on the line where the command occurs.

Once you have inserted a new page break, you can change your mind about its location and move it, or simply delete it altogether. To move the page break, select the line containing the ∗NEW PAGE∗ instruction and move it just like any other text line. First Choice will recognize the command at its new location and break the page there. If you wish to delete the page break, select the ∗NEW PAGE∗ command, and choose **Erase this line** from the Edit menu or use the Alt-L speed key combination. Once you delete a new page command, the text that followed the command is automatically reformatted and the pagination is readjusted.

# Using Bookmarks in Long Documents

When working with long documents, it is sometimes necessary to keep track of sections or certain items within your document. To help you find an item, you can use one of First Choice's special features, the *bookmark*. For example, you can set a bookmark in a long document, leave the document and work in another application such as the spreadsheet or database, and then jump right back to that bookmark. First Choice allows you to set up to nine different bookmarks in a single document, or between applications. In Chapter 14, you'll learn how to use the bookmark feature within a database. For now, let's review the simple steps for adding a bookmark to your working document.

1. Move the cursor to the exact position where you want to leave a marker. You can't insert a bookmark into a blank space or on a blank line. A good place for a bookmark is the first letter of the first word at the beginning of a paragraph.
2. Open the Features menu with the mouse or press F3.
3. Choose **Set bookmark**. The Bookmark box will appear, as shown in Figure 3-11.
4. Type the number for the bookmark (from 1 to 9), and then press Enter.

First Choice records the bookmark and returns to the working document. You will notice that the letter where you placed the bookmark will appear highlighted on your screen. If you enter a bookmark number that has been previously used, First Choice will override the original bookmark and replace it with the new one.

Once a bookmark is inserted into your document, you can continue to work on your document, add text, edit text, format text, or leave the document entirely to use one of the other First Choice applications. When you wish to return to the specific location where the bookmark was set, simply open the Features menu a second time and choose **Find bookmark**. From the Bookmark box, you can indicate the number of the bookmark by typing its number or using the arrow keys and pressing Enter. First Choice then returns to the working document at the exact location of the bookmark.

*Tip:* If you remember which number is assigned to a specific bookmark, you can use the speed key method by typing Alt followed by the bookmark number. For example, Alt-1 will go directly to the first bookmark.

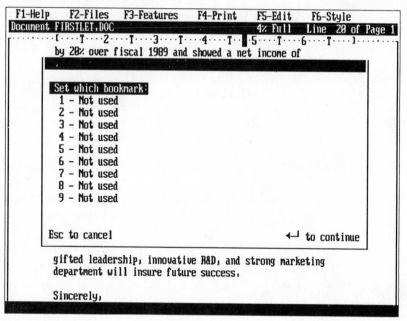

**Figure 3-11.** The Bookmark box.

# Saving Documents

In Chapter 2 you learned the importance of saving your documents. Beginners should save their work often, say every 5 minutes or so. If you forget to save your work, and some unforeseen disaster occurs, such as the computer's power suddenly going off during an electrical storm, then the only work you will lose will be what you've done since the last executed save.

To save your work, complete the following steps:

1. Open the Files menu with the mouse or press F2.

2. Choose **Save a copy of this document**. The Directory Assistant will appear on your screen.

3. At the **Save as** prompt, type a name that indicates the contents of the document that you are about to save. Remember, the file name may be one to eight characters long. You don't need to add the DOC. file extension, since First Choice adds it automatically.

*Note:* For systems with more than one disk drive, you can easily save a copy of the working document to a disk inserted into drive B (or another hard disk). To do this, simply type the name of that disk drive followed by a colon and the file name. For example, type `B:MTHLYRPT` at the **Save as** prompt to save the document named MTHLYRPT on a disk inserted into drive B.

4. Press Enter. First Choice will save the document as specified.

*Alt-Q saves the current document.*

If you have previously saved the current working document, you can use the speed key, Alt-Q, to quickly save any recent changes to the document. Remember, though, all changes will be saved and the previous version of the working document will be lost. If you wish to keep the original version safe on your disk, then you must save the new version of the working document with a different name or to a different disk.

## Saving a Portion of the Document

*You can even create a "baby file."*

You can save all of a document or only a part of it. This ability can be handy if you wish to divide a long document, such as a business plan or a research paper, into smaller, more manageable documents. For example, you may wish to save and print only the executive summary of a complicated business report as an individual document for quick review. To do this, you must select the portion of the document that you wish to save, choose the **Save selected text only** option from the Files menu, and then enter a file name different from the original name. When the Directory Assistant saves the selected text using this unique name, a new file is created. The original document containing the entire file is stored safely on the disk.

## Saving a Document in a Different Format

Businesses commonly need to save documents in file formats different than the ones they are in so they can be used with other programs, such as WordPerfect, WordStar, and other popular word processors. To achieve this goal, save your document either in ASCII format (a format that saves your document as straight text, without any styles such as boldface) or one of the other formats available on the conversion disk that you received in your original First Choice package. If you don't have the conversion disk (available from Software Publishing Corporation when you return your registration card), then you must use the ASCII format option. To save a document in a different format, complete these steps:

1. If you have a hard disk, simply copy the Conversion disk into the same directory that First Choice resides in. Following installation instructions (see Appendix A if necessary), this directory is likely named CHOICE. If you have a system with two floppy drives, then place the Conversion disk into drive B.

2. Make sure that the document that you wish to save is indeed the working document on the screen. If it is, open the File menu and choose the **Save as different type of file** option. The Directory Assistant should appear on your screen.

3. At the **Save as** prompt, type the drive destination, any optional directory, and the file name (type `C:\SALES\REPORT1.DOC`, for example). The name cannot exceed eight characters, and should include a three-character file name extension.

4. Press Enter. A list of available file formats will appear, as shown in Figure 3-12. Choose the name of the format that corresponds to the word processor that you wish to export the current file to, and then press Enter.

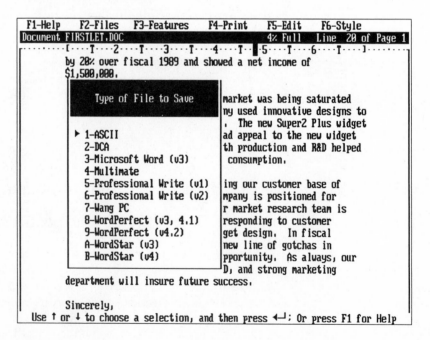

**Figure 3-12.** You can save your documents in many different formats.

# An Exercise in Saving a Modified Document

You have now learned how to use many of the editing and formatting tools that First Choice has to offer. For practice, let's review the file named FIRSTLET.DOC in order to make some subtle changes. It appears that the Wikley Company has changed the focus of their business from widgets to temporary employment services. Use any of the First Choice tools to modify your first letter until it looks like Figure 3-13. You will notice a change in some of the text, as well as the addition of a header and a footer in boldface font. Try your best to catch all the changes. Once you have made your changes, use the First Choice spell checker to double check your work, and then save the document with the file name WIKLEYLT.DOC. You will use this new document in later chapters.

```
                                      Wikley Company--Quarterly Report


          April 1, 1990


          The Wikley Company
          101 Main Street
          New York, NY  10022

          Dear Stockholder:

          Fiscal 1989 was a very successful year for the Wikley
          Company.  We reported record revenues and profits due to the
          acceptance of our product as the standard widget in the U.S.
          market today.  The Wikley Company increased its market share
          by 20% over fiscal 1989 and showed a net income of
          $1,500,000.

          At the time when the U.S widget market was being saturated
          by our competitors, Wikley Company used innovative designs to
          expand our universe of customers.  The new Super2 Plus widget
          was especially found to have broad appeal to the new widget
          customer.  Its general use in both production and R&D helped
          spawn a new generation of widget consumption.

          While we are committed to servicing our customer base of
          installed widgets, the Wikley Company is positioned for
          strong growth in the future.  Our market research team is
          listening, and more importantly responding to customer
          requests for improvements in widget design.  In fiscal
          1990, we will introduce a brand new line of gotchas in
          response to this unique market opportunity.  As always, our
          gifted leadership, innovative R&D, and strong marketing
          department will insure future success.

          Sincerely,


          Kelly Wikley
          President and Chief Executive Officer


                                    1
```

**Figure 3-13.** The modified WIKLEYLT.DOC.

# Printing Documents

Once you have edited and formatted your document until it sounds and looks just right, you are ready to complete the last step in word processing—printing your document.

*Here's a checklist to help you before you print for the first time.*

Using First Choice to print your documents is easy, as explained in Chapter 2. Sometimes, however, it's difficult to set your printer up properly the first time you print. To help, review the following checklist before you instruct First Choice to print your documents.

*A port is like a jack.*

- Be sure the correct port has been specified for your printer. For this you need to know which type of printer you have—serial or parallel. (Most dot-matrix printers are serial and most letter quality printers are parallel.) First Choice is automatically set up to be used with a parallel printer connected to a port called PRN (also called LPT1). For more details, review the section on installing your printer in Appendix A.

- Is your printer type even supported by First Choice? If your printer type is not listed (in the list you choose from during the setup procedure), then you may be able to choose another printer that emulates your printer. Contact Software Publishing Corporation and read your printer's manual for help.

- Check to see that your printer cable is firmly attached to both your computer and your printer, and to the correct printer port as detailed in the First Choice setup procedure.

- Be sure that the printer is indeed plugged in and that it is turned on. If the printer is turned on, an on-line light (or similar light such as Ready, SEL for select, or Print On) should be on to indicate that the printer is ready to receive input from the computer. If the printer has an Alert light, it must be off (the Alert light often indicates that paper is not properly installed into the printer or that there is no paper in it at all).

- Check to see that your computer paper is properly aligned and fed into your printer. You may be using fanfold sheets; or you may be using single sheets of paper that need to be hand fed; or you may have one of the many laser printers that have an automatic single sheet feeder that should be checked for levels of paper. If you have fanfold paper, be sure it fits snugly into the tractor feed and runs properly through the paper alert mechanism to signal when the paper runs out.

- Check your printer's ribbon and cartridge (the ribbon should be between the paper and the print wheel or print head). A document looks much better when the printing is clear due to a fresh ribbon.

- If you have trouble installing your printer or printer ribbon, or properly aligning your paper, consult your printer's manual.

Before you tell First Choice to print your document, you should be aware that First Choice does offer several printing options in addition to merely printing on paper a complete copy of your letter in this exact form. The ones that you might conceivably use at this point include printing selected text only, printing form letters, and printing a picture of your screen (a "screen dump"). (Later you will learn about other printing options, including ones for printing long documents and for printing to something other than paper, such as another file.)

## Printing the Working Document

Now that you are convinced that your printer is properly installed and set to go, you are ready to print your working document. To do this, complete the following steps:

1. Make sure that the working document that appears on your screen is indeed the one that you wish to print. If not, you must return to the Main menu and use the **Get an existing file** command to retrieve the file that you wish to print. As an exercise, retrieve the file, WIKLEYLT.DOC, and make it the working document if it's not already.

2. Open the Print menu by using the mouse or pressing F4. The word processor print options are displayed, as shown in Figure 3-14. To print the working document on your screen, choose item 1, **Print this document**.

3. The menu of Print Options soon appears on your screen, as shown in Figure 3-15. As on other menus, the Tab key (or mouse) moves you from one option to another. For our example, move to the option, **Draft or correspondence quality (D/C)** and type **C**. This option is a little slower than the other one, but it will include all of the formatting options given to your document and the other one won't. Table 3-1 lists all of the print options and their meanings.

4. Press Enter to begin the printing process. First Choice will alert you if there are any problems. Remember, the on-line switch must be set in its ready position.

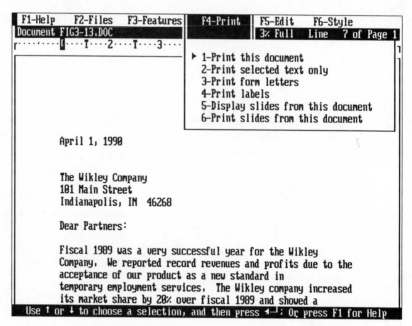

**Figure 3-14.** The word processor print menu.

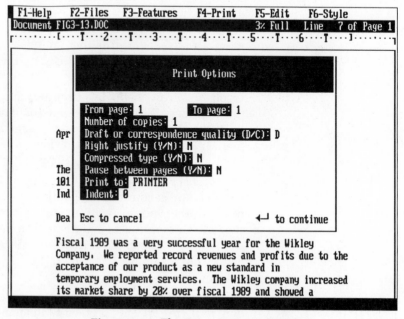

**Figure 3-15.** The Print Options dialog box.

*Press Esc once to stop printing temporarily, twice to stop altogether.*

The above steps are simple enough to follow for printing standard working documents. Once printing begins, you can temporarily halt the printing by pressing the Esc key. To restart the printing, press Enter. If you wish to cancel the printing job altogether, simply press the Esc key twice.

**Table 3-1.** Printing Selections in the Print Options Box.

| Option Name | Description |
|---|---|
| From page/To page | Tells First Choice what page or pages to print. If you wish to print only a single page, say page 5, type a 5 in both of these options |
| Number of copies | You can accept the default 1, or type another number for multiple copies. |
| Draft or correspondence quality (D/C) | Most printers can print in either of these modes. Draft mode is faster but usually offers poorer quality and may not print all character formats. Correspondence mode produces the best possible quality at the slower speed. |
| Right justify | Means full justification (both the left and right margins justified). First Choice adds spaces to each line of your document where necessary. Don't confuse this with flush right. |
| Compressed type | Means that up to 132 characters will fit on a line instead of the usual 70 (on a standard 8-1/2 X 11 page). Not all printers can print in compressed mode. |
| Pause between pages | Used if you are inserting individual pages into your printer manually. Press Y to tell the printer to stop after it prints each page. Press Enter when you're ready to print the next page. |
| Print to | To have the printer print, leave this option set to the default. Change it when you want to print to another device, such as SCREEN or FILE. To print to a file, enter the name of the disk file. |
| Indent | To indent each line of your document, type a number for the number of spaces that you wish to set indentation of the left margin. |

## Printing Selected Text

First Choice gives you the option of printing only a portion of the text within a document. To do this, before you choose any command from the Print menu, you must first select the text as follows:

1. Select the desired text in the usual way. For example, press Alt-S and then move the cursor with the arrow keys to highlight the text to be selected.
2. Open the Print menu with the mouse or press F2. Choose **Print selected text only**.
3. From the Print Options menu, change any options you need to and then press Enter.

## Printing Long Documents

First Choice offers a special printer command that is useful for printing long documents, called *JOIN*. For example, suppose you have previously broken up a large document, such as a book, into more manageable separate files, such as individual chapters. (Once in a while you may need to break up a file that simply gets too big from a memory standpoint too.) Instead of repeating the print procedures for each file, you can print a collection of files by joining them together with the *JOIN* command. To use this command, simply type:

```
*JOIN filename*
```

(where Filename is the name of the second file that you are printing) exactly in the place in your working document where you wish to join the second file to the working document itself. (You can abbreviate the *JOIN* command by just entering *J filename*.)

For instance, suppose you wish to print three chapters of a book that are named CHAP1.DOC, CHAP2.DOC, and CHAP3.DOC. To do this, open the first file, or CHAP1.DOC, thus making it the working document. Then, move the cursor to the end of the document and type the following:

```
*JOIN CHAP2.DOC*
*JOIN CHAP3.DOC*
```

Next, you would choose the standard **Print this document** option from the Print menu to begin the print process. After the current working document (CHAP1.DOC) is printed, then First Choice will read the first *JOIN* command and print the second file, or CHAP2.DOC. Once it has printed the second file, it will encounter the last *JOIN* instruction and print the third file.

Keep in mind that the printer will use the page numbering sequence and header or footer formats of the working document. That is, it ignores any page numbering scheme in the joined file. In contrast, however, it uses the margin and tab settings specified in the joining files. Therefore, before you begin to print with the *JOIN* command, it might be a good idea to check to be sure that all document files use the same formatting settings.

The *JOIN* command differs from the **Merge another document** command listed in the File menu. This command immediately merges a second file into the working document on your screen *before* any printing begins (such as adding a spreadsheet to a word processing document). The *JOIN* command, on the other hand, simply waits for your working document to be printed, and then prints the next "joined" file. The *JOIN* command does not add the second file to the working copy on your screen, and it only comes into play when First Choice encounters the special printing code.

The *JOIN* command is not limited to use at the end of the working document. You can insert it anywhere; the printing of the joined file will begin whenever First Choice "sees" the *JOIN* command. If you insert a join command in the middle of a document, when First Choice finishes printing the second document it will return to the first, so that the rest of it is not skipped.

*Be sure the correct path is specified.*

One last caution: Be sure that the *JOIN* command specifies the correct diskette or directory for the file you are joining, if it is located in a different place than the working file. For example, if your working file is in the BUDGET subdirectory and you are joining a file named PAGE2LTR.DOC located in a subdirectory named REPORTS in drive C, you need to use this command:

```
*JOIN C:\REPORTS\PAGE2LTR.DOC*
```

## Printing Form Letters and Labels

*Chapter 14 walks you through generating a form letter and its accompanying mailing labels.*

You print form letters and mailing labels using two of First Choice's applications, the word processor and the database. We will defer our detailed discussion of this topic to Chapter 14. For now, you need to know simply that creating a form letter or a label begins with the word processor in a fashion to that employed in creating FIRST-LET.DOC. In the case of a form letter, for example, draft and format the letter in the usual way, except that instead of typing specific information that can change (such as a name or an address), you type a *field name*, which is a word that functions in a very specific way in a database. A field name stands for the same *kind* of information each time it occurs (for instance, a typical field name is **address**). The field names themselves are enclosed within a pair of asterisks (*).

For example, suppose only the address block and salutation of your form letter will change. You might begin your form letter with the following field designations:

```
*first* *last*
*address*
*city*, *state* *zip*
Dear *abbr.* *last*:
```

All the punctuation outside the asterisks will appear in the body of the document. You can, of course, insert field names anywhere that you wish within a document. Once you have written your form letter, you will develop a database to store the actual information that will replace the field names. The command that inserts data from the database and replaces the field names with it is the **Print form letters** option from the Print menu.

## Printing to Another File

Sometimes it is desirable to print or send output to a file rather than to paper. The reasons for this vary. For example, you might want to send a document over the telephone line to another computer using First Choice's communications feature. Or, you might wish to "dump" the document into another word processing file (either in First Choice or another program) for someone to edit. (This procedure is particularly useful when you save the word processing document in ASCII format; this is true even though ASCII ignores any format- ting.) Later in this book, you will learn how to print both a database file and a spreadsheet file to a disk. It is helpful to know how to do this because there's a good chance you'll need to merge one or both of these kinds of files into a word processing document to create a single fairly sophisticated report.

To print a file to a disk, simply type a file name (instead of the printer port such as LPT1) in response to the **Print to** option found on the Print Options screen. The file does not have to already exist; you can be creating it on the spot. The **Print to** option allows you to print your output to paper (the printer port), to a disk file (type the file name and any extension, such as LETTER.ASC for ASCII files), or to the screen itself to get an idea of what the file will look like when printed (type SCREEN).

## Stopping the Printer

You may wish to stop the printing of a document, either temporarily, or altogether. To stop the printing temporarily, press the Esc key once; to restart the printing, simply press Enter. If you don't wish to continue with the printing process, press the Esc key twice. Notice that pressing the Esc key does not stop the printer immediately. The reason is this: most printers have a buffer, which is an area of internal memory that holds a small number of the characters transferred from the computer to the printer until the actual printing occurs. When you press the Esc key, characters stop being sent from the computer to the printer, but all the characters in the buffer continue to print until the buffer has emptied.

## More Special Printer Codes

As handy as First Choice is, the number of fonts and styles available from the Styles menu is fairly limited. Using special printer codes, you can remedy this limitation if your printer has the capability. For example, many laser printers are capable of printing additional fonts such as Chicago or New York and styles such as double-strike, Elite, and double-width. To find out what is available with your printer, first check your printer's manual. The codes for printers vary a great deal and are usually listed in an appendix of the printer manual as either ASCII or DEC decimal numbers.

*Don't forget to turn off your font codes.*

Using the special printer codes is a simple process. You insert the printer codes directly into your text where you want the special printing to occur. Keep in mind that when you insert a code, it must be turned off, or the remainder of the document will continue to use the special printing feature that you have inserted.

As for the format of printer codes, they consist of the PRINTER command (or just P as an abbreviation) followed by the decimal printer code itself, and the whole statement is enclosed within a pair of asterisks (similar to the *JOIN* command). For example,

*PRINTER 27*

is used for printing double strike mode, and

*PRINTER 14*

for printing double-wide length, and

*PRINTER 15*

for printing compressed text. The way this code differs from the printing option **Compressed type** from the Print Options menu is that the latter puts an entire document in compressed type, while the printer code enables you to print selected portions of the document in compressed type.

In summary, there are two important rules to remember when using special printer codes within your document.

1. You must embed the featured text within a pair of printer code commands so that the printer code will turn off. For example, suppose you check your printer's codes and determine that *P 27* will start double strike and that *P 20* will stop double strike and return to normal printing. The instructions for producing this effect in your document will look like this:

   *P 27* lottery winner *P 20*

2. You must check your printer's manual for the proper decimal printer codes. As stated, the codes for stopping or starting a particular type of format vary from printer to printer.

# Summary

- You learned how to retrieve an existing file from storage in order to edit that file.
- You were introduced to all the tools on the Edit menu. In addition, you learned how to use numerous speed key combinations to make your work easier.
- The first step in completing many of the editing tasks is to select the text that you wish to change. You learned how to select text using both the mouse and the keyboard.
- The clipboard is very useful when you need to move or copy text—a process also known as block editing.
- You mastered many methods for erasing text as well as inserting lines.
- Using the Features menu, you learned how to use the **Find and replace** command to make changes quickly throughout your documents, a process that can be either automatic or manual.

- You were introduced to the First Choice utility programs for spell checking and looking words up in the thesaurus. You learned how to create your own personal dictionary as well as how to use the First Choice dictionary.

- You received a tour of many of First Choice's formatting tools, including changing text styles, line spacing, justification, margins, indentation, and tabs, and creating headers and footers.

- You now know that top and bottom margins are changed with the **Set page size, headers, and footers** option from the Features menu, and that page numbers are set by placing them in a header or footer.

- You learned how to force a new page break with the **Start new page** command from the Features menu.

- You learned how to use bookmarks to keep track of specific sections or items within the text when working with long documents.

- You learned several ways to save your document. You can save the entire document or a portion of a document. You can also save your document in a different file format so it can be used with another word processor, such as WordPerfect.

- You received a detailed explanation of all of the options for printing your documents.

# Database Fundamentals

**In this chapter:**

This chapter covers the fundamental concepts you will use in database creation. We begin by looking at a database you have used many times, a phonebook, and continue by designing and creating one of Wikley Company's most important databases: the employee database. The chapter concludes with a discussion of the Wikley Company's partnership database, which contains entries for each of the owners.

## A Common Database

Although you may not have referred to them as such, you have undoubtedly worked with several databases in your everyday activities.

A database is a collection of information on *objects*. Each of these objects has a specific format, and all objects within a database must have the same format. Let's say you have one database consisting of a specific type of object and a second database consisting of objects with a completely different format from those in the first. In general, the objects in the first database are not compatible with those in the second.

Your local phonebook is an excellent example of a database as we have defined it above. Figure 4-1 shows a few entries from a sample phonebook. Each entry has its own name, address, and phone number.

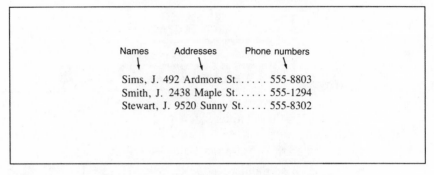

**Figure 4-1.** Entries from a sample phonebook.

First Choice lets you maintain a personal phone directory like this on your PC. Rather than thumbing through a bulky phonebook, you specify the name of the person to call, and—voilà!—that person's address and phone number are displayed. Soon you will learn how to create databases in First Choice, but first we need to discuss some common database terminology.

# Fields Versus Records Versus Files

*Remember to look at a file's extension to determine the type of information it contains.*

You know something about files from your work with several different files in the preceding chapters. *Files* are simply those entries on your disk which contain all your data. A *file name* is specified by an eight-character name followed by an optional three-character extension. For example, the FIRSTLET.DOC file name represented one of the document files you worked with in Chapter 2. In First Choice's database application, you will create files with a .FOL extension.

The phonebook example above showed three entries (Sims, Smith, and Stewart) which you may want to place in a database. Each of those entries may also be referred to as a *record*. Further, each of the records consists of three *fields*: Name, Address, and Phone Number. The relationship between a file, records, and fields is shown graphically in Figure 4-2. (In this database the objects are people who own telephones.)

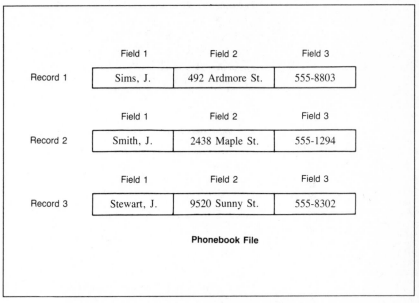

**Figure 4-2.** Relationship between file, records, and fields.

In order to store these phonebook records in a First Choice database you must first create what is known as a *form*.

# What Is a Form?

If you didn't have access to First Choice, you could maintain a personal phonebook using a set of index cards. You could start by writing the field names on each of the index cards as shown in Figure 4-3. (Unlike the First Choice manual, by "field name" this book means the word that functions as the label, such as "Name" or "Address," while the field itself is the area that will receive the information.)

To make your cards easy to use, it is a good idea to have field placement remain consistent across cards. That is, the Name field is at the top of the card above, and it should be in that same location for all cards; this allows you to always look in the same position for the name when you are thumbing through the deck.

```
Name:


Address:


Phone Number:
```

**Figure 4-3.** A phonebook index card.

The same principle applies to electronic card files. This means that you always need to provide field placement information to First Choice. This information, which is called the *database form*, is the template First Choice uses to determine the database record structure.

Now that you are familiar with some of the First Choice database terminology, let's take a look at the layouts for two of Wikley Company's most important databases: the employee database and the partnership database.

# The Wikley Company Databases

As you know, Wikley Company is an agency which finds part-time work for secretarial and accounting specialists. Before Wikley Company begins to find employment for a new client, he or she must complete the questionnaire shown in Figure 4-4.

By using this questionnaire, the Wikley Company personnel department is able to determine each candidate's specialties and work timeframe. After the candidate completes a questionnaire, it is placed in either the secretarial personnel filing cabinet or the accounting personnel filing cabinet. If the candidate specifies skills in both areas, the questionnaire is photocopied and one copy is placed in each cabinet. The questionnaires in each of the cabinets are sorted in alphabetical order. However, this arrangement is really not the most efficient way for Wikley Company to locate the best match for a job opening. For example, if a company requests a part-time accountant to work afternoons and weekends only, there is no quick way to locate a match. The

```
            WIKLEY COMPANY PERSONNEL RECORD

                        Date of Application:  __/__/__

      Name:_____

      Address:_____ _____

      City:_____ State:___ ZIP:_____


      Home Phone:_____   Social Sec No_____


      Do you possess skills in:

              Secretarial Y / N ?   Accounting Y / N ?

                  (circle the appropriate responses)


      When are you available for work?

          From:_____ AM  To:_____ PM


      Are you willing to work weekends?  Y / N

                  (circle the appropriate response)
```

**Figure 4-4.** The Wikley Company personnel record.

Wikley personnel department is looking for some way to solve this and several other information management problems.

In addition to the employee information above, Wikley Company maintains a file folder containing information about company owners, or partners. Each entry in this file contains the information shown in Figure 4-5.

The company was created 27 years ago by two brothers, Joseph and Richard Wikley. Since that time the two brothers have invited many other family members to become partners in the company. In fact, 12 family members are now listed as Wikley Company partners, and that figure increases each year. The partners are not all considered equal. The Ownership Points and Authority Level fields shown in the partner form are used to denote partner seniority. The senior partners have

```
            WIKLEY COMPANY PARTNER RECORD
      Name:_____

      Address:_____

      City:_____ State:___ ZIP:_____


      Home Phone:_____    Social Sec No_____


      Ownership Points:        Authority Level: 1 / 2 / 3
```

**Figure 4-5.** The Wikley Company partner form.

more Ownership Points than the newer ones, and the Authority Level field contains one of three values:

1. This represents a new owner who just recently purchased a partnership in the company; partners at this level have very limited voting rights.

2. This represents a seasoned owner with full voting rights; however, partners at this level are not permitted to participate in financial decisions such as pay raises, equipment purchases, etc.

3. This represents a full partner with full voting and financial decision-making rights.

The partners hold a meeting each quarter to discuss and vote on pressing issues like budgets, promotions, reviews, etc. Before each quarterly meeting one of the Wikley Company secretaries must prepare invitations on her typewriter for each of the partners. This takes quite awhile, and Wikley Company is very interested in how First Choice can expedite the process.

These are the two Wikley Company data files you will be turning into databases in this chapter. Let's take a look at how to create the employee database in First Choice.

# Steps for Creating a Database Form—the Employee Database

*Plan your forms carefully.* The first step in creating the Wikley Company employee database is to define the database form. Careful planning is an important step in creating a database form, because unstructured forms are both unattractive and difficult to use. These are the basic steps you will follow to create any database form:

1. Determine the record structure, field sizes, and field types.
2. Enter First Choice's database application.
3. Enter the form and press F10 to save it.
4. Specify field types and press F10 again to save this information.

We will now explore each of these steps in detail.

## Determining Record Structure, Field Size, and Field Type

The record structure for our employee database must have fields for each of the items that appears in the Wikley Company Personnel Record form, which is shown in Figure 4-4:

- Date of Application
- Name
- Address
- City
- State
- ZIP
- Home Phone Number
- Social Security Number
- Secretarial Skills? (Y/N)
- Accounting Skills? (Y/N)
- Available Work Hours
- Weekend Availability (Y/N)

Once you have identified the fields required for the database record, you must determine the maximum size requirements for each. For example, you as the database designer determine that Wikley Company believes that no employee last name will be longer than 25 characters. They also feel that 25 characters is sufficient space for the address field. Table 4-1 shows the maximum size requirements for each field in the employee database structure. You need to know this information when you build the database form; enough space should be left between field names to accommodate these maximum field sizes.

**Table 4-1.** Maximum Employee Database field sizes.

| Field Name | Maximum Field Size |
|---|---|
| Date of Appl | 8 |
| Name | 25 |
| Address | 25 |
| City | 12 |
| State | 2 |
| ZIP | 5 |
| Home Phone | 8 |
| Social Security Number | 9 |
| Secretarial Skills? | 1 |
| Accounting Skills? | 1 |
| Avl Wrk Hrs (FROM) | 8 |
| Avl Wrk Hrs (TO) | 8 |
| Weekend Avail? | 1 |

*Refer to the section on specifying field types for a detailed discussion of these data types.*

At this point in the form design, you need to make a decision about each field: Will it be standard alphanumeric text or one of these special types?

- Date
- Time
- Numeric
- Yes/No

Although each of the types is fairly self-explanatory, we will go into their specifics and use later in this chapter. If you define a field to be one of these special types, when the keyboard entry person enters data into that field, First Choice performs some special tests (*extra validation*, in database terms) for that field to ensure that the data entered is in the proper format. At this point we should simply note that the following employee database fields could be defined with these special types as shown in Table 4-2.

**Table 4-2.** Employee Database special field types.

| Field Name | Type |
|---|---|
| Date of Appl | Date |
| ZIP | Numeric |
| Social Security Number | Numeric |
| Secretarial Skills? | Yes/No |
| Accounting Skills? | Yes/No |
| Avl Wrk Hrs (FROM) | Time |
| Avl Wrk Hrs (TO) | Time |
| Weekend Avail? | Yes/No |

# Entering First Choice's Database Application

Now that you know the fields you'll use and their maximum length and have singled out which fields will be special types, you are ready to create the form for the Wikley Company employee database. Since you are creating a new database file, you should select option 2, **Create a database**, from the First Choice main menu, which is shown in Figure 4-6, as follows:

Move the cursor to selection 2 with the cursor keys and press Enter

*or*

Press the 2 key

*or*

If you have a mouse, position the mouse cursor over selection 2 and click the mouse button.

The Directory Assistant will be displayed next, as Figure 4-7 shows. You worked with the Directory Assistant earlier, in the first three chapters. (The screen shown here lists more files than the one shown earlier.) Note that when you specify a file name without an extension (for example, EMPLOYEE) for the directory assistant in the database application, .FOL is used as the default extension, instead of the .DOC extension, which is used for document files. (If you acciden-

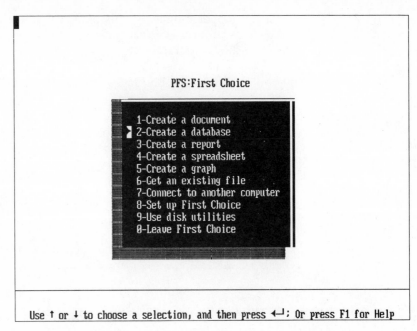

**Figure 4-6.** The First Choice Main menu.

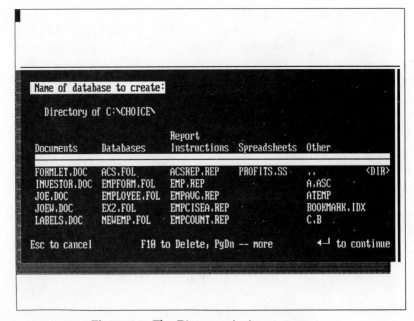

**Figure 4-7.** The Directory Assistant screen.

tally selected the wrong option from the main menu, you can press Escape to go back and try again.)

Since you are going to create the employee database form, use the file name EMPLOYEE.FOL, which will be easy to remember. At the Directory Assistant screen you may enter either EMPLOYEE or the full name EMPLOYEE.FOL and press Enter. The form design screen shown in Figure 4-8 will now be displayed.

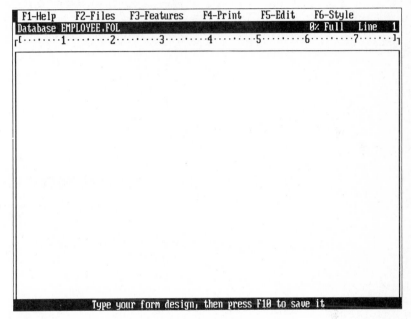

**Figure 4-8.** The Form Design screen.

## Entering and Saving a Form

*Be sure to include the colons in each field name.*

The form design screen is where we will actually enter the fields and other words that will appear on our employee database form. Since you are already familiar with getting around on the screen and entering information from using the word processor application, you should have no problem typing the form to conform to the finished form shown in Figure 4-9. Be sure to type in the exactly what you see in Figure 4-9, including the colons that follow each field name. The colon tells First Choice that what precedes it is a field name. Do not worry that the field names (Name, Address, etc.) are not highlighted as you type them; they will become highlighted when you first save the basic form layout later. (For easier readability, this book will not use the colons in text in discussions of the field names, but it will use the colons when telling you exactly what to type in.)

```
┌────────────────────────────────────────────────────────────────┐
│ F1-Help    F2-Files   F3-Features    F4-Print   F5-Edit   F6-Style│
│ Database EMPLOYEE.FOL                        ·       4% Full  Line  18│
│ ┌[····1····2····3····4····5····6····7····]┐                      │
│ │                                                              │
│ │    *************** EMPLOYEE RECORD ***************            │
│ │                                                              │
│ │    ---------- PERSONAL INFO ----------                        │
│ │   Name:                         Social Security Number:       │
│ │                                                              │
│ │   Address:                      Date of Appl:                 │
│ │                                                              │
│ │   City:          State:         ZIP:                          │
│ │                                                              │
│ │   Home Phone:                                                 │
│ │                                                              │
│ │                                                              │
│ │    ---------- PROFICIENCIES ----------                        │
│ │   Secretarial?:     Accounting?:                              │
│ │                                                              │
│ │                                                              │
│ │    ---------- AVAILABILITY ----------                         │
│ │   From:      To:          Weekends?:                          │
│ │                                                              │
│ │         Type your form design, then press F10 to save it      │
└────────────────────────────────────────────────────────────────┘
```

**Figure 4-9.** The Employee Database form.

The only difference between this and the word processor that you may notice when you enter this form design is that the Tab key does not do anything. In fact, there are no tab markers on the ruler at the top of the screen. You will need to use either the spacebar, cursor keys, or the mouse when you need to move to another field name. Make sure you leave enough space between field names for the maximum field sizes specified earlier.

As noted previously, each of the employee database field names is followed by a colon. The colon is a special character which the form design screen uses to determine the end of a field name and the start of the data entry position for that field. The following rules must be followed when specifying field names:

1. Any character except a colon (:), asterisk (*), or two consecutive spaces (   ) may be used in a field name.
2. The field name must be *followed by* a colon and this colon must be preceded by a non-space character.
3. The field name may be up to one line long.

Table 4-3 shows several valid and invalid field names.

**Table 4-3.** Valid and invalid field names.

| Field Name | Valid/Invalid and Reason |
|---|---|
| `Total:` | Valid |
| `Total :` | Invalid because there is a space before the colon |
| `Length x Width:` | Valid |
| `Length * Width:` | Invalid because the asterisk is an illegal character |
| `Home Phone:` | Valid |
| `Home  Phone:` | Invalid because two consecutive spaces are illegal in a field name |

*Excessive use of background text makes forms look busy and cluttered.*

If we follow the rules in Table 4-3, it would appear that some of the information in Figure 4-9 is invalid. For example, the line

`**************** EMPLOYEE RECORD ****************`

contains asterisks and does not end with a colon. However, these are not field names. The EMPLOYEE RECORD line above is a type of information referred to as *background text*, which is text used to enhance the form design. (You can use asterisks in background text.) First Choice protects both the background text and the field name areas of a database form from change so that you (or a keyboard operator) cannot type over them after you complete the form design.

*Note:* A word about the effect of the colon again. If you mistakenly omit the colon after the field name and then press the spacebar twice or more (or press Enter) to move to another location on the screen, First Choice will think the word is background text. However, if you type a colon as explained earlier and then press Enter or two or more spacebars, First Choice will know that the word is a field name.

The maximum number of lines which First Choice can protect as a region (that is the maximum number of successive lines) is 20. (Your screen shows only 20 lines of a database form at a time.) A *protected region* consists of several lines of background text plus the following line containing a data field name. Therefore, you can only really have a maximum of 19 lines of background text plus one data field line. If you try to create a background text block larger than 19 lines First Choice will display the message, "A protected region cannot be more than 20 lines long." In addition, if you try to create a field name longer than one line, First Choice will treat all lines before the last as background text, meaning that they will not be highlighted after you accept the basic form layout.

The employee database form in Figure 4-4 contains three other lines of background text: PERSONAL INFO, PROFICIENCIES, and AVAILABILITY. Actually, the PERSONAL INFO and EMPLOYEE RECORD lines are treated as a single region of background text since there are no data field names between them.

If you make a mistake or two while typing in the form, you can use any of the editing features discussed earlier for the word processor application to correct it. If you make several typos and just want to start over, you can erase the entire form by selecting **Erase this record** from the Edit menu; First Choice will ask you if you are sure you want to erase the working copy before the contents are actually removed.

After you have successfully typed in the employee database form, save it to disk by pressing the F10 key. After the database form has been saved, you will see the screen shown in Figure 4-10. There are two differences in appearance between it and the Form Design screen when you first saw it: 1) the message at the bottom, which requests that you enter data types for each of the fields; and 2) the field names are now displayed in reverse video. If you try to change them, you'll also notice that they're now protected too.

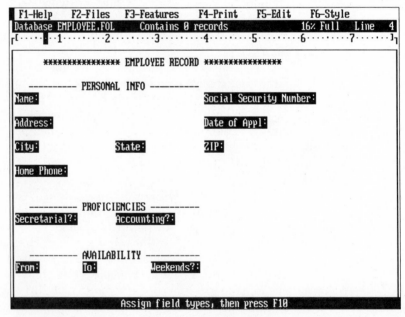

**Figure 4-10.** Field Type Entry screen before specifying types.

# Specifying Field Types

Earlier in this chapter we implied that each field in a database may be either standard text (alphanumeric data) or one of the four special types:

- Date
- Time
- Numeric
- Yes/No

The screen in Figure 4-10 requests that you specify whether each field should be treated as text or as one of these distinctive types. Let's take a look at some of the rules for valid and invalid entries for each of these types.

## Date

*Dates must be specified as numeric entries.*

The **Date of Appl** field in the employee database form will be defined as a date type. "June 22, 1989" is not a valid date. Dates may be specified using either month-day-year format (for example, *6/22/90*) or year-month-day format (for example, *90/6/22*). Further, you may specify the last two digits of the year, as in *6/22/90*, or you may enter all four digits like this: *6/22/1990*.

The month, day, and year numbers may be separated by virtually any non-numeric character; therefore each of these are valid dates:

```
6^2^90
90-6-22
6?22?90
1990*6@22
06+22=1990
6   22   1990
6 22 1990
90y6m22
```

*Notice that two or more spaces are OK in date entries but not in field names.*

As you can see, you can even use one or more spaces as separators for the month, day, and year. First Choice also validates leap years; therefore the date entry *2/29/88* is valid and *2/29/90* is invalid.

## Time

We have determined that two of the fields in the employee database form will be defined as Time types—**From** and **To** under the AVAILABILITY background text. You can specify time in any one of several different formats. Table 4-4 shows some examples of time entries and how First Choice interprets them:

**Table 4-4.** Examples of time entries.

| Time you type | How First Choice interprets it |
|---|---|
| 1:00 | 1:00 AM (because AM is assumed if AM or PM is not specified) |
| 23:25 | 11:25 PM |
| 2:38 PM | 2:38 PM (nothing fancy here) |
| 2:38 pm | 2:38 PM (case is not important) |
| 4 | 4:00 AM (DOS would reject this as a time entry, but First Choice accepts it) |

*As with the date type above, virtually any non-numeric separator may be used between the hours, minutes, and seconds.*

Although each of the examples above show only hours or hours and minutes, you can also specify seconds with any of your time entries if you so desire. However, you must maintain the sequence of hours first, then minutes, and seconds last.

## Numeric

Numeric type data fields can accept integral (whole) numbers or *floating point* numbers (numbers containing a decimal point). These numbers may optionally include a sign character (+ or -) but they must not be a calculation. For example, even though the results are equal,

2

is a valid entry but

4 - 2

is not. First Choice does not understand exponential notation (e.g. 4.35E5) so you cannot use this format for numeric entries. You may use a dollar sign (**$**), comma (**,**), and/or a decimal point (**.**) in numbers. However, be aware that no validation is performed on commas, so that

$100

is equal to

$1,00

and it is also equal to

1,,,00

You may use as many commas as you wish but only one decimal point and only one dollar sign (for example, $1,500,000.00).

In the employee database form we have designated the Social Security Number and ZIP fields as numeric type. Usually you will see a Social Security number written with separating dashes like this: 123-45-6789. First Choice will not recognize the entry

123-45-6789

as a valid number, so Social Security number data will have to be entered without the dashes. We could get around this necessity: the Social Security number with dashes would be acceptable if the text field type was used instead of numeric. However, Wikley Company wants to use the Social Security number in a calculation to generate a unique employee ID number for its security program, so we must define it as numeric.

## Yes/No

Yes/No data field entries are restricted to one of the following:

YES NO Y N

in any combination of upper- or lowercase characters. We will be using this special data type for the **Secretarial Skills?**, **Accounting Skills?**, and **Weekend Avail?** fields.

## Field Types for Wikley Company

If a data field does not fit into one of these four special types, use text type for it. For example, **Name**, **City**, **State**, and **Home Phone** are all text type fields in the employee database form. When the field is a special type you specify the type by placing the first character of the type name next to the field name. For example, the **Social Security Number** field is numeric so we should place an **N** next to it.

You can now go ahead and specify each of the employee database field types as shown in Figure 4-11. Notice that the Tab key may be used on this screen to quickly jump from one field to the next. Follow these steps to specify the field types:

1. Press the Tab key to move the cursor from the **Name** field to the **Social Security Number** field.

2. Press **N** because **Social Security Number** is a numeric field.

3. Press Tab twice until the cursor moves to the **Date of Appl** field and press **D** (for date type).

4. Press Tab three times to move to the **ZIP** field and press **N** (for numeric type).

5. Press Tab twice to move to the **Secretarial** field and press **Y** (for yes/no type).

6. Press Tab to move to the **Accounting** field and press **Y** (for yes/no type).

7. Press Tab to move to the **From** field and press **T** (for time type).

8. Press Tab to move to the **To** field and press **T** (for time type).

9. Press Tab to move to the **Weekends** field and press **Y** (for yes/no type).

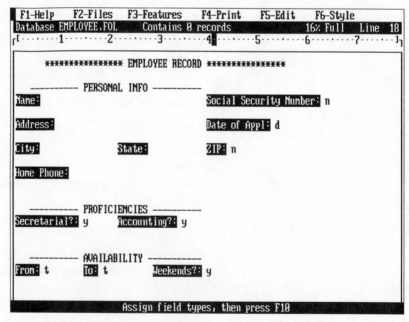

**Figure 4-11.** Employee database field types filled in.

Notice that we do not specify a type for **Name**, **City**, **State**, or **Home Phone**; if no type is specified First Choice defaults to the text type.

*You can quickly move to a specific field via Tab or Shift-Tab.*

If you make a typing mistake just press the backspace key to erase the incorrect entry. If you press Tab after making the **Weekends** entry the cursor moves back to the **Name** field; First Choice knows that **Weekends** is the last field in the employee database record and jumps back to the first field. If you hold the Shift key down and press Tab, the cursor moves to the previous field in the record.

When your type entries match those in Figure 4-11, press the F10 key again to save the type specifications. You are now ready to start adding records to the employee database.

# Adding Records

Once you have saved the type specifications, the screen shown in Figure 4-12 is displayed. Notice how the top of the screen indicates that the database contains no records ("Contains 0 records) and yet it is 12% full. The reason? Although we have not added any records to the database yet, information has already been written to the EMPLOYEE.FOL file. This information includes the form layout, field types, etc.

*Note:* It appears that the percentage full differs from computer to computer. The figures for percentage full on your screen may differ from those shown here.

You can perform several different operations from this screen; first we will use it to add records to the employee database. The following is a partial list of employee applications the Wikley Company has gathered over the years. The list is shown in the database format rather than the personnel record format presented earlier. We will be using the following list to build the employee database:

**Name:** John Adams        **Social Security Number:** 583082856
**Address:** 83 Park Lane      **Date of Appl:** 6/22/85
**City:** Indianapolis        **State:** IN **ZIP:** 46268
**Home Phone:** 555-8490
**Secretarial?:** n            **Accounting?:** y
**From:** 9:00 AM    **To:** 5:00 PM     **Weekends?:** n

**Name:** David Craig
**Address:** 20 N. Main St.
**City:** Indianapolis
**Home Phone:** 555-3367
**Secretarial?:** n
**From:** 8:00 AM    **To:** 6:00 PM

**Social Security Number:** 527835661
**Date of Appl:** 12/05/87
**State:** IN **ZIP:** 46390

**Accounting?:** y
**Weekends?:** y

**Name:** Kelly Craig
**Address:** 2309 Emerson Rd.
**City:** Carmel
**Home Phone:** 555-8679
**Secretarial?:** y
**From:** 9:00 AM    **To:** 12:00 PM

**Social Security Number:** 496882034
**Date of Appl:** 3/12/88
**State:** IN **ZIP:** 46032

**Accounting?:** n
**Weekends?:** y

**Name:** Tim Smith
**Address:** 1314 Grouse Dr.
**City:** Zionsville
**Home Phone:** 555-4590
**Secretarial?:** n
**From:** 8:00 AM    **To:** 5:00 PM

**Social Security Number:** 233184409
**Date of Appl:** 11/20/80
**State:** IN **ZIP:** 46121

**Accounting?:** y
**Weekends?:** y

**Name:** Mary Zale
**Address:** 2304 Maple St.
**City:** Speedway
**Home Phone:** 555-6620
**Secretarial?:** y
**From:** 8:00 AM    **To:** 6:00 PM

**Social Security Number:** 335121905
**Date of Appl:** 1/13/89
**State:** IN **ZIP:** 46090

**Accounting?:** y
**Weekends?:** n

You can enter these records into the database by following the following steps:

1. Type in the applicant's name, John Adams, and press the Tab key to move to the **Social Security Number** field.
2. Type in the applicant's Social Security number, 583082856, and press the Tab key to move to the **Address** field.
3. Type in the date of application, 6/22/85, and press the Tab key to move to the **City** field and so forth.

Keep entering each of the data fields listed above for John Adams until you enter n for the **Weekends** field.

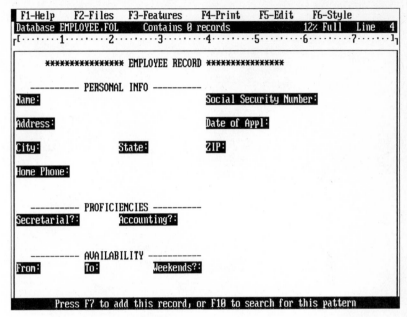

**Figure 4-12.** The finished Employee Database entry screen.

## Moving Through the Database Entry Screen

Notice how the Tab key moves the cursor from one field to the next, just as it did previously in the field type screen (Figure 4-5). The Tab key provides one of the easiest ways of moving from one field to another, but other avenues are available as well. The Enter key will move from one field to the next unless the fields are separated by a blank line. For example, if you move the cursor into the Social Security number field and press Enter, the cursor will move to the blank line between the **Name** and **Address** fields. Therefore, the Enter key is not much help when working with a form containing blank lines. If you have a mouse on your computer, you can use it to move from one field to another. In fact, a mouse will let you jump directly to the destination field without having to stop at every other field along the way.

So if the cursor is sitting at the **Name** field and you want to hop to the **Home Phone** field you simply position the mouse cursor over the **Home Phone** field and press one of the mouse buttons.

*Unlike some applications, First Choice responds to either the left or right button.*

# If You Make a Mistake

You can press Shift-Tab to move the cursor backwards one field. If you make a mistake entering data, use any of the standard editing features (such as the Backspace key) to make corrections. At this point, you should make sure the entries for John Adams match those listed above. Once you are satisfied that your entries are correct, press the F7 key to add the record.

If First Choice finds your entries valid, the record will be written to the database and the form on the screen will be cleared so that another record may be entered. However, if you have made some entries that are invalid according to the rules explained previously, for example typing Z instead of Y, as shown in Figure 4-13, you have a bit more work to do.

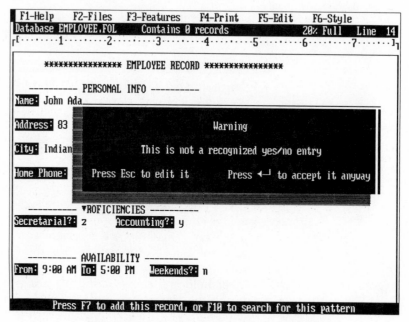

**Figure 4-13.** Invalid **Secretarial** field entry.

Figure 4-13 shows the error message displayed by First Choice when an erroneous entry is made for the **Secretarial** field. As you can see, we accidentally entered the value Z instead of a valid yes/no response. To correct this error, you must first press the Escape key to tell First Choice you want to fix the problem. Next, enter the correct response, N in this case. Finally, press F7 again to add the record. Any other field error you may encounter should be fixed in this manner.

Go ahead and enter the fields for the next record in the listing of employee data, David Craig, and press F7 to save it to the database. Enter the other records for Kelly Craig, Tim Smith, and Mary Zale in the same fashion. Once you have completed these steps, the information for each of these applicants is stored in the EMPLOYEE.FOL file.

# Retrieving an Existing Database

When you want to leave First Choice's database application all you need do is keep pressing Escape until the Main menu (Figure 4-1) is displayed. If you are in the middle of a modification and you try to leave the database application First Choice will display an error message like the one shown in Figure 4-14.

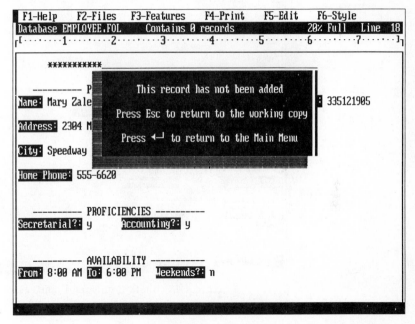

**Figure 4-14.** Error message displayed when leaving database application before completing a record.

Follow the error message directions to either abort your changes or apply them.

Now that we are back at the Main menu, how can we retrieve the employee database file we've been using? Select option 6, **Get an existing file**, from the Main menu to display the Directory Assistant screen. We can retrieve our employee database via this screen in one of two ways:

Enter the file name EMPLOYEE.FOL and press Enter.

*or*

Move the file selection cursor to the EMPLOYEE.FOL entry via the cursor keys or mouse. You'll find EMPLOYEE.FOL in the Databases section on the Directory Assistant screen.

After you've specified the file name above, the database application screen will be displayed with a copy of a blank form (Figure 4-15).

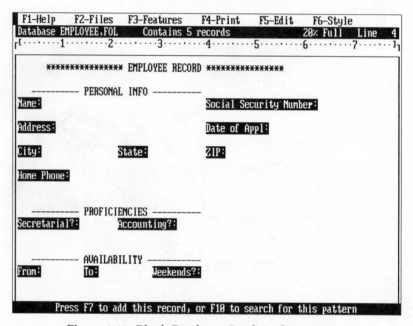

**Figure 4-15.** Blank Employee Database form screen.

This is the same screen we worked with earlier; it allows you to add records, perform search/sort requests, etc. In Chapter 5 we'll see another way to verify that the employee database was successfully saved to disk (by stepping through the entries with the F10 and F9 keys).

# Creating the Partnership Database

Now that you know the basics of creating and working with a database, let's create the Wikley Company Partnership database. We should be able to do this fairly quickly. The document in Figure 4-16 shows the current format of Wikley Company's partner record, and Table 4-5 shows the field types and maximum field sizes for each of the partner record fields.

```
              WIKLEY COMPANY PARTNER RECORD
    Name:_____

    Address:_____

    City:_____ State:____ .ZIP:_____


    Home Phone:_____    Social Sec No_____


    Ownership Points:          Authority Level: 1 / 2 / 3
```

**Figure 4-16.** The Wikley Company partner form.

**Table 4-5.** Partner Record field sizes and types.

| Field Name | Maximum Field Size | Type |
|---|---|---|
| Name | 25 | Text |
| Address | 25 | Text |
| City | 12 | Text |
| State | 2 | Text |
| ZIP | 5 | Numeric |
| Home Phone | 8 | Text |
| Social Security No. | 9 | Numeric |
| Ownership Points | 4 | Numeric |
| Authority Level | 1 | Numeric |

Follow these steps to create the partner form:

1. Press the Escape key one or more times until you return to the First Choice Main menu.
2. Select option 2, **Create a database**, from the Main menu, and the Directory Assistant screen is displayed.
3. Enter the file name PARTNER at the Directory Assistant screen and press Enter to proceed to the Form Design screen.
4. Type in the field names as shown in Figure 4-17 and press F10.

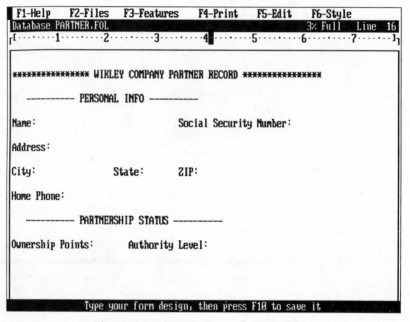

**Figure 4-17.** Partner Form design screen.

5. Type in the field types shown in Figure 4-18 and press F10.

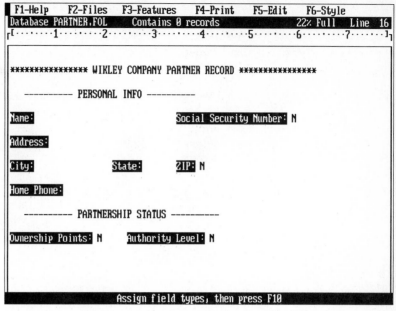

**Figure 4-18.** Partner Form field type screen.

Now go ahead and enter the partner records shown in the following list:

**Wikley Company Partner Records**

**Name:** Joseph Wikley          **Social Security Number:** 217497270
**Address:** 9831 Aylesworth Ct.
**City:** Indianapolis           **State:** IN **ZIP:** 46268
**Home Phone:** 555-2009
**Ownership Points:** 2500        **Authority Level:** 3

**Name:** Richard Wikley         **Social Security Number:** 339038909
**Address:** 98 Norton St.
**City:** Indianapolis           **State:** IN **ZIP:** 46230
**Home Phone:** 555-1190
**Ownership Points:** 2500        **Authority Level:** 3

**Name:** Paul Wikley            **Social Security Number:** 178334509
**Address:** 452 Altaview Ave.
**City:** Lafayette              **State:** IN **ZIP:** 43090
**Home Phone:** 555-2330
**Ownership Points:** 200         **Authority Level:** 1

**Name:** Lisa Wikley     **Social Security Number:** 886298086
**Address:** 8088 Parker Way
**City:** Chicago     **State:** IL **ZIP:** 60025
**Home Phone:** 555-3890
**Ownership Points:** 100     **Authority Level:** 1

**Name:** Wally Wikley     **Social Security Number:** 546842689
**Address:** 2008 Sidneywood Rd.
**City:** Carrollton     **State:** OH **ZIP:** 45445
**Home Phone:** 555-5022
**Ownership Points:** 500     **Authority Level:** 2

The partner database will be used to generate a mailing list for Wikley Company's annual report in Chapter 14, *Program Integration*. Chapter 5, *Searching and Sorting Database Records*, explains how to retrieve specific database records in different orders.

# Summary

- This first chapter on database fundamentals explained some of the basic database terminology including forms, fields, records, and files.
- You learned how to create a database form utilizing all of the possible field types: text, numeric, yes/no, date, and time.
- You learned the difference between background text and field names.
- You created Wikley Company's employee database and added several records.
- Finally, you defined and created Wikley Company's partner database. It will be used to generate an annual report mailing list in Chapter 14.

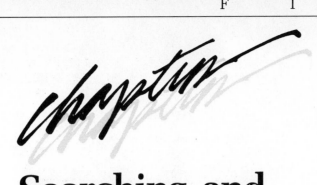

# Searching and Sorting Database Records

**In this chapter:**

- Searching the Employee Database
- Sorting the Employee Database
- Search and Sort Combined
- Printing Your Data
- Summary

In Chapter 4 you created the Wikley Company employee database. Now we can discuss the notions of searching through, sorting, and printing employee entries. These features allow database users to "pick and choose" specific records for reports, upkeep (*maintenance*, in database terminology), etc. These search and sort techniques may be used to retrieve records for screen display or hard copy printout.

## Searching the Employee Database

Recall that the bottom of the screen shown in Figure 4-13 says "Press F7 to add this record, or F10 to search for this pattern." Up to now you have been entering data for each of the employee records and pressing the F7 key to add them to the database. Now that you have added each of the five records listed above, when you load the EMPLOYEE.FOL database, your screen should look like the one shown in Figure 5-1.

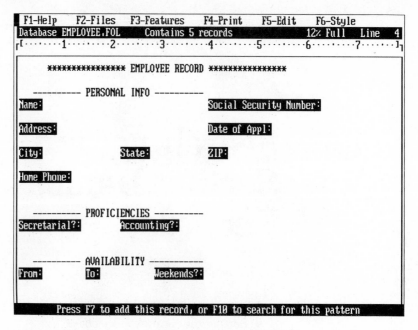

**Figure 5-1.** Screen displayed after adding five employee records.

*Percentages full may differ from PC to PC.*

Notice that the top of the screen indicates that the database "Contains 5 records" and is "12% full." Although you have added five records, the full percentage has not changed; this is because our records are small enough that five of them don't even constitute one percent of the memory available in a First Choice database.

## Viewing the Employee Database Sequentially

If your screen looks like Figure 5-1, press the F10 key without filling in any of the fields. What happened? Your screen should look like the one in Figure 5-2.

This screen shows the contents of the first record you added to the database. All the information for John Adams is displayed exactly as you entered it. The prompt at the bottom of Figure 5-2 says to "Press F10 to continue to the next record, or F9 to get the previous one." Press F10 again and the record for David Craig is displayed (see Figure 5-3).

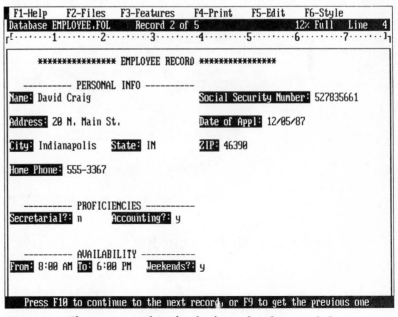

```
 F1-Help     F2-Files   F3-Features    F4-Print    F5-Edit     F6-Style
Database EMPLOYEE.FOL       Record 1 of 5                    12% Full   Line   4
 ┌[·······1········2········3········4·······5········6········7·····]┐

          *************** EMPLOYEE RECORD ***************

          ---------- PERSONAL INFO ----------
     Name: John Adams                Social Security Number: 583082856

     Address: 83 Park Lane           Date of Appl: 6/22/85

     City: Indianapolis   State: IN    ZIP: 46268

     Home Phone: 555-8490


          ---------- PROFICIENCIES ----------
     Secretarial?: n      Accounting?: y


          ---------- AVAILABILITY ----------
     From: 9:00 AM  To: 5:00 PM    Weekends?: n


     Press F10 to continue to the next record, or F9 to get the previous one
```

**Figure 5-2.** The screen that appears after you press F10 when the screen
in Figure 5-1 is displayed.

```
 F1-Help     F2-Files   F3-Features    F4-Print    F5-Edit     F6-Style
Database EMPLOYEE.FOL       Record 2 of 5                    12% Full   Line   4
 ┌[·······1········2········3········4·······5········6········7·····]┐

          *************** EMPLOYEE RECORD ***************

          ---------- PERSONAL INFO ----------
     Name: David Craig               Social Security Number: 527835661

     Address: 20 N. Main St.         Date of Appl: 12/05/87

     City: Indianapolis   State: IN    ZIP: 46390

     Home Phone: 555-3367


          ---------- PROFICIENCIES ----------
     Secretarial?: n      Accounting?: y


          ---------- AVAILABILITY ----------
     From: 8:00 AM  To: 6:00 PM    Weekends?: y


     Press F10 to continue to the next record, or F9 to get the previous one
```

**Figure 5-3.** The next record in the database after the record shown
in Figure 5-2.

Now press F9 to go backwards. The record for John Adams is re-displayed (see Figure 5-2).

When you first pressed the F10 key in this chapter you told First Choice to display the first record of the employee database. This illustrates the fact that anytime you are looking at the screen in Figure 5-1 the F10 key may be used to *invoke* (start) the search feature. Once the first record (for John Adams) is displayed the F10 key still searches but in a slightly different way: F10 is used to search forward in the database for the next record. On the other hand, the F9 key searches backwards through the database. You can keep pressing the F10 key until you reach the last record in the database.

If you press F10 while viewing the last record, the error message in Figure 5-4 is displayed. A similar error is displayed if you press F9 to search further backwards while viewing the first record.

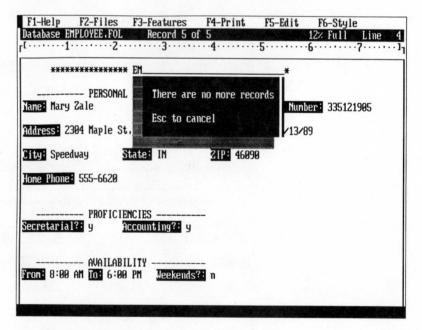

**Figure 5-4.** Pressing F10 at the last record results in this error message.

## Changing an Existing Record

While perusing the employee database you might notice that you mis-keyed one of the records. For example, I erroneously entered Kelly Craig's Social Security number; her number really is 495882034, not 496882034, as it is in Figure 5-5, and as you entered it in Chapter 4.

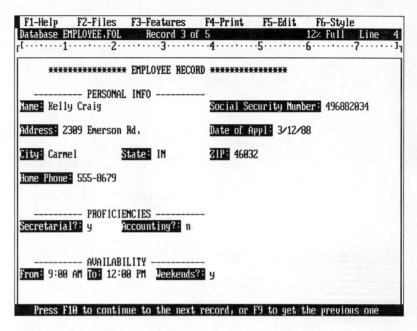

**Figure 5-5.** Incorrect Social Security number in Kelly Craig's record.

To correct this mistake press the Tab key once to move to the **Social Security Number** field and move the cursor to the right until it is under the **6**. Enter a **5** and press the F10 key. The next record (Tim Smith) is displayed and the correction for Kelly Craig is saved to the EMPLOYEE.FOL file. You can verify this correction by pressing F9 at the Tim Smith record to redisplay Kelly Craig's information. You could have made the correction and pressed F9 instead; the correction would be saved and instead of displaying the next record, the previous one would be shown (David Craig).

## Search Specifications

The preceding examples show the simplest use of the search function. In reality, it is much more useful to search for specific records rather than sequentially viewing the database. For example, you may wish to know how many applicants are willing to work weekends. In order to do this, you need to know how to *specify search criteria* for First Choice—in other words, to tell First Choice what to look for.

## Exact Matches

If you are in the middle of the previous sequential search, press the Escape key to return to the screen without any employee data that is shown in Figure 5-1. Move the cursor to the **Weekends?** field and enter the value y. If you now press the F10 key, your screen should look like Figure 5-6.

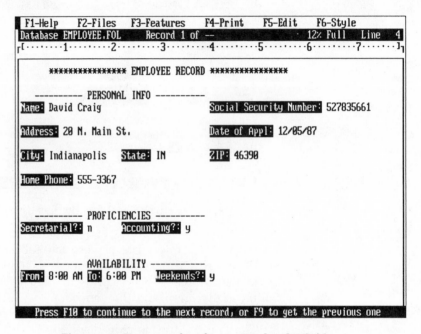

```
 F1-Help    F2-Files   F3-Features   F4-Print    F5-Edit    F6-Style
 Database EMPLOYEE.FOL      Record 1 of --                   12% Full   Line   4
 [········1·······2·······3·······4·······5·······6·······7······]

           ************** EMPLOYEE RECORD **************

           ---------- PERSONAL INFO ----------
 Name: David Craig                    Social Security Number: 527835661

 Address: 20 N. Main St.              Date of Appl: 12/05/87

 City: Indianapolis   State: IN       ZIP: 46390

 Home Phone: 555-3367


           ---------- PROFICIENCIES ----------
 Secretarial?: n      Accounting?: y


           ---------- AVAILABILITY ----------
 From: 8:00 AM  To: 6:00 PM   Weekends?: y


      Press F10 to continue to the next record, or F9 to get the previous one
```

**Figure 5-6.** First record with **y** in **Weekends?** field.

*F9 and F10 work the same in a search for a specific value as they do in a sequential search.*

Rather than displaying the first record in the database, First Choice has found the first record with a y value in the **Weekends?** field. Because the first record (John Adams) contains an n value for **Weekends?**, it is skipped and the second record is checked. The second record (David Craig) contains a y value for **Weekends?** so it is the first record displayed. Press F10 again and Kelly Craig's record is displayed, because hers is the next one in the file with a y for **Weekends?**. If you press F9 after retrieving Kelly Craig's record, David Craig's record will be redisplayed. As you can see, F9 and F10 still have the same meaning within a search whether or not you specify any search criteria. By pressing these keys it is easy to determine that only three of the five records in the employee database contain y responses for the **Weekends?** field: David Craig, Kelly Craig, and Tim Smith.

Did you notice that in the first several screens in the chapter a message at the top of the screen identified the record you were looking at as, for example, Record 3 of 5? First Choice does not do this during a search of the type just described. It does not specify how many records meet the search criteria until you try to go beyond the last one. Notice that until you try to search beyond the last record (Tim Smith's), the top of the screen shows that you are currently viewing "Record X of —" where X is either 1, 2, or 3.

Now let's say that the Wikley Company wants to determine which *secretarial* applicants are willing to work weekends. If you performed the search above, press the Escape key to return to the screen in Figure 5-1. Now specify y values in *both* the **Secretarial?** and **Weekends?** fields and press F10 to invoke the search. If your entries are correct, Kelly Craig's record should be displayed. And her record is the only one that fits the two-part criteria of a secretarial applicant willing to work weekends.

These search specifications are referred to as *exact matches* because a unique value is listed for each search field. Actually, "exact" match is somewhat of a misnomer for the yes/no field, and for the text and time fields as well. For example, you specified the value y for both the **Weekends?** and the **Secretarial?** fields, but here are the other values you could have used instead: yes, YES, YeS, Yes, YEs, yEs, yeS, or yES. First Choice searches are not case sensitive for exact matches so any of the affirmative values above are OK. Because of this lack of case sensitivity you could search for Kelly Craig's name with this specification: kElLy CrAiG.

You may recall from Chapter 4 that time fields may be specified in one of many different formats. As a result, it is possible to specify search criteria in any of the valid formats and First Choice will understand your specifications and be able to make comparisons to database records. For instance, if the Wikley Company wants to determine which applicants will work from 9:00 AM to 5:00 PM the search criteria could be written in any of the following formats:

> **From: 9:00 AM**     **To: 5:00 PM**
> *or*
> **From: 9:00**     **To: 17:00**
> *or*
> **From: 9:00**     **To: 5:00 PM**

As you can see, First Choice understands all of the valid time formats for searches. The same rule holds true for date search criteria, so that when you specify exact match values for date fields you don't have to maintain a consistent date format. All our applicant's dates are specified in the format MM/DD/YY so if you want to see who applied on December 5, 1987, you could specify the value as 12/05/87. If you invoke this search, you will find that David Craig applied on that date. However, you could specify that date with any of the following search values as well:

    12-05-87

    12/5/87

    12 05 87

    1987-12-05

Now that you know how to specify exact matches for search criteria, how would you find all applicants with the last name of Craig? In order to do this you must know how to specify partial matches.

## Partial Matches

First Choice provides two mechanisms for stipulating partial match search criteria:

    ..

    ?

The dot-dot (..) operator is used to specify a variable number of *wildcard* characters, and the question mark represents one wildcard character. For example, to determine which applicants have the last name "Craig" you would place

    ..Craig

in the **Name** field and then press F10 to invoke the search. If you perform this search, First Choice returns the records for David Craig and (after you press F10 again) Kelly Craig. If you press F10 again, you will see a message telling you that there are no more records, which tells you that there are no more people with the last name Craig. In short, the ..Craig Name specification tells First choice to find all entries whose **Name** field ends with "Craig."

Actually, this specification is not perfect. Remember, our goal was to find all applicants with the last name Craig. Although the search did return the two records we expected it would, what would have happened if one of the applicant record's **Name** field was Jerry McCraig? If you think Mr. MrCraig's record would also match the search criteria you are correct; this is because ..Craig returns all values ending with

"Craig" regardless of what appears before the "Craig." The best way to search for applicants with the last name Craig would be to specify the search criteria like this:

```
.. Craig
```

with a space before the "Craig." You should note that, as in exact matches, which we discussed previously, partial match searches are not case sensitive. So, you could specify the criteria like this too:

```
.. cRaIg
```

The dot-dot operator may appear at the end of the field as well, like this:

```
Tim..
```

which would return all values starting with "Tim" like Tim, Timothy, time, etc. You may also place dot-dots at both the beginning and end of a field like this:

```
..88..
```

which you could specify in the **Social Security Number** field to determine which applicants have an 88 in their Social Security number. When you invoke this search, the warning message in Figure 5-7 is displayed.

The warning message in Figure 5-7 tells you that First Choice does not recognize the dot-dot operator as a numeric value. If you go ahead and press Enter, the 88 will be treated as text (which is what you want to happen) and Kelly Craig's record will be retrieved since it contains an 88 in the **Social Security Number** field.

*The dot-dot operator can be used to retrieve only those records with data in the specified field.*

One last note about the dot-dot operator: If you use it by itself like this:

```
..
```

it will return all records with an entry in that field. For example, if you specify dot-dot by itself in the **Home Phone** field, only applicant records with phone numbers will be retrieved. Those applicants who did not provide a Home Phone value will be skipped in the search. Notice that the use of the dot-dot by itself differs from the sequential search where no specifications were entered; in the latter, all records are retrieved regardless of field contents.

The other partial match operator, the question mark (?), works similarly to dot-dot except that each question mark represents one and only

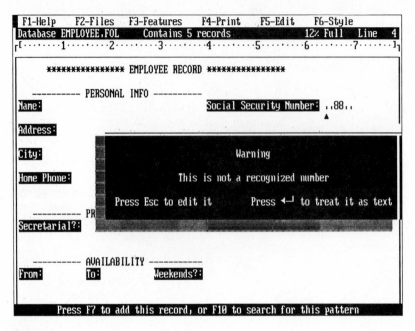

**Figure 5-7.** Warning displayed when dot-dot is used with a numeric field.

one character. For instance, if you want to determine which applicants provided a State value beginning with the letter I, you could use this specification in the **State** field:

        I?

All five of our sample applicant records specified "IN" as their home states so all should be retrieved in this search. If you accidentally spelled out the word "Indiana" when you added the records, none of them would be found because I? retrieves only those records with a two-character **State** field value whose first character is "I" (or "i"). Since the question mark represents one character, it may be duplicated to provide a request for several characters. For example, this specification in the **Home Phone** field would retrieve all records with a phone number starting with 555-6:

        555-6???

Actually, you could have used the dot-dot operator instead, like this:

**555-6..**

The important thing to remember is that the question mark always specifies one character, so that **555-6???** is not the same as **555-6????**.

The dot-dot and question mark operators are quite handy when used together in searches. For example, if you wanted to find all applicants with a four-character last name starting with the letter "Z" you could place this in the **Name** field for the search:

**.. Z???**

## Relative Matches

Although partial matches may be specified for non-text fields, as we saw with the search for the Social Security number with 88 in it, the *relative match* type specification may be used to clarify these search objectives.

First Choice provides three operators for use in relative matches:

**>**

**<**

**=**

If the Wikley Company wants to determine which applicants have zip codes less than 46200 (indicating they live outside the city limits), you could use this relative match specification in the **ZIP** field:

**<46200**

This request works in this particular database because all the records are in the Indianapolis area. If for some reason there was an applicant who lived in a zip code beginning with 3, you would have to include a lower limit in your criteria also. This request retrieves the records for Kelly Craig, Tim Smith, and Mary Zale. The **<** and **>** operators may be coupled with the **=** operator to request "greater than or equal to" or "less than or equal to" searches as well. Be sure to place the **<** or **>** before the **=** like this:

**>=**

*or*

```
<=
```

because First Choice will not accept => or =<.

If the Wikley Company wants to know what applicants have hometowns that come after Indianapolis alphabetically, you could specify this search instruction in the **City** field:

```
>Indianapolis
```

Since relative matches are not case sensitive you could have specified Indianapolis in any case format. The search above retrieves the records for Tim Smith and Mary Zale.

Be careful when using relative matches for text field searches. If you think this search specification:

```
>Tim Smith
```

in the **Name** field will retrieve Mary Zale's record because Zale would appear after Smith in an alphabetical sort, you're wrong! When First Choice performs the comparison between "Tim Smith" and every Name entry, it simply compares characters from left to right. So, the "T" in "Tim Smith" is compared with the "M" in "Mary Zale" and, since T appears after M in the alphabet, Mary Zale's record is not retrieved. If the Wikley Company wants to do searches like this, the last name should be entered ahead of the first name (for example, Smith, Tim) when adding records to the database.

## Range Matches

The Wikley Company wants to find which applicants live in cities with first letters from A to M (the first half of the alphabet). You might think that this could be done by cleverly specifying the criteria via relative matches (e.g. combinations of <, >, and =). Instead, First Choice offers a special operator, ->, to specify search criteria ranging from one value to another. If, for example, the Wikley Company would like to determine which applicant's zip codes range from 46100 to 46200 you could specify the search criteria as:

```
46100->46200
```

in the **ZIP** field. This search will retrieve one record: Tim Smith. The Wikley Company would also like to know which applicants filed their applications in 1985. You could retrieve these records by specifying:

```
1/1/85->12/31/85
```

in the **Date of Appl** field. As you may have guessed, the beginning and ending values are inclusive in the search. That is, applications filed on 1/1/85 or 12/31/85 would also be retrieved in the previous search.

Performing this search illustrates the importance of specifying field types carefully. Since you defined the **Date of Appl** field as a date type First Choice knows to interpret 1/1/85 as the first day of January in the year 1985. If you had accidentally left this field as a text type, First Choice would have to compare the search string to each record's **Date of Appl** field on a character-by-character basis; this would not necessarily retrieve the records with dates between 1/1/85 and 12/31/85. (The reason is, if this field were a text type, a value like Jan. 3, 1985 would be accepted as a valid date for that field, and then First Choice would not know how to include that date in the 1/1/85 to 12/31/85 search.)

Let's look at one last example of range matches—this time for text fields. How would you retrieve all applicant records whose first name is alphabetically between David and Kelly? This specification in the **Name** field would do the trick:

```
David->Kelly
```

As with the other search types, range matches are not case sensitive, so you don't have to capitalize the D in David and the K in Kelly. Also note that you don't have to explicitly state your indifference to what appears after "David" or "Kelly"; in other words, you want to retrieve all Davids with any last name, all Joannas with any last name, all Johns with any last name, etc. Think of this as an invisible dot-dot operator after both David and Kelly in the search instruction above. So, in the specification:

```
David->Kelly
```

only the first five characters of the **Name** field in each record are significant and compared (since both David and Kelly are five characters long).

Similarly, consider this specification:

```
Bob->Larry
```

If the first three characters of the **Name** field in a record are alphabetically after "Bob" (i.e. "Bon" in "Bonnie Boyle") and the first five characters are alphabetically before "Larry" (i.e. "Bonni" in "Bonnie Boyle"), the record will be retrieved. Put another way, my point is that the lower range (Bob) has three *significant* characters and the upper range (Larry) has five *significant* characters.

*Check your range specifications if the search doesn't return the expected records.*

One final note for range matches: make sure the lower range value appears on the left side and the higher range value appears on the right side of the -> operator. If you mix them up like this:

    Larry->Bob

First Choice will not alert you to the error and no records will be retrieved.

## Negative Matches

Many of the previous match types may be negated via the *negative match* operator, the forward slash (*/*). For example, if you want to determine which applicants have the first name John, you would specify this search criteria in the Name field:

    John..

However, if you want to see which applicants do *not* have the first name John, you would use the negative match operator like this in the Name field:

    /John..

This search would return the records for David Craig, Kelly Craig, Tim Smith, and Mary Zale.

Similarly, while you can determine which applicants have names starting with the letters A through M by specifying this search for the **Name** field:

    A->M

you might guess now that you could retrieve those applicants with names starting with N through Z like this:

    N->Z

or this:

    /A->M

You probably won't need to use the / operator with relative match selections like >=, <, etc. because they provide their own opposites implicitly. For example, the opposite of "greater than or equal to" (>=) is "less than" (<). However, you can use the negative operator with **>=** to act like **<** if you choose, and the same principle applies for "less than or equal to."

The ability to search for and retrieve records is one of the fundamental requirements of a database application. We'll now discuss another fundamental requirement, the ability to sort records.

# Sorting the Employee Database

When we sequentially viewed the employee database earlier, the five records were displayed in the same order we added them to the file. Specifically, John Adams' record was displayed first, followed by David Craig's, etc. You can display the records in a *sorted* order by stipulating sort specifications just like you stipulated search criteria above.

## Performing a Primary Sort

For example, suppose that you want to sort the database in order of the **Date of Appl** field, from earliest to most recent. To do this you need to place the **[1A]** sort specification in the **Date of Appl** field, as shown in Figure 5-8, and press the F10 key.

The **1** in **[1A]** tells First Choice to sort the file using the **Date of Appl** field as the *primary key*. The **A** in **[1A]** tells First Choice to sort in an *ascending* fashion. In other words, you're telling First Choice to find the record with the oldest Date of Appl value and display it first. Find the record with the next oldest Date of Appl value and display it second, etc.

Once the database has been sorted the first record is displayed. You can then press F10 or F9 to proceed forward and backward through the sorted database. Now instead of displaying the five records in the sequential order in which they were added:

**Name**
John Adams
David Craig
Kelly Craig
Tim Smith
Mary Zale

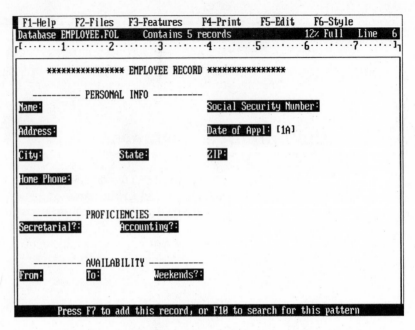

**Figure 5-8.** Designating a sort specification with [1A].

the records are displayed in order of the **Date of Appl** field as follows:

| Name: | Date of Appl: |
| --- | --- |
| Tim Smith | 11/20/80 |
| John Adams | 6/22/85 |
| David Craig | 12/05/87 |
| Kelly Craig | 3/12/88 |
| Mary Zale | 1/13/89 |

*First Choice offers both a primary field sort and a secondary field sort for more detailed record arrangements.*

First Choice allows us to sort by either one or two fields. For example, you could sort the employee database by the City field by placing [1A] next to **City** and pressing F10. If you do this First Choice will sort this field alphabetically. Browsing through the records, you'll see the database sorted in this order:

| Name: | City: |
| --- | --- |
| Kelly Craig | Carmel |
| John Adams | Indianapolis |
| David Craig | Indianapolis |

|              |           |
|--------------|-----------|
| Mary Zale    | Speedway  |
| Tim Smith    | Zionsville |

As you can see, you have two residents from Indianapolis. Since our sort specification sorts by the City field only, these two records are arranged in the order that First Choice encounters them in the database. Remember when you used the F10 key to browse through the unsorted database earlier? John Adams' record appeared before David Craig's and that is why John's appears before David's in the sorted list above.

## Performing a Secondary Sort

Rather than listing records with identical **City** entries in the order they appear in the database, perhaps you would prefer to sort those records by the **Social Security Number** field. You can do this by adding a *secondary sort* to the sort specification above. To add this secondary sort place a [2A] next to the **Social Security Number** field, as shown in Figure 5-9 and press F10.

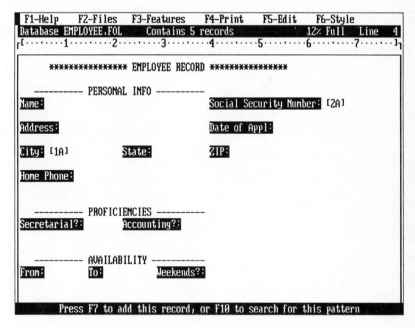

**Figure 5-9.** Specifying a secondary sort with [1A] and [2A].

If you browse through the list now, you will see that the records are sorted in this order:

| Name | City | Social Security Number |
|------|------|------------------------|
| Kelly Craig | Carmel | 495882034 |
| David Craig | Indianapolis | 527835661 |
| John Adams | Indianapolis | 583082856 |
| Mary Zale | Speedway | 335121905 |
| Tim Smith | Zionsville | 233184409 |

Notice that David Craig's and John Adams' records are switched from the order in the previous sort. Notice too that the ordering of the rest of the database remains unchanged from the previous sort. The secondary sort (**[2A]**) that you placed in the **Social Security Number** field has no effect until records with identical primary sort fields (**[1A]**) are encountered. When this occurs, those records with identical primary sort fields (in this case, the **City** field) are sorted by the secondary sort field. Since David Craig's Social Security number (527835661) is less than John Adams' (583082856), David's record appears before John's in the sorted list.

The sort examples just given list the database records in an ascending order based upon the specified sort field(s). You can also sort in a descending order by replacing the A's with D's in the sort specifications. For example, to sort in descending order based upon the **Date of Appl** field you would type **[1D]** next to **Date of Appl** and press F10. The list of records is now sorted in this order:

| Name: | Date of Appl: |
|-------|---------------|
| Mary Zale | 1/13/89 |
| Kelly Craig | 3/12/88 |
| David Craig | 12/05/87 |
| John Adams | 6/22/85 |
| Tim Smith | 11/20/80 |

*You don't need to put **A** in ascending sort instructions.*

Actually, there is a shortcut to the techniques just discussed. First Choice will sort records in ascending order by default, so [1A] is equal to [1] and [2A] is equal to [2]. Table 5-1 lists each of the sort instructions recognized by First Choice.

**Table 5-1.** Sort instruction definitions.

| Sort Instruction | Meaning |
|---|---|
| [1] or [1A] | Primary sort field (ascending) |
| [1D] | Primary sort field (descending) |
| [2] or [2A] | Secondary sort field (ascending) |
| [2D] | Secondary sort field (descending) |

If the sort field is a text type, you have the option of either sorting alphanumerically or numerically. For example, sorting the employee database by specifying a [1] next to the Address field results in this record order:

| **Name:** | **Address:** |
|---|---|
| Tim Smith | 1314 Grouse Dr. |
| David Craig | 20 N. Main St. |
| Mary Zale | 2304 Maple St. |
| Kelly Craig | 2309 Emerson Rd. |
| John Adams | 83 Park Lane |

These addresses are sorted alphanumerically on a character-by-character basis. Tim Smith's address is first in the list because the 1 in 1314 Grouse Dr. is alphabetically *less than the first character* in any of the other addresses. You can also sort the database by the Address field in a numerical fashion. Place a [1N] next to the **Address** field and press F10. The database is now sorted in this order:

| **Name:** | **Address:** |
|---|---|
| David Craig | 20 N. Main St. |
| John Adams | 83 Park Lane |
| Tim Smith | 1314 Grouse Dr. |
| Mary Zale | 2304 Maple St. |
| Kelly Craig | 2309 Emerson Rd. |

In this numeric sort, the *numbers* in the **Address** field are compared rather than the characters. Since 20 is less than 83, 1314, etc., David Craig's record is placed at the beginning of the list above.

The numeric modifier (N) may be used with any of the recognized sort instructions discussed earlier.

# Search and Sort Combined

Now that you know how to search for specific entries in a database and how to sort the records in different orders, a logical question might be, "How can I search and sort at the same time?" The answer is simple: Place the search and sort instructions together on the screen and press F10.

Suppose that the Wikley Company needs to know which employees live in Indianapolis. Further, they would like these employee records listed in reverse chronological order of application to the firm. This requirement involves a search (**City:** Indianapolis) and a sort (**Date of Appl:** [1D]). Simply enter these search/sort instructions as shown in Figure 5-10 and press F10.

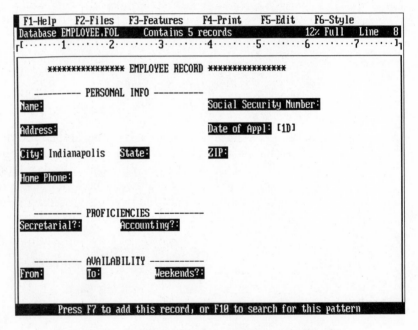

**Figure 5-10.** Search and sort instructions combined.

By pressing F10 again you can see that two records were found: David Craig's and John Adams's. David and John both live in Indianapolis and David's record is listed before John's because the former applied with the Wikley Company before the latter.

*You can even put both search and sort instructions in the same field.*

Let's take this combination further by specifying search and sort instructions in the same field. The Wikley Company wants a list of those employees who do not live in Indianapolis. This list should be in reverse chronological order and should not include anyone who applied before January 1, 1987. You can find these records by placing

    /Indianapolis

in the **City** field and

    [1D] >=1/1/87

in the **Date of Appl** field. The latter field contains both a search (>=1/1/87) and a sort specification ([1D]). You can place both these specifications in one field as long as the sort requirements appear before the search requirements. This search/sort request results in the following list of records:

| Name: | Date of Appl: |
|-------|---------------|
| Mary Zale | 1/13/89 |
| Kelly Craig | 3/12/88 |

# Printing Your Data

Now let's take a look at how to print database records, including lists of records generated by search/sort instructions.

## Printing One Record

You have seen how to make database inquiries to retrieve specific records. This is certainly quite useful and is a fundamental aspect of using any database, but often you may need a written version of what you've found. How can you print a record once it has been retrieved? The answer is simple: use the Print menu and answer a few questions. Once the record you want to print is displayed, press the F4 key to select the Print menu, which is shown in Figure 5-11.

Since the menu cursor is automatically positioned beside the first selection, **Print this record**, press the Enter key or click on the selection. The Print Options dialog box shown in Figure 5-12 is then displayed.

**Figure 5-11.** The Print menu for the database.

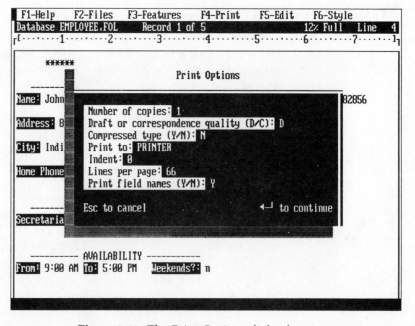

**Figure 5-12.** The Print Options dialog box.

This dialog box closely resembles the one displayed in the word processing application. The following two items which require a response are unique to the database application's Print Options dialog box:

**Lines per page**    Unless you specify otherwise, First Choice will use 66. Use 66 if you are using 8-1/2 x 11 paper. If you're using legal size paper (8-1/2 x 14), specify 84.

**Print field names**    Leave the default value (yes) in this field, because you want to show the field names next to the field values on the printed page.

When you are satisfied with your dialog box responses, press Enter to print the record. If your printer is properly connected, the record is printed exactly as it appears on the screen.

## Printing Several Records

You can print the entire employee database by selecting the Print records option from the Print menu; press F4 and then select option 2 to select this option. The Print Options dialog box shown in Figure 5-12 is displayed. Enter any necessary changes to the default values and press Enter. This displays a screen with a message at the bottom requesting information on which records to print, shown in Figure 5-13.

Because you want to print all the records, you do not need to enter any criteria. Just press F10, and all the records in the database will be printed.

## Printing with Search/Sort Instructions

*All of the search and sort specifications you worked with earlier can also be used for printing database records.*

As the prompt in Figure 5-13 indicates, you can specify search and sort instructions for printing. The last search/sort specifications you worked with were for a list of employees living outside of Indianapolis. The records were sorted in reverse chronological order of the **Date of Appl** field. Let's see how to print this list. Select the **Print records** option from the Print menu and press Enter at the Print Options dialog box. Now enter the search/sort specifications shown

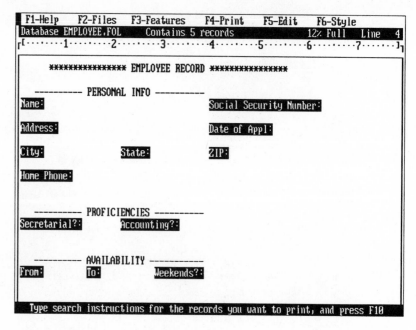

**Figure 5-13.** Search/Sort Print Specifications screen.

in Figure 5-14. Press F10 and the records for Mary Zale and Kelly Craig are printed in that order.

# Summary

- We used the employee database entries from Chapter 4 to illustrate the powers of searching and sorting in the database application.

- First Choice allows you to search for virtually any type of match or non-match condition.

- You also may re-order database records by sorting on one or two separate fields. Search and sort specifications may be combined to provide a sorted list of specific records.

- You may route database records to your system printer to provide you with a hard copy of your entries. You can print either a single record or a list of records generated by search/sort specifications.

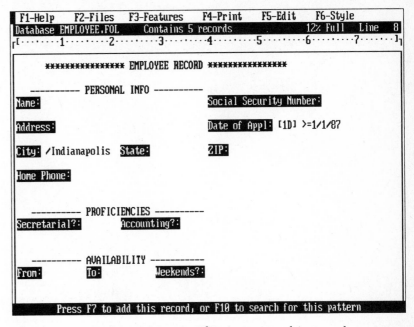

**Figure 5-14.** Search/sort print specifications entered in two places on the screen.

# More Database Operations

**In This Chapter:**

- Removing One Record
- Copying a Form to Create a New Database
- Copying Records to Another Database
- Removing Several Records
- Ditto-ing Fields and Records
- Changing a Form Design
- Using Table View
- Merging Another File
- Records and Document Files
- Saving and Retrieving ASCII Data Files
- Summary

This chapter covers advanced features of First Choice's database application and discusses efficient database management techniques in detail. You will learn how to remove unwanted records, change form designs, and transfer data from one database file to another. All of the menu items unique to the database application are also explained. In addition, you'll learn how to convert your First Choice database files into a format recognizable by other database applications. Let's start by examining how to delete records from a database.

*Remember, a file is a set of records.*

*Note:* In this chapter you'll be manipulating files as a whole. If most of your computer experience is with word processors, you may need to guard against a tendency to think of a file as a single item. In word processing a file is the smallest unit you handle, but in the database, the smallest unit you handle is a *record*, and the term "file" refers to a *collection* of records. In other words, when thinking about the database, don't confuse a file with a record.

# Removing One Record

In Chapter 4 we discussed how to add and change database records. First Choice also provides the ability to delete a record from a database, via the Features menu. Figure 6-1 shows Tim Smith's record, which the Wikley Company wants to remove from the employee database because he recently moved out of town. (Remember, your computer likely will show a different percentage full than the screens in this book, due to differences between systems.)

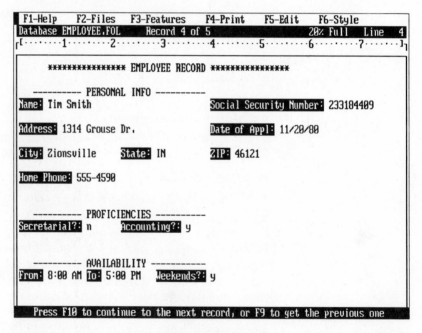

**Figure 6-1.** Tim Smith's record.

To delete this record from the employee database, select option 4, **Remove this record**, from the Features menu. After this option is selected, the warning message in Figure 6-2 is displayed.

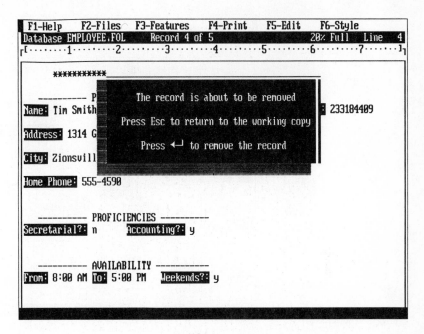

**Figure 6-2.** Record deletion warning message.

*Even experienced database managers exercise care when deleting records.*

This message warns you that you are about to remove a record from the database. This means that the information listed for that record will be lost forever, so proceed with extreme caution! If you really didn't mean to select the record removal option, press Escape and the screen in Figure 6-1 will be re-displayed. If you want to remove the record from the database press the Enter key. However, I recommend you leave this record in for now, because we'll be using it later in the chapter. In your database work when you do remove a record, you can verify the record has been deleted by trying to search for an item, (in this example, you would search for the name Tim Smith).

Removing a record via option 4 of the Features menu is different from erasing a record via option 9 (**Erase this record**) of the Edit menu. The erase option in the Edit menu will delete all field entries for the current record, but it will not remove that record from the database file. Figure 6-3 shows a new record added to the employee database to illustrate this point.

The top of Figure 6-3 indicates that the employee database contains 6 records. Select option 9, **Erase this record**, from the Edit menu. Figure 6-4 shows the warning message displayed when the erase option is selected; this message is very similar to the warning displayed when

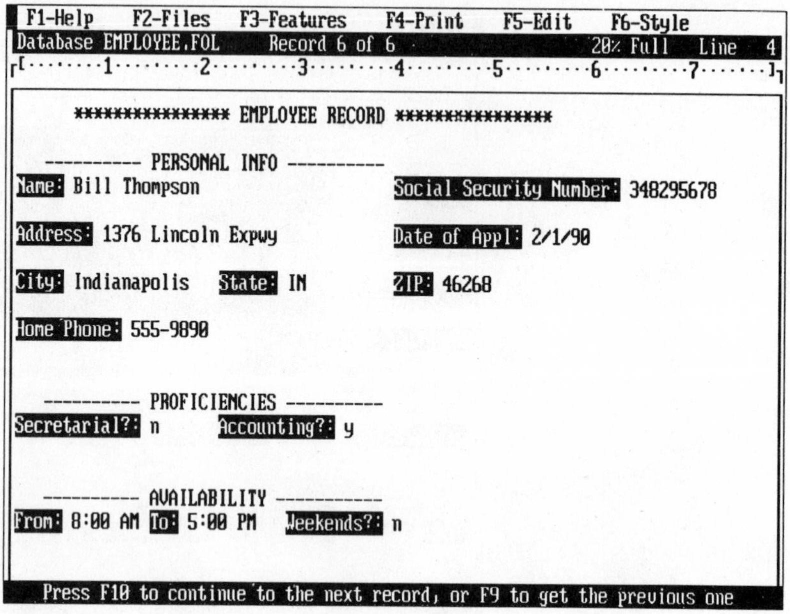

```
 F1-Help     F2-Files    F3-Features    F4-Print    F5-Edit    F6-Style
 Database EMPLOYEE.FOL      Record 6 of 6                  20% Full   Line    4
 r[········1········2········3········4········5········6········7·····]7

         *************** EMPLOYEE RECORD ***************

          ---------- PERSONAL INFO ----------
     Name: Bill Thompson              Social Security Number: 348295678

     Address: 1376 Lincoln Expwy      Date of Appl: 2/1/90

     City: Indianapolis   State: IN   ZIP: 46268

     Home Phone: 555-9890


          ---------- PROFICIENCIES ----------
     Secretarial?: n     Accounting?: y


          ---------- AVAILABILITY ----------
     From: 8:00 AM  To: 5:00 PM   Weekends?: n


    Press F10 to continue to the next record, or F9 to get the previous one
```

**Figure 6-3.** A new temporary employee record.

removing a record. After Enter is pressed to continue with the erase, the screen in Figure 6-5 is displayed showing a blank form.

*The* **Erase this record** *selection doesn't remove a record from the database—it only clears the record's fields.*

Notice that the top of Figure 6-5 indicates that the database still contains six records. This is because the steps you just performed replaced the new record with a blank record. Even if you leave the database application and return via option 6 of the Main menu (**Get an existing file**) you will see that the database still contains six records. Browsing through the database with F10 shows each of the original five records followed by the blank one. You can remove this blank record with option 4 of the Features menu, **Remove this record**, as described above.

*There is no easy way to undo an accidental deletion from a database.*

When you press Enter at the screen in Figure 6-2 the record is removed from the database file on your disk. Since accidents can and do happen it is a good idea to maintain backup copies of all your First Choice files. Refer to the Disk Utilities section of Chapter 12 to see how to create backup copies of your data files.

Removing one record at a time is handy if you don't have to delete very many. In reality, database maintenance involves the deletion of many records at once. The single record removal feature would be a cumbersome alternative if the Wikley Company wants to purge all applicant records two years after the application date. Unfortunately,

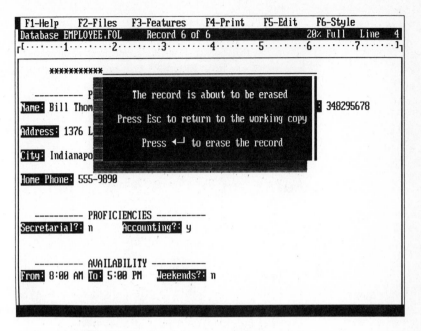

**Figure 6-4.** Record erase warning message.

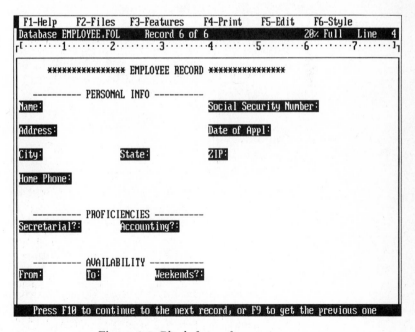

**Figure 6-5.** Blank form after erasure.

First Choice does not provide a quick and easy method of multiple record removal like the single record removal feature. First Choice does offer the capability of copying the records of one database to another database file. Further, you can use search and sort specifications to denote which and in what order records should be copied to the destination file. Creative use of this process will allow you to delete several records from a database file at once. Let's take a close look at each step involved.

# Copying a Form to Create a New Database

Before records can be copied from one database file to another, the format of the *destination file* (file you are copying to) must be defined. This means that there must be a form definition in the destination file. For example, suppose you want to copy all the records from EMPLOYEE.FOL to a file called NEWEMP.FOL. Before we can do this you must define the form structure of NEWEMP.FOL. This definition may be performed in one of two ways:

Select option 2, **Create a database**, from the Main menu and create the form for NEWEMP.FOL as you did for EMPLOYEE.FOL in Chapter 4.

*or*

Use option 4, **Copy form design**, in the Files menu to copy the form design from EMPLOYEE.FOL to NEWEMP.FOL.

If you choose the first method, you must be careful to define the form design for NEWEMP.FOL exactly as you did for EMPLOYEE.FOL, including field types and sizes. The second method assures you that these specifications will be the same in both databases. Since you already know how to create a form design via the first method, let's take a look at how to copy one with the second method:

1. Once the employee database is loaded you can select option 4, **Copy form design**, from the Files menu. After this selection the Directory Assistant is displayed (Figure 6-6).

2. Enter the file name NEWEMP.FOL at the prompt **Database to copy form design to:** and press Enter. This displays the screen shown in Figure 6-7. This screen shows a message indicating the form copy was successful. Press Enter to complete the form copy process.

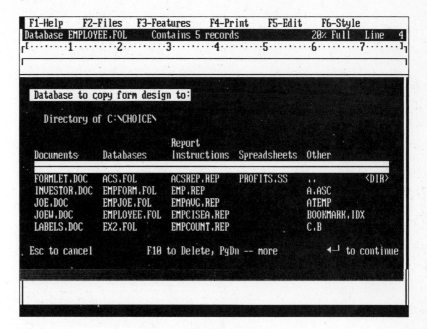

**Figure 6-6.** The Directory Assistant with the request for the database you want to copy the form design to.

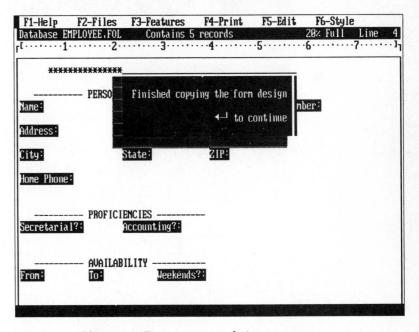

**Figure 6-7.** Form copy completion message.

Let's verify that NEWEMP.FOL contains a copy of the EMPLOYEE.FOL form design. Press Escape to leave the employee database and return to the Main menu. Select option 6, **Get an existing file**, and the Directory Assistant is displayed (Figure 6-8). Notice the entry for our new database file NEWEMP.FOL. The screen in Figure 6-9 is displayed when you retrieve the NEWEMP.FOL file from the Directory Assistant above.

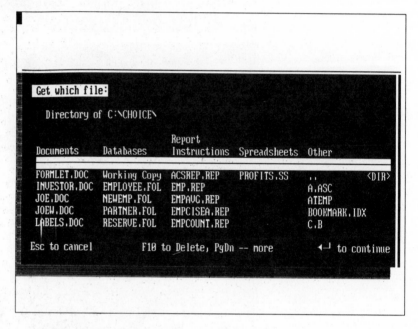

**Figure 6-8.** Directory Assistant with NEWEMP.FOL added.

# Copying Records to Another Database

As you can see in Figure 6-9, the NEWEMP.FOL database file contains zero records, but the form design from our original employee database is displayed. You could add records to NEWEMP.FOL by entering the data fields and pressing F7 as you did in Chapter 4. However, our goal with NEWEMP.FOL is to copy records directly from EMPLOYEE.FOL without having to manually enter them. Let's find out how this task is accomplished.

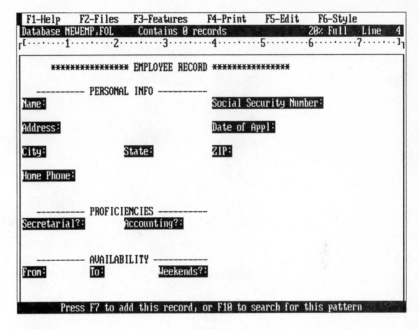

**Figure 6-9.** Form design for NEWEMP.FOL. Notice that the file has no records in it currently.

## Copying an Entire Database

Press Escape to leave the NEWEMP.FOL database and return to the Main menu. Then follow these steps to copy an entire database:

1. Select option 6, **Get an existing file**, and choose EMPLOYEE.FOL from the Directory Assistant to retrieve our original employee database file. Since the form design has already been copied to NEWEMP.FOL, this new employee database file is ready to receive copies of the records from EMPLOYEE.FOL.

2. Select option 5, **Copy records**, from the Files menu. The Directory Assistant is displayed, as shown in Figure 6-10.

3. Select the NEWEMP.FOL file from the Directory Assistant. This displays the screen in Figure 6-11. This is the same screen you used to specify search and sort commands in Chapter 5.

4. Press F10 with no search/sort specifications to copy the entire set of records in our employee database to the NEWEMP.FOL file. The screen in Figure 6-12 is displayed when First Choice is finished copying the records from EMPLOYEE.FOL to NEWEMP.FOL. As you can see in Figure 6-12, all five records were copied to our new employee database.

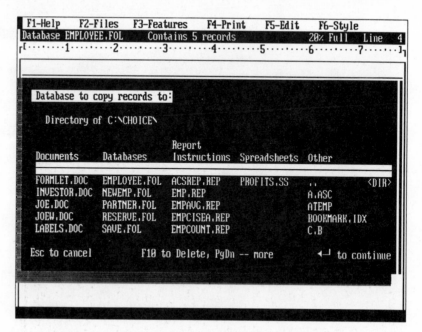

**Figure 6-10.** The Directory Assistant for copy records.

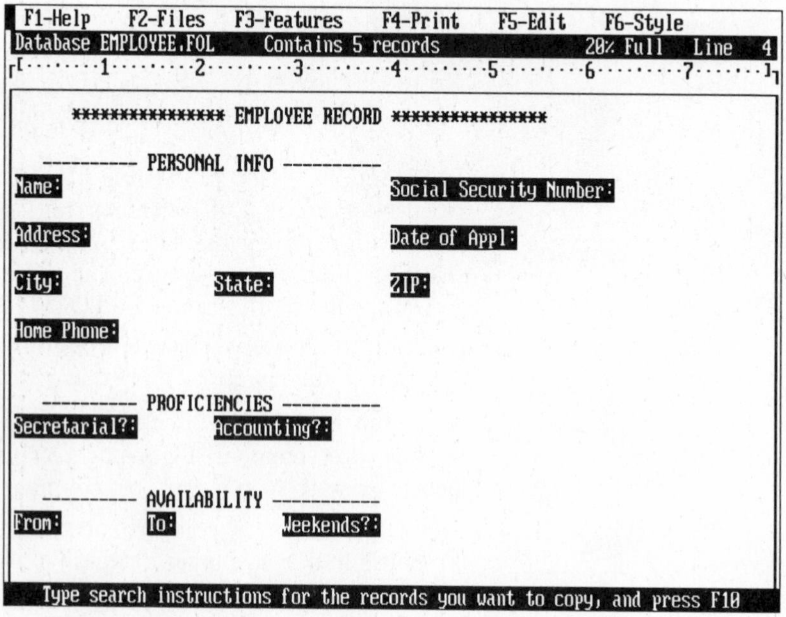

```
 F1-Help    F2-Files    F3-Features    F4-Print    F5-Edit    F6-Style
Database EMPLOYEE.FOL      Contains 5 records           20% Full   Line   4
[·······1·······2·······3·······4·······5·······6·······7·····]


           *************** EMPLOYEE RECORD ***************

         ---------- PERSONAL INFO ----------
  Name:                            Social Security Number:

  Address:                         Date of Appl:

  City:            State:          ZIP:

  Home Phone:



         ---------- PROFICIENCIES ----------
  Secretarial?:       Accounting?:



         ---------- AVAILABILITY ----------
  From:       To:         Weekends?:


   Type search instructions for the records you want to copy, and press F10
```

**Figure 6-11.** Search/sort specifications screen for copying.

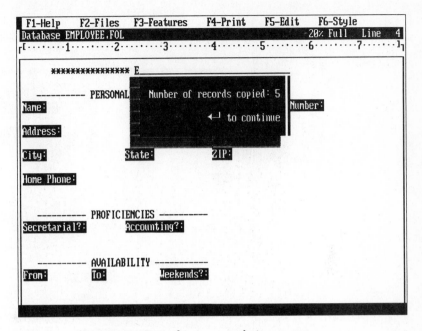

**Figure 6-12.** Record copy completion message.

Now let's verify that all the employee database records were indeed copied to NEWEMP.FOL:

1. Press Enter to acknowledge the message on Figure 6-12 and then press Escape to return to the Main menu.

2. Select option 6, **Get an existing file**, choose the NEWEMP.FOL file from the Directory Assistant, and voilà, the screen in Figure 6-13 is displayed. This screen indicates that this database contains five records. If you like, verify that the records were copied correctly by browsing through the database with the F10 key.

## Copying Portions of a Database

Rather than simply pressing F10, you could have entered search and sort specifications on the screen shown in Figure 6-11 to copy particular records in a specific order. Before trying this you should create a new .FOL file to use as a destination in the copy process. To copy the employee database's form design to this new file, NEWEMP2.FOL, follow these steps:

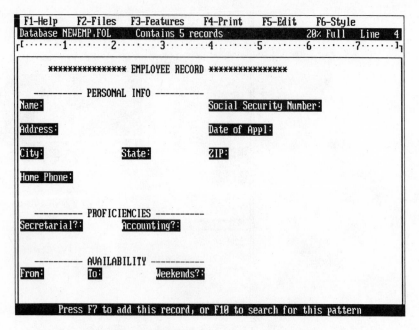

```
 F1-Help   F2-Files   F3-Features   F4-Print   F5-Edit   F6-Style
Database NEWEMP.FOL      Contains 5 records              20% Full  Line   4
r[·······1·······2·······3·······4·······5·······6·······7·····]

    *************** EMPLOYEE RECORD ***************

        ---------- PERSONAL INFO ----------
    Name:                        Social Security Number:

    Address:                     Date of Appl:

    City:             State:     ZIP:

    Home Phone:


        ---------- PROFICIENCIES ----------
    Secretarial?:     Accounting?:


        ---------- AVAILABILITY ----------
    From:        To:         Weekends?:



        Press F7 to add this record, or F10 to search for this pattern
```

**Figure 6-13.** The NEWEMP.FOL form screen, this time showing that there are five records in the database.

1. Return to First Choice's Main menu and select option 6, **Get an existing file**.

2. Specify the file name EMPLOYEE.FOL in the Directory Assistant.

3. Select option 4, **Copy form design**, from the Files menu.

4. Specify the new file name NEWEMP2.FOL in the Directory Assistant.

5. Press Enter to acknowledge the form copy completion message.

Now NEWEMP2.FOL contains our employee database form design and you can copy records to it.

At this point, you can use any of the search and sort specifications discussed in Chapter 5 to copy specific records in a particular order to NEWEMP2.FOL. One of those examples involved finding all applicants who do not live in Indianapolis. Further, the list was sorted in reverse chronological order and did not include anyone who applied before January 1, 1987. Let's use these specifications to copy selected records to NEWEMP2.FOL:

1. Select option 5, **Copy records**, from the Files menu.

2. Specify the destination file name NEWEMP2.FOL in the Directory Assistant.

3. Specify the search and sort instructions shown in Figure 6-14 and press F10.

4. Press Enter to acknowledge the copy completion message.

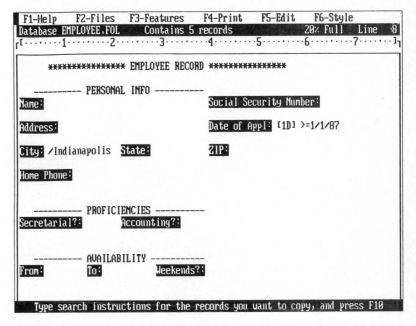

**Figure 6-14.** Search/sort specifications for copying selected records in a particular order into a new database.

The copy completion message indicates that two records were copied to NEWEMP2.FOL. This coincides with the results of these specifications in Chapter 5. Let's verify the correct records were written to NEWEMP2.FOL by following these steps:

1. Press Escape to return to the Main menu and select option 6, **Get an existing file**.

2. Specify the file name NEWEMP2.FOL in the Directory Assistant.

3. Step through the database with F10 and verify that the records for Mary Zale and Kelly Craig appear in that order.

# Appending to an Existing Database

*Use the Files menu to quickly switch between files without returning to the Main menu.*

The NEWEMP2.FOL database now contains two records: Mary Zale and Kelly Craig. What would happen if you use the steps above to copy Tim Smith's record from EMPLOYEE.FOL to NEWEMP2.FOL? Before you try this experiment, there is a quicker way to hop between the EMPLOYEE.FOL and NEWEMP2.FOL databases. Here's how to switch from one file to another without returning to the Main menu:

1. Select option 3, **Get an existing file**, from the Files menu.
2. When the Directory Assistant is displayed, select the file you want to load (EMPLOYEE.FOL).

After you make the Directory Assistant selection, the new file's form is displayed on the screen. The file which was previously loaded is closed and you can perform operations on the selected file. The two steps just given bring about the same results as returning to the Main menu to retrieve an existing file.

Now that the EMPLOYEE.FOL database is loaded let's return to the task of copying Tim Smith's record to NEWEMP2.FOL:

1. Select option 5, **Copy records**, from the Files menu.
2. Specify the destination file name NEWEMP2.FOL in the Directory Assistant.
3. Specify the search instruction shown in Figure 6-15 and press F10.
4. Press Enter to acknowledge the copy completion message.

Now switch to the NEWEMP2.FOL database using option 3, **Get an existing file**, from the Files menu. If you press F10 and browse through NEWEMP2.FOL, you'll see that it now contains records for Mary Zale, Kelly Craig, and Tim Smith. We have proven that if you copy records to an existing database they are appended to the file and the original records are not disturbed. This fact is one of the positive aspects of copying records from one database to another, but there are some negative ones as well. For instance, if you now copy Mary Zale's record from EMPLOYEE.FOL to NEWEMP2.FOL again, NEWEMP2.FOL will have two separate entries for her. Try this and prove it to yourself.

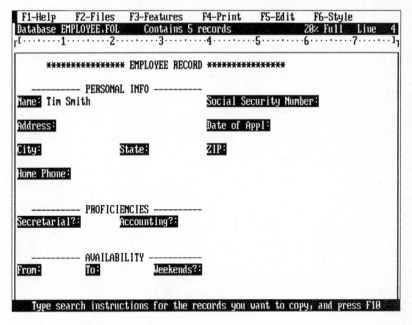

**Figure 6-15.** Copy search instruction.

# Copying Files to Help Perform Other Tasks

It is useful to know how to copy files for other reasons too. Sometimes you want to perform a task that would be tedious if you did it in a straightforward way, and you can use copying methods to accomplish your goal much more quickly.

## Deleting Unwanted Database Files

*Prune unnecessary files from your disk often.*

Since disk space is often a precious commodity, you should always try to keep your disk free from unnecessary files. You have created a couple of working databases which may now be deleted from your disk: NEW-EMP.FOL and NEWEMP2.FOL. You can quickly delete these files via the Directory Assistant as follows:

1. Press Escape to return to the Main menu, and select option 6, **Get an existing file**.

2. When the Directory Assistant is displayed, enter NEWEMP.FOL or position the cursor over its name in the file list.

3. Press F10 to delete the file. The "About to erase" message in Figure 6-16 is displayed.

4. Press Y to delete the file.

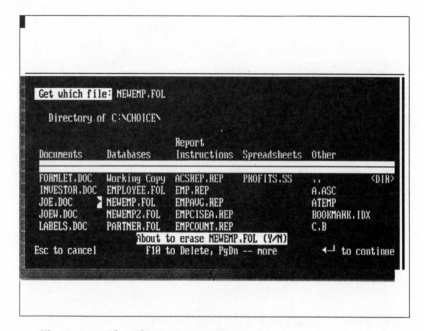

**Figure 6-16.** The **About to erase** Directory Assistant message.

This message is a warning giving you the opportunity to cancel the deletion request. If you press N, the warning disappears and the Directory Assistant waits for your next instruction. This warning is your last opportunity to back out of the deletion. Once a database file has been deleted, its contents are lost. So, be absolutely certain you want to remove your file before pressing Y! After deletion the Directory Assistant screen is re-displayed, this time without the NEWEMP.FOL entry. You can use the same steps above to delete the NEWEMP2.FOL database.

## Organizing a Database

In Chapter 5 you used sort specifications to reorder the records in the employee database file. This was useful to display and print records in various orders. The Wikley Company wants to rearrange the database by Social Security number in ascending order. They don't want to have to specify sort instructions every time they use the database. Further, the

Wikley Company wants the database stored on the disk in the rearranged order so that they can browse through it via F10. As you know, the sorting examples we discussed in Chapter 5 didn't rewrite the file to the disk in sorted order; they simply re-ordered the records for that request. Here are the general steps you must perform to re-order the database file:

1. Copy the form design to a new database (SORTEMP.FOL).
2. Copy all the records in the database to the new database with sort specifications (for our example, **Social Security Number: [1A]**).
3. Delete the original database (EMPLOYEE.FOL).
4. Rename the new database with the original database name.

Let's take a look at each of these steps in detail.

## Copying the Form Design to SORTEMP.FOL

You have already performed this step a few times in this chapter. Follow these steps:

1. Return to First Choice's Main menu and select option 6, **Get an existing file**.
2. Specify the file name EMPLOYEE.FOL in the Directory Assistant.
3. Select option 4, **Copy form design**, from the Files menu.
4. Specify the new file name SORTEMP.FOL in the Directory Assistant.
5. Press Enter to acknowledge the form copy completion message.

## Copying the Sorted Records to SORTEMP.FOL

Follow these steps to copy the EMPLOYEE.FOL records to SORTEMP.FOL in ascending order of Social Security number:

1. Select option 5, **Copy records**, from the Files menu.
2. Specify the destination file name SORTEMP.FOL in the Directory Assistant.
3. Specify the search instruction shown in Figure 6-17 ([1A]) and press F10.
4. Press Enter to acknowledge the copy completion message.

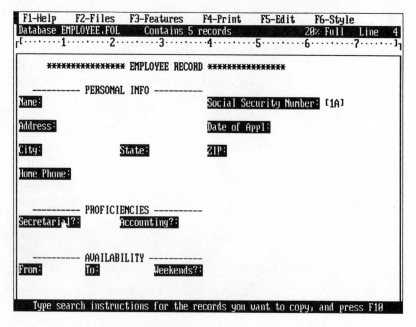

**Figure 6-17.** Copy sort instructions, here [1A].

## Deleting the EMPLOYEE.FOL Database

Before deleting this database, let's make sure the SORTEMP.FOL database contains all our records:

1. Select option 3, **Get an existing file**, from the Files menu.
2. Specify the file name SORTEMP.FOL in the Directory Assistant.
3. Press F10 to browse through the new sorted database and confirm that the records appear in this order:

| Name: | Social Security Number: |
|---|---|
| Tim Smith | 233184409 |
| Mary Zale | 355121905 |
| Kelly Craig | 495882034 |
| David Craig | 527935661 |
| John Adams | 583082856 |

*Always be careful when deleting files. You don't want to lose a lot of work!*

It is very important that you make certain the new database contains all five records before deleting the old database. Why? Once you delete the old database from the disk the records contained within it are lost for ever. This may not be much of a problem with a small database, but it can be a major dilemma if you accidentally delete a large one.

Once you are satisfied that SORTEMP.FOL contains all the data in EMPLOYEE.FOL, follow these steps to delete EMPLOYEE.FOL:

1. Return to First Choice's Main menu and select option 6, **Get an existing file**.

2. At the Directory Assistant, enter `EMPLOYEE.FOL` or position the cursor over its name in the file list.

3. Press F10 to delete the file; the **About to erase** message is displayed.

4. Press `Y` to delete the file.

## Renaming SORTEMP.FOL to EMPLOYEE.FOL

Looking at the Directory Assistant screen, you'll now see that the entry for EMPLOYEE.FOL is gone and a new entry for SORTEMP.FOL exists. At this point you could tell the Wikley Company to use the SORTEMP.FOL database file whenever they want to work with the employee database but that would probably confuse them. Remember, they are used to specifying a file named EMPLOYEE.FOL.

*See Chapter 12 for more details on the rename function.*

How can you rename the file SORTEMP.FOL to EMPLOYEE.-FOL? Use set of tools called the Disk Utilities, which may be accessed via the Main menu or the Files menu within the database application. Figure 6-18 shows the Disk Utilities menu.

Follow these steps to rename the SORTEMP.FOL file to EMPLOYEE.FOL:

1. Return to First Choice's Main menu and select option 9, **Use disk utilities**.

2. When the screen in Figure 6-18 is displayed select option 3, **Rename a file**.

3. When the Directory Assistant screen that asks which file you want to rename (rename source) is displayed (Figure 6-19), select the file to rename (SORTEMP.FOL).

4. When the Directory Assistant asking for what you want to rename it as (*rename destination*) is displayed (Figure 6-20), type the file's new name (EMPLOYEE.FOL).

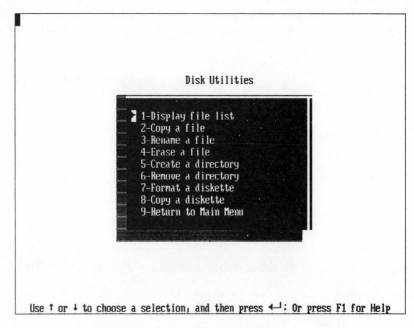

**Figure 6-18.** The Disk Utilities menu.

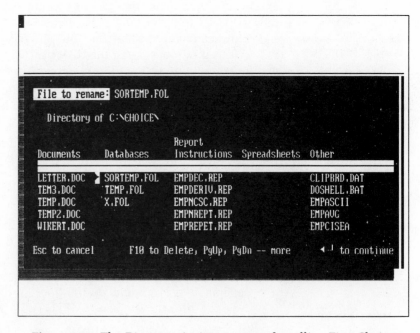

**Figure 6-19.** The Directory Assistant screen for telling First Choice which file you want to rename.

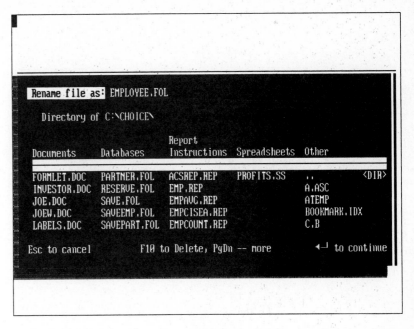

**Figure 6-20.** The Directory Assistant screen for providing the new name.

If the rename is successful, the Disk Utilities menu will be redisplayed (Figure 6-18).

The file rename operation is significantly different than the database record copy operation. When you copy all the records from EMPLOYEE.FOL to another database file the result is two separate database files on the disk. When a file is renamed the result is one database file on the disk with a new name.

When the Directory Assistant is displayed as shown in Figure 6-19, you can select the file to rename from the list of file names. When the Directory Assistant is displayed as in Figure 6-20, you have to type in the new name. You cannot select any of the listed file names as the destination for the rename, because the destination file name must be the name of a file which does not currently exist. Your computer can only differentiate files by their names so two files cannot share the same file name. The list of file names in Figure 6-20 is presented to show you what names are already in use and are therefore illegal destination file names. If you accidentally specify the name of an existing file as the destination file name, the error message in Figure 6-21 will be displayed.

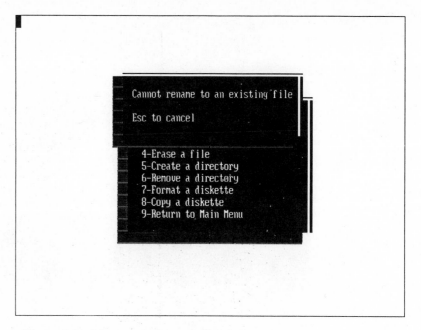

**Figure 6-21.** Message indicating illegal destination file name during
file rename.

Press Escape if the error in Figure 6-21 is displayed; this returns
you to the screen in Figure 6-19, where you may re-enter the source
file name.

By the way, the Disk Utilities may also be directly accessed
within the database application via the Files menu option 8, **Use disk
utilities**. However, one shortcoming exists if you try to rename the
SORTEMP.FOL file via the Files menu: You *cannot* rename the currently active application file by loading the SORTEMP.FOL database;
selecting option 8, **Use disk utilities**, from the Files menu; selecting
option 3, **Rename a file**, from the Disk Utilities menu; and specifying
the source file to rename as SORTEMP.FOL in the screen in Figure
6-22. If you try to do this, the error message in Figure 6-23 will be
displayed. This error message occurs because First Choice cannot
rename the file currently loaded by the database application; you can
rename any other file listed by the Directory Assistant, however.

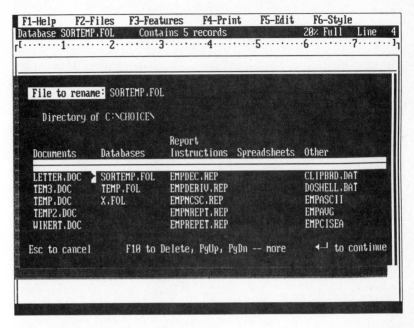

**Figure 6-22.** The Source Rename Directory Assistant screen within the database application.

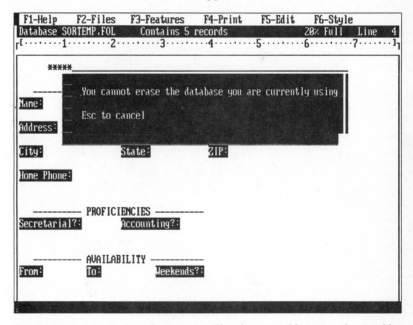

**Figure 6-23.** Message indicating an illegal source file name during file rename within the database application.

Notice that the error message in Figure 6-23 uses the word "erase" in connection with the database you are currently using. The error message is more meaningful if you substitute the word "rename" for "erase." Hopefully Software Publishing Corporation will fix this message in a future release of PFS: First Choice.

Once you have successfully renamed SORTEMP.FOL to EMPLOYEE.FOL you can get into the database application with EMPLOYEE.FOL as you have previously. The only difference is that the employee records in EMPLOYEE.FOL are now sorted in ascending order of Social Security numbers.

# Removing Several Records

*Here's a powerful purging technique.*

Earlier in this chapter we discussed how to remove one record at a time from a database file. We mentioned that single record removal is accomplished via option 4, **Remove this record**, in the Features menu. However, no menu option is provided to remove more than one record at a time. If you can express which records to *not* delete in the resulting database, you can use these steps to remove several records at once:

1. Copy the form design to a new database (TEMP.FOL).
2. Copy the records you want to keep in the database to the new database with search (and, optionally, sort) specifications.
3. Delete the original database (EMPLOYEE.FOL).
4. Rename the new database to the original database name.

Steps 1, 3, and 4 have already been discussed in other sections of this chapter. We have also previously examined the major concept behind step 2, copying selected records to another database file. Use this implementation of the record copy procedure to remove unwanted records. For example, suppose the Wikley Company wants to clean up its employee database by removing all applicants who applied before January 1, 1986. Once you have copied the database form to a new temporary file (step 1 above) you could use the search instructions in Figure 6-24 to copy the records Wikley Company wants to keep.

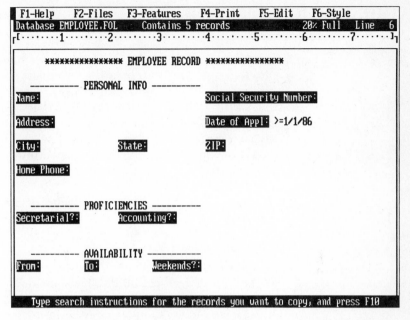

**Figure 6-24.** Search instructions for file purge of applications made before January 1, 1986.

Continue with the record copy process by pressing F10. The copy completion message indicates that three records were copied. If you now retrieve the TEMP.FOL and browse through it, you will see that the following records were copied:

| Name: | Date of Appl: |
|---|---|
| Mary Zale | 1/13/89 |
| Kelly Craig | 3/12/88 |
| David Craig | 12/5/87 |

You could now execute steps 3 and 4 above to rename this "current" version of the database as EMPLOYEE.FOL. You have been able to remove, or purge, the unwanted records from the employee database via the record copy operation. As you can see, this process is more complicated than the single record removal operation but it is a powerful way of creating databases without unwanted records.

# Ditto-ing Fields and Records

Even though First Choice makes database maintenance relatively simple, this operation can be a time-intensive and repetitious task. This is especially true when you must add many records to the database at one sitting. Quite often you may find that some of the records contain similar or even identical field information. When this occurs you can save keystrokes by using First Choice's *ditto* feature. For example, let's say you are in the process of adding records to the employee database and you just finished adding the following record:

**Name:** John Wilson          **Social Security Number:** 286004892
**Address:** 1323 Market St.    **Date of Appl:** 8/28/89
**City:** Carmel               **State:** IN   **ZIP:** 46032
**Home Phone:** 555-2889
**Secretarial?:** n            **Accounting:** y
**From:** 9:00 AM  **To:** 5:00 PM   **Weekends?:** y

Now you are about to add the following record:

**Name:** Amy Wilson          **Social Security Number:** 762097902
**Address:** 1323 Market St.    **Date of Appl:** 8/28/89
**City:** Carmel               **State:** IN   **ZIP:** 46032
**Home Phone:** 555-2889
**Secretarial?:** n            **Accounting:** y
**From:** 9:00 AM  **To:** 5:00 PM   **Weekends?:** y

John and Amy Wilson are married and therefore much of the data in both records is the same. You just pressed F7 to add John's record to the database and you don't want to have to retype much of the same information for Amy. If you press Alt-E, the record ditto shortcut key, the information you entered for John is displayed on the screen (Figure 6-25).

Although the information for John Wilson is displayed in Figure 6-25, you are not actually working with John's record. You have copied John's data to the form on the screen in Figure 6-25. Now you can follow these steps to make the necessary changes for Amy's record:

1. Type Amy's name over John's and delete the **n**.
2. Press Tab to move to the **Social Security Number** field.
3. Type Amy's Social Security number over John's.
4. Press F7 to add Amy's record to the database.

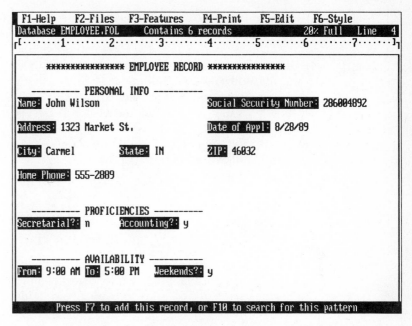

```
F1-Help    F2-Files   F3-Features   F4-Print   F5-Edit   F6-Style
Database EMPLOYEE.FOL      Contains 6 records          20% Full   Line   4
[·······1·······2·······3·······4·······5·······6·······7·······]

         *************** EMPLOYEE RECORD ***************

          ---------- PERSONAL INFO ----------
 Name: John Wilson                  Social Security Number: 286004892

 Address: 1323 Market St.           Date of Appl: 8/28/89

 City: Carmel         State: IN     ZIP: 46032

 Home Phone: 555-2889



          ---------- PROFICIENCIES ----------
 Secretarial?: n      Accounting?: y



          ---------- AVAILABILITY ----------
 From: 9:00 AM  To: 5:00 PM   Weekends?: y



        Press F7 to add this record, or F10 to search for this pattern
```

**Figure 6-25.** Result of pressing record ditto key after adding John Wilson's record.

Browse through the database with F10 to see that the records for John and Amy have been successfully added. The record ditto shortcut key, Alt-E, is quite handy in situations like John and Amy Wilson's since their records are almost identical.

*This process may be repeated as many times as needed to copy individual fields from the previous record.*

What about situations where only one or two fields are the same between consecutive records to add? For example, many of the Wikley Company's applicants are from Indianapolis. The person adding records to the database must type that lengthy city name over and over again. You probably wouldn't want to use the record ditto key to copy the entire previous record because only one field is the same. Fortunately First Choice offers a *field ditto* shortcut key, Alt-D. If you want to copy one field at a time from the previously entered record, follow these steps:

1. Position the cursor at one of the fields and press Alt-D.
2. Move to the next field and press Alt-D again to copy that field's data from the previous record.

The previous examples show how the ditto keys can be used when you are adding two consecutive records with identical fields.

These keys can also be used to extract information from the last record retrieved in a search. Mary Zale's record was added to the database on January 13, 1989. On September 28, 1989 her twin sister, Terry, visited Wikley Company to seek employment. Terry's personnel information is identical to Mary's with the obvious exception of her name and Social Security number. Here's how you could copy Mary's data into a new record for Terry via the record ditto key:

1. Initiate a search for Mary Zale's record by placing her name in the **Name** field and pressing F10.
2. When Mary's record is displayed, press Escape to terminate the search and display a blank form.
3. Press the record ditto shortcut key (Alt-E) to copy Mary's data to the blank form.

Now you can type Terry's name and Social Security number over Mary's and press F7 to save the new record. You can use the same sequence of steps to copy single fields from the previous record with the Alt-D key.

# Changing a Form Design

You can change a form design in several ways. We'll illustrate one in detail.

## Adding A Field

The Wikley Company is very favorably impressed with First Choice's database capabilities. Now that you've got the employee and partner databases created they throw a wrench into the works: Wikley Company forgot to tell you that they wanted to add another field to the employee form! It seems they want to include the minimum hourly rate desired by each applicant. What can you do now? Fortunately you've only added a few records to the employee database so you could start all over by creating the new form and adding the records again. But what if you had already added a few hundred records? What if the company changes the form design again in the future? Fortunately First Choice offers a relatively easy method of modifying a form design via option 5, Change form design, in the Features menu.

*Always make a backup copy of your database before changing its form design.*

You should always make a backup copy of your database before changing its form design. Refer to the previous sections in this chapter for copying the form and all records to a backup file. Once you have made a backup copy of the database, follow these steps to add the new field to the employee database:

1. Retrieve the employee database and select option 5, **Change form design**, from the Features menu.

2. The warning message in Figure 6-26 is then displayed to remind you to make a backup copy of the database before proceeding. If you have made a backup copy, press Enter to continue; otherwise press Escape to abort the form change process.

3. Select option 1, **Add fields**, from the Change Form Design menu shown in Figure 6-27.

4. Position the cursor and type the new field, **Min. Rate:**, as shown in Figure 6-28, and press F10.

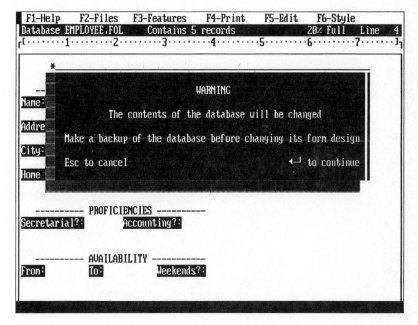

**Figure 6-26.** Reminder to make a backup before modifying the form design.

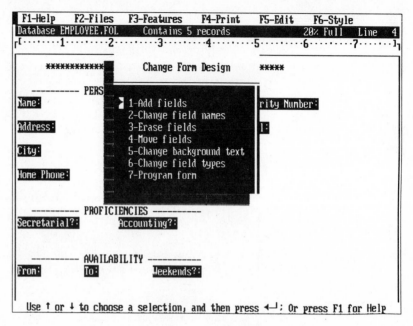

**Figure 6-27.** The Change Form Design menu.

```
 F1-Help    F2-Files   F3-Features   F4-Print   F5-Edit    F6-Style
 Database EMPLOYEE.FOL     Contains 5 records        20% Full   Line   10
┌·······1·······2·······3·······4·······5·······6·······7·······┐

         *************** EMPLOYEE RECORD ***************

          ---------- PERSONAL INFO ----------
    Name:                           Social Security Number:

    Address:                        Date of Appl:

    City:            State:         ZIP:

    Home Phone:                     Min. Rate:


             ---------- PROFICIENCIES ----------
    Secretarial?:        Accounting?:


              ---------- AVAILABILITY ----------
    From:      To:           Weekends?:

          Type new fields where you want them, then press F10
```

**Figure 6-28.** The new employee database form design, after adding a
field for minimum pay rate.

First Choice actually starts changing the database record formats when you press F10 in step 4. Each record is quickly displayed as it is being processed. A blank copy of the new form is displayed after all records have been modified. At this point you may add new records, initiate a search, etc.

*By default, all fields added to an existing form are defined as text type.*

Press F10 to browse through the database and make certain all the records are present. Notice that the new **Min. Rate** field is blank for all entries. At this point you could place an entry in each record's **Min. Rate** field to store these figures in the database. However, it would seem that the **Min. Rate** field should be a numeric type, and you never defined it as numeric. Don't worry, you didn't miss anything. Remember that the Change Form Design menu in Figure 6-27 contains selections for both **Add fields** (selection 1) and **Change field types** (selection 6). First Choice does not provide any way of denoting special field types when adding fields via selection 1.

Adding a non-text field to a form is really a two-step process. You must first add the field, as you have done above, then change the field type via the **Change field types** selection in the Change Form Design menu. Follow these steps to change the **Min. Rate** field to numeric type:

1. Select option 5, **Change form design**, from the Features menu.
2. The warning message in Figure 6-26 is then displayed to remind you to make a backup copy of the database before proceeding. If you have made a backup copy, press Enter to continue; otherwise press Escape to abort the form change process.
3. Select option 6, **Change field types**, from the Change Form Design menu shown in Figure 6-27.
4. Press Tab 8 times to move to the **Min. Rate** field and enter **N** to designate the field as numeric type.
5. Press F10 to save the type specifications.

Now enter numeric values in the **Min. Rate** field for each of the applicant records as shown here:

| Name | Min. Rate |
|------|-----------|
| David Craig | 8.50 |
| Kelly Craig | 5.00 |
| John Adams | 9.00 |
| Tim Smith | 7.50 |
| Mary Zale | 7.00 |

# Making Other Changes in Form Design

The following selections are also available in the Change Form Design menu for redesigning your form layout:

- **Change field names**. Figure 6-29 shows the screen displayed when this option is selected. You should type the new field names next to the existing field names (where your data would normally be placed) and press F10 to save the changes.

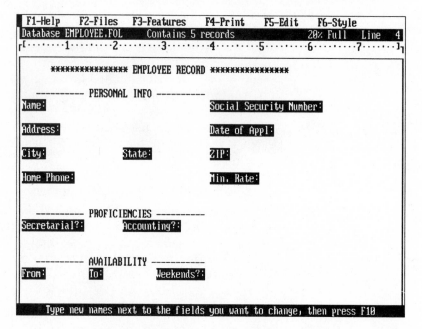

**Figure 6-29.** The Change Field Names screen.

- **Erase fields**. Figure 6-30 shows the screen displayed when this option is selected. You should type either **erase** or **e** next to each field to you want erased. Then press F10 to erase the designated fields. Note that all data previously available for the erased fields is no longer available after the erasure is complete. Therefore, use this option with extreme caution. Also notice that the erased fields leave empty space on the form design; the remaining fields are not shifted up or over to fill in the blank areas. The remaining fields may be moved via the next menu option, **Move fields**.

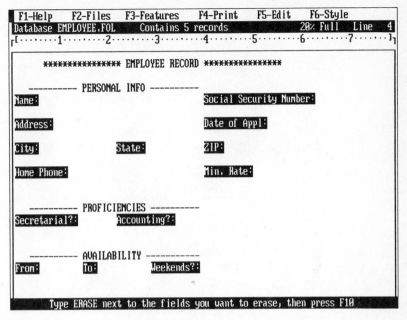

**Figure 6-30.** The Erase Fields screen.

- **Move fields**. Figure 6-31 shows the screen displayed when this option is selected. Move the cursor where you want the existing field(s) moved to and type the full field name, including the colon. Then press F10 to move the field(s) to the new position(s). This option permits movement of fields only; background text must be modified via the next selection, **Change background text**.

- **Change background text**. Figure 6-32 shows the screen displayed when this option is selected. You can type new background text or move existing text via the clipboard (choose selections 2 and 4 in the Edit menu to Move and Paste respectively). Press F10 to save the background text changes.

- **Program form**. This option will be thoroughly discussed in Chapter 7, *Form Programming*.

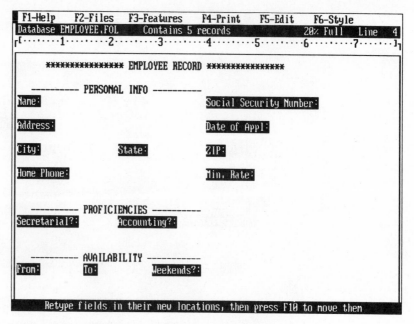

**Figure 6-31.** The Move Fields screen.

```
 F1-Help    F2-Files   F3-Features    F4-Print    F5-Edit    F6-Style
Database EMPLOYEE.FOL      Contains 5 records              8% Full   Line    4
┌[·······1·······2·······3·······4·······5·······6·······7·····]┐

        *************** EMPLOYEE RECORD ***************

        ---------- PERSONAL INFO ----------
    Name:                             Social Security Number:

    Address:                          Date of Appl:

    City:            State:           ZIP:

    Home Phone:                       Min. Rate:


        ---------- PROFICIENCIES ----------
    Secretarial?:        Accounting?:


        ---------- AVAILABILITY ----------
    From:        To:          Weekends?:


                Change the background text, then press F10
```

**Figure 6-32.** The Change Background Text screen.

# Using Table View

The F10 and F9 keys permit us to step through a database one record at a time—forwards and backwards respectively. This is sufficient if you only want to view one record on each screen. But what do you do if you want to view more than one record at a time? The answer to this question is First Choice's *table view* option.

Retrieve the employee database and select option 6, **Show table view**, from the Features menu. Figure 6-33 shows the screen displayed when this view option is selected. The table view of the employee database in this screen shows each record on a horizontal line. Each column represents a different field in the form. This view makes it much easier to compare field values for different records than looking at each record individually.

```
 F1-Help     F2-Files    F3-Features    F4-Print    F5-Edit    F6-Style
 Database EMPLOYEE.FOL       Record 1 of 5                        3% Full
 [·······1·T·····2·T·····3·T····4···T···5····T··6·····T··7·····T·
 Name      |Social Se>|Address  |Date of A>|City     |State |ZIP    |Ho

 Tim Smith |233184409|1314 Grou>|11/20/80 |Zionsville|IN    |46121  |55
 Mary Zale |335121905|2304 Mapl>|1/13/89  |Speedway  |IN    |46090  |55
 Kelly Cra>|495882034|2309 Emer>|3/12/88  |Carmel    |IN    |46032  |55
 David Cra>|527835661|20 N. Mai>|12/05/87 |Indianapo>|IN    |46390  |55
 John Adams|583082856|83 Park L>|6/22/85  |Indianapo>|IN    |46268  |55




             Press F1 for Help; or press ◄┘ to go back to current record
```

**Figure 6-33.** A table view of the employee database.

The default width of each column is 10 characters. As a result, some of our data is only partially displayed. For example, Kelly Craig's name is displayed as:

```
Kelly Cra>
```

The > (greater than) symbol indicates that the column width is too narrow to show the entire field value. This symbol is also used to denote field names which are too wide to completely display (such as **Social Se**>). In a moment we'll see how to define our own table view to fix this problem.

*The Home and End keys will move to the leftmost and rightmost positions in the table view respectively.*

You may also notice that Figure 6-33 does not show all the fields for the employee records. If you look to the right of the **ZIP** field's column, it appears that the first couple of characters of the **Home Phone** fields are displayed. You can press the right arrow key (→) to move to the right side of the table view. If you hold down the right arrow key long enough, the remaining fields will come into view. You also could press the End key once to move to the rightmost position in the table view, instead of holding down the right arrow key.

You can print this table view via option 1, **Print this table view**, of the Print menu. After this option is selected, the Print Options dialog box is displayed. Make any necessary changes to the default entries in the Print Options dialog box and press Enter to print the table view. Unless you have a wide carriage printer (wider than 80 columns), this printout will look exactly like the table view in Figure 6-33. Since only the first seven fields will show, this printout is not very useful. Let's look at how you can modify the table view so the results are more valuable.

## Defining a Table View

Once the default table view is displayed (Figure 6-33) you can select option 1, **Define table view**, from the Features menu to create a new table view. The screen in Figure 6-34 is displayed when this selection is made.

You could instead press the shortcut key for **Define table view**, Alt-T, to display the screen in Figure 6-34. Make entries in the screen shown in Figure 6-34 to specify the order and size of fields to include in the table view. The Wikley Company would like to see just the **Name, Min. Rate, Accounting?**, and **Home Phone** fields on a table view. You will therefore use the following table view specifications:

| | |
|---|---|
| **Name:** | 1w25 |
| **Min. Rate:** | 2w10 |
| **Accounting?:** | 3w11 |
| **Home Phone:** | 4w11 |

The number preceding each of the **w**s in the specifications designates the position you desire for that field in the new table view. The positions may be numbered from 1 to 9999, although only a maxi-

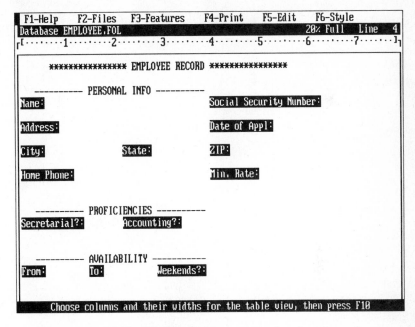

**Figure 6-34.** Table View Definition screen, for changing column widths.

mum of 64 fields and/or 250 characters will be placed in the table view. The position numbers increase from left to right so the leftmost position is number 1, the next position to the right is number 2, etc. The numbers after the **ws** in the specifications denote the width for that column. For example, the specification for the **Home Phone** field,

   4w11

means 1) the Home Phone values should be placed in the fourth column from the left and 2) that column has a maximum width of 11 characters. Enter the table view specifications as shown in Figure 6-35 and press F10 to generate the new table view shown in Figure 6-36.

The new table view in Figure 6-36 lists the four fields **Name**, **Min. Rate**, **Accounting?**, and **Home Phone** from left to right as you defined them in the specifications. Also, our width specifications are large enough to shown the largest values allowable in each field. Actually, the **Accounting?** and **Home Phone** field widths were set to 10 and 11 respectively to display the entire field names rather than the field values.

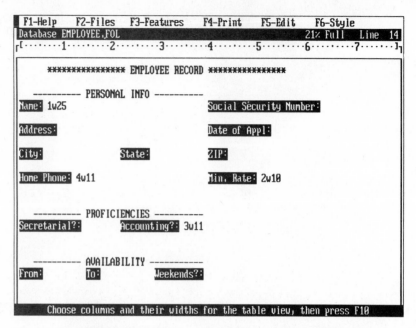

**Figure 6-35.** Specifications for the new table view.

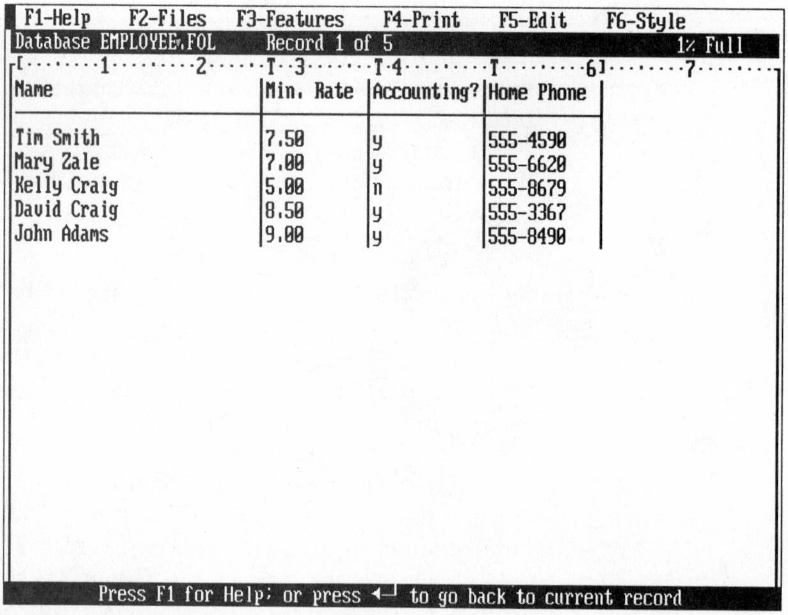

**Figure 6-36.** The new user-defined table view, with widths changed
and only selected columns displayed.

This new table view is much more useful for the Wikley Company because it wants to be able to find the phone numbers quickly for all applicants with accounting backgrounds. Now you can look through the **Accounting?** column for all Y entries to locate accounting applicants and their phone numbers.

Let's take this table view one step further by including a search specification. Since Wikley Company is only interested in viewing accounting applicants, you can suppress the display of non-accounting applicants with these steps:

1. If your screen looks like the one in Figure 6-36, you can press Escape twice to return to the blank form screen.

2. Enter a Y next to the **Accounting?** field as shown in Figure 6-37.

3. Press the table view shortcut key, Alt-T. The new table view of accounting applicants is shown in Figure 6-38.

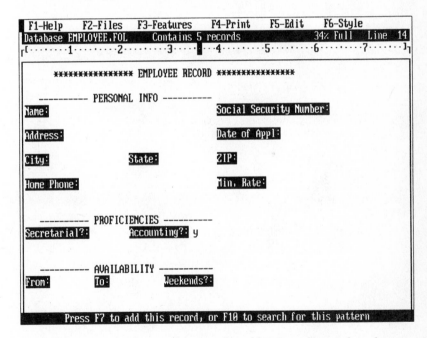

**Figure 6-37.** Search specifications for table view, designed to show only accounting applicants.

*Table view specifications are stored with the database file.*

Did you notice that you didn't have to re-enter your last set of table view specifications? Your *table view* specifications are stored in the database file (such as EMPLOYEE.FOL) so you don't have to re-enter them even if you leave First Choice and open the database again

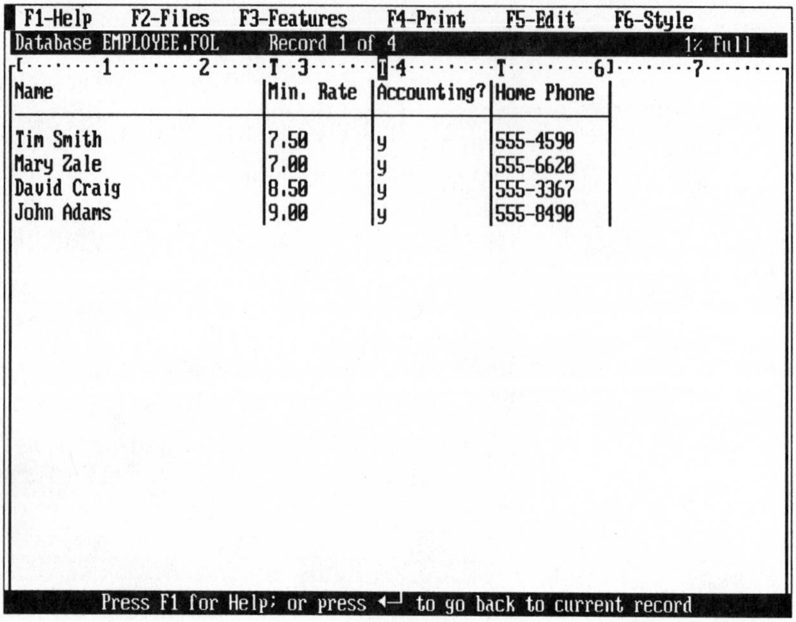

```
 F1-Help    F2-Files    F3-Features    F4-Print    F5-Edit    F6-Style
Database EMPLOYEE.FOL        Record 1 of 4                        1% Full
[·······1······2·····I··3·····I·4·····I·······6]·····7·····
Name                  |Min. Rate |Accounting?|Home Phone |

Tim Smith             |7.50      |y          |555-4590
Mary Zale             |7.00      |y          |555-6620
David Craig           |8.50      |y          |555-3367
John Adams            |9.00      |y          |555-8490




            Press F1 for Help; or press ←┘ to go back to current record
```

**Figure 6-38.** Accounting applicants table view.

later. In contrast, the *search* specifications you used for this new table view are not stored with the database so you would have to re-enter those for later table views. Although you only used a simple search specification here, you can use any of the search and sort instructions discussed in Chapter 5.

*A table view is a very useful tool.*

The table view in Figure 6-38 is just what Wikley Company wanted to see. Now they can even print the table view for later reference. In addition, instead of directing the print output to a printer the Wikley Company could write the output to a disk file; this would allow them to edit the table view as a document file in First Choice's word processor. Follow these steps to write the table view to a file named EMPTABLE.DOC:

1. Select option 1, **Print this table view**, from the Print menu.

2. Press Tab three times to move to the **Print to** entry in the Print Options dialog box.

3. Type the file name EMPTABLE.DOC, as shown in Figure 6-39 and press Enter.

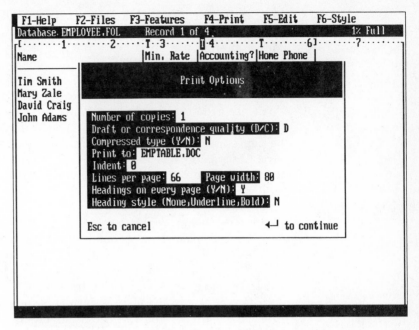

**Figure 6-39.** Print Options dialog box for table view file output.

Although you can't make modifications to a record while looking at it in a table view, First Choice allows you to quickly retrieve a record for modifications. For example, let's say you are looking at the table view in Figure 6-38 and you need to modify David Craig's record. You can move the cursor to any field in the row with David's entry and press Enter to retrieve his record and make modifications.

# Merging Another File

Part of our previous discussion about First Choice's word processor included how to merge another document into the working document. You may recall that this operation was performed via the **Merge another file** option in the Files menu. This same option is available in the Files menu in the database application.

*These ASCII files are readable by First Choice's word processor.*

You may think this menu selection could be used to bring records from another database into the working database. However, the **Merge another file** selection simply retrieves ASCII data from a file and places it at the cursor's position. An ASCII file is a file consisting solely of printable characters (that is, letters, numbers, symbols, etc.), in contrast to a non-ASCII file, which includes codes for printing bold type, printing running heads, etc. Let's see how the **Merge another file** option uses ASCII files.

The Wikley Company's personnel manager is in his office speaking with a potential client corporation. This corporation would like to know which of Wikley's applicants live in the 46268 zip code. They don't need the information until later this afternoon so the personnel manager is going to make a note of the request and get to it later. After he hangs up he realizes he can't find a pencil so he quickly starts up First Choice and selects **Create a document** from the Main menu. He then types in the number 46268, saves the document as ZIP.DOC and rushes off to an important meeting.

Later that afternoon he remembers the client corporation wanted information about applicants in a certain zip code. He also remembers that he saved the zip code in a file named ZIP.DOC, so he starts up First Choice and retrieves the employee database. He positions the cursor at the **ZIP** field and selects option 2, **Merge another file**, from the Files menu. He then selects the ZIP.DOC file from the Directory Assistant and presses Enter. His screen now looks like the one shown in Figure 6-40. As you can see, the contents of ZIP.DOC have been copied to the **ZIP** field. The personnel manager can now press F10 to initiate a search for that zip code.

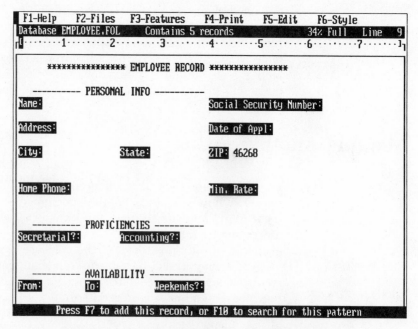

**Figure 6-40.** After merging ZIP.DOC file into the **ZIP** field.

The **Merge another file** selection is useful for copying ASCII data from another file for searches like this. (Keep in mind that this selection does not allow you to copy non-ASCII kinds of data into your database however.)

# Records and Document Files

Now that you know how to bring document file information into a database, let's see how to write a database record to a document file.

## Writing a Record to a Document File

Option 1, **Save a copy of this record**, of the Files menu allows you to save a database record to a document file. When a database record is displayed, you may select this option or press the shortcut key, Alt-Q, to save the record as a document file. The Directory Assistant then requests a file name for the record document file. If you specify an existing file the Directory Assistant warns you that the database record will overwrite the previous contents of the file.

## Bringing a Database Record into an Existing Document

The purpose of the last option discussed, writing a record to a document file, is to create or overwrite an existing document file. However, you cannot append to or insert into an existing document file with this option. Follow these steps to pull a database record into an existing document file:

1. Retrieve the database containing the record you want to place in a document file.
2. Retrieve the database record to place in the document file. Choose Option 1, **Select Text**, and highlight the entire record. Then copy it to the clipboard via option 3, **Copy selected text to clipboard**, in the Edit menu.
3. Return to the Main menu and retrieve the document file in which you want to insert the database record.

4. Position the cursor where you want the record to be placed and select option 4 from the Edit menu, **Paste from clipboard**, to paste the database record in the document file.

Earlier in the word processing discussion, you learned the value of the clipboard for copying from one location in a document file to another. Now you can see the value of the clipboard in copying data from one First Choice application (the word processor) to another (the database).

# Saving and Retrieving ASCII Data Files

As you know, First Choice stores your database information in files with a .FOL extension (as in the file name EMPLOYEE.FOL). Behind the scenes, so to say, First Choice uses its own conventions for specifying the form layout and record information in .FOL files; these conventions are not necessarily compatible with other database applications (for example, dBASEIII+). Therefore, a file created by one database application may not be readable by, or compatible with, files created by another database application.

## Saving a Database as a Delimited ASCII File

You can get around these differences because there are two ways to take a First Choice database file and make it readable for other database applications. The first of these operations is done via option 7, **Save ASCII data**, of the Files menu. Note, however, that the ASCII file created by this selection does not contain any form layout information such as field lengths, field types, etc.

Let's take a look at the steps involved in creating an ASCII file for the employee database:

1. Load the employee database and select option 7, **Save ASCII data**, from the Files menu.
2. At the Directory Assistant screen enter the file name EMPASCII for our ASCII file and press Enter.

*A delimiter is a character that is used to separate two fields.*

3. The Choose Delimiter Characters dialog box is then displayed (Figure 6-41). Press Enter to accept the default values.
4. The Search/Sort Instruction screen is then displayed. Press F10 to specify all records to be written to the ASCII file.

5. Press Enter to acknowledge the completion message shown in Figure 6-42.

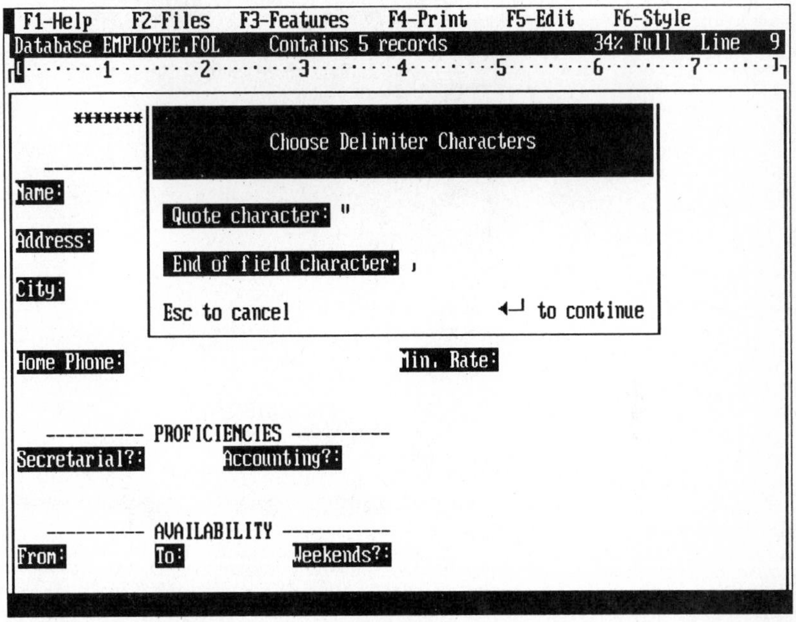

```
║ F1-Help    F2-Files   F3-Features   F4-Print   F5-Edit   F6-Style
║Database EMPLOYEE.FOL      Contains 5 records            34% Full   Line   9
 ┌[····· 1 ······· 2 ······· 3 ······· 4 ······· 5 ······· 6 ······· 7 ···· ]┐

        ******
                           Choose Delimiter Characters
        ---------
    Name:
                       Quote character:  "
    Address:
                       End of field character:  ,
    City:
                    Esc to cancel                    ←┘ to continue

    Home Phone:                             Min. Rate:


         --------- PROFICIENCIES ----------
    Secretarial?:        Accounting?:


         --------- AVAILABILITY ----------
    From:        To:            Weekends?:
```

**Figure 6-41.** Choose Delimiter Characters dialog box.

*Commas separate fields from each other; a pair of quotation marks surrounds each non-numeric field.*

As mentioned above, First Choice uses its own conventions for specifying form layout including field length, etc. in its .FOL files. The EMPASCII file created above does not use First Choice's conventions to show field lengths. Rather, fields are separated by a delimiter in EMPASCII. By default, First Choice uses the comma (,) character as the delimiter in ASCII database files. Further, First Choice uses another delimiter to mark the beginning and end of each *non*-numeric field in an ASCII database file. The default character for this delimiter is the double quote (" and ").

You can view the EMPASCII file in the word processor to see how our records look in ASCII format. Follow these steps to load EMPASCII into the word processor:

1. Return to the Main menu and select option 6, **Get an existing file**.

2. Select the file EMPASCII from the Directory Assistant. Note that since EMPASCII has no file extension (e.g., .DOC), it appears in the **Other** column of the Directory Assistant.

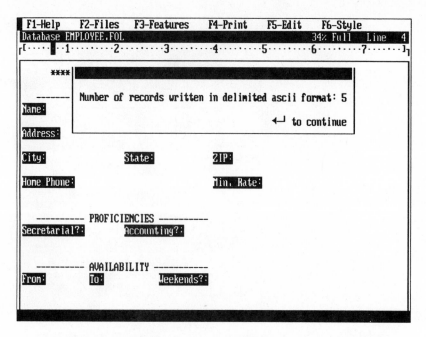

**Figure 6-42.** ASCII file copy completion message, indicating the number of records written in delimited ASCII format.

3. The Type of File To Get menu in Figure 6-43 is displayed next. Select option 1, **ASCII - Preserve carriage returns**, to retrieve EMPASCII "as is."

4. The EMPASCII file is then displayed, as shown in Figure 6-44.

Each line in Figure 6-44 shows the fields for a different record in our employee database.

If you so desire, you can specify other delimiter characters instead of the defaults (see the Choose Delimiter Characters dialog box in Figure 6-41). Notice that all fields are separated by commas and each non-numeric field is surrounded by double quotes. We refer to EMPASCII as a delimited ASCII file because of the delimiters used to separate fields. Before we discuss the other type of ASCII database file that First Choice can create, let's see how to retrieve delimited ASCII files into a database.

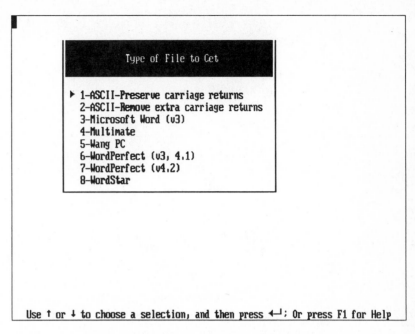

**Figure 6-43.** The Type of File To Get menu.

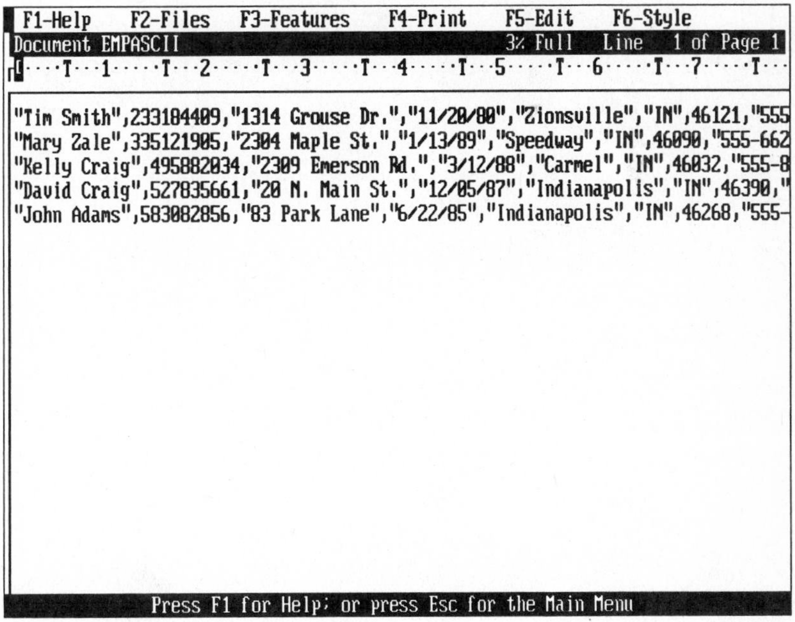

**Figure 6-44.** The EMPASCII file in the word processor. Note the Document designation at the top left corner.

# Retrieving a Delimited ASCII File into a Database

For this discussion, let's assume that the EMPASCII file created above was actually generated by another database package that the Wikley Company had experimented with before discovering First Choice. The company now wants to load this EMPASCII file into a First Choice database so it won't have to rekey all the entries.

As you might guess, before you can load an ASCII file into a First Choice database you must define the form design. This would usually mean building the form using the steps in the section entitled "Steps to Creating a Database Form" in Chapter 4. But since you have already created the employee database, you can simply copy the form to a new database file with these steps:

1. Once the employee database (in this case, the one you created in Chapter 4) is loaded, you can select option 4, Copy form design, from the Files menu to display the Directory Assistant.

2. Enter the file name NEWEMP.FOL and press Enter to start the form copy process.

3. When the form copy is finished, the message in Figure 6-7 is displayed.

Now follow these steps to load the NEWEMP.FOL file which contains a form layout with no database records:

1. Press Enter to acknowledge the form copy completion message in Figure 6-7.

2. Press Escape to return to the Main menu.

3. Select option 6, **Get an existing file**, and from the Directory Assistant select the NEWEMP.FOL file.

Now you are at the same point you would be at if you manually built the form: you have a .FOL file with a form layout and no records. To load the EMPASCII file into the NEWEMP.FOL database, follow these steps:

1. Select option 6, **Get ASCII data**, from the Files menu to display the **Delimited or fixed length ASCII** question, shown in Figure 6-45.

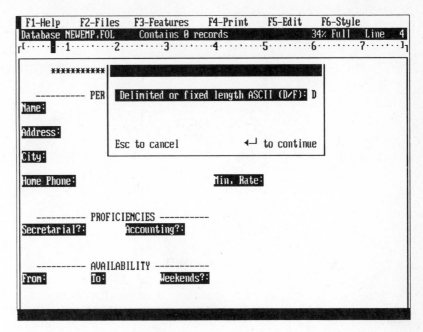

**Figure 6-45.** Question asking you to choose between delimited and fixed length ASCII.

2. Press Enter to accept the default value (**D**, for delimited ASCII) in Figure 6-45.

3. Select the EMPASCII file from the Directory Assistant screen and press Enter.

4. The Choose Delimiter Characters dialog box (Figure 6-41) is displayed next. Press Enter to accept the default delimiters (" and ,) and start the retrieval process.

5. The completion message shown in Figure 6-46 is displayed when the retrieval process is complete. Press Enter to acknowledge this message.

When the ASCII data retrieval process is complete, you can browse through the database via F10 to verify that all the data in EMPASCII was retrieved. Now let's take a look at how to save and retrieve fixed length format ASCII data files.

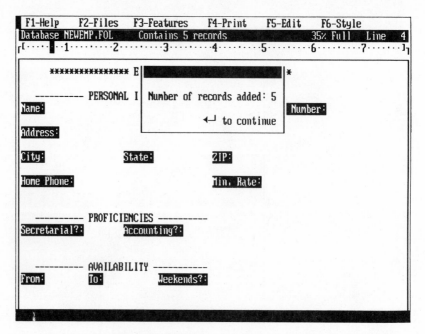

**Figure 6-46.** The get ASCII data completion message, indicating the number of records that were added.

## Saving a Database as a Fixed Length ASCII File

The second way of saving a database file as an ASCII file is as a *fixed length* ASCII file. By definition, in a delimited ASCII file, fields are separated by a special character (First Choice uses the comma by default). Fixed length ASCII files do not use delimiters; rather, each field is a specific number of characters wide. This specific character width is usually the same as the field's maximum size. For example, the maximum length of the Name field in our employee database is 25 characters. If you save the employee database in a fixed length ASCII file, you should allow for names of up to 25 characters. This sounds like the size requirements we discussed earlier for table views, doesn't it? In fact, fixed length ASCII files created by First Choice are generated from table view information. Follow these steps to create a table view of the employee database with maximum field lengths:

1. Load the employee database and select option 6, **Show table view**, from the Features menu.

2. When the table view is displayed select option 1, **Define table view**, from the Features menu.

3. Enter the table view specifications shown in Figure 6-47 and press F10.

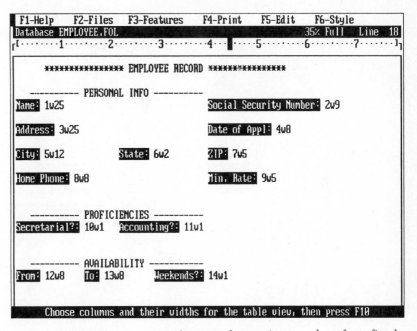

**Figure 6-47.** Table view specifications for maximum values for a fixed length ASCII file.

*Press End to check the rightmost portion of the table view.*

Take a look at this new table view field to make sure the field widths are large enough to show all the field values. It's OK if some of the field names are abbreviated with the greater than (>) symbol, but none of your field values should be cut short with >. Be sure to check all the widths in the table view. Once you are satisfied all your data is shown, follow these steps to create the fixed length ASCII file:

1. Select option 1, **Save table view as an ASCII file**, from the Files menu (or press Alt-Q, the shortcut key for this selection).

2. At the Directory Assistant screen enter the file name EMPFLASC for the fixed length ASCII file and press Enter.

A **Saving...** message will briefly be displayed while the fixed length ASCII file is being written. The table view will be redisplayed when the copy process is complete. Follow these steps to see what the fixed length ASCII file looks like in the word processor:

1. Return to the Main menu and select option 6, **Get an existing file**.

2. Select the file EMPFLASC from the Directory Assistant. Note that since EMPFLASC has no file extension (e.g., .DOC), it appears in the OTHER column of the Directory Assistant.

3. The Type of File To Get menu in Figure 6-43 is displayed next. Select option 1, **ASCII - Preserve carriage returns**, to retrieve EMPFLASC "as is."

4. The EMPFLASC file is then displayed, as shown in Figure 6-48.

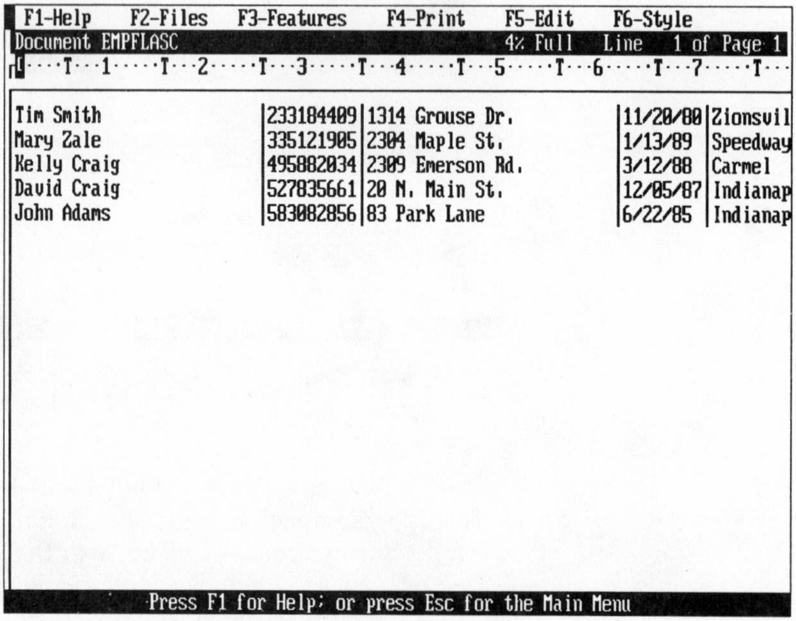

```
 F1-Help    F2-Files   F3-Features   F4-Print    F5-Edit   F6-Style
 Document EMPFLASC                        4% Full    Line   1 of Page 1
 [····T···1····T···2····T···3····T···4····T···5····T···6····T···7····T··

 Tim Smith           233184409 1314 Grouse Dr.        11/20/88 Zionsvil
 Mary Zale           335121905 2304 Maple St.         1/13/89  Speedway
 Kelly Craig         495882034 2389 Emerson Rd.       3/12/88  Carmel
 David Craig         527835661 20 N. Main St.         12/05/87 Indianap
 John Adams          583082856 83 Park Lane           6/22/85  Indianap











              Press F1 for Help; or press Esc for the Main Menu
```

**Figure 6-48.** The EMPFLASC fixed length ASCII file. Notice how the fields line up neatly.

Note that vertical bars separate field entries in each record in Figure 6-48. Each column shows the maximum width for that field in each record. Recall that the delimited ASCII file, which is shown in Figure 6-44, did not appear in a columnar format like Figure 6-48. This illustrates the chief difference between delimited and fixed length ASCII files. Fixed length ASCII files do not use delimiters to separate field values. Rather, field values are written to the fixed length ASCII file in a space-filled fashion so all the like fields are the same length. That is, all the **Name** fields are the same length; all the **Address** fields are the same length, and so forth. Now let's see how to bring this fixed length ASCII file into a database.

## Retrieving a Fixed Length ASCII File into a Database

As we discussed in the delimited ASCII file section, before you can load an ASCII file into a First Choice database, you must define the form layout. This usually means building the form using the steps in the section called "Steps to Creating a Database Form" in Chapter 4. But, since you have already created the employee database you can simply copy the form to a new database file with these steps:

1. Once the employee database is loaded, you can select option 4, Copy form design, from the Files menu to display the Directory Assistant.

2. Enter the file name `NEWEMP2.FOL` and press Enter to start the form copy process.

3. When the form copy is finished, the message in Figure 6-7 is displayed.

Now follow these steps to load the NEWEMP2.FOL file, which contains a form design with no database records:

1. Press Enter to acknowledge the form copy completion message in Figure 6-7.

2. Press Escape to return to the Main menu.

3. Select option 6, **Get an existing file**, and from the Directory Assistant, select the NEWEMP2.FOL file.

Now you are at the same point you would be at if you had manually built the form: you have a .FOL file with a form design and no records. Follow these steps to load the EMPFLASC file into the NEWEMP2.FOL database:

1. Select option 6, **Get ASCII data**, from the Files menu to display the **Delimited or fixed length ASCII** question in Figure 6-45.

2. Type **F** and press Enter to specify a fixed length ASCII file value.

3. Select the EMPFLASC file from the Directory Assistant screen and press Enter.

4. Enter the first and last column values for each field as shown in Figure 6-49 and press F10.

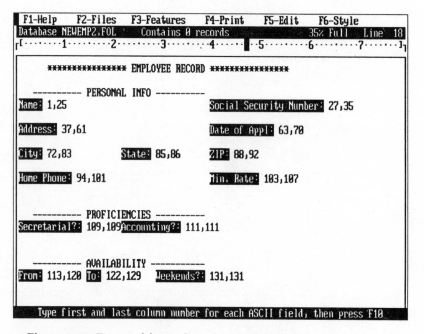

**Figure 6-49.** First and last column specifications for retrieval of EMPFLASC.

5. The completion message shown in Figure 6-50 is displayed when the retrieval process is complete. Press Enter to acknowledge this message.

When the ASCII data retrieval process is complete, you can browse through the database via F10 to verify that all the data in EMPFLASC was retrieved.

One of the major differences between retrieving delimited files and retrieving fixed length ASCII files is illustrated in Figure 6-49. First Choice needs to know where one field ends and the next field begins to properly load the ASCII information into the database. This first/last column information is specified like this for the **Name** field:

1,25

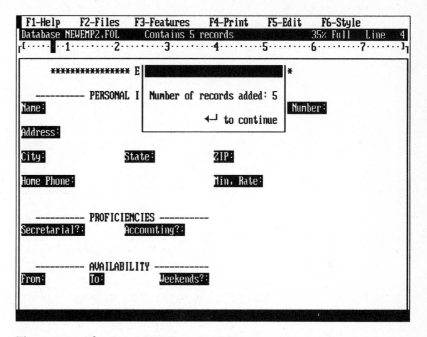

**Figure 6-50.** The Get ASCII Data Completion message, indicating the number of records that have been added.

where the first number (1) is the start column and the second number (25) is the end column. The start and end column numbers must be separated by either a comma, space, or dash (—).

*Be careful to determine start and end positions accurately.*

First Choice uses the specifications in Figure 6-49 to fill each field regardless of whether your entries in Figure 6-49 are correct. Exercise care on this point. If you count incorrectly for one field and then base your counts for all subsequent fields on that erroneous count, those fields will be filled with bogus data.

Although we mentioned earlier (in the discussion of creating the fixed length ASCII file) that you must define your table view with the maximum field widths, it is worth noting again here. Field data not visible in a table view (that is, abbreviated with the ⟩ symbol) will not be written to the fixed length ASCII file. Therefore, that missing data is not available for retrieval into a database.

You may recall that the Search/Sort Specifications screen was one of the screens displayed in the creation of a delimited ASCII data file. You can use any of the search/sort options discussed in Chapter 5 to selectively write records to the delimited ASCII file. You may be wondering, "What about search/sort specifications for fixed length ASCII data files?" Well, you can do that here too. Once you defined the table view, there was no opportunity to specify search/sort information before writing the fixed length ASCII data file. Follow these steps to specify search/sort information before writing to the fixed length ASCII data file:

1. With the table view displayed, press Escape to return to the Form screen.

2. Press Escape again to clear the form so that search/sort information may be entered.

3. Enter your search/sort specifications and press Alt-T, the table view shortcut key, to display the new table view.

You can now select option 1, **Save table view as an ASCII file**, from the Files menu to create a fixed length ASCII data file based upon your search/sort specifications.

Now that we are finished discussing ASCII data files you can delete the temporary databases (NEWEMP.FOL and NEWEMP2.FOL) and ASCII data files (EMPASCII and EMPFLASC) by following these steps:

1. Press Escape to return to the Main menu.

2. Select option 6, **Get an existing file**, to display the Directory Assistant.

3. Specify the file name NEWEMP.FOL and press F10 to delete it.

4. Press Y to acknowledge the deletion warning message.

5. Specify the file name NEWEMP2.FOL, press F10, then Y.

6. Specify the file name EMPASCII, press F10, then Y.

7. Specify the file name EMPFLASC, press F10, then Y.

8. Press Escape to return to the Main menu.

# Summary

- Record erasure differs from record removal in that the former only clears fields in a record, and the latter deletes the record from the database.

- A database's form design may be copied to a new database file, and records may be copied from one database file to another. Search and sort specifications may be used in this copy process to selectively copy records in a particular order to the destination database.

- Perform file deletions with caution: once a file is deleted its contents are lost.

- The previously maintenanced record can be quickly copied to the current form screen by the record ditto shortcut key, Alt-E. This option is also available via selection B, **Ditto entire record**, in the Edit menu.

- Individual fields from the previously maintenanced record can be quickly copied to the current form screen by the field ditto shortcut key, Alt-D. This option is also available via selection A, **Ditto field**, in the Edit menu.

- Selection 5, **Change form design**, in the Features menu allows you to perform the following form modifications: add fields, change field names, erase fields, move fields, change background text, and change field types. You should create a backup copy of the database file before performing any of these modifications.

- First Choice offers a table view of your database files, in which each record is displayed as a row and fields are shown in columnar format. Once a table view is displayed, you can change the table view via option 1, **Define table view**, of the Features menu.

- Search and sort specifications may be used to define contents and order records in a table view.

- The **Merge another file** selection, 2 in the Files menu, may be used to "pour" an ASCII data file into a database.

- The current record may be written to an ASCII file via option 1, **Save a copy of this record**, in the Files menu, or with the shortcut key Alt-Q. Once a record has been written to a document file, you can use or alter it in the word processor.

- Database files may be saved as either delimited or fixed length ASCII data files for use by other database applications.

# Form
# Programming

**In this chapter:**

- What Is Form Programming?
- Programming Concepts
- A Simple Form Program: Social Security Number Validation
- Using Remarks
- Referencing Database Fields
- Conditional Statements
- GOTO Statements
- Error Messages: @ERRBOX
- Adding **ZIP** and **State** Validation
- Keywords
- Generating the Employee ID Security Number
- Other Variables and a Special Keyword
- The Final Employee Form Program
- Summary

This chapter covers one of the more interesting and flexible features of First Choice's database application: form programming. Form programs are short programs used in databases that cause certain events to occur automatically when a record is added to or modified in a database. These events are designed to guard against "typos" and other mistakes in data entry, among other things, and can include displaying custom error messages, calculating field values, and more. Throughout this discussion we will gradually build a single sophisticated form program for the Wikley Company's employee database to:

- validate the **Social Security Number**, **State**, and **ZIP** field entries to ensure data integrity,
- generate an employee ID security number,
- require the user to specify a value in the **Name** and **Social Security Number** fields,
- default the **Date of Appl** field to the current date, and
- validate the **Home Phone** field entry.

This program will run each time a record is added or modified.

# What Is Form Programming?

We have seen how First Choice's database application allows us to define a database form layout, or design, and add and maintain database records. To add a record to a database all you need do is enter the field values on a blank form screen and press F7. If the entered field data *passes validation* (is accepted by the program as "legal") for each of the field types (numeric, date, etc.), the record is written to disk and is available for search/sort retrieval or further maintenance.

What if you wanted something else to happen between the time F7 is pressed and when the record is written to the database file? You might want to do this if you wanted to make certain checks of the entered data. For instance, suppose that the Wikley Company wanted to make sure that only valid Social Security numbers are entered for each applicant. (Social Security Number validation must ensure that the entered data is both numeric and within the range: 000-00-0000 and 999-99-9999.) Recall that the **Social Security Number** field is defined as a numeric type so the form does not call for the operator to enter the dashes. Therefore, the acceptable range is 0 through 999999999. Since you defined the **Social Security Number** field as a numeric field a non-numeric entry will be flagged as an error when F7 is pressed to add the record. But how can you prevent the database user from adding a record with a Social Security number outside the valid range of 0 through 9999999999? The answer to this question is simple: write a form program that displays an error message if the Social Security Number data is not within the valid range.

*Alt-R will also run a form program.*

A form program is a set of instructions automatically performed by First Choice when a database record is added or modified. For example, you can write instructions to validate field data and display an error message for invalid entries. If you are familiar with computer programming languages such as BASIC, the form programming concepts discussed in this chapter will be fairly straightforward. However, if you are a programming novice you must understand a few programming concepts and terms before diving into form programming

# Programming Concepts and Terms

*As when following instructions for assembling a bike, you must follow each instruction to properly assemble a program.*

A form program, like any other computer language program, is a list of steps to be followed when performing an operation. In form programming, we refer to one step or instruction as a *statement*. Therefore, a form program is a list of one or more statements or instructions which First Choice follows when a database record is added or modified.

A few other "ground rules" will be useful for readers new to programming to know.

1. Programming requires a different kind of thinking than operating software. You need to tell the program everything very explicitly.

2. The wording (grammatical structure) of a programming statement is called its *syntax*. You'll learn soon about something called a syntax check, which is a check to be sure the program is using "grammar" that the First Choice can understand.

3. A term you'll run into is *function*. This means a single word that has a whole formula packed into it that performs a certain operation such as find a square root or make a statistical or financial calculation.

4. All programming languages have *keywords*, which are words that the program reserves to be used in certain very specific ways by it and that you can't use for other purposes in the instructions that you write. For example, **@DATE** is a common keyword and exists in First Choice. If your company sold dates and figs and you used the word **date** in a form program, this might confuse First Choice when it wanted to use its internal @DATE function for some operation.

5. Remember back in Chapter 4 when you were designating fields as text, numeric, etc.? You may have noticed that the numerals in an applicant's address were handled the same way as the street name

—that is, as text. It will help you to know right now that in form programming, you also need to think about whether you want a number to be treated for its numerical value or as text.

## Branching and Conditional Statements

First Choice form programs may contain several different types of statements. Two of the more commonly used types are *branching* and *conditional* statements.

*Use branching and conditional statements when you want the program to "skip around."*

In a form program, statements are performed one at a time from the top (the beginning) of the program to the bottom (the end). A branching statement may be used to alter this sequence and cause another statement, other than the next sequential one, to be performed. It is somewhat like what happens when you're making a long trip and you exit off the interstate highway to get gas or do something else related to your trip and then return to the interstate.

A conditional statement evaluates an expression and determines whether the expression is true or false. The expression being evaluated may be something like "Is the Social Security Number data outside the range of 0 to 999999999?" Conditional statements are used to perform one set of statements when the expression evaluates to true and a different set when the expression is false. To make another traveling comparison, a conditional statement is what a driver does who checks the fuel gauge to see whether the gas tank has enough gas in it to make it to the next exit. The driver does one thing if the answer is yes and another if the answer is no.

Did you notice any similarities between branching and conditional statements? Actually, a conditional statement must incorporate a branching statement to cause a statement other than the next sequential one to be executed—in other words, to do any good. For example, an entire conditional statement may be something like "If the Social Security number data is outside the range of 0 to 999999999 then display an error message; otherwise, perform the next form program statement." The clause "If the Social Security number data is outside the range of 0 to 999999999" is a conditional statement. The next portion, "then display an error message;" implies the use of a branching statement to display a special error message and is performed when the expression is true—that is, when the conditional statement applies. The final portion of the conditional statement, "otherwise, perform the next form program statement," is performed when the expression is false—that is, when the conditional statement does not apply. To illuminate these concepts, let's take a look at a form program example which uses these statements.

# A Simple Form Program—Social Security Number Validation

The first form program we will discuss is designed to validate Social Security number data by accepting only entries within the valid range of 0 to 999999999. Follow these steps to enter the form program:

1. Load the employee database and select option 5, **Change form design**, from the Features menu.

2. Press Enter to acknowledge the backup warning and select option 7, **Program form**, from the Change Form Design menu (Figure 7-1).

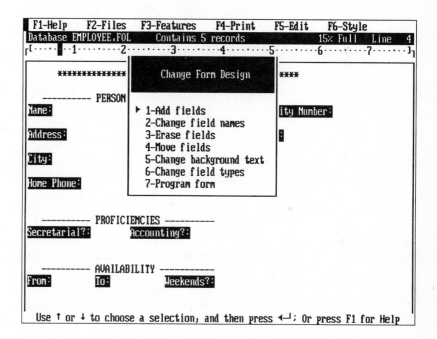

**Figure 7-1.** Change Form Design menu.

3. Enter the form program listed in the form program entry screen in Figure 7-2. Be sure to include the semicolons at the left of the screen and the colon after the word number. Although uppercase and lowercase do not matter to the form program *interpreter* (this is what translates and runs the program), you should follow the

case conventions used in this and subsequent form programs. It's a good habit to get into, in case you use other languages or software in the future, and it makes for readability, but most importantly, it creates a habit of care and precision.

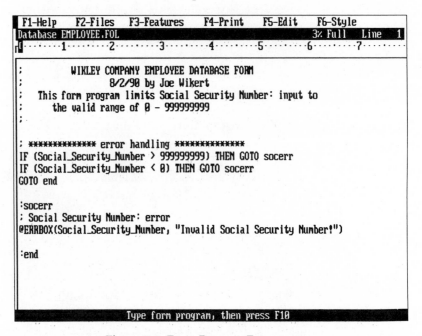

```
F1-Help    F2-Files   F3-Features    F4-Print   F5-Edit   F6-Style
Database EMPLOYEE.FOL                              3% Full    Line    1
0........1........2........3........4........5........6........7........

;          WIKLEY COMPANY EMPLOYEE DATABASE FORM
;                  8/2/90 by Joe Wikert
;   This form program limits Social Security Number: input to
;         the valid range of 0 - 999999999
;


; ************ error handling *************
IF (Social_Security_Number > 999999999) THEN GOTO socerr
IF (Social_Security_Number < 0) THEN GOTO socerr
GOTO end

:socerr
; Social Security Number: error
@ERRBOX(Social_Security_Number, "Invalid Social Security Number!")

:end




               Type form program, then press F10
```

**Figure 7-2.** Form Program Entry screen.

4. When you are satisfied that your form program looks like the one shown in Figure 7-2, press F10, and First Choice will check the program's syntax.

5. If your program passes First Choice's syntax check (for example, if you haven't mistakenly entered an illegal character), the dialog box shown in Figure 7-3 is displayed. We will discuss the details of this dialog box later; for now, enter an n and press Enter, and a blank form screen is displayed.

Before we discuss the specifics of the form program in Figure 7-2 let's see it at work—by looking at what effect it has on Social Security number data entries. Enter the record data shown in Figure 7-4 including the Social Security Number entry of 8764278556.

Press F7 to add the record to the database. What happened? If your form program matches the one in Figure 7-2 the error message in Figure 7-5 should be displayed.

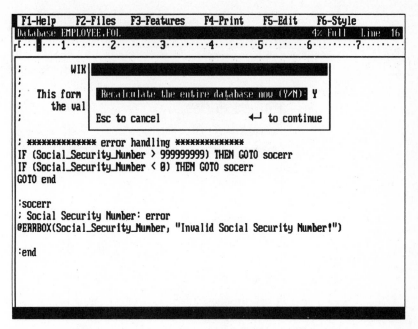

**Figure 7-3.** Form Program Recalculation dialog box.

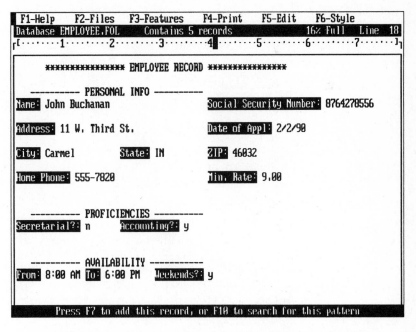

**Figure 7-4.** Employee record with long Social Security number.

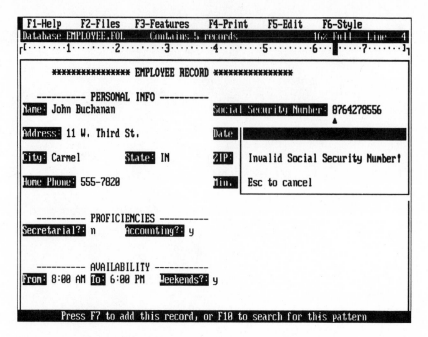

**Figure 7-5.** Social Security Number error message .

Press Escape and try entering the Social Security Number with a minus sign in front, as shown in Figure 7-6. Press F7 again to add this version of the record to the database. The same error shown in Figure 7-5 is displayed if your form program was entered correctly.

Well, it appears that this form program does in fact prevent Social Security Number entries outside the valid range of 0 through 999999999, as it is designed to do. Now let's take a look at each of the program statements to see how the form program works.

# Using Remarks

*Remarks are optional but highly recommended.*

The first few lines of the form program are *remarks*, which are program lines that are not instructions to the computer. The purpose of remarks is to document the form program's purpose and functionality so that another person reading the program will know what its purpose is (also, even the smartest people can't remember everything, and you may create some programs that you won't look at for six or twelve months, in which case the remarks will prove very helpful). The remarks are

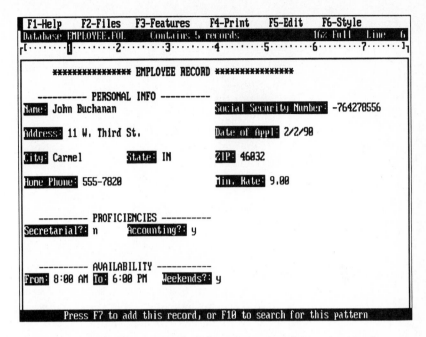

**Figure 7-6.** Employee record with negative Social Security Number.

```
;          WIKLEY COMPANY EMPLOYEE DATABASE FORM
;                 8/02/90 by Joe Wikert
;     This form program limits Social Security Number: input to
;          the valid range of 0 - 999999999
;
```

A remark line starts with a semicolon (;). When First Choice sees a semicolon as the first character on a form program line it ignores that entire line. It is a good idea to precede the logic, or instructional portion, of a form program with a remark block like this to identify the date the form was written, who wrote it, and what it does.

Remarks should appear throughout your form programs to explain the reasoning behind the form program logic. In fact, the next line of the form program:

```
; ************** error handling ***************
```

is a remark which refers to the next block of the form program. Before we discuss this next block, let's see how to refer to database field names in a form program.

# Referencing Database Fields

In most cases, when you want to refer to a database field in a form program, simply type the full name of the field as it appears on the form but *without* the trailing (ending) colon. Thus you could refer to the field for the applicant's zip code as Zip, zip, ZiP, etc. (remember, the form programming interpreter is not case sensitive).

If the field name contains spaces, like **Social Security Number**, the spaces should be replaced by underscores (_) when referring to the field in a form program. Thus, **Social Security Number:** becomes

    Social_Security_Number

Although my testing proved otherwise, the makers of First Choice (Software Publishing Corporation) claim that only the first 12 characters of a field name are used by the form program interpreter to differentiate between fields. To use a rather imaginative example, this means that if for some reason you had one field named ABCDEFGHIJKLX and another field named ABCDEFGHIJKLZ, the interpreter would not see the difference between the two fields when you use their names in a form program, because the first 12 characters in each are identical.

If true, this fact is both good and bad. First the (possibly) good news: It is possible to abbreviate your longer field names to only the first 12 characters. Instead of spelling out Social_Security_Number as shown in Figure 7-2, you could refer to that field as

    Social_Secur

Abbreviating the field in this manner could save keystrokes if you have to keep typing the same lengthy name over and over again. However, it is usually a good idea to completely spell out a field name in a form program, because Social_Security_Number is more readable and meaningful than Social_Secur.

The downside of this 12-character recognition limit arises when you have lengthy field names that are similar. For example, if you have two fields in a form named

**Date of Job Application:**

and

**Date of Job Offer:**

there is no way to clearly differentiate between the two in a form program since the first 12 characters of each are identical. The solution to this dilemma is to rename either one or both of the fields so that the first 12 characters in each are different; for instance, the fields above could be renamed to

**Application Date:**

and

**Offer Date:**

Nonetheless, as I mentioned earlier, I have run tests with lengthy similar field names and found that the form program interpreter was able to distinguish between the fields.

My tests also have shown that you can abbreviate a long field name to only the first 12 characters and First Choice will know which field you are referring to—that is, (and this probably won't surprise you) *if* the first 12 characters of all field names in the form are unique. For example, you could abbreviate `Social_Security_Number` to `Social_Secur` in a form program and First Choice will know you are referring to the **Social Security Number** field. This is because no other field name's first 12 characters match `Social_Secur`. However, if you have the fields

**Date of Job Application:**

and

**Date of Job Offer:**

in a form you cannot use the abbreviation `Date_of_Job` in a form program since it is unclear to which field you are referring. However, you can still use either `Date_of_Job_Application` or `Date_of_Job_Offer` in a form program and First Choice will look beyond the first 12 characters to differentiate between the two fields. Be careful though, because the supposed 12-character limitation may be enforced in future versions of First Choice.

Try to avoid using any mathematical symbols in field names (such as +, −, *, /, =). These characters can be misconstrued by the form program interpreter and may lead to unpredictable results.

Now that you know how to handle a field name in a form program, let's see how a field name is used in the next line of the form program in Figure 7-2.

# Conditional Statements

The next line of the employee form program:

```
IF (Social_Security_Number > 999999999) THEN GOTO socerr
```

is a conditional statement commonly referred to as an *IF..THEN* statement. An IF..THEN statement checks a condition and, if that condition (in the example above, `Social_Security_Number > 999999999`) is true, it performs the instructions in the clause that appears after the `THEN`—in this example, `(GOTO socerr)`. In more general terms, in form programming the syntax for an IF..THEN statement is

IF (Condition) THEN GOTO Label

A label refers to a sort of heading for another section of the program, and the label in the statement we are discussing is **socerr**.

The condition in the IF..THEN statement may contain one or more of the logical operators shown in the following list:

*In <= and >=, remember to place the equal sign after the < or >.*

**Logical operators for IF..THEN statements**

| Operator | Meaning |
|---|---|
| = | equal to |
| < | less than |
| > | greater than |
| <= | less than or equal to |
| >= | greater than or equal to |
| <> | not equal to |

The first IF..THEN statement checks to see if the Social Security Number value is greater than 999999999 by using the > logical operator. You may have noticed that the next line in the form program:

```
IF (Social_Security_Number < 0) THEN GOTO socerr
```

uses the **<** logical operator to determine whether the Social Security Number entered is less than 0. Together these two statements are responsible for determining whether the Social Security number entered is between the valid range of 0 through 999999999.

First Choice offers three other logical operators for more complex conditional statements:

**Additional logical operators for complex IF..THEN statements**

| Operator | Meaning |
|----------|---------|
| AND | each condition must be true for entire expression to be true |
| OR | only one of the two expressions must be true for the entire expression to be true |
| NOT | negates a condition |

By the way, you may have guessed that you could combine the two IF..THEN statements into one by using the AND operator like this (The line is too long to fit on one line in this book, but on a computer screen it *must* be kept on a single line):

```
IF (Social_Security_Number > 999999999) AND
    (Social_Security_Number < 0) THEN GOTO socerr
```

*Short and simple statements fit on the screen and are easier to understand.*

As you can see, however, this is a rather lengthy expression. If you enter it into the form program you will see that it is too long to be fully displayed on your screen. Unlike in some programming languages, you *cannot* split the statement across two lines like this:

```
IF (Social_Security_Number > 999999999) AND
(Social_Security_Number < 0) THEN GOTO socerr
```

because in First Choice each form program statement is limited to one line. As a result, I recommend that you do not try to combine conditions into complex IF..THEN statements. The two separate IF..THEN statements in the employee form program are much more readable and manageable than the lengthy complex example above.

What about the portion of the IF..THEN statement that appears after THEN—the (GOTO socerr) part? This segment is actually another statement itself, and is called the GOTO statement.

# GOTO Statements

In form programming, the syntax of a GOTO statement is

```
GOTO Label
```

where Label is an *alphanumeric identifier* (that is, a word composed of numbers and/or letters) with a maximum length of 21 characters.

Although Software Publishing Corporation's own documentation says that "a label can be from 1 to 12 characters long," my testing proves otherwise. I found that all characters in a 21-character label are significant and that if you try to use a label any longer than 21 characters the error message at the bottom of the screen in Figure 7-7 is displayed.

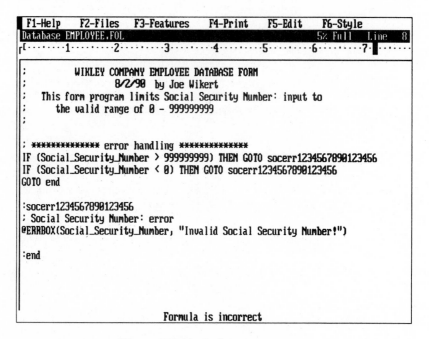

**Figure 7-7.** Formula error message.

In Figure 7-7, the label is

socerr1234567890123456

The word socerr has six characters and there are 16 numbers, so the last number, 6, is the 22nd character. The message Formula is incorrect indicates an error with the form program. When this error message appears, the cursor is positioned at the point where the error was discovered. In this case, the cursor is located at the 22nd character in the label (it does not show up in this book, however).

*Later you'll see how GOTO can appear as a statement by itself.*

A label is an identifier used to indicate the start of a segment in a form program. As pointed out earlier, statements in a form program are executed one after another from the top of the program to the bottom. The GOTO statement gives you, the form programmer, the ability to modify this top-to-bottom flow. With GOTO, you can write a form program to jump from one statement to another; and the statement jumped to need not be in any specific position relative to the GOTO statement (in other words, a GOTO can jump to a statement before or after it in the program). The label in a GOTO statement determines where to jump to in the form program. For example, the statement

```
IF (Social_Security_Number > 999999999) THEN GOTO socerr
```

jumps to the label **socerr** if the Social Security number is greater than 999999999. Look further down the form program and you will see the label **socerr** preceded by a colon (:) like this:

```
:socerr
```

The next statement after this label statement,

```
; Social Security Number: error
```

is the first one that First Choice looks at to see if it needs to pay attention to it after the GOTO statement. We will refer to **:socerr** as a *label statement* (because it is preceded by a colon), and we will differentiate it from the **socerr** *label* in the GOTO statement. A label statement simply tells First Choice where it should look next for a statement to carry out after a GOTO is executed. (Put another way, the **GOTO socerr** and the **:socerr** together form a sort of bridge or overpass that guides the program to where you want it to go.)

So, if the value 1234567890 is entered for an applicant's Social Security number, the statement

```
IF (Social_Security_Number > 999999999) THEN GOTO socerr
```

will catch this error and jump to the statement following the **socerr** label. The statement after the **socerr** label happens to be a remark:

```
; Social Security Number: error
```

How do you know it's a remark? Because the first character on the line is a semicolon! You may also recall that a remark line is completely ignored by the form program interpreter. Therefore, it and our discussion move on to the next statement, which is an @ERRBOX statement.

# Error Messages—@ERRBOX

The next statement in your employee form program

```
@ERRBOX(Social_Security_Number, "Invalid Social Security Number!")
```

is an @ERRBOX statement. It displays an error at the specified field. In First Choice the syntax for @ERRBOX is

```
@ERRBOX(Fieldname,"Message")
```

where **Fieldname** is the name of the field where the message is displayed. Thus our example statement means that in the field for Social Security number the message `Invalid Social Security Number` will appear. You can place a string of up to 75 characters in the message; anything over 75 characters is chopped off since the message is limited to one line on the screen. A string is a series of alphanumeric or special characters (special characters being the comma, forward slash, curly braces, square brackets, etc.).

@ERRBOX is a built-in function of the form program interpreter. You will see many other functions, or keywords, which are preceded by the "at sign" (**@**). Although the **@** preceding ERRBOX and these other keywords is optional, I recommend that you always use it, for greater ease in distinguishing your labels and field names from the built-in keywords.

The earlier discussion about IF..THEN statements mentioned that a GOTO should appear after the THEN. An @ERRBOX statement can be placed after THEN instead of GOTO. You could combine the IF..THEN with @ERRBOX like this (Once again, the line is too long to fit on one line in this book, but it can and should be fit on a computer screen on a single line):

```
IF (Social_Security_Number > 999999999) THEN @ERRBOX
    (Social_Security_Number, "Invalid Social Security Number!")
```

Since the entire statement must be placed on one line this statement is not very readable on your PC's screen. The same is true of the IF..THEN statement comparing the Social Security Number to 0. Both IF..THEN statements use the same @ERRBOX message so it makes sense to simply use GOTO statements for each to jump to the same @ERRBOX statement.

It should be pretty clear that the same @ERRBOX statement is executed whether the Social Security Number is less than 0 or greater than 999999999. But what happens when a valid Social Security Number is entered? The first IF..THEN statement's condition results in a false value, so the next IF..THEN statement is executed. This IF..THEN statement's condition is also false, so the next statement:

```
GOTO end
```

is executed. This is an example of an *unconditional* GOTO—since it is not used with an IF..THEN statement. The purpose of this GOTO is to branch around the Social Security Number @ERRBOX statement. Since there are no statements after the

```
:end
```

label statement the form program is finished.

# Adding ZIP and State Validation

Now let's build on this form by adding validation for two more fields. The next couple of items that the Wikley Company would like verified during employee database maintenance are the **State** and **ZIP** fields. It would like to ensure that the State entry is abbreviated to a maximum of two characters. Also, it wants only ZIP values between 0 and 99999 to be accepted by the form program. The solution to this additional validation requirement is shown in the following form program:

**Listing 7-1.** Enhanced form program with State and ZIP validation.

```
;        WIKLEY COMPANY EMPLOYEE DATABASE FORM
;                    8/05/90
;
;   This form program:
;            1 - limits Social Security Number: input to
;                the valid range of 0 - 999999999
;            2 - limits the State: entry to a maximum of
;                2 characters
;            3 - limits ZIP: input to the valid range of
;                0 - 99999
;
```

```
; ************* error handling ***************

; ** Social Security Number: **
IF (Social_Security_Number > 999999999) THEN GOTO socerr
IF (Social_Security_Number < 0) THEN GOTO socerr

; ** State: **
IF (@LENGTH(State) > 2) THEN GOTO staterr

; ** ZIP: **
IF ((Zip > 99999) OR (Zip < 0)) THEN GOTO ziperr
GOTO end


; ************* error message display *************

:socerr
; Social Security Number: error
@ERRBOX(Social_Security_Number, "Invalid Social Security Number!")
GOTO end

:staterr
; State: error
@ERRBOX(State, "Cannot exceed 2 characters!")
GOTO end

:ziperr
; ZIP: error
@ERRBOX(Zip, "Invalid ZIP Code!")

:end
```

This form program includes the same Social Security Number error handling presented in the first form program. In fact, all form programs in this chapter will build upon the previous ones. We have modified the remark block at the top of the program to describe the new logic for **State** and **ZIP**.

The remainder of the form program is split into two sections: error handling and error message display. These sections are identified by the remark blocks:

```
; ************* error handling ***************
```

and

```
; ************** error message display **************
```

The first portion of the error handling section contains the IF..THEN statements which validate the Social Security Number entry. The next two lines:

```
; ** State: **
IF (@LENGTH(State) > 2) THEN GOTO staterr
```

are for validation of the entry in the **State** field. Notice that each block of statements for field validation in the error handling section starts with a remark containing that block's field name (for example, **;** **\*\* State: \*\***). The IF..THEN statement for State validation contains an identifier you have not seen before: @LENGTH. A detailed discussion of this keyword is presented in the next section. For now, all you need to know is that this IF..THEN statement can determine how many characters were entered for **State**; if more than two characters were entered, the GOTO staterr clause is executed.

The next block:

```
; ** ZIP: **
IF ((Zip > 99999) OR (Zip < 0)) THEN GOTO ziperr
GOTO end
```

identifies the **ZIP** field validation and checks to see if the number entered for ZIP is between 0 and 99999; if the number lies outside this range the GOTO ziperr clause is performed; otherwise, a branch is made to the end label.

Notice that since all validation is in one consecutive block of statements you can perform the necessary checks on each field in an efficient manner. That is, as a good record passes through the validation section, each successive IF..THEN statement is executed without any branching.

The error message display block contains what are called @ERRBOX *calls* for each of the **Social Security Number**, **State**, and **ZIP** fields. Notice that the error statements for Social Security Number and State both contain GOTO end statements; these GOTO statements are used to skip over all subsequent @ERRBOX calls. For example, if the record has an invalid Social Security number, you want to perform the @ERRBOX statement after the socerr label but you don't want to perform the ones after staterr and ziperr.

*Regardless of the number of errors in a database record, only one @ERRBOX error can be displayed at a time.*

The previous discussion illustrates the fact that @ERRBOX is called only once each time the form program is executed; this is regardless of whether more than one field contains erroneous data.

You might think you should rewrite the form program so that multiple errors can be displayed at the same time. However, only one error can be displayed at a time in a form program. Even if you place two @ERRBOX statements together like this in a form program:

```
@ERRBOX(State, "Cannot exceed 2 characters!")

@ERRBOX(Zip, "Invalid ZIP Code!")
```

the **State** field error will be the only one displayed. This is consistent with First Choice's standard handling of field type errors. For example, if you try to add a record with non-numeric Social Security number and ZIP entries only the error for the Social Security number is displayed first.

# Keywords

*A parameter is a value that you include with a function to make the function do what you want.*

Now let's explore a few of First Choice's built-in keywords, including @LENGTH. The @LENGTH keyword has the following syntax:

```
@LENGTH(String)
```

where String is either a *literal string* (a series of characters that appears on the screen but is not a field name—for example, "Hi there") or a text type field name. Items specified between parentheses after the keyword are called *keyword parameters*. A parameter is a word that you place after a function (or command) to tell it what to act upon. If a literal string (as opposed to a *variable name*, which we'll look at later) is specified as @LENGTH's parameter the characters must be enclosed in double quotes. Since **State** is a text type field you were able to use it as the parameter for @LENGTH in the previous form program without quotation marks, like this:

```
IF (@LENGTH(State) > 2) THEN GOTO staterr
```

*Note:* When using a keyword you should always include the @ sign in front of it to clearly distinguish it from any other identifiers such as labels and field names.

The result of @LENGTH is the number of characters in its parameter. Therefore, if the three-character value

```
FLA
```

is entered for the **State** field, here is what goes on "behind the scenes" within the program: the IF..THEN statement

```
IF (@LENGTH(State) > 2) THEN GOTO staterr
```

simplifies to

```
IF (3 > 2) THEN GOTO staterr
```

and since 3 is greater than 2, a branch is made to the `staterr` label. Then, on-screen you see the staterr message.

First Choice provides several keywords for operations ranging from string manipulation (working with alphanumeric text) to mathematical calculations. Each of these keywords is discussed in Chapter 10, *Advanced Spreadsheet Topics*, because the keywords available to the form programmer are included in those available in the spreadsheet application.

Keywords used in this chapter are described with the form program they appear in. For a complete description of all keywords, however, you should refer to Chapter 10.

# Generating the Employee ID Security Number

When we designed the form for Wikley Company's employee database we noted that the **Social Security Number** field should be numeric. This is because the company wants to use the **Social Security Number** field to generate an employee ID number for each applicant. Let's first take a look at the steps required to add this new field to the employee form:

1. Select option 5, **Change form design**, from the Features menu.
2. If you have made a backup copy of the database press Enter to acknowledge the backup warning message; otherwise press Escape to abort the form change process.
3. Select option 1, **Add fields**, from the Change Form Design menu.
4. Type the new field, `ID Number:`, as shown in Figure 7-8, and press F10.

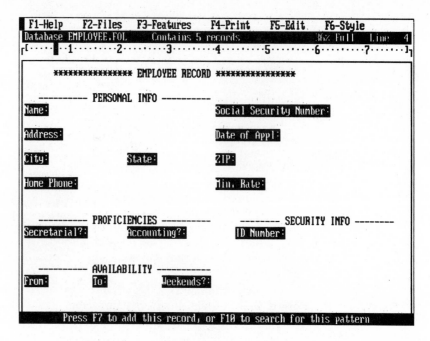

**Figure 7-8.** Employee form with **ID Number** field.

Notice that you've added the background text

---- SECURITY INFO ----

above the ID number in Figure 7-8. Follow these steps to add this
background text:

1. Select option 5, **Change form design**, from the Features menu.
2. If you have made a backup copy of the database press Enter to
   acknowledge the backup warning message; otherwise press
   Escape to abort the form change process.
3. Select option 5, **Change background text**, from the Change Form
   Design menu.
4. Enter the ---- SECURITY INFO ---- background text shown in
   Figure 7-8 and press F10.

We will treat the **ID Number** field as a text type. Since this is the
default field type you don't have to go through the steps of modifying
it to another type.

Before we look at the form program changes required to generate this ID number let's see how the Wikley Company currently calculates it. It uses the following procedure:

1. Add the rightmost digit to the two rightmost digits.
2. Add some random number between 0 and 1000 to the result of step 1 above.

For example, for an applicant with a Social Security Number of 123456789, if the random number were 693, the ID number would be 791 and is calculated as follows:

| Rightmost Digit | Rightmost 2 Digits | Random Number between 0 and 1000 | Result |
|---|---|---|---|
| 9 | + 89 | + 693 | = 791 |

The random number used in this calculation is some random number between 0 and 1000 that Wikley Company adds to the sum of the rightmost digits to make it more difficult for other people to guess an applicant's ID number. Here's the form program containing the changes necessary to automatically generate ID Number values:

**Listing 7-2.** Enhanced form program with State and ZIP validation plus ID Number generation.

```
;        WIKLEY COMPANY EMPLOYEE DATABASE FORM
;                    8/09/90
;

;    This form program:
;            1 - limits Social Security Number: input to
;                the valid range of 0 - 999999999
;            2 - limits the State: entry to a maximum of
;                2 characters
;            3 - limits ZIP: input to the valid range of
;                0 - 99999
;            4 - generates an ID Number: based upon the
;                Social Security Number: and a random number
;                between 0 and 100
;
```

```
; ************* error handling ***************
; ** Social Security Number: **
IF (Social_Security_Number > 999999999) THEN GOTO socerr
IF (Social_Security_Number < 0) THEN GOTO socerr

; ** State: **
IF (@LENGTH(State) > 2) THEN GOTO staterr

; ** ZIP: **
IF ((Zip > 99999) OR (Zip < 0)) THEN GOTO ziperr

; ********** generate ID number *************
IF (ID_Number <> "") THEN GOTO end
@V1 = @MOD(Social_Security_Number, 10)
@V2 = @M.)D(Social_Security_Number, 100)
ID_Number = @STRING((@V1 + @V2 + (@RANDOM * 1000)), 0)
GOTO end

; ************* error message display **************
:socerr
; Social Security Number: error
@ERRBOX(Social_Security_Number, "Invalid Social Security Number!")
GOTO end

:staterr
; State: error
@ERRBOX(State, "Cannot exceed 2 characters!")
GOTO end

:ziperr
; ZIP: error
@ERRBOX(Zip, "Invalid ZIP Code!")

:end
```

Be sure to keep remarks up to date with any changes you make to a form program.

The remark block at the start of this form program has been updated to reflect the changes for generating the ID number. All the other differences from the previous form program are in this block:

```
; *********** generate ID number *************
IF (ID_Number <> '"') THEN GOTO end
@V1 = @MOD(Social_Security_Number, 10)
@V2 = @MOD(Social_Security_Number, 100)
ID_Number = @STRING((@V1 + @V2 + (@RANDOM * 1000)), 0)
GOTO end
```

We'll examine this six-line block a line or two at a time. The first line, of course, is a remark. The second line, the IF..THEN statement, protects an ID that has already been calculated from being replaced. We'll return to this thought shortly; for now all you need to know is that if there is no ID number already in the **ID Number** field on the form screen, the program will execute the remainder of the block.

The next two statements, the ones on the lines beginning with @V1 and @V2, are almost identical. They both use the @MOD keyword, which has the following syntax:

Value = @MOD(Numerator, Denominator)

where Value is the remainder after Numerator is divided by Denominator. For example, if the value 123456789 is entered for the **Social Security Number** field the result of

@MOD(Social_Security_Number, 10)

is 9 (since 123456789 divided by 10 equals 12345678 with a remainder of 9). The other statement with @MOD reads

@V2 = @MOD(Social_Security_Number, 100)

What is the result of

@MOD(Social_Security_Number, 100)

if the Social Security Number is 123456789? If you guessed 89, you're correct! This is because 123456789 divided by 100 equals 1234567 with a remainder of 89. These two statements have provided you with the one rightmost and two rightmost digits of the **Social Security Number** field.

There are still a couple of things about the @MOD statement that may be unclear to you. For example, what do the @V1, @V2, and the equal sign (=) represent? Let's take a look at @V1 and @V2 first.

## Local Variables

The @V1 and @V2 are *local variables*. A *variable* is a named area in memory that stores a value or string. In a First Choice form program, a *local* variable is one whose value is maintained only for a limited period of time. For instance, if you place the value 3 in the variable @V1 in a form program, that value will *not remain in @V1 if you switch to the word processor and then return to the database application. (This is opposed to some other database programs, in which the variable retains its value until it is changed.) First Choice provides four local variables named @V1, @V2, @V3, and @V4. As with keywords, the @ preceding the V1, V2, V3, and V4 is optional, but I strongly suggest you use it to prevent future confusion with field names.

*Note:* Software Publishing's own documentation states that "Local variables are cleared when you open the database." They further say that local variables "are not reset for every record but retain the value from the previous record, until you leave the database." However, my testing has proven that this last statement is not entirely true. It appears that these local variables are reset every time a search operation is performed.

*I highly recommend that you always use the @ character to help distinguish local variables from field names.*

As mentioned above, variables hold either text or numeric values. You have seen how a keyword statement may use field names as parameters, as in

```
IF (@LENGTH(State) > 2) THEN GOTO staterr
```

In this statement the field name **State** is the parameter for the keyword @LENGTH. A keyword statement may also specify a local variable as a keyword statement parameter, as in

```
IF (@LENGTH(@V2) > 2) THEN GOTO staterr
```

In this statement the local variable **@V2** is the parameter for the keyword @LENGTH. Because a parameter occurring after a keyword is either a field name or a local variable, it helps you and people who will be reading your program in the future if you always precede local variables with the at sign.

In addition, field names and local variables may be used in another type of statement, *assignment* statements.

# Assignment Statements

The equals sign is used to place a value in a field name or a local variable. The equals sign (=) in the statement

```
@V1 = @MOD(Social_Security_Number, 10)
```

causes the value returned by the @MOD keyword to be placed in the @V1 local variable. When a value is placed in a field name or variable like this we refer to it as an *assignment statement*. The syntax of an assignment statement is

```
Receiver = Expression
```

where **Expression** is some statement which represents a value (in database terminology, a *value statement*). This expression may be as simple as a number such as 7, or as complex as the result of a keyword like @LENGTH. The result of the expression is assigned to the receiver.

To illustrate assigning a value to a local variable, you could set the local variable @1 equal to 7 like this:

```
@V1 = 7
```

In this case, the value statement is simply the number 7.

To illustrate assigning a value to a field, you can also use assignment statements to place values in database fields like this:

```
State = "IN"
```

or

```
Min. Rate = 8.50
```

The first assignment statement places the string IN in the **State** field. (A string, you remember, is a series of alphanumeric characters.) Notice that when a string is assigned to a field name or a variable it must be enclosed in double quotes.

An example of a more complex assignment statement is

```
@V1 = @LENGTH(State)
```

where the value returned by the keyword @LENGTH is placed in the @V1 variable. For example, if the letters IN were entered for the **State** field, this assignment statement would place the value 2 in @V1.

Now you know the logic behind the second and third statements in the new lines in the form program, whose purpose is to produce the rightmost and two rightmost digits of the applicant's Social Security number.

## Mathematical Operators

Moving to the third statement (the fourth line of the block), we see something we haven't encountered previously in our tour of form programming—a plus sign:

```
ID_Number = @STRING((@V1 + @V2 + (@RANDOM * 1000)), 0)
```

The plus sign is one of several mathematical operators that First Choice offers which allow you to create even more complex statements. And the one needed for creating the Wikley Company's applicant ID number *is* rather complex. This number may be expressed as the sum of

rightmost digit of Social Security Number

+

two rightmost digits of Social Security Number

+

some random number between 0 and 1000

You have seen how the @MOD keyword may be used to determine the first two pieces of this sum. The way you add them together is with the plus sign. First Choice provides the symbols shown in Table 7-1 for this and other mathematical operations.

**Table 7-1.** Form programming mathematical operators.

| Symbol | Mathematical Operation |
| --- | --- |
| + | Addition |
| − | Subtraction |
| * | Multiplication |
| / | Division |
| ^ or ** | Exponentiation |

Let's look at some examples of the use of these operators. To add 3 plus 4 and place the result in @V1 you would write

```
@V1 = 3 + 4
```

You can also use variables or field names on the right side of the equals sign like this:

```
@V1 = @V2 + Zip
```

which adds @V2 to the ZIP value and places the result in @V1.

As you can see, First Choice provides two different symbols for exponentiation: the caret (^) and double asterisks (**). So, you can place the value of 4 squared in @V1 like this:

```
@V1 = 4^2
```

or like this:

```
@V1 = 4**2
```

## Precedence of Mathematical Operators

An important point to know about mathematical operators is how First Choice prioritizes them. Here's what I mean. In a simple statement like this:

```
@V1 = 4 + 3 - 2
```

First Choice evaluates the result from left to right. That is, 4 is added to 3 resulting in 7. Then 2 is subtracted from 7 resulting in 5, which is placed in the @V1 variable. You would get the same result if you reversed the order of the last two operations. That is, 4 − 2 + 3 also equals 5.

In contrast, there are some expressions in which the order of the operations affects the answer. For example, in this more complex statement:

```
@V1 = 4 + 3 * 2
```

You get one result (14) if you perform the addition first and the multiplication second, and another result (10) if you multiply first and then add. A human being doing this problem might do it one way on one day and the other way the next day, because humans can choose which way to do problems like this. First Choice, however, will do this problem the same way each time because of built-in instructions that tell it which kinds of operations to carry out before certain other ones. In this case, it will use the 3 in multiplying 3 times 2 and never will get around to adding 4 plus 3. This is because in First Choice multiplication has a higher *precedence* than addition. Table 7-2 shows the order of mathematical operator precedence from highest to lowest.

**Table 7-2.** Mathematical operator precedence.

| Operator | Precedence |
|----------|------------|
| ^ or ** | Highest |
| * and / | Middle |
| + and − | Lowest |

As you can tell from the table, First Choice evaluates the statement:

@V1 = 4 + 3 * 2

as follows: Multiply 3 times 2. This equals 6. Then add 4 to 6, resulting in 10.

If all operations within an expression have the same precedence (for example, @V1 = 4 + 7 − 3 + 2) First Choice evaluates the expression from left to right. Otherwise, the higher precedence operations are performed first.

## Use of Parentheses

There is a way to alter the order in which First Choice performs operations within a complex statement: by using parentheses. You saw earlier how the statement:

@V1 = 4 + 3 * 2

places the value 10 in @V1 because the multiplication is performed before the addition. What if you actually wanted to add 4 to 3 and multiply that sum (7) by 2 instead? You can use parentheses like this:

@V1 = (4 + 3) * 2

to *force* First Choice to add 4 to 3 and multiply the result, 7, times 2. This statement places the value 14 in @V1.

*First Choice starts with the innermost parentheses first.*

Parentheses are very handy when working with complicated expressions. Give yourself a little quiz now—how would First Choice evaluate this expression:

@V1 = (7 + 3 * ((4 − 2) * 3))

The secret to evaluating an expression like this is to start with the innermost operation and work outwards. Multiple sets of parentheses like those in this example cause operations to be nested within other operations. For example, the subtraction operation:

(4 − 2)

is nested within the multiplication operation:

((4 − 2) * 3)

which in turn is nested within the right side of the expression. Therefore the subtraction operation is nested within three sets of parentheses. Since no other operation is nested that deeply it is performed first. Once you perform the subtraction the expression is simplified to

@V1 = (7 + 3 * (2 * 3))

The multiplication operation

(2 * 3)

is inside two sets of parentheses. Since it is the most deeply nested operation remaining it is performed next. Now the expression is simplified to

@V1 = (7 + 3 * 6)

The remaining operations, addition and multiplication, are both within one set of parentheses. Therefore the mathematical operator precedence rules illustrated in Table 7-2 must be used to determine the next operation. Since multiplication has higher precedence than addition, the operation

(3 * 6)

is performed next and the expression simplifies to

```
@V1 = (7 + 18)
```

Finally, the addition is performed and the result, 25, is placed in the variable @V1. Is that what you got?

Now that you understand mathematical operators and their precedence, let's resume our discussion of the new portion of the employee form program.

# The ID Number Assignment

As you know, the statements

```
@V1 = @MOD(Social_Security_Number, 10)
@V2 = @MOD(Social_Security_Number, 100)
```

place the rightmost digit of the Social Security number value in @V1 and the two rightmost digits of the Social Security number value in @V2.

You also probably guessed this about the next statement in the ID number generation block:

```
ID_Number = @STRING((@V1 + @V2 + (@RANDOM * 1000)), 0)
```

The plus sign will add the two local variables (@V1 and @V2) and the value generated by the expression following the second plus sign. Let's take a look at this entire expression now, starting with this portion:

```
(@RANDOM * 1000)
```

*Unlike @LENGTH and @MOD, @RANDOM doesn't need any parameters.*

This is the most deeply nested operation so you should evaluate it first. The @RANDOM keyword has the following syntax:

```
@RANDOM
```

Because @RANDOM has no parameters, there is no need to place parentheses after it. The First Choice @RANDOM function always returns a value between 0.0 and 1.0. However, you want a random number between 0 and 1000, so you need to multiply the result of @RANDOM by 1000.

Let's assume the Social Security number entered is 123456789 and @RANDOM has returned the value .4. The complex statement can now be simplified to

```
ID_Number = @STRING((@V1 + @V2 + (.4 * 1000)), 0)
```
or

```
ID_Number = @STRING((@V1 + @V2 + 400), 0)
```

You also know that @V1 and @V2 equal 9 and 89 respectively for our example Social Security number of 123456789. That allows you to simplify the statement to

```
ID_Number = @STRING((9 + 89 + 400), 0)
```

or

```
ID_Number = @STRING(498, 0)
```

*Remember, the field for the ID number is a text field.*

As you can tell, this is an assignment statement (because of the equals sign), and the right side of the statement is a function with a parameter after it, in parentheses, of course. The **ID Number** field will receive the result of the @STRING keyword. But what does the @STRING keyword do? @STRING converts a numeric value to a text value and has the following syntax:

```
@STRING(Number, DecPlaces)
```

In this function the `Number` parameter is converted to a text string. The `DecPlaces` (meaning decimal places) parameter specifies how many digits should appear to the right of the decimal point after `Number` is converted to a string.

Our example shows @STRING called with the parameters 498 and 0. @STRING converts the numeric value 498 to a string 498 with 0 digits to the right of the decimal point. As a result, the text value 498 is assigned to the **ID Number** field. We are using 0 as the DecPlaces parameter to prevent ID Number from containing any fractional data.

Now the ID number has been assigned. The last line in the new block is

```
GOTO end
```

This GOTO statement causes all the error handling statements to be skipped. It does this because you don't need them (because if the program has gotten to the point of generating an ID number, it has already proceeded through the other checks). Here the form program ends.

Now let's get back to that first GOTO statement in the ID number generation block, which I promised to explain. It reads

```
IF (ID_Number <> "") THEN GOTO end
```

This is here for three reasons: 1) if a value already exists in the **ID Number** field you don't need to put it in again, and 2) if the program goes through the random number routine again, the ID number very probably will change. (Remember, a form program is automatically executed each time a record is added or changed.) This could be confusing and havoc-wreaking. Therefore, once an ID number has been assigned to an employee, you don't want to change it just because another field has been modified.

Third, this IF..THEN statement allows Wikley Company to assign an ID number different than the one that would be generated by the form program; if an ID number is entered on the form screen independently of the form program this way, this IF..THEN statement will skip the statements that would normally generate and assign the number.

After you've added the new statements for this form program press F10 and First Choice will check for any syntax errors. If no errors are detected, the dialog box shown if Figure 7-3 is displayed. This time, rather than answering no (N) as you did earlier in the chapter, press Enter to accept the default yes response.

Now you get to view the fruits of your labor. The form program is running against every record in the employee database. You want to do this to generate ID Number values for all the existing employee records. Notice that each record is briefly displayed. If you watch closely, you can see each new ID number that is generated. When this recalculation is complete, use the F10 key to step through the database and verify that each record now has an ID Number entry.

A little later on, we'll add more functionality to this form program. But for now, let's look at other variables and another special keyword that you might want to use in your form programming.

# Other Variables and a Special Keyword

We've already discussed the temporary, or local, variables @V1 through @V4, which are *initialized* (made freshly available and ready to receive a value) at the start of the database application and after a search operation. First Choice also offers a *permanent variable* for form programming, which is called @DISKVAR.

## The @DISKVAR Variable

At first the term "permanent variable" may seem to contradict itself. If something is permanent how can it also be variable? Here's why it's called "permanent": @DISKVAR is a variable which resides in your database file. Therefore, when you assign a value to it you are actually placing this value in the database file. This is in contrast to the local variables @V1 − @V4; when you assign a value to these local variables you are modifying a temporary storage area of memory in your computer. Local variable values are not stored in your database file. If you assign a value to @DISKVAR it will remain there until you assign a new value to @DISKVAR. Even if you turn your computer off for the day the value will be stored in @DISKVAR for the next time you run the database application.

Now for the reason it's a "variable": @DISKVAR may be used like the local variables @V1 − @V4 and can hold either a numeric value or a text value (of up to 240 characters). If you're clever you might use @DISKVAR to hold a password or a count of how many records have been added to the database. Let's take a look at a special form programming keyword which can help you keep track of record additions.

One way of using @DISKVAR is to display a warning when the database reaches a certain number of records. For example, the Wikley Company might consider manually purging the employee database when the file grows larger than 10,000 records. If so, the program would use the statement

```
IF @DISKVAR > 10000 THEN GOTO COUNTWARNING
```

# The @OLDREC Keyword

*As with any IF..THEN statement, if the condition is not true, the next sequential statement is executed immediately.*

The @OLDREC keyword determines whether the current record being processed by the form program is new or is being updated. In other words, @OLDREC tells the program whether the form program is being executed for a record add or record update modification. (A bit later on you'll see how the ability to do this helps the Wikley Company, but for now we're using @OLDREC for another purpose.) @OLDREC is TRUE if the record already exists and is being updated. @OLDREC is FALSE if the record is being added to the database. Therefore, this form program block:

```
; Maintain Record Addition Count
IF @OLDREC = TRUE THEN GOTO end
@DISKVAR = @DISKVAR + 1
        .
        .
        .
:end
```

would increment @DISKVAR every time a new record is added to the database. In this block, @DISKVAR *does* represent how many records have been added to the database but it *does not* necessarily represent how many records are in the database. Why not? @DISKVAR is incremented each time a record is added but it is not decremented when a record is deleted. Unfortunately, there is no good way to maintain a record count in @DISKVAR since the form program is executed only for record adds and updates. Put another way, @DISKVAR is where First Choice stores the number of records that have ever been in the database.

*Note:* The vertical ellipsis (three periods in a row) means that you can put one or more other program statements between @DISKVAR = @DISKVAR + 1 and :end.

Now let's look at one other form programming variable, @DECIMALS.

# The @DECIMALS Variable

The way you tell a form program how many significant digits you want it to use after the decimal point in numeric data is with a variable called @DECIMALS. Up to 15 digits may be used to specify a numeric value—this includes digits before and after the decimal place. The @DECIMAL variable may be assigned either a numeric value or the string "FLOAT." Table 7-3 shows the results of using different @DECIMALS values.

**Table 7-3.** Examples of @DECIMALS values.

| @DECIMALS Value | Number Before Conversion | Number After Conversion |
|---|---|---|
| 0 | 123.9840 | 124 |
| 1 | 123.9840 | 124.0 |
| 2 | 123.9840 | 123.98 |
| 3 | 123.9840 | 123.984 |
| FLOAT | 123.9840 | 123.984 |

In the first example in Table 7-3 @DECIMALS is set to 0. This tells First Choice to display zero digits to the right of the decimal point. Why isn't the number 123.9840 converted to 123 in this case? Because First Choice performs a bit of number rounding before dropping the digits to the right of the decimal point. In this case, any number greater than or equal to 123.5 is going to be rounded up to 124.

The next example in Table 7-3 shows what happens with the same number when @DECIMALS is set to 1. The result here is similar to what happened when @DECIMALS was set to 0. The only difference is that one digit (0) is shown to the right of the decimal point.

What happens to 123.9840 when @DECIMALS is set to 2? As you would expect, only 2 digits are shown to the right of the decimal point but no rounding occurred. Why not? Rounding only occurs when the first digit to be chopped off (4 in this case) is greater than or equal to 5. Since the first digit to be chopped off is less than 5, no rounding is done and the extra digits are simply discarded.

The last two examples in Table 7-3 result in the same number after conversion. When @DECIMALS is set to 3 the number 123.9840 is converted to 123.984. Since the first digit to be chopped off is 0 no rounding is done. Why does the converted number equal 123.984 when @DECIMALS is set to FLOAT? The FLOAT assignment tells First Choice to drop all trailing zeros. Thus you wind up with 123.984 if the original number is 123.9840, or 123.98400, or even 123.9840000000.

*@DECIMALS has no effect on fields not assigned values in the form program.*

The @DECIMALS variable affects only values assigned in the form program. For example, assume a @DECIMALS value of 0. If a Min. Rate value of 4.25 is entered for an applicant and this field is not modified by the form program the value will not be changed.

However, if for some reason the form program multiplies the Min. Rate by 2 and places the result back in Min. Rate the result will be 9. (4.25 times 2 equals 8.50, which rounds up to 9.) The same holds true for simple assignment statements. The result of these form program statements:

```
@DECIMALS = 0
Min._Rate = 4.25
```

is a value of 4 in the Min. Rate field.

# The Final Employee Form Program

Now let's take a look at the final version of Wikley Company's employee form program, which includes some nifty features. The company has a few more items that it would like to place in the program. It wants to ensure that the Name and **Social Security Number** fields contain data when a record is added or modified. It would also like to avoid having to enter the current date for the **Date of Appl** field; it feels the computer should be intelligent enough to automatically fill this field in with today's date. Finally, they want to make sure that a valid Home Phone value (that is, one which consists of three digits followed by a dash followed by four more digits) is entered.

## The Program Listing

Here's the final version of Wikley Company's form program which incorporates these requirements:

Listing 7-3. The final Wikley Company Employee database form program.

```
;        WIKLEY COMPANY EMPLOYEE DATABASE FORM
;                    8/20/90
;
; This form program:
;           1 - Limits Social Security Number: input to
;               the valid range of 0 - 999999999
```

```
;              2 - limits the State: entry to a maximum of
;                  2 characters
;              3 - limits ZIP: input to the valid range of
;                  0 - 99999
;              4 - generates an ID Number: based upon the
;                  Social Security Number: and a random number
;                  between 0 and 1000
;              5 - requires a Name: and Social Security
;                  Number: entry
;              6 - defaults the Date of Appl: field to the
;                  current date
;              7 - validates the Home Phone: entry
;

; ************** error handling ***************

; ** Name: **
IF Name = "" THEN GOTO namerr
; ** Social Security Number: **
IF (Social_Security_Number > 999999999) THEN GOTO socerr1
IF (Social_Security_Number < 0) THEN GOTO socerr1
IF Social_Security_Number = "" THEN GOTO socerr2

; ** State: **
IF (@LENGTH(State) > 2) THEN GOTO staterr

; ** ZIP: **
IF ((Zip > 99999) OR (Zip < 0)) THEN GOTO ziperr

; ** Home Phone: **
IF Home_Phone = "" THEN GOTO calcid
@V1 = Home_Phone
IF @LENGTH(@V1) > 8 THEN GOTO phonerr
IF (@MID(@V1, 3, 1) <> "-") THEN GOTO phonerr
IF (@VALUE(@LEFT(@V1, 3))) = @ERROR THEN GOTO phonerr
IF (@VALUE(@RIGHT(@V1, 4))) = @ERROR THEN GOTO phonerr

:calcid
; ********** generate ID number *************
IF (ID_Number <> "") THEN GOTO end
@V1 = @MOD(Social_Security_Number, 10)
@V2 = @MOD(Social_Security_Number, 100)
ID_Number = @STRING((@V1 + @V2 + (@RANDOM * 1000)), 0)
; ********** default Date of Appl: **********
```

```
IF @OLDREC = TRUE THEN GOTO end
Date_Of_Appl = @NOW
GOTO end

; ************* error message display *************
:namerr
; Name: error
@ERRBOX(Name, "Must specify a name!")
GOTO end

:socerr1
; Social Security Number: error (invalid)
@ERRBOX(Social_Security_Number, "Invalid Social Security Number!")
GOTO end

:socerr2
; Social Security Number: error (not entered)
@ERRBOX(Social_Security_Number, "Must specify a Social Security Number
GOTO end

:staterr
; State: error
@ERRBOX(State, "Cannot exceed 2 characters!")
GOTO end

:ziperr
; ZIP: error
@ERRBOX(Zip, "Invalid ZIP Code!")
GOTO end

:phonerr
; Home Phone: error
@ERRBOX(Home_Phone, "Invalid Phone Number!")

:end
```

Now let's discuss the modifications to this version of the form program.

## Making the Modifications

First of all, more information has been added to the remark block at the top of the program. Items 5 through 7 in this block describe the new features of the program: compulsory Name and Social Security number entry, default Date of Appl value, and validation of the **Home Phone** field.

The first non-remark line of the new form program:

```
If Name = "" THEN GOTO namerr
```

causes an error to be displayed if no Name is provided. (The value **""** is sometimes referred to as a *null string* because it doesn't contain any characters.)

The **namerr** block referred to in the GOTO clause looks like this:

```
:namerr
; Name: error
@ERRBOX(Name, "Must specify a name!")
GOTO end
```

and simply causes the program to display the message "Must specify a name!" when it detects the absence of a name when an operator is entering data.

The next validation block, for **Social Security Number**, has a few modifications. Rather than performing GOTOs to **socerr** you have changed the identifier (label) to **socerr1**. This is because you now have two different possible types of Social Security Number errors—no number and an invalid number. A third IF..THEN statement has been added to the block and reads:

```
IF Social_Security_Number = " " THEN GOTO socerr2
```

As with the Name field, if the value for Social Security Number is a null string an error will be displayed. The error for no Social Security Number is immediately after the **socerr2** identifier:

```
:socerr2
; Social Security Number: error (not entered)
@ERRBOX(Social_Security_Number, "Must specify a Social Security Number
GOTO end
```

This @ERRBOX error looks almost identical to the one after **socerr1**; the only difference is the error message.

Immediately after the ZIP validation we have added validation for the **Home Phone** field. This block reads:

```
; ** Home Phone: **
IF Home_Phone = "" THEN GOTO calcid
@V1 = Home_Phone
IF @LENGTH(@V1) > 8 THEN GOTO phonerr
IF (@MID(@V1, 3, 1) <> "-") THEN GOTO phonerr
IF (@VALUE(@LEFT(@V1, 3))) = @ERROR THEN GOTO phonerr
IF (@VALUE(@RIGHT(@V1, 4))) = @ERROR THEN GOTO phonerr
```

If no Home Phone value is specified (Home_Phone equals ""), a GOTO calcid is performed; this causes the Home Phone validation to be skipped. (Note that calcid is a new identifier which immediately precedes the ID number generation block.)

The Home Phone validation starts by placing the Home Phone value in @V1. (I do this to save myself some keystrokes in the next few statements.) The next statement checks to see if the length of @V1 is greater than 8 (via @LENGTH); if this is true then the @ERRBOX after the **phonerr** identifier is executed.

The next statement:

```
IF (@MID(@V1, 3, 1) <> "-") THEN GOTO phonerr
```

uses the @MID keyword to make sure the fourth character in the **Home Phone** field is a dash (-). @MID's syntax is

```
@MID(String, Start, NumChars)
```

@MID returns NumChars characters from String starting in Start position. The position of the leftmost character in String is considered 0, not 1. So this statement:

```
@V1 = @MID("playground", 4, 6)
```

means "In the word *playground*, take six characters in a row starting with the fourth character; and put that string of characters in the area called @V1." Because @MID starts counting with the leftmost character (which is *p*) as number 0, the fourth character is the G. It places the string "ground" in @V1.

Since you expect the fourth character in the **Home Phone** field to be a dash, the statement

*More niftiness in programming.*

```
IF (@MID(@V1, 3, 1) <> "-") THEN GOTO phonerr
```

jumps to the **phonerr** identifier if it is not a dash.

The remaining two statements in the Home Phone validation block look very similar to one another. They are also fairly complex so let's dissect them and perform one operation at a time. In the first one:

```
IF (@VALUE(@LEFT(@V1, 3))) = @ERROR THEN GOTO phonerr
```

the @LEFT keyword is the most nested operation, so First Choice starts out with it. The @LEFT keyword has the following syntax:

```
@LEFT(String, NumChars)
```

@LEFT returns the *NumChars* leftmost characters from `String`. For instance, this statement:

```
@V1 = @LEFT("Baseball", 4)
```

means "In the word *Baseball*, place the four leftmost characters in the area called @V1." It places the string "Base" in @V1.

In your form program, (@LEFT(@V1, 3) refers to the three-digit prefix in the phone number. The value returned by @LEFT is then passed as a parameter to the @VALUE keyword, whose syntax is

```
@VALUE(String)
```

@VALUE simply converts a text value, String, into a numeric value. If `String` does not represent a numeric value, @VALUE returns @ERROR. The program then performs the GOTO phonerr operation. The result is that an error message appears on-screen if the keyboard entry person mistakenly types letters instead of digits for the first part of the home phone number.

*The @ERROR keyword has some unique and useful properties.*

@ERROR is a rather unique keyword which is not actually a function that performs some operation. Rather, it is a value that is returned by another keyword (for example, @VALUE) when something "does not compute," such as letters trying to enter a numeric spot. It's as if your computer is saying to itself, "Now wait a minute—this can't be!" The instructions after the word @ERROR (GOTO phonerr) tell it where to go after it says this to itself.

The last statement in the Home Phone validation block looks like this:

```
IF (@VALUE(@RIGHT(@V1, 4))) = @ERROR THEN GOTO phonerr
```

Rather than using the keyword @LEFT this statement uses @RIGHT, whose syntax is the same as @LEFT's:

```
@RIGHT(String, NumChars)
```

@RIGHT returns the **NumChars** rightmost characters in the String parameter.

As you have probably figured out, this last statement in this validation block ensures that the rightmost four characters of Home Phone are numeric. If they are not numeric, a `GOTO phonerr` is performed to display an error message.

Turning to the part of the program listing that generates the ID number, let's consider the **calcid** identifier. This has been added to the start of the ID number generation block because sometimes the program needs to skip the Home Phone validation, and it needs a label to skip to (remember the `GOTO calcid` at the start of Home Phone validation?). Nothing else in the ID number generation block has been changed in this version of the form program.

The block of statements after the ID number generation are new and were added to place today's date in the **Date of Appl** field. We use the @OLDREC keyword, which is discussed earlier in this chapter, to determine whether the record processed is being added (new) or changed (existing). If @OLDREC returns a TRUE value (that is, if the record being processed is indeed old), the Date of Appl default statement:

```
Date_Of_Appl = @NOW
```

is skipped. As you recall, @OLDREC is TRUE if the record is being updated; you don't want to automatically change the **Date of Appl** field for an existing record. If @OLDREC returns FALSE you know the record is being added to the database and you want to make the application date today's date by default (that is, automatically). The keyword @NOW returns the current date stored in your PC's internal clock. (So if the date is set incorrectly on your PC this field will contain erroneous data. Use DOS' DATE command to set the date in your PC.)

This final version of the employee database form program does everything that the Wikley Company requested. It also contains some very useful features and techniques that I hope you will find helpful in your own form programs. Before starting the next chapter, which is about reports, or printed versions of your database, take some time to study the following summary information to ensure that you thoroughly understand form programming concepts.

# Summary

- A form program is a set of instructions carried out by First Choice when a database record is added or modified.

- A form program, like any other computer language program, is a list of steps to be followed when performing an operation.

- In form programming, we refer to one step or instruction as a statement.

- In a form program, statements are performed one at a time from the top of the program to the bottom.

- Remarks are an optional feature of form programming which should be used to document the form's purpose and functionality. A remark line starts with a semicolon.

- In most cases, when you want to refer to a database field in a form program, simply type the full name of the field as it appears on the form without the trailing colon. If the field name contains spaces, like **Social Security Number**, the spaces should be replaced by underscores (_).

- The IF..THEN statement, in conjunction with the GOTO statement, may be used to alter the top to bottom sequence and cause another statement, other than the next sequential one, to be performed.

- A label statement provides a place for the program to "jump to" and start in on another instruction after a GOTO is executed.

- @ERRBOX is a built-in function, or keyword, of the form program interpreter.

- Keywords are preceded by the "at sign" (@). Although the @ preceding ERRBOX and these other keywords is optional, it is recommended that you always use it.

- A variable is a special type of word which is used to hold values. First Choice provides four local variables. These may be used to hold text or numeric values.

- When a value is placed in field name or variable like this we refer to it as an assignment statement.

- First Choice provides the symbols +, -, *, /, ^, and ** for mathematical operations. Each operation has a certain priority level, or precedence, associated with it. Higher precedence operations are performed before lower precedence ones in complex expressions. However, parentheses may be used to alter the order of precedence.

- @DISKVAR is a "permanent variable," a variable which resides in your database file.
- The @OLDREC keyword determines if the current record being processed by the form program is new or is being updated.
- @DECIMALS is a variable you can use to specify the number of significant digits after the decimal point in numeric data.

# Database Reports

**In this chapter:**

- Creating a Simple Report: Name and Phone Number
- Print Options
- Columns
- Headings and Calculations
- Search Specifications
- Reusing and Deleting Report Instructions
- Summary

Reports are printed summaries of database information. As such they are extremely useful. In this final chapter on First Choice's database application we will discuss the reporting function, for which First Choice provides a great deal of flexibility. We will start off by creating a report that includes the Name and Home Phone values for each record in Wikley Company's employee database. Then we will discuss in detail each of the steps involved in creating a report, from print options through search specifications. Finally, you will learn how to reuse and delete report specification files.

# Creating a Simple Report: Name and Phone Number

Wikley Company would like to generate a report each week that shows the Name and Home Phone values for each entry in its employee database. It would like this report to resemble the following list:

### Phone Listing

| Name | Home Phone |
| --- | --- |
| David Craig | 555-3367 |
| John Adams | 555-8490 |
| Kelly Craig | 555-8679 |
| Mary Zale | 555-6620 |
| Tim Smith | 555-4590 |

*Reports are more flexible than table views.*

Actually, it is possible to create a report very similar to this by using a table view. You could create a table view of the employee database that includes only the Name and Home Phone fields. You could then print the table view but you wouldn't get the "Phone Listing" heading for the entire report. Further, only one table view may be defined for a database at one time whereas several report definitions, or *instruction sets*, may exist simultaneously.

Before going any further you should make sure that your printer is properly hooked up to your computer, the paper is properly fed, and the power switch is on. Once your printer is ready to go, follow these steps to create the Phone Listing report:

1. Select option 3, **Create a report**, from the Main menu.
2. Select the employee database file, EMPLOYEE.FOL, from the Directory Assistant.
3. Press Enter to accept the default values in the Print Options dialog box shown in Figure 8-1.
4. Type 1 next to the **Name** field and 2 next to the **Home Phone** field on the columns screen (Figure 8-2) and press F10.
5. Type the heading Phone Listing in the **Report title** field at the top of the headings and calculations screen (Figure 8-3) and press F10.
6. Press F10 at the Search Specifications screen (Figure 8-4) and the Save Report warning message (Figure 8-5) is displayed.

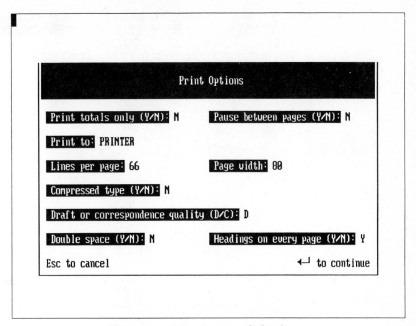

**Figure 8-1.** Print Options dialog box.

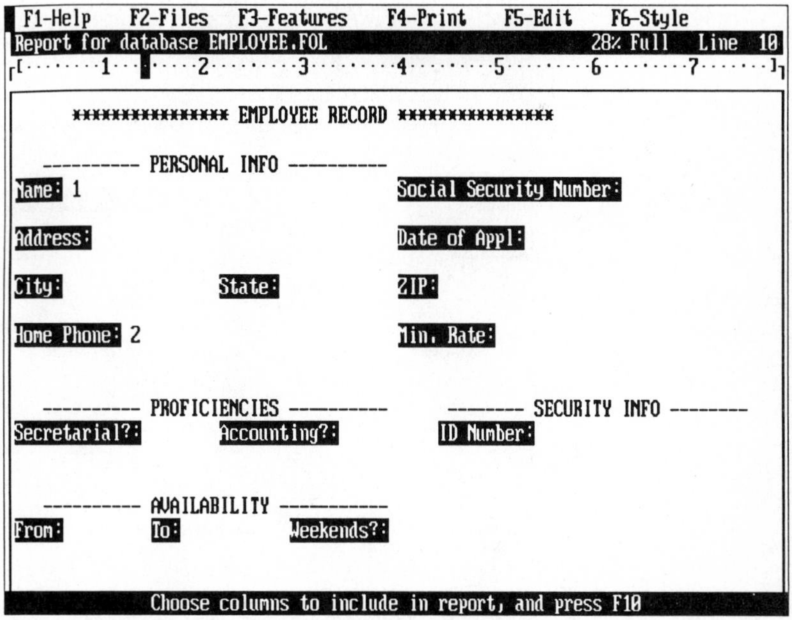

```
 F1-Help    F2-Files   F3-Features   F4-Print   F5-Edit   F6-Style
 Report for database EMPLOYEE.FOL                    28% Full   Line  10
 r[·····1····|·····2·····3·····4·····5·····6·····7·····]₁

          *************** EMPLOYEE RECORD ***************

          ---------- PERSONAL INFO ----------
   Name: 1                              Social Security Number:

   Address:                             Date of Appl:

   City:              State:            ZIP:

   Home Phone: 2                        Min. Rate:


          ---------- PROFICIENCIES ----------        -------- SECURITY INFO --------
   Secretarial?:        Accounting?:             ID Number:


          ---------- AVAILABILITY ----------
   From:       To:              Weekends?:


              Choose columns to include in report, and press F10
```

**Figure 8-2.** Columns screen, requesting that the names appear in column
1 and the phone numbers appear in column 2.

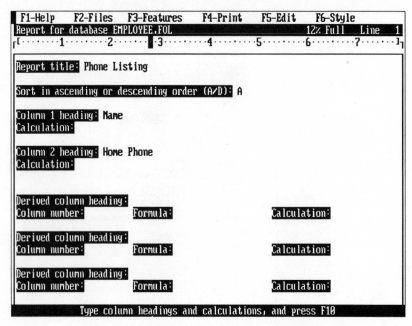

**Figure 8-3.** Headings and Calculations screen for the Phone Listing report.

```
 F1-Help    F2-Files   F3-Features   F4-Print   F5-Edit    F6-Style
 Report for database EMPLOYEE.FOL                         28% Full   Line   4
 ┌[····1····|····2····|····3····|····4····|····5····|····6····|····7····]┐


            *************** EMPLOYEE RECORD ***************

             ---------- PERSONAL INFO ----------
         Name:                            Social Security Number:

         Address:                         Date of Appl:

         City:              State:        ZIP:

         Home Phone:                      Min. Rate:


             ---------- PROFICIENCIES ----------        -------- SECURITY INFO --------
         Secretarial?:       Accounting?:        ID Number:


             ---------- AVAILABILITY ----------
         From:       To:          Weekends?:


                 Type search instructions for the report, and press F10
```

**Figure 8-4.** Search Specifications screen.

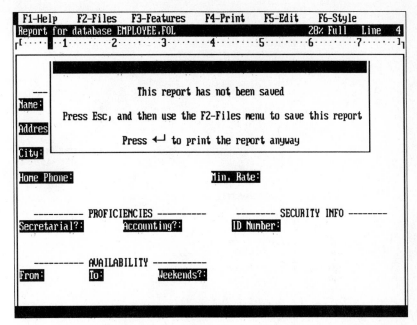

**Figure 8-5.** Save Report warning message.

7. Press Enter to acknowledge the warning message in Figure 8-5. A couple of other messages (selecting records and printing pages) are displayed during the printing process.

When this process is complete your printer should produce a report which looks like the one in Figure 8-6. Notice that it sports a heading, which the table view is incapable of providing, and that there are horizontal lines (rules) under the column headings.

Now let's take a closer look at what you just did in order to take a tour of all of the database reporting options available in First Choice.

# Print Options

Many of the selections in the Print Options dialog box (Figure 8-1) should look familiar to you; we've seen them in Print Dialog boxes for the word processor and database applications earlier in this book.

The first option in the Print Options dialog box (**Print totals only**) determines whether a detailed report or special total summary report is

```
                        Phone Listing

                  Name            Home Phone
                  -----------     ----------
                  David Craig     555-3367
                  John Adams      555-8490
                  Kelly Craig     555-8679
                  Mary Zale       555-6620
                  Tim Smith       555-4590
```

```
                          Page 1
```

**Figure 8-6.** The Wikley Company's Phone Listing report.

generated. You selected in favor of the detailed report; we will show examples of the total summary report in the Headings and Calculations section later in this chapter.

The next option, **Pause between pages**, should be set to yes (Y) if you want your printer to pause after each page of the report is printed. This option is useful if you want to print single sheets of paper rather than the continuous variety.

*Write the report to a file if you want to edit it in the word processor.*

The **Print to** option is identical to **Print to** options we've seen in other Print Option dialog boxes. Leave this set to Printer if you want the report sent to the printer. Alternatively you could enter the name of a disk file where the report should be written (for example, C:MYR-EPORT), or specify Screen to display the output of the report on your monitor.

The **Lines per page** selection also appeared in the database Print Options dialog box. In general, you should set this to 66 for 8-1/2 X 11 inch paper or 84 for 8-1/2 X 14 inch legal paper.

The next option, **Page width**, has a default value of 80. This option's value may range from 1 to 255 for the use of narrow paper or a wide carriage printer.

Normally, report output is horizontally spaced at a rate of 10 characters per inch. The **Compressed type** option allows you to change this spacing to 17 characters per horizontal inch. Specify an N for this option if you wish to print at 10 characters per inch or Y if you want 17 characters per inch (refer to Appendix F of your PFS: First Choice manual to determine whether your printer can print in compressed mode).

The **Draft or correspondence quality** selection allows you to print either a lower-quality output (draft) or higher-quality output (correspondence) report. As with compressed type print, you should refer to Appendix F of your PFS: First Choice documentation to determine whether your printer can print both degrees of quality.

If you want to leave a blank line between each record on a report, you should specify Y for the **Double space** option. Select N for this option if you want each record to appear immediately after the previous one with no blank lines in between.

The final selection in the Print Options dialog box is **Headings on every page**. The heading for our report, Phone Listing, was specified in the Headings and Calculations screen (Figure 8-3), which we will discuss shortly. If you specify Yes for this print option the heading and column titles (the column titles are the field names) will be printed on every page of the report. If you specify No here, the heading and column titles are printed only on the first page of the report.

# Columns

The columns screen shown in Figure 8-2 allows you to define which, and in what order, fields should be included in the report. Fields are shown in columnar format in reports, just as they are in table views. You may include up to 20 different fields in a report.

To include a field in a report place a position number from 1 to 20 next to it, as shown in Figure 8-2. Fields become columns in a report and are ordered from left to right based upon position numbers. In this example, you have specified **Name** and **Home Phone** as fields 1 and 2 respectively. As a result, the Name values are in the left-most column of the report and the Home Phone values are to the right. If you switch the positions of Name and Home Phone the new report will look like the one shown in Figure 8-7.

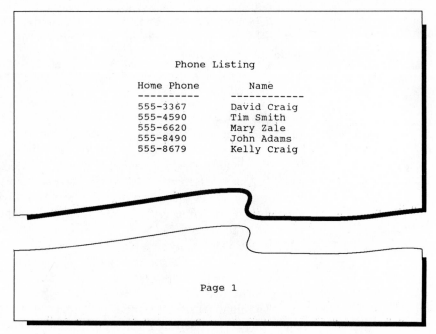

```
                        Phone Listing

                Home Phone           Name
                ----------           ----------
                555-3367             David Craig
                555-4590             Tim Smith
                555-6620             Mary Zale
                555-8490             John Adams
                555-8679             Kelly Craig
```

Page 1

**Figure 8-7.** The Wikley Company's Phone Listing report with columns reversed.

Now let's add some information. Follow these steps to add the **Address** field to the report:

1. Select option 3, **Create a report**, from the Main menu.
2. Select the employee database file, EMPLOYEE.FOL, from the Directory Assistant.
3. Press Enter to accept the default values in the Print Options dialog box shown in Figure 8-1.
4. Place a 1 next to the **Name** field, a 2 next to the **Address** field, and a 3 next to the **Home Phone** field on the columns screen (Figure 8-8) and press F10.

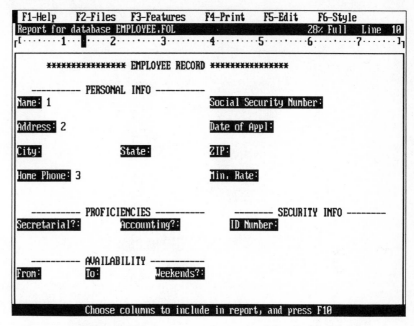

**Figure 8-8.** Columns screen (with address added).

5. Type the heading Phone Listing (with Address:) in the **Report title** field of the headings and calculations screen (Figure 8-9) and press F10.

6. Press F10 at the search specifications screen (Figure 8-4); the Save Report warning message (Figure 8-5) is displayed.

7. Press Enter to acknowledge the warning message in Figure 8-5.

Your new report with the **Address** column should look like the one in Figure 8-10.


## How are Report Records Organized?

*Records are sorted in a report based on the values in columns 1 and 2.*

The records in the first report, the phone listing (Figure 8-6), appear in the same order as those in the third—the address and phone listing (Figure 8-10). But did you notice that the records in the second report—the phone listing with the columns reversed (Figure 8-7)—appear in a completely different order? For example, Tim Smith's record is second in the second report and is last in the first and third reports.

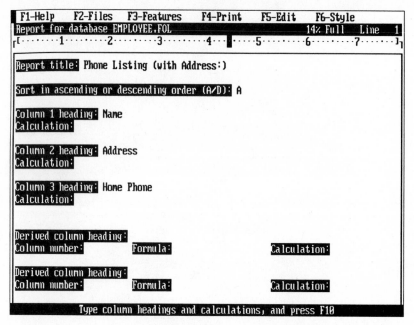

**Figure 8-9.** Headings and Calculations screen (with address added).

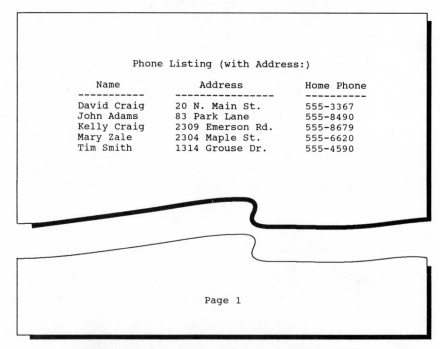

**Figure 8-10.** Phone Listing report (with **Address** field).

The reason for this discrepancy is that report records are sorted by the entries in columns 1 and 2. Column 1 is the *primary sort* field. Records with identical column 1 values are further sorted by column 2 values, the *secondary sort* field. Since **Name** is the first column in the first and third reports, these records are sorted by Name values. However, Home Phone is the first column in the report in the second report, so the records are sorted by phone numbers.

The records in each of the previous reports are sorted in ascending order. You'll see how to change this to descending order later in the Headings and Calculations screen section.

## Reporting in Database Storage Order

What if you don't want to sort the records based upon columns 1 and 2? You might want to print the report records in the same order they appear in the database. Recall that we reordered the records in the employee database in Chapter 5 because Wikley Company wanted them to appear in ascending order by Social Security number. Now how can you print the Phone Listing report in this same order? If you don't specify any field to appear in columns 1 or 2, First Choice will report the records in the same order as they are stored in the database. Follow these steps to create the Phone Listing report with the records in the same order as they are stored in the database:

1. Select option 3, **Create a report**, from the Main menu.
2. Select the employee database file, EMPLOYEE.FOL, from the Directory Assistant.
3. Press Enter to accept the default values in the Print Options dialog box shown in Figure 8-1.
4. Place a 3 next to the **Name** field, a 4 next to the **Address** field, and a 5 next to the **Home Phone** field on the columns screen (Figure 8-11) and press F10.
5. Type the heading Phone Listing (database order) in the **Report title** field of the headings and calculations screen (Figure 8-12) and press F10.
6. Press F10 at the Search Specifications screen (Figure 8-4); the Save Report warning message (Figure 8-5) is displayed.
7. Press Enter to acknowledge the warning message in Figure 8-5.

This new unsorted report is shown in Figure 8-13.

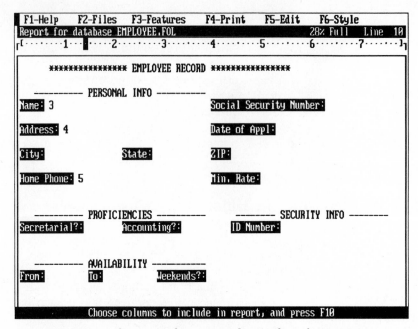

**Figure 8-11.** Skipping columns 1 and 2 on the columns screen.

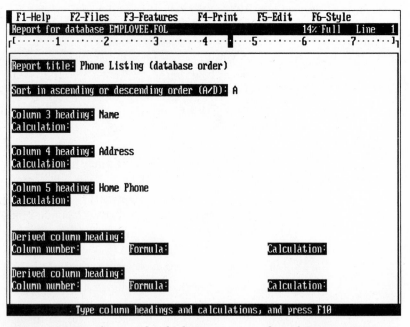

**Figure 8-12.** Headings and Calculations screen when skipping columns 1 and 2.

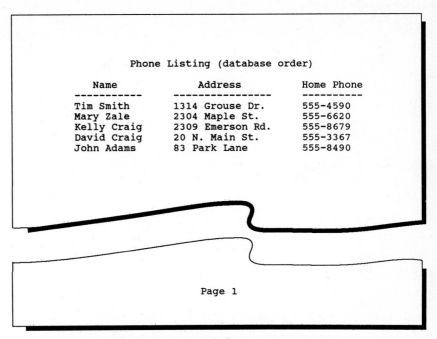

```
              Phone Listing (database order)

          Name              Address          Home Phone
        -----------     ----------------     ----------
        Tim Smith       1314 Grouse Dr.      555-4590
        Mary Zale       2304 Maple St.       555-6620
        Kelly Craig     2309 Emerson Rd.     555-8679
        David Craig     20 N. Main St.       555-3367
        John Adams      83 Park Lane         555-8490
```

```
                          Page 1
```

**Figure 8-13.** Unsorted Phone Listing report.

Notice that although you didn't specify fields for columns 1 and 2 in this report, no blank columns or "holes" are printed. This is because First Choice automatically shifts all columns to the left so the field with the smallest position number is in the leftmost column of the report. In fact, rather than using position numbers 3, 4, and 5 in the previous report, you could have used 4, 7, and 15 respectively and achieved the same results.

# Headings and Calculations

Now that you know all the reporting options available via the Columns screen, let's discuss the flexibility of the Headings and Calculations screen.

## Report Title

The first entry request on a typical Headings and Calculations screen (Figure 8-3) is **Report title**. The report title is the heading that appears at the very top of the report ("Phone Listing" was the first title we saw in this chapter). You can specify whatever title you desire here and it will be printed at the top of the first page of the report. If you selected yes (Y) at the **Headings on every page** option in the Print Options dialog box, the report title will print at the top of every page in the report.

## Ascending or Descending Order

In the earlier discussion about sorting by columns 1 and 2, we noted that all our reports have been sorted in ascending order. The second entry request on the headings and calculations screen is **Sort in ascending or descending order**. The previous reports have all been sorted in ascending order because **A** is the default response. Change this option to **D** if you wish to sort in a descending order.

## Column Headings

*Although field names are used for column headings by default, you can modify the headings as needed.*

A **Column X heading** entry request appears on the Headings and Calculations screen for each field included in the report. The **X** in **Column X heading** represents the unique position number for each selected field.

By default, First Choice uses the form design field names (without the trailing colon) for column headings. However, you can change these headings to be more descriptive and more meaningful. For example, if you use the column headings shown on the screen in Figure 8-14, the report in Figure 8-15 is the result.

## Calculations

*Let First Choice do your arithmetic for you.*

You can tell First Choice to total numbers in a column or make other calculations for you for each report field. You do this via the 12 different calculation options, which may be used either alone or in conjunction with each other. (The section on mixing calculation options later in this chapter discusses combining calculations.) To specify a calculation for a column, place the calculation's abbreviation in the **Calculation** field. These abbreviations are shown in parentheses next to each calculation option below.

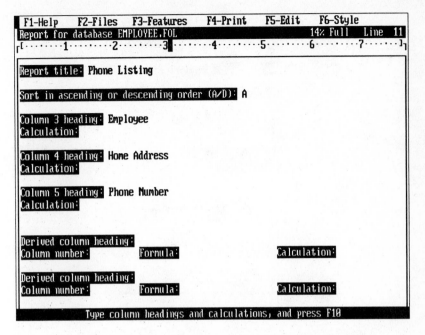

**Figure 8-14.** Screen with more meaningful column headings.

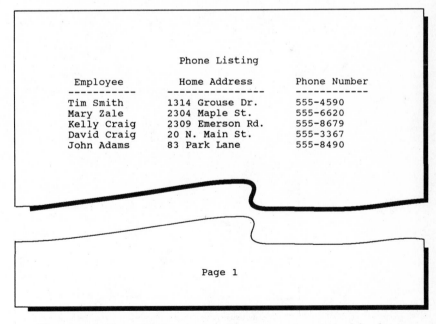

**Figure 8-15.** Phone Listing report with new, more meaningful column headings.

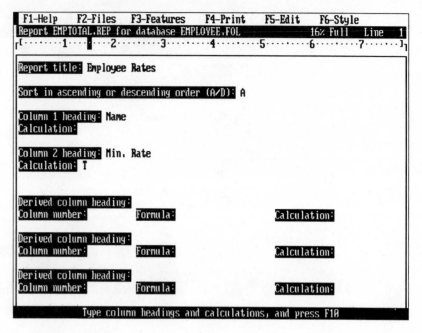

**Figure 8-16.** Screen specifying a total calculation for the Min. Rate column.

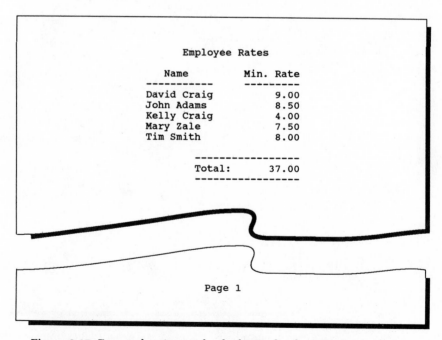

**Figure 8-17.** Report showing total calculation for the Min. Rate column.

## Total (T)

Use the total calculation option when you want a total printed for a numeric column. When you specify a total calculation for the **Min. Rate** field, as shown on the screen in Figure 8-16, you produce the report in Figure 8-17.

You can also print a report consisting solely of totals by using the total option in conjunction with the **Print totals only** option of the Print Options dialog box. By changing the **Print totals only** response from No to Yes the new report looks like the one shown in Figure 8-18.

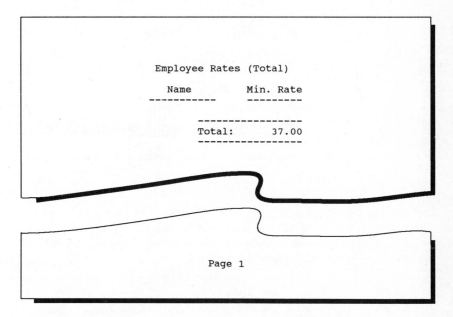

```
                Employee Rates (Total)

            Name            Min. Rate
        ------------        ---------


                        -----------------
                Total:       37.00
                        -----------------




                        Page 1
```

**Figure 8-18.** Totals only report for the Min. Rate column.

## Subtotal (ST)

*This option also prints a grand total, like the total option discussed earlier.*

The subtotal calculation option should be used when you want to print a numeric column's subtotal each time column 1's value changes. For example, specifying a subtotal calculation for the **Min. Rate** field (Figure 8-19) produces the report shown in Figure 8-20. This figure also arranges the minimum rates by city, an operation you will learn how to do later.

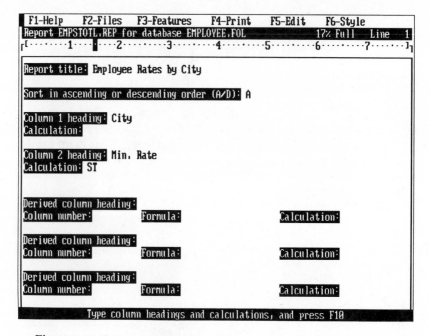

**Figure 8-19.** Screen specifying a subtotal calculation for the Min. Rate column.

The report in Figure 8-20 shows minimum pay rate subtotals by city for the employee database (although the report uses the word "total"). The subtotal calculation option for Min. Rate causes a subtotal to be printed each time a new city is encountered. Did you notice that the string "Indianapolis" was only printed once even though two entries from that city were printed? This feature can be used to make a report more readable by allowing you to quickly locate new values in column 1. (If you want to disable this feature and cause duplicate column entries to print, use the repeat option, which will be discussed shortly.)

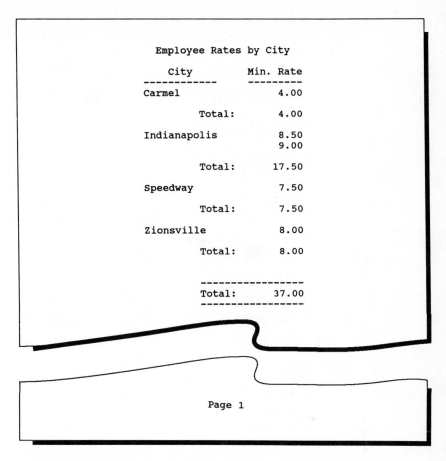

```
          Employee Rates by City

              City          Min. Rate
          -------------     ---------
          Carmel                4.00

                    Total:      4.00

          Indianapolis          8.50
                                9.00

                    Total:     17.50

          Speedway              7.50

                    Total:      7.50

          Zionsville            8.00

                    Total:      8.00


                    ------------------
                    Total:     37.00
                    ------------------
```

Page 1

**Figure 8-20.** Report with subtotal calculation for the Min. Rate column.

## Average (A)

The average calculation option may be used when you want to print a numeric column's average. When you specify an average calculation for the **Min. Rate** field (Figure 8-21), you get the report illustrated in Figure 8-22.

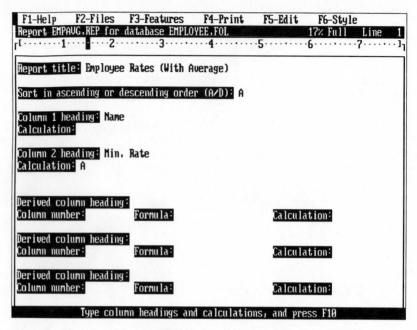

**Figure 8-21.** Specifying an average calculation for the Min. Rate column.

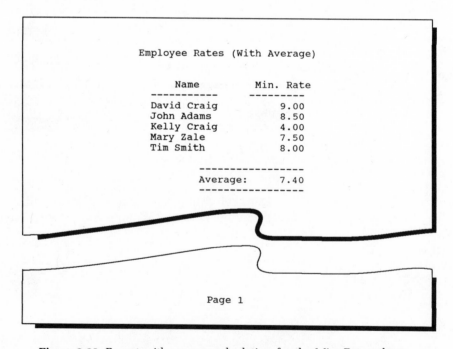

**Figure 8-22.** Report with average calculation for the Min. Rate column.

## Subaverage (SA)

This option also prints an overall average, like the average option discussed earlier.

The subaverage calculation option should be used when you want to print a numeric column's subaverage each time column 1's value changes. For example, specifying a subaverage calculation for the **Min. Rate** field, as shown in the screen in Figure 8-23, produces the report in Figure 8-24. (The report uses the word "average" even though it is showing subaverages.)

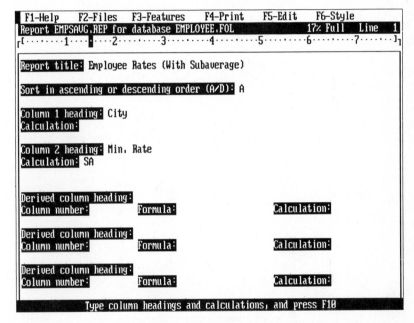

**Figure 8-23.** Screen specifying a subaverage calculation for the Min. Rate column.

## Count (C)

The total number of entries in a column is printed when the count calculation option is used. When this option is used for the **Name** field (Figure 8-25), the report in Figure 8-26 is generated.

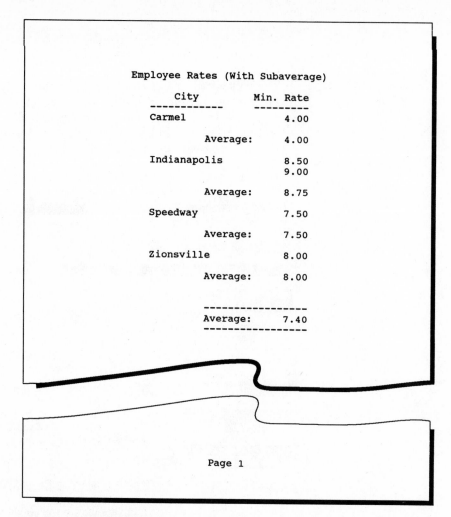

```
          Employee Rates (With Subaverage)
                City          Min. Rate
          -------------       ---------
          Carmel                 4.00

                      Average:   4.00

          Indianapolis           8.50
                                 9.00

                      Average:   8.75

          Speedway               7.50

                      Average:   7.50

          Zionsville             8.00

                      Average:   8.00


                          -------------------
                  Average:   7.40
                          -------------------




                          Page 1
```

**Figure 8-24.** Report showing subaverage calculation for the Min. Rate column.

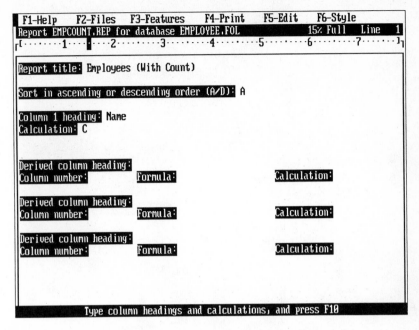

**Figure 8-25.** Screen specifying a count for the Name column.

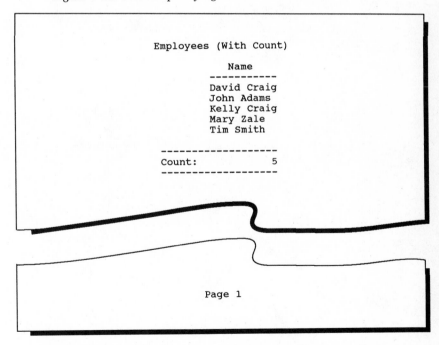

**Figure 8-26.** Report with count calculation for the Name column.

## Subcount (SC)

*This option also prints a total count, like the count option discussed earlier.*

The subcount calculation option should be used when you want to print a column's subcount each time column 1's value changes. For example, the result of specifying a subcount calculation for the **Min. Rate** field (Figure 8-27) is the report in Figure 8-28. (This type of report uses the word "count" even though it shows subcounts.)

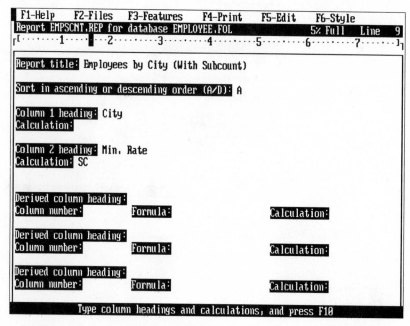

**Figure 8-27.** Screen specifying a subcount for the Min. Rate column.

## Repeat (R)

By default, column 1 and 2 values will not print if they match the values from the same columns in the previous report line. You saw this feature in the previous discussion of the subaverage calculation option; the report in Figure 8-20, entitled Employee Rates by City, shows that "Indianapolis" was printed only once even though two records appear in the report for that city. The repeat calculation option may be used to override this feature and cause duplicate entries to print. First let's look at a report without the repeat option. When you select the **City** and **Secretarial** fields with no calculation options (Figure 8-29), you produce the report in Figure 8-30.

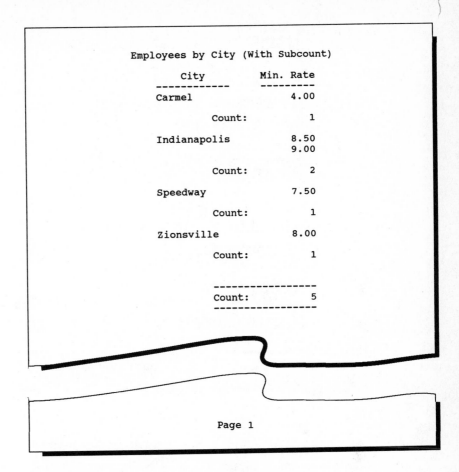

```
            Employees by City (With Subcount)

                      City          Min. Rate
                   -------------     ---------
                   Carmel               4.00

                              Count:       1

                   Indianapolis         8.50
                                        9.00

                              Count:       2

                   Speedway             7.50

                              Count:       1

                   Zionsville           8.00

                              Count:       1


                              ------------------
                              Count:       5
                              ------------------
```

Page 1

**Figure 8-28.** Report showing subcount calculation for the Min. Rate column.

Although our employee database contains five records only four entries are printed in the City and Secretarial report in Figure 8-30. This is because two employees in the database are from Indianapolis and are not secretaries. This report is sorted by city since that field appears in column 1. Therefore you would have expected to see two identical entries like this:

Indianapolis      n

Indianapolis      n

for David Craig and John Adams. But since the values in columns 1 and 2 for both these records are identical, only one line printed. What

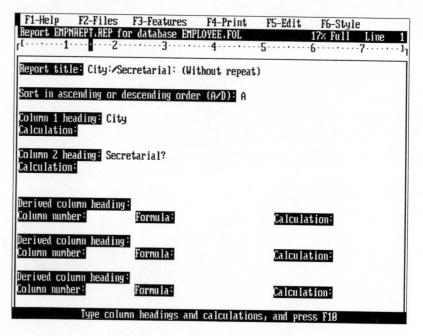

**Figure 8-29.** Screen selecting the City and Secretarial fields with no calculation options.

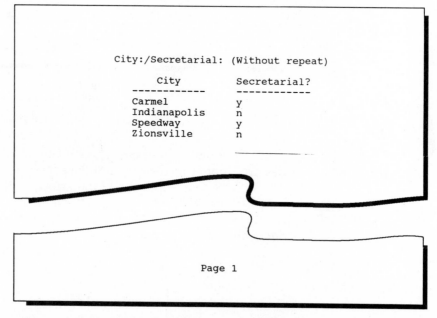

**Figure 8-30.** City and Secretarial report without repeat.

do you think would happen if you added a third column to the report? The screen shown in Figure 8-31 illustrates selecting the **City**, **Secretarial**, and **Accounting** fields with no calculation options, and the report in Figure 8-32 shows the result.

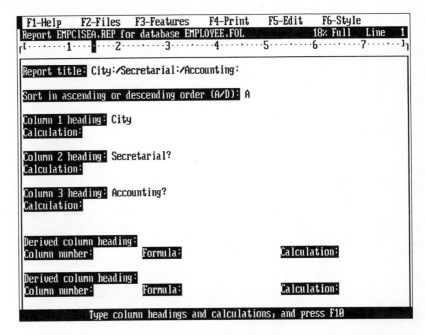

**Figure 8-31.** Screen selecting the **City**, **Secretarial**, and **Accounting** fields without calculation options.

When you add the Accounting column to the report, all five entries are printed, in spite of the fact that David Craig and John Adams share the same values in the **Accounting?** and **Secretarial?** fields. The addition of this third column (Accounting) forced First Choice to print records for both workers. This is because the report will skip printing an entry only if all of the following conditions are met:

1. The report contains only 1 or 2 columns.
2. The values to be printed for one record match those of the previous record.
3. The repeat calculation option is not used.

*Use repeat to force printing of duplicate records.*

Now let's use the repeat calculation option to redo the City and Secretarial report shown in Figure 8-30. The screen in Figure 8-33 shows selecting the **City** and **Secretarial** fields with the repeat calculation option (Figure 8-33), and the report in Figure 8-34 is the result.

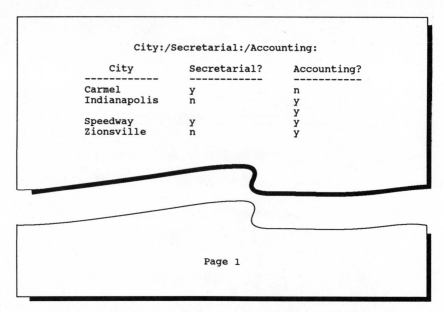

```
                City:/Secretarial:/Accounting:

        City            Secretarial?         Accounting?
        ------------    -------------        -----------
        Carmel          y                    n
        Indianapolis    n                    y
                                             y
        Speedway        y                    y
        Zionsville      n                    y
```

Page 1

**Figure 8-32.** City, Secretarial, and Accounting report without calculation options.

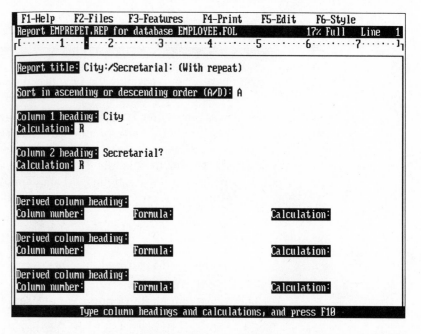

**Figure 8-33.** Screen showing the use of repeat with the City and Secretarial column.

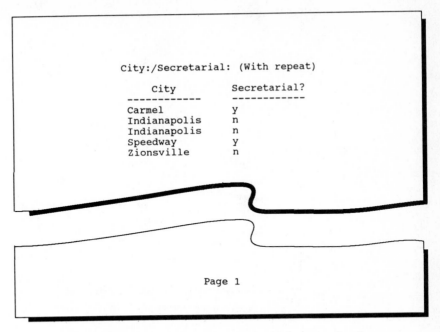

```
                    City:/Secretarial: (With repeat)

                         City          Secretarial?
                    ------------        ------------
                    Carmel             y
                    Indianapolis       n
                    Indianapolis       n
                    Speedway           y
                    Zionsville         n
```

Page 1

**Figure 8-34.** City and Secretarial report with repeated values.

The only difference between the reports in Figure 8-30 and Figure 8-34 is the duplicate entry:

Indianapolis     n

which is caused by specifying the repeat option shown on the screen in Figure 8-33.

## Width (W) and Line (L)

First Choice makes report columns wide enough to accommodate the largest of either

the column heading

*or*

the largest data value printed for the column

The width option allows you to manually set column widths. The syntax for width is Wxxx where xxx is some number from 1 to 255. The report shown in Figure 8-35 shows the **Name** and **Address** fields with default widths.

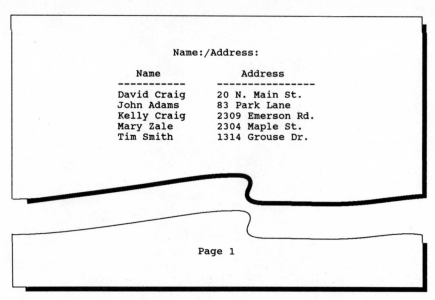

```
                    Name:/Address:

            Name                Address
         -----------         ----------------
         David Craig         20 N. Main St.
         John Adams          83 Park Lane
         Kelly Craig         2309 Emerson Rd.
         Mary Zale           2304 Maple St.
         Tim Smith           1314 Grouse Dr.




                         Page 1
```

**Figure 8-35.** Name and Address report with default widths.

As you can see, the Name column is just wide enough (11 characters) to accommodate the longest names, David Craig and Kelly Craig. The Address column is just wide enough (16 characters) to hold the longest address, 2309 Emerson Rd. (You can tell how wide the address column is by the length of the line at the top of the column.) After manually setting the column widths for Name and Address to 20 (Figure 8-36), you'll receive the report in Figure 8-37.

Occasionally you may need for a column to be rather wide. Although the First Choice documentation states, "When you set the width, First Choice wraps lines too long to fit in the column," my testing has proven otherwise. I found that if you do manually set the width of a column, and a value for that column is too wide to fit onto the remainder of a line, that value is truncated. It appears that the only way to get value wrapping to a second line to occur is if you do *not* manually set the column width *and* the value is longer than 40 characters.

*The line option prevents line wrap.*

The time to use the line option is if you don't want to manually set the width and you do not want a line wrap to occur.

## Page (P)

Use the page option to make the printer skip to the top of the next page every time the value in column 1 changes. This is a very nice formatting option which makes it easy to find the start of a new block

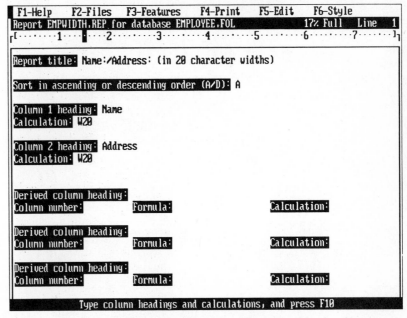

**Figure 8-36.** Screen defining 20-character column widths for the Name and Address columns.

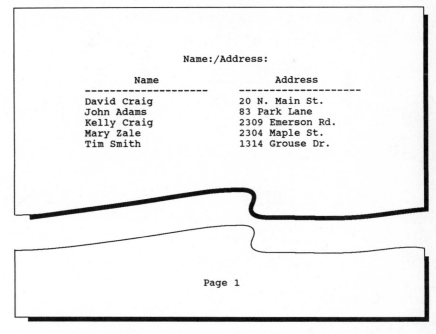

**Figure 8-37.** Name and Address report with 20-Character column widths.

of data in a report. This option may only be used in the Calculation entry for column 1 only.

### Invisible (I)

The invisible option provides some very powerful reporting features. We'll see later how this option can be creatively used for *derived* columns (columns whose content depends on that of others) but first let's see how you can use it to solve a simpler problem.

Suppose the Wikley Company wants to generate an employee database report consisting of only one column—Name. But it wants this report to be sorted in ascending order by city. You know that reports are sorted based upon the values in columns 1 and 2 but how can you prevent the values in a column from printing? (Remember, you want this report to show names only.) The answer is simple: Select the **City** and **Name** fields as columns 1 and 2 respectively, and specify the invisible option for the ZIP column (Figure 8-38). The report generated by these specifications is shown in Figure 8-39.

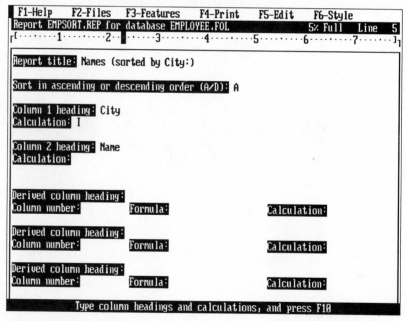

**Figure 8-38.** Screen specifying the invisible option in the City column.

The invisible option can be used when you want to include a field in a report for some reason other than printing its contents.

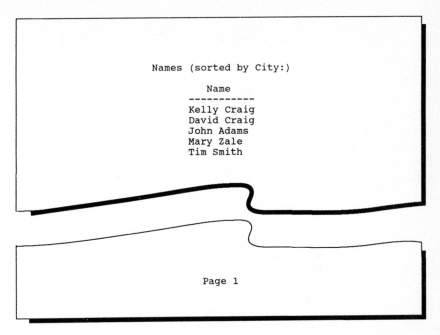

```
              Names (sorted by City:)

                      Name
                 -----------
                 Kelly Craig
                 David Craig
                 John Adams
                 Mary Zale
                 Tim Smith




                    Page 1
```

**Figure 8-39.** Name report with invisible city column.

## Decimals (D)

You can change the number of decimal places printed in a report via the decimals option. The syntax for decimals is Dxx where xx is some number from 0 to 15. Setting this field's decimals option to 0 (Figure 8-40), produces the report in Figure 8-41. Notice how the Min. Rate values are affected.

When the decimals option is used to truncate numbers as in Figure 8-41, it will also automatically perform any necessary rounding (notice that John Adams' and Mary Zale's minimum rates were rounded up to 9 and 8 respectively).

## Mixing Calculation Options

The foregoing 12 calculation options may be used in combination with each other. For example, if you combine the total and average options in the Min. Rate column, as shown in Figure 8-42, you'll obtain the results shown in the report illustrated in Figure 8-43.

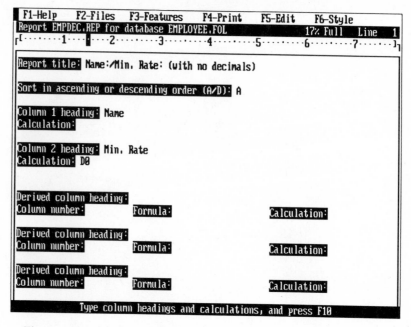

**Figure 8-40.** Screen specifying 0 decimal places for the Min. Rate column.

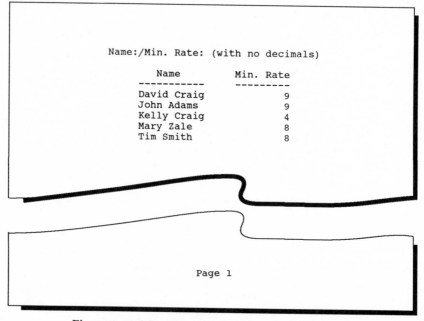

**Figure 8-41.** Min. Rate report with 0 decimal places.

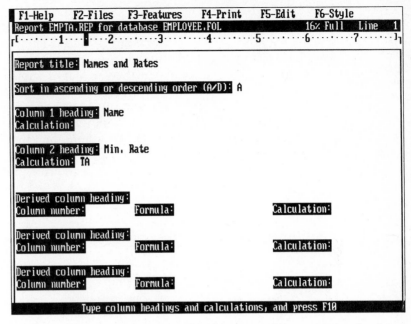

**Figure 8-42.** Screen using total and average options together for the Min. Rate column.

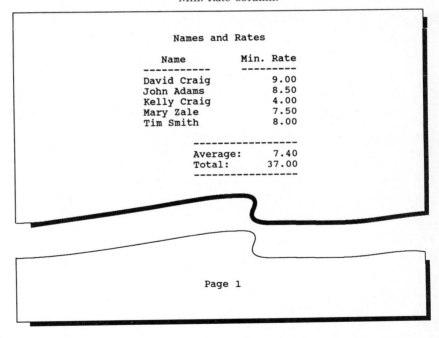

**Figure 8-43.** Min. Rate report with total and average options.

# Derived Columns

*You can have as many as three different derived columns in a report.*

The final section of the headings and calculations screen (Figure 8-3) deals with derived columns. A derived column is a numeric column whose value depends on the value(s) of another column or columns.

Let's explore a reporting problem where a derived column may be used. Wikley Company wants to print a report showing each applicant's name, minimum rate, and a rate called the Wikley charge rate. The Wikley charge rate is $4.00 more than the Min. Rate value and is the hourly rate that the company charges to clients who employ its temporary workers in order to make a profit. The result of the derived column entry in Figure 8-44 appears in the report in Figure 8-45.

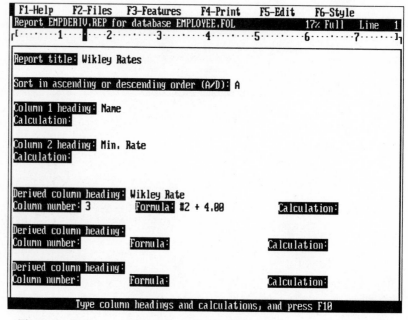

**Figure 8-44.** Screen illustrating deriving the Wikley Rate column from the Min. Rate column.

First Choice requests four separate items for each derived column:

- derived column heading
- column number
- formula
- calculation

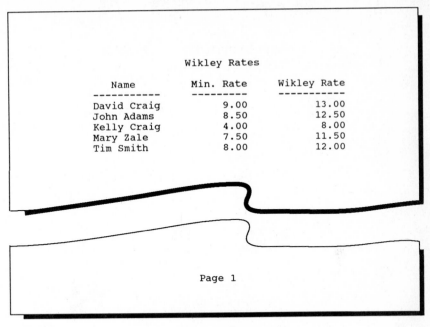

```
                        Wikley Rates

                 Name        Min. Rate    Wikley Rate
              -----------    ---------    -----------
              David Craig       9.00         13.00
              John Adams        8.50         12.50
              Kelly Craig       4.00          8.00
              Mary Zale         7.50         11.50
              Tim Smith         8.00         12.00




                         Page 1
```

**Figure 8-45.** Wikley Rate report.

## Derived Column Heading and Column Number

The Derived column heading is the heading to be printed at the top of the derived column; this is just like the Column X heading entries you've seen before. The derived column heading specified in Figure 8-44 (**Wikley Rate**) appears at the top of the derived column in the report in Figure 8-45.

*Refer to the previous section on Calculations for a complete discussion of all the calculation options available.*

When you want to obtain a derived column, use the same position indicators you use on the Columns screen for regular (non-derived) columns (see Figure 8-2). Place a number from 1 to 20 in the **Column number** field to specify where you want the derived column located. If you want to specify any special calculation options for the derived column, place them in the **Calculation** field.

## Derived Column Formula

*Use the pound sign in front of a column number.*

The only derived column field entry in Figure 8-3 whose meaning may need explanation is **Formula**. On the screen in Figure 8-44 you specified this formula:

    #2 + 4.00

which tells First Choice to take the value in column 2, add $4.00 to it and place the result in the derived column (column 3). You must precede a column number with a pound sign (#) in derived column formulas; otherwise First Choice cannot differentiate between column numbers and numeric values. You must put a derived column formula to the right of all columns referenced in the formula. That is, the formula for a derived column in column 3 may reference columns 1 and 2 only. You can use any of the mathematical operators shown in Table 8-1 for formula expressions.

**Table 8-1.** Mathematical operators for derived column formulas.

| Symbol | Mathematical Operation |
|--------|------------------------|
| ^ | Exponentiation |
| * | Multiplication |
| / | Division |
| + | Addition |
| – | Subtraction |

*You can also use parentheses in formulas.*

The operators shown in Table 8-1 are listed from highest precedence (top) to lowest precedence (bottom). (Chapter 7, *Form Programming*, explains operator precedence, or order of priority.) The only mathematical operator available in form programming that is not available in derived column formulas is the exponentiation asterisks (**). However, you can use the caret (^) in both form programming and derived column formulas, so this is not much of a problem. You can also use parentheses in derived column formulas to change operator precedence, and/or to prevent expression ambiguity.

## Combining Invisible and Derived Columns

Remember the report that lists names sorted by city (Figure 8-39) where you used an invisible column (City) to report only employee names sorted by city? Let's suppose that the Wikley Company wants to generate another report sorted by the worker's minimum rates in ascending order. To do so, you remember, you need to put the minimum rate in the leftmost column and make it invisible. However, if you do this, how can you also have a Min. Rate column to the right of the applicant's names? The solution is to make the Min. Rate column that's not invisible a derived column. Figure 8-46 shows a screen with entries telling First Choice to print such a report.

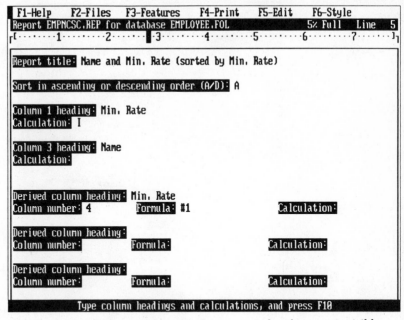

**Figure 8-46.** Screen showing deriving a value from an invisible column.

As Figure 8-46 shows, you don't need to use any mathematical operators in a derived column formula. This is a pretty handy trick to use whenever you want to print the column on which your report was sorted in a non-leftmost column. The result of these entries looks like the report shown in Figure 8-47.

# Search Specifications

The place where you enter search criteria for record inclusion and/or exclusion in reports is on the Search Specifications screen (Figure 8-4). These specifications may be expressed in the same fashion as those discussed in Chapter 5, *Searching and Sorting Database Records*. Keep in mind that the screen in Figure 8-4 accepts search specifications only; you cannot enter any sort specifications on this screen. As we discussed earlier, First Choice sorts reports only by the values in columns 1 and 2.

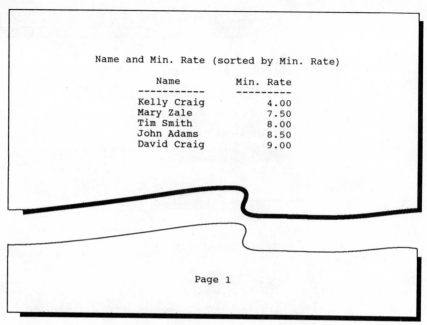

```
Name and Min. Rate (sorted by Min. Rate)

             Name          Min. Rate
          -----------      ---------
          Kelly Craig         4.00
          Mary Zale           7.50
          Tim Smith           8.00
          John Adams          8.50
          David Craig         9.00
```

```
                        Page 1
```

**Figure 8-47.** Proposed Name and Minimum Rate report sorted by Min. Rate.

# Reusing and Deleting Report Instructions

*First Choice uses the extension .RPT for report instruction files.*

The options you specify for a report, also called the *report instructions,* can be saved to a disk file. This allows you to run the report again in the future without having to type in information for the columns, title, search specifications, etc. all over again. Follow these steps to save your report instructions:

1. Once you've specified search specifications (Figure 8-4), press F10. The Save Report warning message (Figure 8-5) is displayed.

2. Press Escape; then select option 1, Save this report, from the Files menu. The Directory Assistant appears.

3. Specify a report instruction file name (for example, type EMPNAMES.RPT), and press Enter. (As you may have guessed,

you can omit the .RPT file extension in the report instruction file name and First Choice will add it for you.) The Search Specifications screen is redisplayed.

4. Press F10 to print the report.

To delete a report instruction file, select the file on the Directory Assistant screen and press F10. Then press Y to acknowledge the deletion warning message.

# Summary

- You can print useful summaries of database information with the report feature of First Choice.
- The reports Print Options dialog box has several options, which provide flexibility in report output.
- The Columns screen allows you to define which, and in what order, fields you want the report to include.
- Report records are sorted by the entries in columns 1 and 2. Column 1 is the primary sort field. Records with identical column 1 values are further sorted by column 2 values, the secondary sort field.
- The Headings and Calculations screen is where you specify the report title, sort order, and additional columnar information.
- Twelve different calculation options enable you to perform such operations as columnar totaling, averaging, counting, and special formatting, among others.
- A derived column is a numeric column whose value is derived from the value(s) of another column or columns. You can have as many as three different derived columns in a report.
- You may enter search specifications to include specific types of records in (or exclude them from) the report.
- You can save the options specified for a report, also called the report instructions, to a disk file. This allows you to run the report again in the future without having to retype information for the columns, title, search specifications, etc.

# Building Blocks
# for Spreadsheets

**In this chapter:**

- What Is a Spreadsheet?
- The Spreadsheet Screen
- Creating a Spreadsheet
- Understanding Formulas
- Saving Your Spreadsheet
- Printing Your Spreadsheet
- Summary

This chapter introduces you to the spreadsheet feature of First Choice. It describes the spreadsheet, discusses how to move the cursor around and defines the type of information that you put in a spreadsheet. Once you learn the basics, you will learn how to save and print a spreadsheet.

## What Is a Spreadsheet?

A spreadsheet is simply an electronic version of a columnar pad—the same type that accountants use when working with rows and columns of information. A columnar pad requires that the accountant manually perform mathematical calculations, but with a spreadsheet a computer completes most of the work. Because of its ability to quickly recalculate values and lower margin for error, the spreadsheet has become a standard tool in many areas of business today.

To get a good idea of the value of a spreadsheet, imagine that you must keep track of a budget or balance sheet with dozens of entries. An electronic spreadsheet enables you to change a single value to test "What-If?" scenarios and instantly see the change's impact on the bottom line. Suppose you are calculating a business loan and the interest rate changes from 9 to 10 percent. To complete a what-if-analysis, you can change the interest rate and use the spreadsheet to quickly recalculate the loan.

In order to complete a what-if-analysis, the spreadsheet uses mathematical formulas and equations to help it "remember" values and to calculate new ones. However, you don't have to be a math whiz to create and use a spreadsheet. You will soon discover that this is a simple process.

# The Spreadsheet Screen

Once you select item 4, **Create a spreadsheet**, from First Choice's Main menu, the initial spreadsheet screen will appear as shown in Figure 9-1. (Note: You can also open an existing spreadsheet by selecting the **Get an existing file** option and then choosing the file from the Spreadsheet column within the Directory Assistant.) An empty spreadsheet consists of several components: the work area, menu bar, information line, column headings area, row headings area and the cursor.

You should take a moment to study each of these components (especially if you're a beginner), described as follows:

*The Work Area*—The large empty area in the middle of your screen is the spreadsheet itself. This area, sometimes called the *work area*, is a series of rows and columns that form a rectangular grid. The rows are identified by R1, R2, etc. and the columns are C1, C2, etc. The intersection of a row and column is called a *cell*. Thus, the first cell in the spreadsheet is at a location identified by R1C1. The location is referred to as the cell's *coordinates*. Cells are used to store information, such as numbers, text and formulas. You can even give a cell a name in order to help identify its contents. The work area is where you enter data and formulas and perform calculations to solve your business needs.

The area of the spreadsheet that you see on your screen is actually just a small portion of the size of the First Choice spreadsheet. The size of the spreadsheet will vary depending on the amount of available memory of your computer. The maximum size is 1024 rows and 768 columns. Since the size of the spreadsheet is so large, you will only see a portion of it on your screen at one time. Note that the number of cells

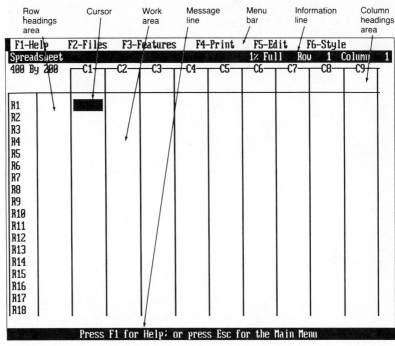

**Figure 9-1.** The initial spreadsheet screen.

that you can use in your spreadsheet also depends on the complexity of the information that you put in them. The *percentage full* message on the information line is a good indicator of how much of the spreadsheet you've filled (see *Information Line* below).

*The Menu Bar*—Across the top of the speadsheet screen, you'll see the same familiar menu items that are available with the First Choice word processor—Files, Features, Print, Edit and Style. Although the operations some of these menu options perform are similar to the word processor operations, you will find many of the commands are specifically for spreadsheet functions. The procedure for accessing the commands, as well as using the standard Help function located on the far left side of the menu bar, remains the same. As we progress through the spreadsheet operation, you will learn about all the commands available on the menu bar in detail.

*Information Line*—The line that appears just below the menu bar provides information or a description of the "status" of the specific application in use. At the far right of the information line, a message tells the percentage of the spreadsheet that is being used (initially 1%), as well as the position of the cursor. The initial position of the cursor is row 1, column 1 or R1C1. On the far left side of the information line, the application name **Spreadsheet** appears. If you open an existing file, the file name is also displayed there.

*Column/Row Headings Area*—Just below the column numbers (C1, C2, etc.) is the column headings area. This row of blank space, labeled row 0, is used to enter column headings. Similarly, the left-hand blank column is column 0, where you enter a row heading.

*The Cursor*—The spreadsheet cursor is the rectangular box that first appears in row 1 and column 1 of a new spreadsheet. To select a cell, you simply move the cursor to that cell. Later, you will learn that you can use the *edit cursor*, or the same blinking line that appears in the word processor, to edit text within a cell.

## Moving the Cursor

In order to get any work done with the spreadsheet, you must first learn how to navigate around the spreadsheet. In fact, before you can enter data into a cell or change its contents, you must move the cursor to that cell. To move left to right, from one column to another, press the Tab key (press Shift-Tab to move back one column). To move from one row to another, press Enter (or Ctrl-Enter to move up a row). You can use a variety of cursor control keys to move around your spreadsheet as detailed in Table 9-1. In addition, the **Go to cell** option on the Features menu or the speed key Alt-G moves the cursor to a specific cell. Once you press Alt-G, simply type the cell's row and column location.

## Creating a Spreadsheet

As discussed, a spreadsheet consists of rows and columns of individual cells forming a type of grid. When you create a spreadsheet, you input information into the cells. Individual cells may contain three types of information:

- *labels*, which are any strings of text characters (non-numeric), typically used for headings and names or an address to describe a row or column
- *values*, or any number (for example, 100, 1.75, or 0)
- *formulas*, which are mathematical expressions that perform calculations

The following sections explore all three types of information and tell how to enter the information into your spreadsheet.

**Table 9-1.** Moving the spreadsheet cursor.

| To Move Cursor: | Press This Key: |
|---|---|
| One column to the right | Tab |
| One column to the left | Shift-Tab |
| Down one row | Enter or Down Arrow |
| Up one row | Ctrl-Enter or Up Arrow |
| Right one space | Right Arrow |
| Left one space | Left Arrow |
| Right one screen | Ctrl-Right Arrow |
| Left one screen | Ctrl-Left Arrow |
| Previous screen | Page Up |
| Next screen | Page Down |
| Top of the current column | Ctrl-Page Up |
| Bottom of the current column | Ctrl-Page Down |
| Beginning of current row | Home |
| End of current row | End |
| Beginning of spreadsheet (R1C1 location) | Ctrl-Home |
| End of spreadsheet (lower right corner of spreadsheet) | Ctrl-End |

# Entering Headings

Once you have decided to create a spreadsheet, you need to give some thought to how the spreadsheet should look. In other words, plan the spreadsheet's layout. The layout of the spreadsheet depends on what information you wish to emphasize. For example, if you are tracking the monthly sales of several products, you may wish to place the names of the products on individual rows with the months of the year as columns across the top of the spreadsheet.

Keep the reader in mind when planning your spreadsheet. Organize the spreadsheet to provide the information in a clear and logical way. Meaningful labels or headings help readers understand spreadsheet contents, so you should start by entering the headings for the rows and columns.

*If you have a mouse, you can easily point at a cell and click to move the cursor. Then you can enter or correct information as you wish.*

To enter a heading, move the cursor to the desired location in the column or row heading area, and then type the heading. Keep in mind that the initial width of a column is six characters long. If you enter a heading that is longer than six characters, First Choice will automatically increase the size of the cell to up to 20 characters to accommodate the longer heading. If you make a mistake as you type the headings, use the Backspace key to erase one character at a time and type the correction as needed. If you press the Delete key, the entire entry in the cell is erased. You can also use Ctrl-Tab to move one column at a time to the left and edit the headings just like any text.

As an example, complete the following steps to enter the first six months of the year as column headings.

1. Move the cursor to the heading area just below column C1. To do this, simply press the Up Arrow key once. If your cursor is not in the Home position (location R1C1) when you begin, press Ctrl-Home prior to pressing the Up Arrow key.

2. Type Jan and press Tab once. The cursor will move one column to the right.

3. Type Feb and press Tab once. The cursor will again move one column to the right.

4. Continue typing the remaining months of the year (Mar, Apr, May, Jun) separately within columns. Remember to press the Tab key once to move one column to the right. When finished, your column headings will look like Figure 9-2.

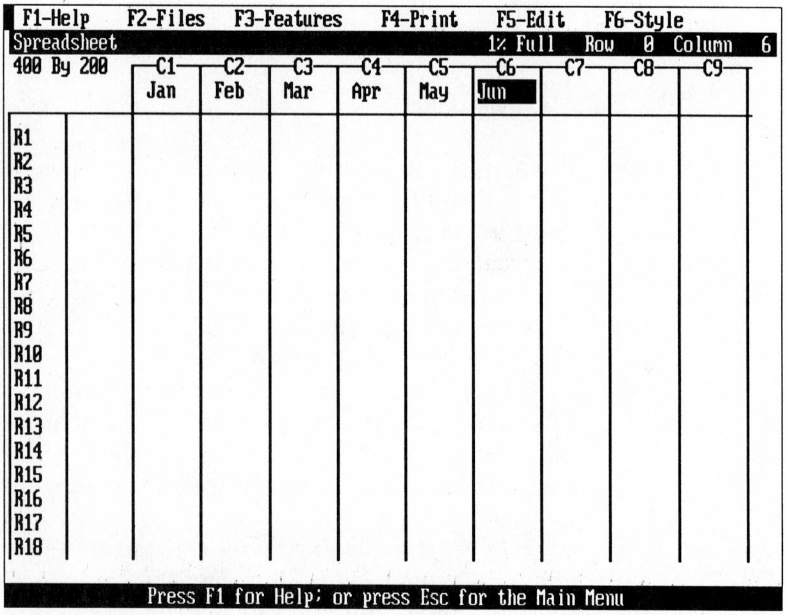

**Figure 9-2.** Entering the months as column headings.

To enter a heading for a row, follow a similar procedure. The length and height of a cell within a row will depend upon how much information you wish to input. As stated, the width of a row may be 20 character spaces. As you reach the end of a cell's width, the text will wrap around to the next line. The maximum number of lines in a cell is five. Thus, the maximum size of a heading is 100 characters—20 characters long and five lines deep. To practice entering row headings, complete the following steps:

1. Move the cursor to the first row heading area (the column just to the right of R1). To move it quickly, press Ctrl-Home to move back to R1C1 and then press Shift-Tab to move the cursor one column to the left. Of course, you can also point and click with a mouse.

2. Type the heading for the first row. For our example, type Widget and then press Enter. The cursor will move to the next row.

3. Type the heading for the second row. In this case, type Gadget and press Enter. Your spreadsheet will now include column as well as row headings, as shown in Figure 9-3.

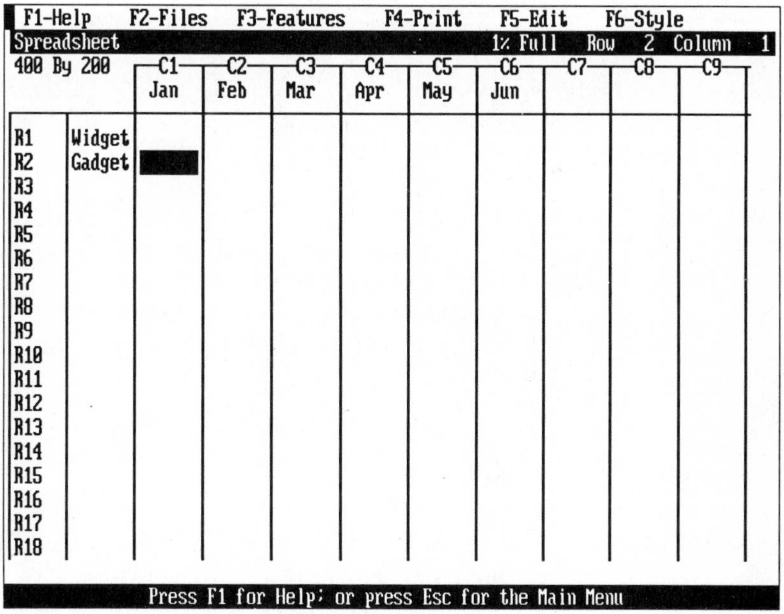

```
┌─────────────────────────────────────────────────────────────────────┐
│ F1-Help    F2-Files   F3-Features    F4-Print    F5-Edit    F6-Style │
│ Spreadsheet                              1% Full   Row  2  Column   1 │
│ 400 By 200 ┌─C1──┬─C2──┬─C3──┬─C4──┬─C5──┬─C6──┬─C7──┬─C8──┬─C9──┐    │
│            │ Jan │ Feb │ Mar │ Apr │ May │ Jun │     │     │     │    │
│                                                                       │
│ R1  │Widget│                                                         │
│ R2  │Gadget│████│                                                    │
│ R3  │                                                                │
│ R4  │                                                                │
│ R5  │                                                                │
│ R6  │                                                                │
│ R7  │                                                                │
│ R8  │                                                                │
│ R9  │                                                                │
│ R10 │                                                                │
│ R11 │                                                                │
│ R12 │                                                                │
│ R13 │                                                                │
│ R14 │                                                                │
│ R15 │                                                                │
│ R16 │                                                                │
│ R17 │                                                                │
│ R18 │                                                                │
│          Press F1 for Help; or press Esc for the Main Menu           │
└─────────────────────────────────────────────────────────────────────┘
```

**Figure 9-3.** Adding products as row headings.

# Entering Values

When working with a spreadsheet, the terms *number* and *value* mean the same thing. To keep things simple, we will refer to values as numbers. Entering a number in a cell is as simple as entering headings. Before you begin, however, review the following rules:

- A number must begin with a numeric character (0-9), a decimal point (.), a plus (+) or a minus (−) sign.
- Don't include blank spaces, commas, the percent sign or currency symbols. First Choice will enter the necessary items for you.
- Always move the cursor to the exact cell where you wish to input a value before you begin to type.
- The maximum number of digits that you can enter is 20. If you enter too many, the value **** will appear in the cell. In this case, reenter the correct value.
- First Choice provides additional flexibility that will help you enter values. One option is to change the default number of decimal places (from two) specified for the cell's style. To do this, choose the **Set global style** command from the Style menu before you begin to type.
- As a handy time saver, use the First Choice quick entry feature to place the same group of values quickly into cells. This feature is discussed shortly.

To enter a value in a spreadsheet, move the cursor to the desired cell and type the value. Remember, each value is limited to a maximum of 20 characters, including commas and the decimal point. For practice, use the following steps to enter values in the sample spreadsheet that you created with instructions from the previous section on row and column headings:

1. Move the cursor to the R1C1 cell. Press Ctrl-Home to move it there quickly.
2. Type **10000** and then press the Tab key once. Do not include a comma or decimal point. Notice that First Choice properly formats the value for you when you press Tab.
3. Type **25000** for the column labeled **Feb** (R1C2) and press Tab. Continue to enter the remaining values for row 1 as follows:

| For: | Enter: |
|------|--------|
| R1C3 | 15000 |
| R1C4 | 22000 |
| R1C5 | 18000 |
| R1C6 | 20000 |

4. After you type the last value for row 1, press Enter to move down to the second row. Enter all the values for this row as follows:

| For: | Enter: |
|------|--------|
| R2C1 | 5000 |
| R2C2 | 7500 |
| R2C3 | 6000 |
| R2C4 | 9000 |
| R2C5 | 8000 |
| R2C6 | 3000 |

Once you have entered all the values using the preceding steps, your spreadsheet will look like Figure 9-4.

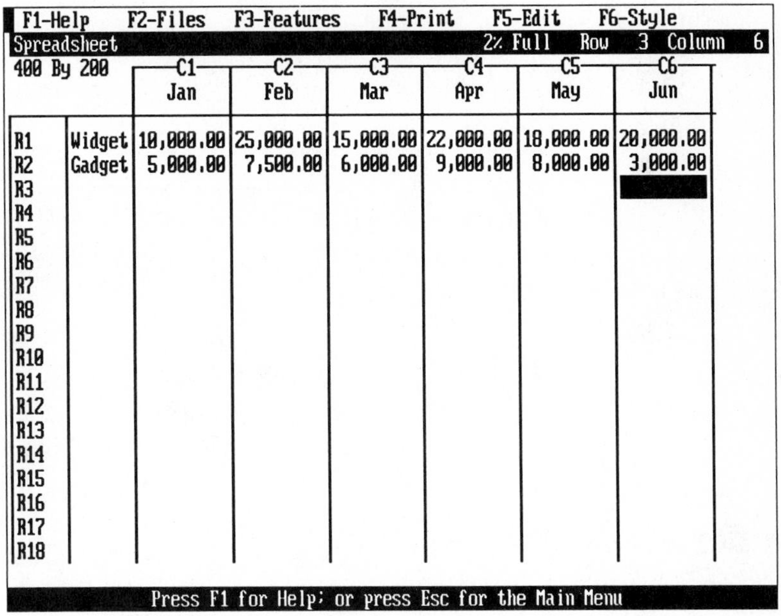

**Figure 9-4.** Sample spreadsheet with two rows of values.

## Using The Quick Entry Feature

To help you enter either headings or values more efficiently, First Choice offers a *quick entry feature*. For example, if you begin to enter a series of related headings, you can enter the first heading (such as **Jan**) and then use the quick entry feature to automatically enter the remaining headings for you (First Choice would enter **Feb**, **Mar**, **Apr**, **May**, **Jun**, etc. into respective headings). To do this, you simply move the cursor to the cell where the headings are to begin, type the first heading, press Alt-Q to start the quick entry feature, and then press Tab (or Enter) to move to the next heading cell. Each time that you move to the next cell (pressing Tab or Enter), First Choice will automatically enter the next heading in sequence for you.

Whatever type of heading and specific format that you enter, First Choice will "read" and then offer the next heading in sequence. For example, if you type January instead of Jan, then First Choice will enter February instead of Feb as the next heading entry. Similarly, Qtr1 would be followed by Qtr2, Qtr3, etc. Basically, the quick entry feature works with most common headings, such as the days of the week, months of the year and so on. If you wish to use a heading other than one that is naturally sequenced, simply end the heading with a numeral that can be incremented, such as Total1, Total2, etc.

## Adding Underlines

To help make your spreadsheets easier to read or to simply make them look neater, you may wish to add underlines to certain areas. To add an underline, you can use either the hyphen (-) or the equal sign ( = ) characters. To illustrate, complete these steps to add an underline at the bottom of the sample spreadsheet we've been building.

1. Move the cursor to the cell where you wish to begin the underline. In this case, move it to R3C1.
2. Type the equal sign until the entire row is underlined through column 6. The result would look something like Figure 9-5.

# Understanding Formulas

*You can also use \*\* instead of ^ for exponentiation.*

To use a spreadsheet's real power, you can add a *formula* to perform calculations on the contents of a worksheet cell. A formula may contain any of the following mathematical operators:

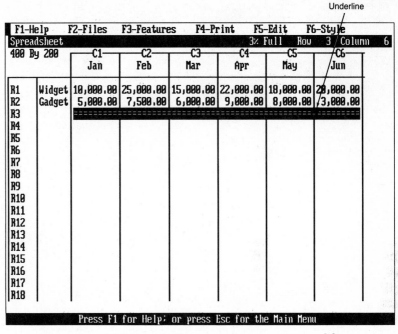

**Figure 9-5.** Adding underlines to enhance your spreadsheet.

+ addition

− subtraction

* multiplication

/ division

^ exponentiation

A formula can operate on specific values within a cell or even reference other cells. A formula may also include one or more of First Choice's special built-in functions, called *keywords*.

Formulas are one of a spreadsheet's most powerful features. The type of formula that you use depends upon the type of spreadsheet that you are creating. In general, you create a formula to perform a particular type of calculation in a cell, and the resulting value appears in that cell. The following are examples of simple formulas:

| Formula | Description |
| --- | --- |
| R1C1 + R1C2 + R1C3 | Adds the values in cells R1C1, R1C2 and R1C3. |

| | |
|---|---|
| R5C1 − R4C1 | Subtracts the value in R4C1 from the value in R5C1. |
| SALES − EXPENSES | Subtracts the value in the cell named EXPENSES from the value in the cell named SALES. |
| @SUM(R1C1..R5C1) | Sums the contents of a range of cells (for example sums the values of the cells R1C1, R2C1, R3C1, R4C1, R5C1). Note that this example uses the built-in function, @SUM, instead of listing five cell locations with the addition sign. |
| Total*R2C2 | Multiplies the value in the cell named Total by the value in cell R2C2. |
| (R1C1 + R2C2)/2 | Adds the value in cell R1C1 to the value in R2C2 and then divides the sum by 2. |

When working with mathematical operators in your formulas, it is important to keep in mind the order of precedence in which calculations are performed. For example, the formula 4+6*2 results in 16, because First Choice multiplies first (6*2 produces 12), and then adds 4 to get 16. First Choice follows this standard order of precedence used in all mathematics.

Some operators have the same level of precedence, such as / (division) and * (multiplication). If two operators of the same level appear on the same line in a formula, then the operators are calculated in left to right order. For example, the formula 24/2*3 produces the value 36. Table 9-2 shows the order of precedence.

**Table 9-2.** Order of precedence for operators.

| Operator | Meaning | Precedence | Example |
|---|---|---|---|
| ^ or ** | Exponentiation | 1 | 6 + 4^2 = 22 |
| - | Negative number | 2 | -8 * 2 = -16 |
| + | Positive number | 2 | +2−1 = 1 |
| * | Multiplication | 3 | 9−2*3 + 1 = 4 |
| / | Division | 3 | 10 + 6/3 -2 = 10 |
| + | Addition | 4 | 2 + 5 + 2 = 9 |
| − | Subtraction | 4 | 2 + 5−4 = 3 |

If you wish some control over the order of precedence, you can use parentheses to override some of the rules. When First Choice encounters a set of parentheses in a formula, the calculation within the parentheses is performed first. For example, the formula $(5+7)*2$ yields 24. If the formula was written as $5+7*2$, the order of precedence would result in 19.

Finally, if a formula is complex and contains many operators, you may wish to nest multiple pairs of parentheses to determine the order of precedence. First Choice allows you to use up to 15 pairs of parentheses in a single formula.

## Entering Formulas

To create a formula, you must use the *Formula box*. All formulas are entered via the Formula box. To enter a formula in a cell, position the cursor in the cell where you want the formula to appear and then choose **Type or edit cell formula** from the Features menu, or simply use the speed key Alt-F. The Formula box is displayed on your screen as shown in Figure 9-6. You can type a formula up to 240 characters long, including spaces, in the Formula box. Long formulas will wrap around inside the formula box.

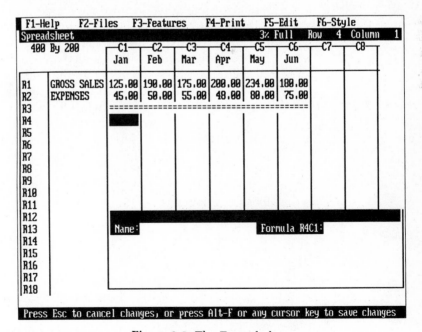

**Figure 9-6.** The Formula box.

Examine Figure 9-6 and notice that we need to add the formula that will compute the net sales for the months from January through June. To do this, you would use the following steps to enter a formula.

1. Position the cursor in the cell where you wish to add a formula. In the example, move the cursor to cell R4C1. (We're using row 4 because row 3 contains the equal sign (=) as a divider.)

2. Open the Formula box by pressing Alt-F or using the **Type or edit cell formula** command from the Features menu.

3. Type the following formula to subtract the values in GROSS SALES from the values in the rows labeled EXPENSES (see Figure 9-7):

    R1C1–R2C1

*To exit the Formula box without inserting a formula into a cell, press the Esc key.*

4. Press the Tab key to move the cursor to the next column in the row. Notice that the correct value now appears in the previous cell as **80.00**. The formula box for the new column also appears as shown in Figure 9-8.

*To move from one cell to another to type another formula, press the Tab, Enter, Ctrl-Enter or Shift-Tab key.*

5. To complete the spreadsheet, you can type similar formulas in each of the columns for the months Feb through June, or simply use the quick entry feature to do the work for you. To use the quick entry feature, position the cursor in the cell containing the formula, such as cell R4C1 in our example. If necessary, open the Formula box by pressing Alt-F. If it's already open, the current formula should still appear there. Next, press Alt-Q to turn on the quick entry feature. Press the Tab key to move the cursor to each cell where you wish to copy the formula in R4C1. Each time you press Tab (or Shift-Tab to move to the left or Enter to move down one row), the formula is entered in that particular cell. Once you have completed copying the formula, you can press Enter to turn off the quick entry feature. Pressing Alt-F turns off the quick entry feature, saves the changes you've made and leaves the formula box. Upon completion, the spreadsheet looks like Figure 9-9.

## Selecting Cells

To complete many tasks easily, you need to know how to select a group or *range* of cells. The ability to select a range of cells will become important when you wish to move or copy cells (remember the quick entry feature illustrated above). For example, you may wish

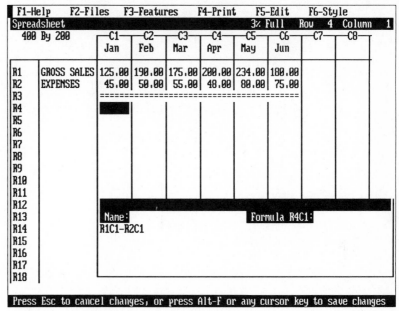

**Figure 9-7.** Enter formulas in the Formula box.

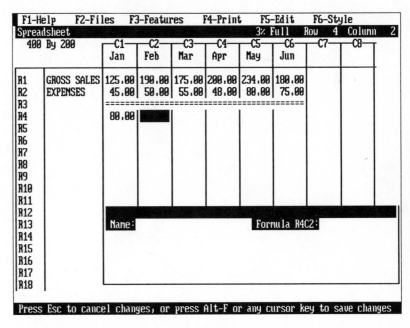

**Figure 9-8.** The correct answer is calculated and placed in cell R4C1.

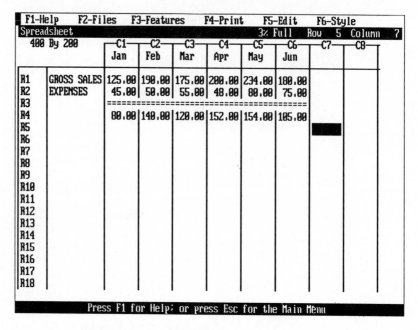

**Figure 9-9.** Completed sample spreadsheet.

to move, insert or delete an entire column or row of cells from one place to another. You can even use the clipboard to move data from one spreadsheet to another. (These operations are discussed in the next chapter.) You can select a range of cells using either the keyboard or the mouse:

### Keyboard Method

1. Position the cursor in the cell where you wish to begin high-lighting a range of cells. Use the arrow keys to move the cursor.

2. Press F5 to open the Edit menu and then choose **Select cells**. You can also complete this step by simply choosing the speed key, Alt-S.

3. Highlight the range of cells that you wish to select by moving the cursor with the arrow keys. If you change your mind about selecting cells, simply press the Esc key or choose **Unselect cells** from the same Edit menu.

**Mouse Method**

1. Position the cursor in the cell where you wish to begin highlighting a range of cells.
2. Hold down the mouse button as you drag across the cells that you wish to highlight. Don't release the mouse button until the entire range of cells has been highlighted.
3. Release the mouse button, and the highlighted range is selected.

# Naming and Referencing Cells

You have learned that a First Choice formula uses cell coordinates to tell it where to find the data to use in a calculation. In a previous example, we referenced a specific cell using the cell's coordinates (for example, the values stored in the cell R2C1, were subtracted from the values stored in the cell R1C1). In other words, the formula referenced the value in a cell in one coordinate location (R2C1) to subtract it from the value in a cell at another location (R1C1). The coordinates of the individual cells become the names of those cells within the formula.

Now suppose you can't remember the specific coordinates of a cell. First Choice provides the option of giving a name to a cell and using that name in a formula. You may find it much easier to remember a formula that looks like this:

(SALES – EXPENSES)/MONTHS

rather than (R12C4 – R18C4)/R18C12. The value stored in the cell named EXPENSES (or R18C4) is to be subtracted from the value stored in a cell named SALES (or R12C4), and then divided by the number of MONTHS (R18C12) used in the spreadsheet calculation. It's apparent that assigning names to cells rather than using a cell's coordinates simplifies reading and writing long formulas, especially when you need to reference a cell often in the same formula.

You need to follow these simple guidelines when naming cells:

- A name can be up to 13 characters but cannot include spaces.
- If a name is to consist of two different words, separate the words with an underscore or simply run the words together. For example, if you wish to use the words Gross Sales, then either use the underscore method, as Gross_Sales, or run them together as GrossSales.

- A name must always begin with a letter and may consist of any combination of uppercase or lowercase characters, numerals or the underscore character.
- No two cells in the same spreadsheet can use the same cell name.
- You can't assign a cell the name of one of First Choice's keywords, such as TOTAL.

To assign a name to a cell, complete the following steps:

1. Position the cursor on the cell that you wish to name.
2. Choose **Type or edit cell formula** from the Features menu or press the speed key, Alt-F. The Formula box soon appears on your screen.
3. Press the Up Arrow key to move the cursor to the **Name** prompt in the Formula box.
4. Type the name that you wish to assign to the cell. Remember, this name must not exceed 13 characters and must be unique to this spreadsheet.
5. When finished with typing the name, you have two options: Either press the Down Arrow key to move the cursor to the Formula item in order to add a formula for this cell (not necessary if the cell already contains a formula), or simply press Alt-F to exit the Formula box and assign the name to the cell. If you change your mind altogether about assigning the name to the cell, simply press Esc to cancel the name and close the Formula box.

*Note: You can quickly erase a cell's name and contents by positioning the cursor on that cell and pressing Alt-W.*

You can easily assign names to cells using the steps above. If you wish to assign names to several cells at once, simply press the Tab key in step 5 instead of Alt-F. Then, repeat steps 3 and 4 and press Tab and/or Enter to move the cursor from left to right and down the spreadsheet until all the cells are assigned names as you wish. If you wish to change the name of a cell or erase the name altogether, use Alt-F to display the Formula box, move the cursor to the **Name** prompt as before and edit the name just like any other text. Once you have completed assigning (or changing) names to the cells in your spreadsheet, press Alt-F to close the Formula box.

## Specifying Ranges

If you need to refer to more than one cell at a time, you just specify a group of cells as a *range*. A range refers to an area of cells on your spreadsheet. Such an area might be a single column or row, or a group of columns and rows. To refer to a range, you use the cell coordinates for the first cell in the range followed by two periods (..), and then the coordinates for last cell in the range. For example, if you wish to refer to the first 10 cells in column 1, you could write the range as:

`R1C1..R10C1`

Similarly, you could refer to a block of cells within a spreadsheet with something like: `R5C3..R10C8`.

In Chapter 10, you will learn about First Choice's library of built-in formulas. One such formula, TOTAL, can be used to sum the values within a range of cells. Such a formula might be written as: `@TOTAL(R1C2..R12C2)` which tells First Choice to sum all the values in the second column from row 1 through row 12. Clearly, using ranges saves time when you enter formulas.

# Saving Your Spreadsheet

Just as you saved documents you created with First Choice's word processor, you need to save your spreadsheets in order to reuse them. For safety, you should save your spreadsheet work every 15 minutes or so. How often you save your spreadsheet depends upon your work habits, and just how much information you are willing to risk due to accidental erasure from something like an unexpected power failure. This section gives the steps necessary to save a spreadsheet and retrieve it from storage.

To save a spreadsheet, complete the following steps:

1. Choose **Save a copy of this spreadsheet** from the Files menu. The Directory Assistant will appear on your screen.

2. Select the disk (and disk drive) on which you wish to save the working file. The current drive is indicated on the Directory line. If the current drive is the correct one, go on to step 3.

   If you wish to save your file to a disk located in a different drive, first type the name of that drive. For example, if you wish to save the spreadsheet file to a disk located in drive B, first insert a formatted disk into that drive, and then type:

   `B:`

Note to hard disk users. You can also indicate the exact sub-directory. For example, you can type:

`C:\REPORTS`

to place the spreadsheet file in a subdirectory named REPORTS within drive C (the hard drive).

3. Type the name that you wish to give the file at the **Save As** prompt. The name should be unique unless you wish to replace an old file with the current working file. Using an existing name will always replace an old file with the new file. Don't enter any spaces. It is not necessary to enter any file name extension. First Choice will add the .SS or spreadsheet file extension automatically for you.

4. Press Enter. First Choice saves the file and returns you to the working spreadsheet file. Notice that the upper left-hand portion of the status line will now show the new file name.

Remember to always save your spreadsheet work before leaving the current work session. If you try to exit the application without saving your worksheet, First Choice flashes a warning message to remind you that you haven't saved your spreadsheet. You can press the Esc key to return to the working spreadsheet file, and then choose the appropriate **Save a copy of this spreadsheet** command.

First Choice enables you to save a file in a format that is compat-ible with other popular spreadsheet programs, including Lotus 1-2-3 or Professional Plan. To save in another format, you must choose the **Save as Professional Plan/1-2-3 WKS/WK1** command from the Files menu instead of the customary **Save a copy of this spreadsheet** com-mand. **Save as Professional Plan/1-2-3 WKS/WK1** tells First Choice to save the file using the 1-2-3 compatible .WKS or .WK1 file format extensions instead of First Choice's .SS spreadsheet extension.

## Retrieving Your Spreadsheet File

Once you have safely stored your spreadsheet on a floppy disk or hard disk drive, you can easily retrieve the file and make it the active spreadsheet on your screen. First Choice provides two options to retrieve a file. One option is to choose **Get an existing file** from the Main menu, and the second option is to choose the same command from within the Files menu common to most First Choice applica-tions. Either way, choosing the **Get an existing file** command will produce the Directory Assistant screen as explained in the following steps:

1. First choose the **Get an existing file** command. You can choose this command from either the Main menu or within the spreadsheet module itself. From within the spreadsheet application, open the Files menu and choose the appropriate command. Either way, the Directory Assistant soon appears.

2. The Directory Assistant will list all the current spreadsheet files available on the current active directory (on a hard disk) or from the current floppy disk drive. If you wish to retrieve a file stored on a different floppy disk (or second hard disk and any subdirectory), simply type the name of the drive and subdirectory you want, and then press Enter. For example, to list all the files stored on a disk inserted into drive B, type `B:` and press Enter. To retrieve files stored in a subdirectory named SALES on a hard drive D, type `D:\SALES`.

3. Once the correct list of files appears within the Directory Assistant, move the highlight over the desired file name that you wish to retrieve and then press Enter. If you have a mouse, you can simply point and double-click to retrieve the file. First Choice retrieves the selected file from storage and makes it the active spreadsheet file on your screen, even if another file previously existed on your screen. Any changes or additions to the spreadsheet file will only affect the current working file. The file that remains on your disk stays intact unless you replace it by saving the active file with the same file name, or delete the existing file from the disk.

# Printing Your Spreadsheet

Printing your spreadsheet files to share the information with others is a common need. You can print all of your spreadsheet or just a portion of it. You can print or "output" your spreadsheet to a printer, to a disk or to the screen. Regardless of which mode of print output that you wish to use, the basic print options are found via the **Print this spreadsheet** command on the Print menu. Table 9-3 lists all the options found on the Print menu as well as a discussion of those options.

If you have reviewed the print options from Table 9-3, you can use the following steps to print the entire spreadsheet.

**Table 9-3.** Options on the Print Options box.

| Option | What It Does |
|---|---|
| Print Formulas (Y/N) | Generally, you will want your printout to show the results of formula calculations. However, if you change this value to Y, you can tell First Choice to print the formulas themselves instead of the computed values. This feature is handy for analyzing the spreadsheet computations. |
| Pause between pages (Y/N) | If you are using a printer with single sheets instead of a continuous form of paper, you should change the default selection from N to Y. Choosing Y will tell First Choice to pause between pages and allow enough time to insert a new page of paper. |
| Print to | The default selection for this option, which you will probably use most, is PRINTER. This option tells First Choice to output your spreadsheet to the printer. If you wish to output your spreadsheet to the screen, enter SCREEN. First Choice will show you one screen full of your spreadsheet at a time. The SCREEN option is handy for previewing your spreadsheet before printing it on paper just in case you wish to make some final adjustments. If you wish to output to another disk file, enter FILE instead. The file that is created can easily be edited using the word processor. |
| Lines per page | Use this option for paper of unusual size. The standard 8 1/2″ X 11″ paper uses the default value of 66. Generally, six lines are printed per inch. If you wish to print your spreadsheet continuously without page breaks, enter a 0. |
| Page width | The default value is 80 for a standard width on an 8 1/2″ X 11″ inch sheet of paper. You can enter a value between 1 and 255. If you use compressed type, some wide carriage printers can print the maximum 255 characters wide. |
| Compressed type (Y/N) | Type Y to print your spreadsheet in compressed type. The standard 8 1/2″ X 11″ page can hold 80 regular characters per line. In compressed type, you can fit 132 characters. |
| Print page numbers (Y/N) | To print a page number on each page of the spreadsheet, accept the default Y. |

| Option | What It Does |
|---|---|
| Draft or correspondence quality (D/C) | To print your final copy of the spreadsheet, type **C** for correspondence quality. Choosing correspondence quality will produce a better looking document, but will make your printer work more slowly than choosing **D** for draft quality. |
| Page heading | This option allows you to print a centered one-line heading for each page of your spreadsheet. |

1. Open the Print menu and choose the **Print this spreadsheet** command.

2. Use the Tab or Shift-Tab key (or mouse) to move the cursor around the Print Options screen and change any of the displayed values as needed. For a review of these values, see Table 9-3.

3. Once you are satisfied with all the selected options, press Enter. First Choice prints the spreadsheet.

## Printing A Part of the Spreadsheet

Sometimes you may want to print only a portion of a spreadsheet that is several pages in length. Printing only part of a spreadsheet saves time when the spreadsheet is rather large and you only wish to analyze a few selected cells of information. To print a portion of a spreadsheet, complete the following steps:

*If you wish to include column or row headings in your range of selected cells, you must first move the cursor into the column or row heading (for example C0R0) before you define or anchor the range of cells.*

1. The first step is to select the cells that you wish to print. Move the cursor to the first cell where you will begin your selection—generally the upper left-hand corner of a range of cells.

2. Anchor the beginning of the range of cells by choosing **Select cells** from the Edit menu or using the speed key, Alt-S.

3. Move the cursor to highlight the range of cells that you wish to select.

4. Select **Print selected cells only** from the Print menu. The Print Options screen soon appears as before.

5. Choose any of the options from the Print Options screen and then press Enter.

# Summary

- This chapter introduced the spreadsheet application feature as well as all the parts that make up the spreadsheet screen. You learned how to move the cursor around the spreadsheet from cell to cell using keyboard commands and the mouse.

- When creating a spreadsheet, you input three types of information: labels, values, and formulas.

- You learned how to enter headings at the top of a spreadsheet in columns and on the left side of the spreadsheet in the rows.

- You learned that a value and a number are the same thing and that entering a value is as simple as typing a heading. The chapter gave rules to follow when entering values.

- The upper left-hand corner of the spreadsheet is described by the coordinates R1C1. To reach this cell quickly, press Ctrl-Home.

- First Choice offers a quick entry feature that helps you enter a series of related headings, such as the months of the year. To turn this feature on, press Alt-Q.

- You can also add readability to your spreadsheets by using underlines. To add underlines to portions of your spreadsheet, use the hyphen or equal sign characters.

- You learned that formulas are used to perform calculations on the contents of a cell. You can use many of the typical mathematical operators in the standard order of precedence to perform mathematical calculations.

- You learned that formulas are entered into a formula box. To access this box, you can use the speed key, Alt-F.

- Many spreadsheet tasks begin with selecting cells. First Choice provides the ability to select a single cell, or a group of cells called a range. You can select cells with either the keyboard or the mouse.

- You also learned how to name and reference cells.

- Finally, you learned how to save, retrieve, and print a spreadsheet.

# More on Spreadsheets

**In this chapter:**

- Using Keywords
- Recalculating Your Spreadsheet
- Changing A Cell's Style
- Editing Your Spreadsheet
- Merging Spreadsheets
- The Wikley Company Spreadsheet
- Graphing Your Spreadsheet
- Summary

This chapter goes beyond the basics of learning how to use the spreadsheet. You will learn how to use First Choice's built-in keywords (sometimes called functions) to add power and flexibility to your spreadsheet. In addition, you will learn how to modify and edit your spreadsheets, merge the data between two spreadsheets and create a quick and easy graph of your spreadsheet's data.

## Using Keywords

In Chapter 9 you were introduced to formulas and using the basic mathematical formula operators (+ − / * ^) to perform calculations in cells. To add true power to your formulas, you can use First Choice's built-in library of keywords. Keywords, sometimes referred to as functions, represent a particular type of operation that is performed within a formula. All of the keywords are formatted in the same way and begin with the @ sign (actually, the @ sign is optional, but it is useful for distinguishing keywords from other elements in a formula). For example, the keyword @AVG averages all the numbers in a range, while @TOT calculates the sum total of a range of numbers. Both @AVG and @TOT are mathematical keywords. First Choice offers a variety of keyword types, including mathematical and statistical, date and time, indexes, logical operators, financial, and strings.

Formulas with keywords must include two parts: the name of the keyword and an argument. The name represents the type of operation to be carried out, and the argument is a cell or range of cells holding the values to be calculated. For example, the formula @TOT(R1C1..R10C1) calculates the sum total of the values in the first 10 rows of column 1.

You can also use keywords to operate on more than one argument at a time. Simply enclose the arguments within a set of parentheses and separate them with commas. For example, the formula @PMT(PRINCIPAL, INTEREST, DURATION) can be used to calculate the payment on a typical loan. In this case, the formula includes the financial keyword @PMT and performs a calculation on three arguments. The PRINCIPAL argument is the amount of the loan, INTEREST is the interest rate applied to the loan, and DURATION is the argument representing the term of the loan.

As you enter a formula (and keywords) into a cell, keep in mind that once you enter the formula and move to another cell, the formula does not appear. Only the resulting value of the calculation is shown in the cell where you entered the formula. If you enter a formula that First Choice can't calculate, then the value ERROR appears in the cell. Don't worry. Rather than indicating a mistake in the formula you entered, the ERROR message might mean that the formula can't be computed just yet. For example, if you type the formula @SQRT(S10) to find the square root of the value in cell S10, you would get an ERROR value if cell S10 is empty. (First Choice is unable to find the square root of an empty cell.) To remedy the situation, simply enter a value in cell S10. The trick is to investigate the problem before changing the formula.

Sometimes, however, the formula may indeed be incorrect. For example, if you try to use the same @SQRT keyword to find the square root of cell that contains a negative number, then the ERROR value will also be returned. You can't find the square root of a negative number. Another typical problem is referencing a cell that contains a label instead of a numerical value. In this case, First Choice will return a value of zero for the calculation of that cell.

Using keywords is a simple and powerful method for adding flexibility to your formulas. The First Choice documentation offers a complete listing and explanation of all the available keywords in the First Choice library. You can use Table 10-1 as a quick summary of the keywords that First Choice has to offer. For more information about the syntax, format or usage of a particular keyword, consult your documentation.

**Table 10-1.** Summary of First Choice Keywords

| KEYWORD | OPERATION |
|---------|-----------|
| *Date and Time* | |
| @DATE | Converts numbers to a First Choice date |
| @DATEVAL | Converts a text date to a First Choice date value |
| @DAY | Isolates the day of month from a date value |
| @HOUR | Isolates the hour from a time number value |
| @MINUTE | Isolates the minute from a time number value |
| @MONTH | Isolates the month from a date value |
| @NOW | Determines the current date and time |
| @SECOND or SEC | Isolates the second from a time number value |
| @TIME | Determines the time number from a First Choice time number value |
| @TIMEVAL | Converts the text time value to a First Choice time number value |
| @YEAR | Isolates a year from a date number value |
| *Mathematical* | |
| @ABS | Converts any number to a positive value |
| @ACOS(value) | Isolates a value equal to an angle in radians whose cosine is value |
| @ASIN(value) | Isolates a value equal to an angle in radians whose sine is value |
| @ATAN(value) | Isolates a value equal to an angle in radians whose tangent is value |
| @COS | Isolates the cosine of an angle, given in radians |

*(continued)*

**Table 10-1.** (continued)

| KEYWORD | OPERATION |
|---------|-----------|
| @EXP | Determines the natural exponential or power of e. |
| @FRACT | Isolates the decimal value only of a fraction |
| @INTEGER or INT | Isolates the whole number value only of a fraction |
| @LN | Determines the natural logarithm or base e |
| @LOG | Determines the common logarithm or base 10 |
| @MOD | Isolates the modulus or remainder only of one value divided by another |
| @PI | First Choice uses the value: 3.141592653589793 as PI |
| @ROUND..TO | Rounds a value to the number of places specified |
| @SIN | Isolates the sine of an angle, given in radians |
| @SQRT | Determines the square root of a value |
| @TAN | Isolates the tangent of an angle, given in radians |

Statistical

| KEYWORD | OPERATION |
|---------|-----------|
| @AVERAGE or AVG | Computes the average mean of a range of cells |
| @COUNT | Computes how many non-blank cells in a range of cells |
| @MAX | Computes the largest value in a range of cells |
| @MIN | Computes the smallest value in a range of cells |
| @RANDOM or RAND | Generates a random number between 0.0 and 1.0 |
| @STDEV or STD | Computes the standard deviation |
| @TOTAL or TOT | Computes the sum or total within a range of cells |
| @VARIANCE or VAR | Computes the variance of the values in a range |

**Table 10-1.** (continued)

| KEYWORD | OPERATION |
|---------|-----------|
| | Financial |
| @CTERM | Computes the number of compounding periods required for an initial sum to grow to a particular future value |
| @DDB | Computes depreciation using the double-declining balance method |
| @FV | Computes the future value of regular payments |
| @INTEREST | Computes the interest paid on an amount given a time period of regular payments |
| @NPV | Computes the net present value of an investment (that is, converts future values into today's dollars) |
| @PAYMENT or PMT | Computes the payment on a loan |
| @PV | Computes the present value of a regular annuity (that is, equal payments) |
| @RATE | Calculates the interest rate required to accumulate a specific amount |
| @SLN | Computes depreciation using the straight-line method |
| @SYD | Computes depreciation using the sum-of-the-years' digit method |
| @TERM | Computes the number of payments required to accumulate a specific future value |

Indexing

| KEYWORD | OPERATION |
|---------|-----------|
| @HLOOKUP | Looks up information in a horizontal table |

Note: The information varies depending upon certain criteria.

| KEYWORD | OPERATION |
|---------|-----------|
| @INDEX | Calculates the value of a cell based on its position within a range |
| @VLOOKUP | Looks up information in a vertical table |

Note: The information varies depending upon certain criteria.

*(continued)*

**Table 10-1.** (continued)

| KEYWORD | OPERATION |
|---------|-----------|
| *Logical* | |
| IF..THEN..ELSE | The primary keyword used to make logical decisions in a worksheet. Compares two conditions of a cell and then uses one of two values for the cell based on that comparison |

(Note: The following relational operators can be used in an relational expression: = < > <= >= <> AND OR NOT.)

| KEYWORD | OPERATION |
|---------|-----------|
| @ERROR or ERR | ERROR is equal to the specific value ERROR. Hint: Use this value to trace the effects of a formula since any formula that refers to a cell with the value ERROR will also result in ERROR |
| @FALSE | FALSE is equal to the numerical value FALSE or 0 |
| @ISERR | Used to compare a value to see if it contains the value ERROR |
| @ISNUMBER | Compares a value to see if it's numerical |
| @ISSTRING | Compares a value to see if it's non-numerical or text |
| @TRUE | TRUE is equal to the numerical value TRUE or 1 |
| *String* | |
| @CHARACTER or CHAR | Provides the character whose number is the numerical ASCII value specified |
| @CODE | Provides the numerical ASCII value of the first character in the string of text |
| @EXACT | Compares two strings and returns a value of TRUE if the strings are identical |
| @FIND | Isolates the position at which a string of text first occurs in another string |
| @LEFT | Beginning with the leftmost character, this keyword returns a specified number of characters from a string and truncates it |
| @LENGTH | Returns the total number of characters in a string of text |

**Table 10-1.** (continued)

| KEYWORD | OPERATION |
|---------|-----------|
| @LOWER | Converts a string of text characters to lowercase |
| @MID | Returns a string of specific characters from within a string |
| @PROPER | Converts the first letter of a string of text characters to uppercase and all remaining characters to lowercase |
| @REPEAT | Repeatedly returns the value of a string as many times as you specify |
| @REPLACE | Replaces old text in a string with new text that you specify |
| @RIGHT | Beginning with the rightmost character of a string, this keyword returns a specified number of characters and truncates the original string |
| @STRING or TEXT | Converts a numerical value to a string value and places the number of decimal places you specify to the right of the decimal point |
| @TRIM | Removes or trims any excess space from a string of text, such as leading or trailing blank spaces |
| @UPPER | Converts all letters of a string to uppercase |
| @VALUE | Converts a string value to its numerical value |

# Recalculating Your Spreadsheet

Each time you enter a new value into a cell that is referenced by a formula, the spreadsheet must be recalculated. First Choice provides two options for recalculating your spreadsheet. The first option, *automatic*, is the default option selected by First Choice the first time you begin working with the spreadsheet application. Automatic recalculation adjusts the results of your spreadsheet instantaneously with each change made to a cell. The second option is *manual recalculation*—First Choice waits to recalculate your spreadsheet until you give the appropriate command.

Generally, you will use automatic calculation when you wish to change one variable (such as the interest rate) to test a what-if analysis on short- to medium-sized spreadsheets. However, since automatic recalculation could be time-consuming on larger spreadsheets where several changes might be necessary, it is more productive to switch to manual calculation, make all the changes at one time, and then recalculate the spreadsheet.

*When in manual mode, press the speed key Alt-R each time you wish to recalculate your spreadsheet.*

To change your spreadsheet from the default, automatic recalculation, to manual recalculation, complete the following steps:

1. Open the Features menu and choose **Set manual recalculation**. The Features menu closes. Note: Choosing the manual option will change the Features menu item to **Set automatic recalculation**.

2. Open the Features menu a second time and choose **Recalculate**. You can also use the speed key Alt-R each time you wish to recalculate your spreadsheet in manual mode.

## Changing a Cell's Style

*Styles only apply to cells containing numerical values or formulas. Labels or text entries do not have styles.*

When you begin entering values into cells, First Choice will display those values with a certain format, or style. For example, our early spreadsheet examples displayed the values with commas to designate thousands as well as two decimal places to designate tenths and hundredths (e.g. 10,000.00). First Choice offers several different styles for displaying values. The options are as follows:

- using currency symbols
- displaying numbers with commas
- displaying numbers with % signs
- determining the number of places to the right of the decimal point to display
- displaying numbers in date and/or time format

First Choice provides the option of changing the style settings for individual cells or for the entire spreadsheet. Both of these options are accessed through the Style menu and are discussed next.

# Style Changes to a Single Cell
# or All Cells (Global)

When you first start the spreadsheet application, the entire spreadsheet is set with a default global style for all the cells. The default styles include the following:

- Commas are inserted as necessary.
- Two decimal places to the right of the decimal point are displayed.
- No currency or percent signs are displayed.
- Date and time values are displayed as special numbers.
- Column width is a minimum of 6 characters.

You can choose to change an individual cell from the global style to another style. Or, you can choose to change the entire global style for all cells. Just keep two points in mind. First, any time you change an individual cell's style, that new style will always take precedence over any global style changes that you might make. (In other words, a global style change will not affect individual cells to which you've made style changes.) Second, changing the global style only affects cells where you haven't entered any values yet. Cells that already contain values will not be affected by a global change.

To change the global style, choose the **Set global style** command from the Styles menu. The Set global style menu will appear on your screen as shown in Figure 10-1.

*Use the speed key Alt-T to quickly open the Style menu and choose the **Set cell style** command in one easy step.*

If you wish to change the style of an individual cell or a group of cells, you must first select that cell (or range). For a single cell, first move the cursor to that cell and then choose **Set cell style** from the Styles menu. If you are changing the style of a range of cells, first move the cursor to the first cell in the range, choose the **Select cells** command from the Edit menu (or drag with the mouse), and then move the cursor to the last cell in the range and choose **Set cell style** from the Styles menu. Choosing **Set cell style** will display its screen of options as shown in Figure 10-2.

Once either the Set global style menu or Set cell style menu appears on your screen, you can select several options. The following sections detail the style options.

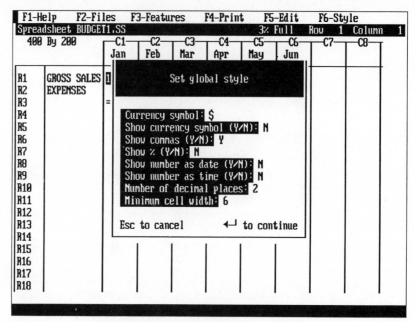

**Figure 10-1.** The Set Global Style menu.

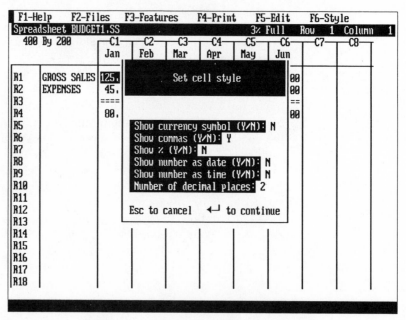

**Figure 10-2.** The Set Cell Style menu.

## Selecting the Currency Format

The first option on both the Set global style and the Set cell style menu sets currency symbols. If you choose to have the symbol displayed (choose Y), the default currency symbol ($) will precede each numerical value. If you wish to display something other than the $ symbol, you must choose the **Set global style** command and choose any symbol from Table 10-2. To turn off symbol display for a particular cell, simply move the cursor to that cell, choose the **Set cell style** command, and then choose Y or N to display the currency symbol or not.

**Table 10-2.** Currency Symbols

| For this value: | Type: |
|---|---|
| Dollar | $ |
| Pound | £ (Hold down the Alt key and press 156 on the numeric keypad to display the £ symbol) |
| Franc | F |
| Franc (French) | FF |
| Franc (Belgian) | BF |
| Franc (Swiss) | SFr |
| Lire | L |
| Lire (Italian) | Lit |
| Mark (German) | DM |
| Krone (Swedish) | Kr |
| Peso | P |
| Peseta (Spanish) | Pts |
| Schilling | S |
| Schilling (Austrian) | öS (Hold down the Alt key and press 148 on the numeric keypad to get the ö symbol) |
| Ruble or Rand | R |
| Yen (Japanese) | Y |

## Displaying Commas

The option for displaying commas is available on both the Set global style menu and the Set cell style menu. To show commas for values of 1,000 or more, leave the default option as Y. Commas will only appear to the left of the decimal point as necessary. The larger the number, the more commas will be inserted. If you wish to omit the commas, simply choose N to turn this option off.

## Displaying the Percent Symbol

Like the commas option, the option to display a percent symbol is available on both global and individual cell style menus. The default selection is N. If your spreadsheet data would be more useful shown as a percentage change, then you may wish to show selected cell values as a percentage of 100. For example, the sales volume from one sales representative over 12 months might show a sales increase or decrease as a percentage of total monthly sales. To display values as a percentage, enter Y for the **Show** % prompt. Choosing Y will instruct First Choice to display each value entered as a percentage (while the value itself is stored as a decimal value). The percentage equals the decimal value multiplied by 100.

## Selecting Date and Time Formats

The first part of this chapter explained how to use several First Choice keywords to generate values for dates and times. (First Choice normally converts dates and times to unique numbers. For example, First Choice would display 07/17/88 as the value 32342). To display the date or time values in a form that you can understand easily, use either the Set global style or Set cell style menus. Choose Y at the Show number as date option or Show number as time option. The date will be displayed in numerical form in regular date format as: month/day/year. Similarly, the time will be displayed in the following time format: hours, minutes, seconds.

## Specifying the Number of Decimal Places

First Choice's default setting is two decimal places to the right of the decimal point. You may wish to change this setting to any number from 0 to 15. Whatever number you choose, keep in mind that First Choice will always show the number of decimal places specified. In other words, if you set the number of decimal places to 3 and you enter 25.1234, the value will be displayed as:

25.123

Similarly, if you enter 25, First Choice will add three zeros to the right of the decimal point and display the value as:

25.000

If you do not wish to show any decimal places, enter 0 at the **Number of decimal places:** prompt. Figure 10-3 depicts our spreadsheet example from Chapter 9 with no decimal places.

```
┌────────────────────────────────────────────────────────────────────┐
│█F1-Help    F2-Files   F3-Features    F4-Print   F5-Edit   F6-Style   │
│ Spreadsheet BUDGET1.SS                         3% Full  Row   5 Column  6│
│    400 By 200    ┌─C1──┬─C2──┬─C3──┬─C4──┬─C5──┬─C6──┬─C7──┬─C8──┐    │
│                  │ Jan │ Feb │ Mar │ Apr │ May │ Jun │     │     │    │
│                  │     │     │     │     │     │     │     │     │    │
│ R1  │GROSS SALES │ 125 │ 190 │ 175 │ 200 │ 234 │ 180 │     │     │    │
│ R2  │EXPENSES    │  45 │  50 │  55 │  48 │  80 │  75 │     │     │    │
│ R3  │            │═════╪═════╪═════╪═════╪═════╪═════╪═════        │    │
│ R4  │            │  80 │ 140 │ 120 │ 152 │ 154 │ 105 │     │     │    │
│ R5  │            │     │     │     │     │     │ ███ │     │     │    │
│ R6  │            │     │     │     │     │     │     │     │     │    │
│ R7  │            │     │     │     │     │     │     │     │     │    │
│ R8  │            │     │     │     │     │     │     │     │     │    │
│ R9  │            │     │     │     │     │     │     │     │     │    │
│ R10 │            │     │     │     │     │     │     │     │     │    │
│ R11 │            │     │     │     │     │     │     │     │     │    │
│ R12 │            │     │     │     │     │     │     │     │     │    │
│ R13 │            │     │     │     │     │     │     │     │     │    │
│ R14 │            │     │     │     │     │     │     │     │     │    │
│ R15 │            │     │     │     │     │     │     │     │     │    │
│ R16 │            │     │     │     │     │     │     │     │     │    │
│ R17 │            │     │     │     │     │     │     │     │     │    │
│ R18 │            │     │     │     │     │     │     │     │     │    │
│           Press F1 for Help; or press Esc for the Main Menu          │
└────────────────────────────────────────────────────────────────────┘
```

**Figure 10-3.** Spreadsheet with no decimal places in cell values.

# Formatting the Cell Width

As you type an entry into a cell, First Choice will automatically adjust the cell's width (and thus the entire column) to accommodate the length of the entry. The minimum width of a column is six characters. If you type an entry that is less than six characters, the width of the cell remains the same. Type an entry greater than six characters and First Choice automatically adjusts the column width to accommodate the length of the entry. However, you can retain some control over the width of a column by setting a minimum cell width. There is no maximum width setting, since First Choice always automatically expands the width of a column according to the widest entry stored in that column.

The option to change the minimum column width from the default of 6 characters is found only on the Set global style menu. To change the minimum cell width, type a number between **6** and **20** at the **Minimum cell width:** prompt. Note that this setting does not affect the row where the column headings appear.

# Editing Your Spreadsheet

From time to time you will find it necessary to make changes to your spreadsheet. Changes may be as simple as correcting a typo in a cell's entry or as complex as adding or deleting an entire row or column of cells. Depending upon what task you need to do, First Choice offers several editing tools and procedures to get the job done. In the sections that follow, we will review all of the editing tasks. Before you begin, though, remember the first step: select the cell or range that you wish to edit.

## Basic Editing

As you build your spreadsheet, it's natural to make mistakes as you type entries into the spreadsheet's cells. You might notice the mistake before you complete the entry or after the entry already exists. Either way, First Choice comes to the rescue with simple spreadsheet editing tools that you can use to correct or change any entries. For example, First Choice allows you to use two of the basic editing keys that you probably used with the word processor, the Backspace and Delete (Del) keys. You can also use the Insert (Ins) key to turn on the Insert mode and insert characters into text or values that have already been typed. One last handy option is the **Erase this cell** command found on the Edit menu (or press Alt-W). All of these keys are used in simple spreadsheet editing when you wish to change the contents of a cell. To review your editing options, refer to Table 10-3. Remember, before you begin to edit any cell's entry, first position the cursor in that cell.

**Table 10-3. Basic Editing Tools.**

| KEY: | TO PERFORM THIS EDITING TASK: |
| --- | --- |
| Backspace | To erase the last character typed. Each time you press Backspace, the character to the left. |
| Delete (Del) | To erase the character at the current cursor position. Each time you press the key, another character is erased. |
| Insert (Ins) | Press the Ins key to change to insert mode. In insert mode, you can add new characters at the location of the Insert cursor (small blinking square). Once you have inserted your characters, press Ins again to turn off insert mode. |
| Alt-W | Alt-W is the speed key combination for choosing **Erase this cell** from the Edit menu. With the cursor placed on a cell, pressing Alt-W will erase its entire contents. You can then type a new entry. |

# Adding Rows and Columns

As you continue to modify your spreadsheet, you may decide that more advanced editing is required. For example, you may discover that you have just completed a lengthy spreadsheet and accidentally omitted an entire row of data. Instead of redoing the entire spreadsheet, you can easily add a new row (or column) at any point. Adding a row or column of cells to a spreadsheet is a simple procedure:

*If adding a row or column will make a formula incorrect, First Choice will give you a warning.*

1. Move the cursor to the row/column where you wish to insert the new row/column. New rows are always added above the cursor position and new columns are always added to the left of the cursor position. For example, to add a blank column between the column headings position (C0) and the first column of data (C1), position the cursor in column 1 (at cell R1C1).

2. Open the Edit menu and choose **Insert row/column**. The Insert Rows or Columns box appears as shown in Figure 10-4.

3. Type R to insert a row or C to insert a column.

4. Press the Tab key to move to the next prompt.

5. Type the number of rows or columns to insert as appropriate. For example, to enter two new columns, type 2.

6. Press Enter. The new rows or columns are inserted as specified.

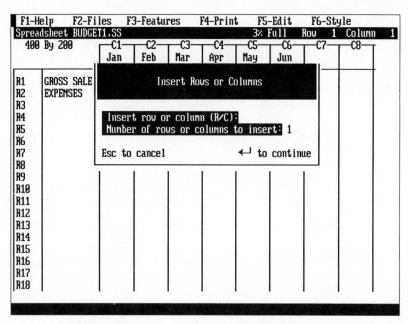

**Figure 10-4.** The Insert Rows or Columns box.

*Before you press Enter, you can easily change your mind about inserting a new column or row by pressing Esc.*

Figure 10-5 depicts our previous spreadsheet example with two blank columns between the column headings and the first column of data. For practice, use the above steps to duplicate this example.

## Erasing Cells or the Entire Spreadsheet

First Choice allows you to erase the contents of a single cell, a range of cells or the entire spreadsheet. As listed in Table 10-3, you can easily erase the contents of a cell by positioning the cursor in the cell, and pressing Alt-W or choosing the **Erase this cell** command from the Edit menu. Once the cell contents are removed in this manner, they are erased forever.

The Alt-W command only works with one cell at a time. To delete the contents of a range of cells, use a safer method—moving the contents of the selected range to the clipboard. First select the cell or cell range with the mouse or use the Alt-S in lieu of the **Select cells** command from the Edit menu. Once the desired range of cells is selected, choose **Move selected cells to clipboard** from the Edit menu or use the speed key, Alt-M. Using this method, the contents of the

```
 F1-Help    F2-Files   F3-Features    F4-Print    F5-Edit    F6-Style
 Spreadsheet BUDGET1.SS                         3% Full   Row   1  Column   1
     400 By 200        C1     C2     C3     C4     C5     C6     C7     C8
                                     Jan    Feb    Mar    Apr    May    Jun

 R1   GROSS SALES ████████         125    190    175    200    234    180
 R2   EXPENSES                      45     50     55     48     80     75
 R3                              =================================================
 R4                               80    140    120    152    154    105
 R5
 R6
 R7
 R8
 R9
 R10
 R11
 R12
 R13
 R14
 R15
 R16
 R17
 R18
              Press F1 for Help; or press Esc for the Main Menu
```

**Figure 10-5.** Sample spreadsheet with two blank columns.

cells are erased and temporarily stored on the clipboard just in case you change your mind.

If you wish to erase the entire spreadsheet, either select the entire spreadsheet and move it to the clipboard, or simply choose the **Erase this spreadsheet** command from the Edit menu. This method erases the current working copy of the spreadsheet permanently and leaves any material on the clipboard intact (until you move something else to the clipboard or leave First Choice.)

## Deleting Rows and Columns

When you wish to delete an entire row or column of text, you have two options. The safer option is to simply select a range of cells (the entire row or column) and then move the contents of those selected cells to the clipboard via the Alt-M speed key command. Using this method gives you a chance to change your mind and retrieve the data from the clipboard (unless you move something else to the clipboard or exit First Choice). A more risky option is to use the **Remove row/ column** command from the Edit menu to permanently erase the entries. With this warning in mind, use the following steps to delete a row or column:

*If recalculation is not on automatic mode, remember to press Alt-R to recalculate the spreadsheet after adding or deleting rows/columns.*

1. Move the cursor to the row (or column) which you wish to delete.

2. Open the Edit menu and choose **Remove row/column**. The Remove Rows or Columns box appears as shown in Figure 10-6.

3. Type R to remove a row or C to remove a column.

4. Press the Tab key to move to the next prompt.

5. Type the number of rows or columns to be deleted. Rows are deleted from the current one down and columns are deleted from the current one moving to the right.

6. Press Enter. The specified rows or columns are deleted and any gaps are automatically closed to keep the spreadsheet looking neat. In other words, columns to the right of a deleted column are shifted to the left and any rows that follow a deleted row are shifted up.

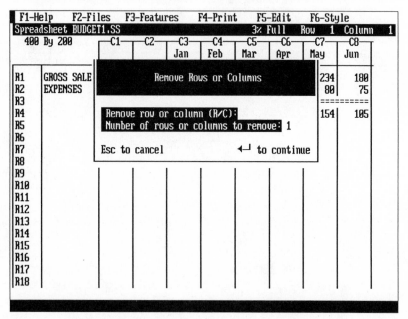

**Figure 10-6.** The Remove Rows or Columns box.

All cell references within a part of a formula are automatically adjusted to reflect the new limits of any specified range. However, if the deleted row or column contained a cell that was the beginning or end of the range, First Choice alerts you with a message that the formula is about to become incorrect. This is a nice safety feature to keep you on your toes.

# Copying Cells

One of the fastest ways to build a worksheet is to copy existing information whenever possible. It's much easier to copy data or formulas into multiple cells than it is to retype the same data over and over. You can use the clipboard to copy a group of cells to another location, or to copy the contents of a single cell into a range of cells. To illustrate both options, we have provided two sample illustrations.

## Copying a Group of Cells to Another Location

As an example, suppose that your sales and expenses data for the first quarter is identical to the data for the second quarter. To make data entry faster, simply enter the data for the first quarter (both sales and expenses) and then copy that information to the second quarter. As shown in Figure 10-7, we have already entered the data for the first quarter. To copy the data to another location, complete the following steps:

1. Move the cursor to the first cell in the group of cells that you are going to copy.

2. Press Alt-S or choose **Select cells** from the Edit menu. You can also use the mouse to select your range of cells by dragging.

3. Move the cursor to the last cell in the range until the entire range is selected. Figure 10-8 depicts a selected range of cells.

4. Copy the cells to the clipboard. You can use the speed key, Alt-C, or choose **Copy selected cells to clipboard** from the Edit menu.

5. This step is important. Move the cursor to the new upper left-hand corner of the range of cells where the data on the clipboard is to be copied. Before you paste the cells from the clipboard, make sure there is enough room to accommodate the range of cells that you are pasting. The first cell where the cursor is positioned will be the upper left-hand cell of the information you will paste. If the new range extends over existing cells, the data in those cells will be lost. For our example, move the cursor to the beginning of the second quarter (Apr at R1C4).

6. Paste the cells from the clipboard to the new range with the speed key, Alt-P, or use the **Paste from clipboard** command from the Edit menu. The result will look something like Figure 10-9.

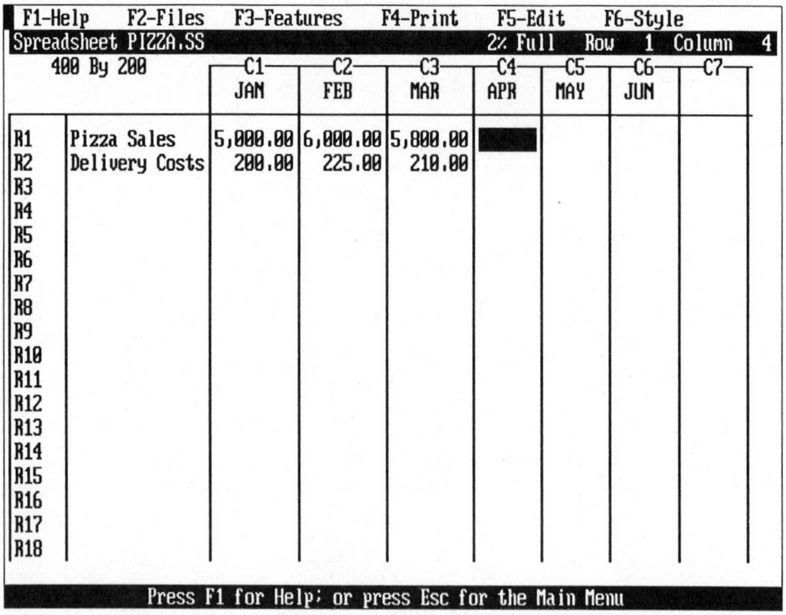

```
│ F1-Help    F2-Files    F3-Features    F4-Print    F5-Edit    F6-Style
│ Spreadsheet PIZZA.SS                              2% Full   Row   1  Column   4
      400 By 200         ┌─C1──┬──C2──┬──C3──┬──C4──┬─C5──┬──C6──┬──C7──┐
                         │ JAN │ FEB  │ MAR  │ APR  │ MAY │ JUN  │      │
│
│ R1  Pizza Sales        │5,000.00│6,000.00│5,800.00│████│    │      │
│ R2  Delivery Costs     │ 200.00 │ 225.00 │ 210.00 │    │    │      │
│ R3
│ R4
│ R5
│ R6
│ R7
│ R8
│ R9
│ R10
│ R11
│ R12
│ R13
│ R14
│ R15
│ R16
│ R17
│ R18
│          Press F1 for Help; or press Esc for the Main Menu
```

**Figure 10-7.** A spreadsheet with 1st Q data entered.

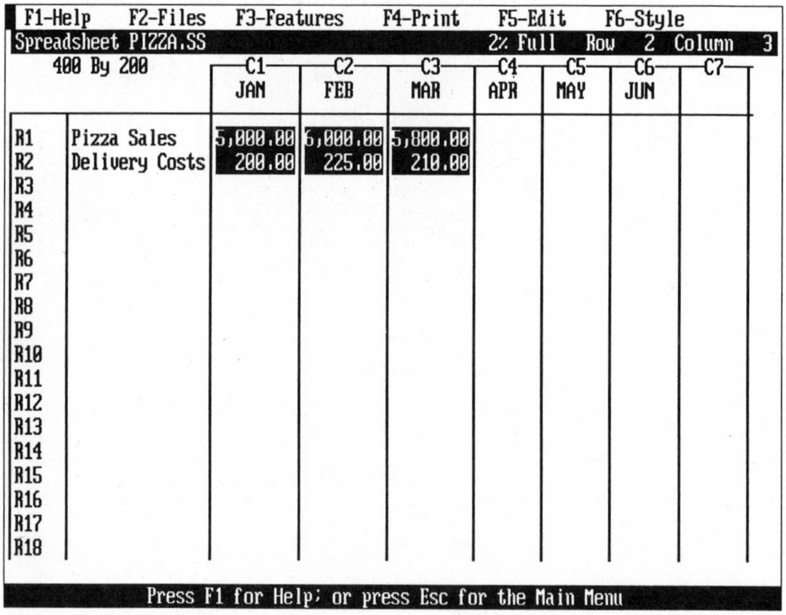

```
│ F1-Help    F2-Files    F3-Features    F4-Print    F5-Edit    F6-Style
│ Spreadsheet PIZZA.SS                              2% Full   Row   2  Column   3
      400 By 200         ┌─C1──┬──C2──┬──C3──┬──C4──┬─C5──┬──C6──┬──C7──┐
                         │ JAN │ FEB  │ MAR  │ APR  │ MAY │ JUN  │      │
│
│ R1  Pizza Sales        │5,000.00│6,000.00│5,800.00│    │    │      │
│ R2  Delivery Costs     │ 200.00 │ 225.00 │ 210.00 │    │    │      │
│ R3
│ R4
│ R5
│ R6
│ R7
│ R8
│ R9
│ R10
│ R11
│ R12
│ R13
│ R14
│ R15
│ R16
│ R17
│ R18
│          Press F1 for Help; or press Esc for the Main Menu
```

**Figure 10-8.** Select the range of cells to be copied.

```
┌─────────────────────────────────────────────────────────────────────┐
│ F1-Help    F2-Files    F3-Features    F4-Print    F5-Edit    F6-Style │
│ Spreadsheet PIZZA.SS                          2% Full    Row  3 Column   1 │
│      400 By 200      ┌─C1──┬─C2──┬─C3──┬─C4──┬─C5──┬─C6──┐             │
│                      │ JAN │ FEB │ MAR │ APR │ MAY │ JUN │             │
│                                                                       │
│ R1  Pizza Sales     │5,000.00│6,000.00│5,000.00│5,000.00│6,000.00│5,000.00│ │
│ R2  Delivery Costs  │ 200.00 │ 225.00 │ 210.00 │ 200.00 │ 225.00 │ 210.00 │ │
│ R3                  │████████│                                        │
│ R4                                                                    │
│ R5                                                                    │
│ R6                                                                    │
│ R7                                                                    │
│ R8                                                                    │
│ R9                                                                    │
│ R10                                                                   │
│ R11                                                                   │
│ R12                                                                   │
│ R13                                                                   │
│ R14                                                                   │
│ R15                                                                   │
│ R16                                                                   │
│ R17                                                                   │
│ R18                                                                   │
│           Press F1 for Help; or press Esc for the Main Menu           │
└─────────────────────────────────────────────────────────────────────┘
```

**Figure 10-9.** Data successfully copied.

## Copying a Single Cell to a Range of Cells

Sometimes you may need to copy the same data from a single cell to an entire range of cells. For example, suppose you are working out the budgets for 10 salespeople, and they all have the same quota for each of the four quarters. Specifically, each sales person must sell 1,200 units in the first quarter, 1,500 units in the second quarter, 1,800 units in the 3rd quarter, and 1,000 units in the 4th quarter. Using the following steps, you can shorten the data entry time by copying the data from one cell into a range of cells.

1. Move the cursor to the cell to be copied. For our example, move the cursor to R1C1. Enter **1200** for the first sales person (Brown) as shown in Figure 10-10. (Note: Our example depicts the spreadsheet with the options for commas and 0 decimal places for a neater look).

2. Select the cell with Alt-S.

3. Copy the contents of the cell to the clipboard by pressing Alt-C.

4. Move the cursor to the first cell in the range where you intend to copy the contents of the clipboard. For our example, move it to R2C1.

5. Select the entire range of cells with the mouse or use Alt-S. Move the cursor to the end of the range to select it. For our example, move it to the bottom of column 1 or to cell R10C1 as shown in Figure 10-11.

6. Copy the data from the clipboard by pressing Alt-P or use the appropriate command from the Edit menu. Pressing Alt-P once will copy the data from the clipboard into each of the cells in the selected range. The result will look something like Figure 10-12. For practice, repeat steps 1 through 6 until the spreadsheet is complete as shown in Figure 10-13.

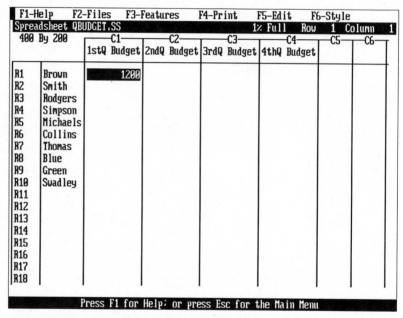

**Figure 10-10.** Type the entry to be copied in the first cell.

# Moving Cells

Just as you can copy the data from a cell or group of cells, you can also move data from cell to cell (or to a group of cells). The primary difference between moving and copying data from one cell to another is that moving data from a cell also erases the contents from the original cell. In other words, when you move data from a cell, the information is temporarily stored in the clipboard until you paste it back into a new location. You are in fact cutting data from your spreadsheet and then pasting it to a new location (or simply leaving it on the clipboard). The steps required to move data are similar to those for copying data:

*Tip: To quickly select an entire spreadsheet, move the cursor to cell ROC0, press Alt-S, and then press Ctrl-End to move to the end of the spreadsheet.*

1. Position the cursor in the cell with data you wish to move (or cut). If you wish to move a range of cells, position the cursor in the upper left-hand corner of the range of cells.

2. Select the cell or range of cells. Use the mouse to highlight the selected cells, choose **Select cells** from the Edit menu or press the speed key, Alt-S. The selected cells will be highlighted.

3. Choose **Move selected cells to clipboard** from the Edit menu or use the speed key, Alt-M. The contents of the selected or highlighted cells will disappear from the screen and will be moved to the clipboard.

4. Next position the cursor at the location where you want the place the contents of the clipboard. If you are moving a range of cells, position the cursor in the upper left hand corner of the new range. Keep in mind that a new range must be large enough to receive the data from the clipboard. Information in any cells in the new location will be overwritten with the moved data.

5. Choose **Paste from clipboard** from the Edit menu or press the speed key, Alt-P. The clipboard contents are moved to the new location in your spreadsheet.

```
 F1-Help    F2-Files   F3-Features   F4-Print   F5-Edit   F6-Style
Spreadsheet QBUDGET.SS                        1% Full   Row  10 Column    1
   400 By 200    ┌──C1──┬──C2──┬──C3──┬──C4──┬─C5─┬─C6─┐
               1stQ Budget 2ndQ Budget 3rdQ Budget 4thQ Budget

   R1   Brown      1200
   R2   Smith
   R3   Rodgers
   R4   Simpson
   R5   Michaels
   R6   Collins
   R7   Thomas
   R8   Blue
   R9   Green
   R10  Swadley
   R11
   R12
   R13
   R14
   R15
   R16
   R17
   R18
                Press F1 for Help; or press Esc for the Main Menu
```

**Figure 10-11.** Select the target range of cells.

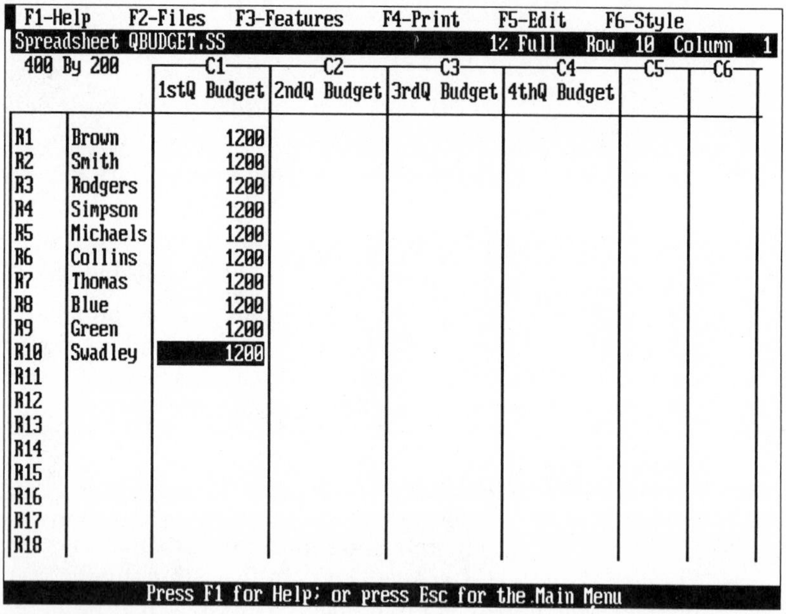

```
┌─────────────────────────────────────────────────────────────────────┐
│ F1-Help    F2-Files   F3-Features    F4-Print    F5-Edit   F6-Style  │
│ Spreadsheet QBUDGET.SS                        1% Full  Row 10 Column 1│
│    400 By 200        ┌─C1──┬──C2──┬──C3──┬───C4──┬─C5─┬─C6─┐          │
│                      │1stQ Budget│2ndQ Budget│3rdQ Budget│4thQ Budget│
│  R1   Brown          │  1200     │           │           │           │
│  R2   Smith          │  1200     │           │           │           │
│  R3   Rodgers        │  1200     │           │           │           │
│  R4   Simpson        │  1200     │           │           │           │
│  R5   Michaels       │  1200     │           │           │           │
│  R6   Collins        │  1200     │           │           │           │
│  R7   Thomas         │  1200     │           │           │           │
│  R8   Blue           │  1200     │           │           │           │
│  R9   Green          │  1200     │           │           │           │
│  R10  Swadley        │  1200     │           │           │           │
│  R11                 │           │           │           │           │
│  R12                 │           │           │           │           │
│  R13                 │           │           │           │           │
│  R14                 │           │           │           │           │
│  R15                 │           │           │           │           │
│  R16                 │           │           │           │           │
│  R17                 │           │           │           │           │
│  R18                 │           │           │           │           │
│         Press F1 for Help; or press Esc for the Main Menu            │
└─────────────────────────────────────────────────────────────────────┘
```

**Figure 10-12.** Paste the contents of the clipboard into each cell.

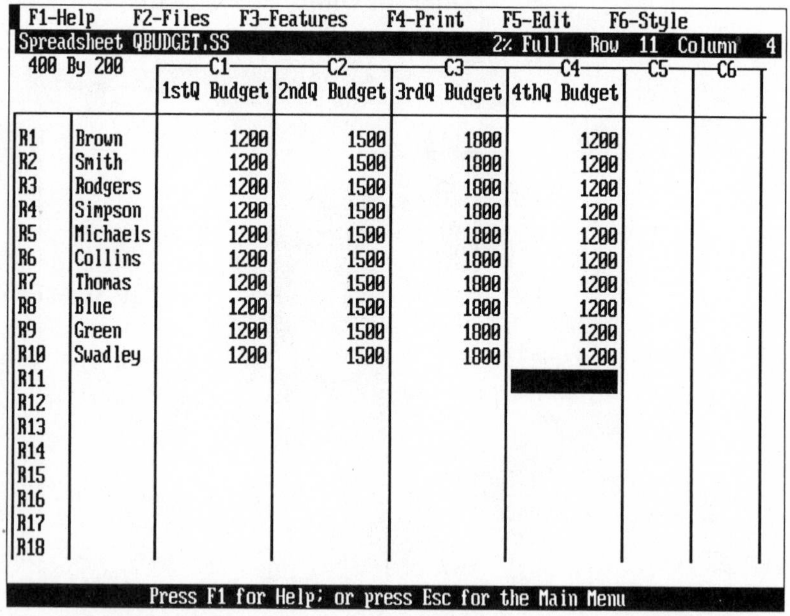

```
┌─────────────────────────────────────────────────────────────────────┐
│ F1-Help    F2-Files   F3-Features    F4-Print    F5-Edit   F6-Style  │
│ Spreadsheet QBUDGET.SS                        2% Full  Row 11 Column 4│
│    400 By 200        ┌─C1──┬──C2──┬──C3──┬───C4──┬─C5─┬─C6─┐          │
│                      │1stQ Budget│2ndQ Budget│3rdQ Budget│4thQ Budget│
│  R1   Brown          │  1200 │  1500 │  1800 │  1200 │           │
│  R2   Smith          │  1200 │  1500 │  1800 │  1200 │           │
│  R3   Rodgers        │  1200 │  1500 │  1800 │  1200 │           │
│  R4   Simpson        │  1200 │  1500 │  1800 │  1200 │           │
│  R5   Michaels       │  1200 │  1500 │  1800 │  1200 │           │
│  R6   Collins        │  1200 │  1500 │  1800 │  1200 │           │
│  R7   Thomas         │  1200 │  1500 │  1800 │  1200 │           │
│  R8   Blue           │  1200 │  1500 │  1800 │  1200 │           │
│  R9   Green          │  1200 │  1500 │  1800 │  1200 │           │
│  R10  Swadley        │  1200 │  1500 │  1800 │  1200 │           │
│  R11                 │       │       │       │       │           │
│  R12                 │       │       │       │       │           │
│  R13                 │       │       │       │       │           │
│  R14                 │       │       │       │       │           │
│  R15                 │       │       │       │       │           │
│  R16                 │       │       │       │       │           │
│  R17                 │       │       │       │       │           │
│  R18                 │       │       │       │       │           │
│         Press F1 for Help; or press Esc for the Main Menu            │
└─────────────────────────────────────────────────────────────────────┘
```

**Figure 10-13.** Spreadsheet completed using the copy method.

When you move data using the preceding steps, First Choice automatically adjusts references to cell coordinates and formulas to reflect the new cell locations.

## Adding Comments

As you work on your spreadsheet, you may decide to add comments to the spreadsheet that explain its contents or point out some important fact. For example, on one spreadsheet you might want to point out that sales significantly increased in the 3rd quarter because of a new product introduction. To add comment lines to your spreadsheet, simply move to the cell where you wish to begin the comment.

The initial cell is important and is referred to as the home cell. Although you can type comments that may cross over several cells and column boundaries (the cells widths remain the same), the home cell is where the actual comment is stored. A comment can contain up to 240 characters. When you wish to start a new line in a comment, press Enter. If a cell already contains a value or formula, you can't type a comment into that cell. You must move to an empty cell. Formulas and values, on the other hand, will override a comment when typed into a cell containing a comment. All other parts of a comment will remain intact unless you enter a value or formula within the home cell of the comment. In this case, the comment will be lost. See Figure 10-14 for an example of a comment that provides further explanation of expenses.

## Setting a Default Spreadsheet

As you begin working with spreadsheets on a daily basis, you might discover that you use one type of spreadsheet for most of your work. For example, suppose you use a spreadsheet to track daily sales and inventory. Once you create this spreadsheet the first time, you can use the **Make this spreadsheet the default** command from the Files menu to save all the specific settings of the current spreadsheet as the default spreadsheet. Then, instead of either recreating the same spreadsheet settings each time you begin to work, or searching through the spreadsheet files column in the Directory Assistant, you can simply refer to the Other column and open the default spreadsheet file.

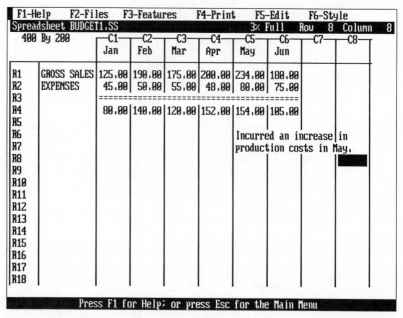

| F1-Help | F2-Files | F3-Features | F4-Print | F5-Edit | F6-Style |
| --- | --- | --- | --- | --- | --- |

Spreadsheet BUDGET1.SS                                    3% Full   Row   8   Column   8

| 400 By 200 | | C1 Jan | C2 Feb | C3 Mar | C4 Apr | C5 May | C6 Jun | C7 | C8 |
| --- | --- | --- | --- | --- | --- | --- | --- | --- | --- |
| R1 | GROSS SALES | 125.00 | 190.00 | 175.00 | 200.00 | 234.00 | 180.00 | | |
| R2 | EXPENSES | 45.00 | 50.00 | 55.00 | 48.00 | 80.00 | 75.00 | | |
| R3 | | ============================================ | | | | | | | |
| R4 | | 80.00 | 140.00 | 120.00 | 152.00 | 154.00 | 105.00 | | |
| R5 | | | | | | | | | |
| R6 | | | | | | Incurred an increase | in | |
| R7 | | | | | | production costs in May. | | |
| R8 | | | | | | | | | |
| R9 | | | | | | | | | |
| R10 | | | | | | | | | |
| R11 | | | | | | | | | |
| R12 | | | | | | | | | |
| R13 | | | | | | | | | |
| R14 | | | | | | | | | |
| R15 | | | | | | | | | |
| R16 | | | | | | | | | |
| R17 | | | | | | | | | |
| R18 | | | | | | | | | |

Press F1 for Help; or press Esc for the Main Menu

**Figure 10-14.** A spreadsheet with comments to help others understand.

*Default files are always stored on a hard disk in the same directory as the First Choice program files.*

As shown in Figure 10-15, the current default file will appear in the Other column in the Directory Assistant as FIRST.DFT. The .DFT extension identifies this file as default. (You can also choose a word-processing or graphic file as the default file using a similar command found within the File menu of those applications.)

To make a file the default file, complete these steps:

1. Open the file that you wish to make the default file.

2. Open the Files menu and choose **Make this spreadsheet the default**. Keep in mind that each time you make changes to the default file and you wish to retain those changes as default, you must choose the **Make this spreadsheet the default** command again. Since the file name extension is .DFT, First Choice will only recognize this file as the default.

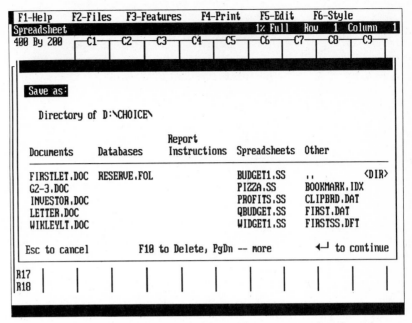

**Figure 10-15.** The default spreadsheet file appears under the Other column.

# Merging Your Spreadsheets

First Choice lets you fully integrate files from one application to another. For example, in Chapter 14 you will learn how to move spreadsheet data into a word processing file, place a database report into a document, and place a graph created with the First Choice graphics feature into a document. You can also use this same integration feature to move data from one spreadsheet to another—or even import data from a different type of spreadsheet file, such as Lotus 1-2-3.

You can easily move data from one First Choice spreadsheet file to another with the help of the clipboard. For example, you can use the procedures to move or copy a range of cells from an existing spreadsheet to the clipboard, open a new or existing spreadsheet file, and then paste the contents of the clipboard into the new file. Each time you make changes to a file, remember to save those changes before you close one file and open another. Using the clipboard to merge file contents only works when both files are the same format, First Choice spreadsheet files. (Note: First Choice offers greater flexibility by allowing you to open and use Lotus 1-2-3 files with the .WKS or .WK1 file format extensions. For many businesses, Lotus 1-2-3 files are recognized as a standard.)

*To learn how to save the incoming file in ASCII format, consult the documentation that was packaged with that particular software.*

Now suppose you wish to merge the data of two files with different file formats (for example, a Microsoft Excel spreadsheet file and a First Choice spreadsheet file). To merge the files, you must import the contents of the other program's spreadsheet file into First Choice as an ASCII file. *ASCII*, or American Standard Code for Information Interchange, is a file format that most programs recognize. When you merge the contents of one spreadsheet into another, the contents are placed at the cursor location and into the cell range to the right. When a carriage return is encountered, the merge starts placing the data in the next row, from the cursor column location to the right.

In order for the First Choice file to know where to put the data from an ASCII file, that is (what data goes into what cell), the data must be separated in some way. The data in an ASCII file is separated or delimited by one of the following methods:

- comma
- semicolon
- two or more spaces
- double quotation marks

To merge an ASCII file into a spreadsheet, complete the following steps:

1. Open the spreadsheet file into which you wish to insert the ASCII file data. Use the **Get an existing file** command to retrieve the file from the Directory Assistant.

2. Position the cursor in the cell where you wish to begin the merge. Remember, the merge will move from left to right and drop down to the next row when a hard return is encountered. If the merge will overlap cells with existing data, be careful, because any existing data will be erased when the new data is placed into the cells.

3. Select **Merge ASCII data** from the Files menu. The Directory Assistant will appear on your screen.

4. From the Directory Assistant, choose the ASCII file that you wish to merge. Press Enter to merge the file at the location of the cursor. If the file is not an ASCII file, then First Choice will tell you that it cannot merge the files into your spreadsheet.

# The Wikley Company Spreadsheet

To get a little practice, let's build the Wikley Company Income Statement for fiscal year 1990. Using the following steps as a guide, your goal is to reproduce the spreadsheet as shown in Figure 10-16.

```
                        The Wikley Company Fiscal 1990 Income Statement

                        QTR1          QTR2          QTR3          QTR4
        INCOME
        Clerical Temps   165,000.00    142,000.00    115,000.00    165,000.00
        Receptionist     108,000.00    110,000.00    201,000.00    165,000.00
        Admin. Assist.   116,000.00    123,000.00    142,000.00    181,000.00
        Accounting Clerks 88,000.00     70,000.00     78,000.00    101,000.00
        CPA Service      357,000.00    175,000.00    150,000.00    249,000.00
                        ------------  ------------  ------------  ------------
        Total Sales      834,000.00    620,000.00    686,000.00    861,000.00

        EXPENSES
        Salaries         342,500.00    342,500.00    359,625.00    359,625.00
        Rent               9,000.00      9,000.00      9,000.00      9,000.00
        Advertising       10,000.00     10,000.00     10,000.00     10,000.00
        Admin. & General   5,000.00      5,000.00      5,000.00      5,000.00

                        ------------  ------------  ------------  ------------
        Total Expenses   366,500.00    366,500.00    383,625.00    383,625.00
                        ============  ============  ============  ============
        NET INCOME BEFORE 467,500.00    253,500.00    302,375.00    477,375.00
        TAXES

        TOTAL NET INCOME 1,500,750.00
        1990
```

**Figure 10-16.** The Wikley Company Income Statement.

1. Position the cursor in R1C1. Type the comment line to describe the spreadsheet. (We skipped the column heading area and placed the comment line in the work area for a uniform look.) As you type, the comment line will cross over cell boundaries. Type:

   `The Wikley Company Fiscal 1990 Income Statement`

2. Move the cursor to R3C1 and enter the following label to represent the first quarter column heading:

   `QTR1`

   Press Tab to move to the next cell, R1C2, and type `QTR2.` Press Tab and enter the appropriate heading in cells R3C3 and R3C4. Use the quick entry method (press Alt-Q to start and Alt-Q or Esc to stop the quick entry process) to enter each successive heading.

3. The next step is to enter all the row headings. Move the cursor to the first row heading cell, R4C0, and type:

   INCOME

4. Press Enter to move the cursor to the next row heading cell, R5C0, and type:

   Clerical Temps

   Press Enter to move to the next row heading cell, R6C0. Continue to enter all headings until your spreadsheet looks like Figure 10-17. When you reach the end of the screen, your spreadsheet will scroll up as you enter new rows of data. Though the existing rows above are not displayed, they are not erased. You can use the arrow keys to scroll back and forth between cells in your spreadsheet.

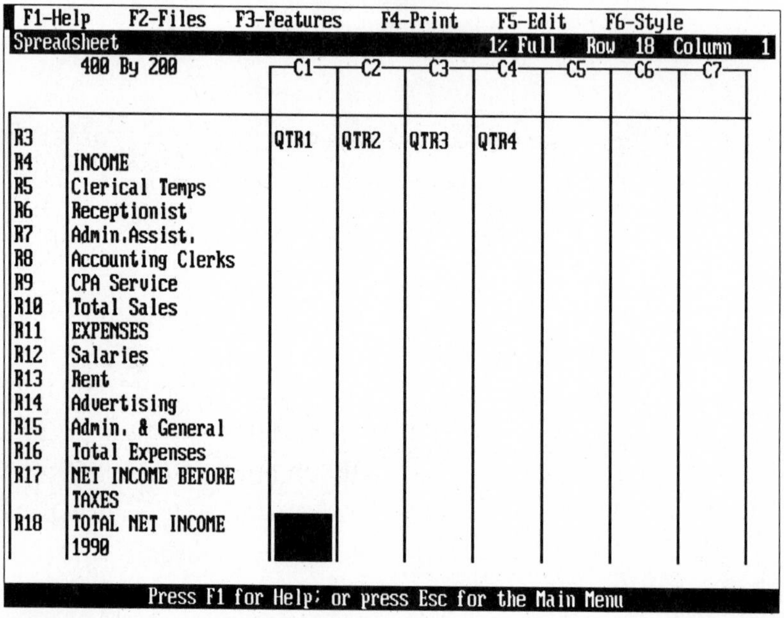

```
 F1-Help    F2-Files   F3-Features    F4-Print    F5-Edit    F6-Style
Spreadsheet                                  1% Full   Row  18  Column   1
           400 By 200          C1    C2    C3    C4    C5    C6    C7

 R3                           QTR1  QTR2  QTR3  QTR4
 R4    INCOME
 R5    Clerical Temps
 R6    Receptionist
 R7    Admin. Assist.
 R8    Accounting Clerks
 R9    CPA Service
 R10   Total Sales
 R11   EXPENSES
 R12   Salaries
 R13   Rent
 R14   Advertising
 R15   Admin. & General
 R16   Total Expenses
 R17   NET INCOME BEFORE
       TAXES
 R18   TOTAL NET INCOME
       1990
            Press F1 for Help; or press Esc for the Main Menu
```

**Figure 10-17.** Spreadsheet with completed row and column headings.

5. Position the cursor in R10C1 and choose **Insert row/column** from the Edit menu. Type R to insert a row and press Enter. The blank row appears above the row labeled Total Sales.

6. Use the same procedures as illustrated in steps 5 and 6 to add blank lines until your screen looks like Figure 10-18.

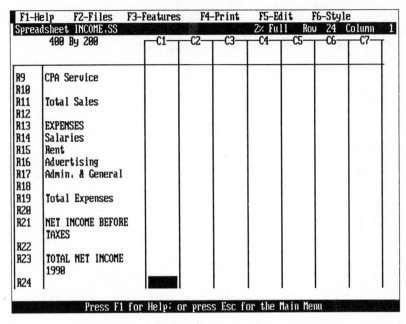

**Figure 10-18.** Add blank rows to separate information.

7. Move the cursor to R5C1 and type the first data entry for Clerical Temps. Type

   165000

   and then press the Tab key. Press Tab or Enter and complete the data entry for the INCOME section as shown in Figure 10-19. Don't worry about the Total Sales row just yet.

8. Move the cursor to the EXPENSES area of the spreadsheet for Salaries and type

   342500

   and then press the Tab key. Press Tab or Enter and complete the data entry for the EXPENSES section. The result should look something like Figure 10-19.

9. The next step is to type the formula to calculate the sum of total income in each of the four quarters. Position the cursor in cell R11C1 and press Alt-F to open the formula box for that cell. Type the following formula:

   TOT(R5..R9)

   Don't press Tab just yet. We also want to name the cell for easy reference later. (If necessary, press Alt-F again to open the

| F1-Help | F2-Files | F3-Features | F4-Print | F5-Edit | F6-Style | |
|---|---|---|---|---|---|---|

Spreadsheet            4% Full    Row   18   Column    1

400 By 200

| | | C1 | C2 | C3 | C4 | C5 |
|---|---|---|---|---|---|---|
| R1 | | The Wikley Company Fiscal 1990 Income Statement | | | | |
| R2 | | | | | | |
| R3 | | QTR1 | QTR2 | QTR3 | QTR4 | |
| R4 | INCOME | | | | | |
| R5 | Clerical Temps | 165,000.00 | 142,000.00 | 115,000.00 | 165,000.00 | |
| R6 | Receptionist | 108,000.00 | 110,000.00 | 201,000.00 | 165,000.00 | |
| R7 | Admin.Assist. | 116,000.00 | 123,000.00 | 142,000.00 | 181,000.00 | |
| R8 | Accounting Clerks | 88,000.00 | 78,000.00 | 78,000.00 | 101,000.00 | |
| R9 | CPA Service | 357,000.00 | 175,000.00 | 150,000.00 | 249,000.00 | |
| R10 | | | | | | |
| R11 | Total Sales | | | | | |
| R12 | | | | | | |
| R13 | EXPENSES | | | | | |
| R14 | Salaries | 342,500.00 | 342,500.00 | 359,625.00 | 359,625.00 | |
| R15 | Rent | 9,000.00 | 9,000.00 | 9,000.00 | 9,000.00 | |
| R16 | Advertising | 10,000.00 | 10,000.00 | 10,000.00 | 10,000.00 | |
| R17 | Admin. & General | 5,000.00 | 5,000.00 | 5,000.00 | 5,000.00 | |
| R18 | | | | | | |

Press F1 for Help; or press Esc for the Main Menu

**Figure 10-19.** Spreadsheet with data for INCOME and EXPENSES.

formula box for this cell). Press Up Arrow to move to the Name item and type the name of the cell as:

Total_Sales1

The result should look like Figure 10-20.

10. Press Tab to move to the next cell. The Formula box will remain open until you press Alt-F a second time to close it. Repeat Step 10 to name each of the remaining cells as Total_Sales2 for column 2, Total_Sales3 for column 3 and Total_Sales4 for column 4. To easily add the formula to compute total income in columns 2 through 4, copy the formula from column 1. First Choice automatically makes the appropriate cell references. For example, move to the cell that you wish to copy, press Alt-S to select it, Alt-C to move its contents to the clipboard, move to the next cell and press Alt-P to paste the contents from the clipboard.

Note: Before you can copy the formula contents of a cell, the formula box must be closed.

11. The next step is to calculate the total expenses for each quarter. To do this, complete the same general procedures as illustrated in steps 9 and 10. Move to the first row for Total Expenses

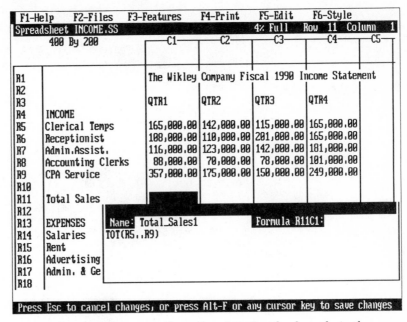

**Figure 10-20.** Naming the cell and typing the formula in the
Formula box.

(R19C1) and press Alt-F to open the formula box for that cell.
Name the cell as Total_Expen1 and then enter the following
formula:

```
TOT(R14..R17)
```

Press Tab to move to the next cell. Name the remaining cells
Total_Expen2, Total_Expen3, Total_Expen4 respectively. Copy
the formula for each of the cells to make data entry easier.

12. Next Position the cursor in R21C1. Press Alt-F to open the
    formula box. Press Up Arrow once and name the cell Gross1Q.
    Press Down Arrow once and type the following formula to
    calculate Net Income for the first quarter as shown in figure
    10-21. Type:

```
Total_Sales1-Total_Expen1
```

Press Tab to move to the next cell.

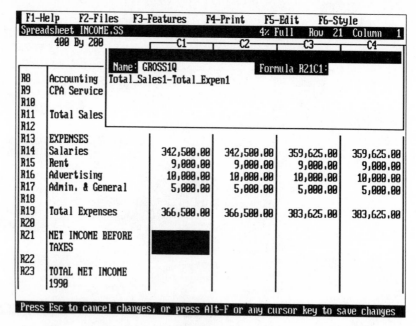

**Figure 10-21.** Entering the formula to calculate net income.

13. With the cursor in cell R21C2, name the cell Gross2Q, then enter the formula for the cell as:

```
Total_Sales2-Total_Expen2
```

Complete the formulas for the third and fourth quarter using the same procedure.

14. Move the cursor to R23C1 and enter the formula to add the net income for all four quarters. Press Alt-F to open the formula box and type:

```
TOT(R21C1..R21C4)
```

Press Tab to enter the formula.

15. The last step is to add some underlines to make your spreadsheet easier to read. Add underlines at rows 10, 18 and 20. Position the cursor in the first cell in row 10 (R10C1) and press the hyphen (-) key until it extends through column 4. Use the same procedure for row 18 and row 20 (but use the equal sign (=) for row 20). Your completed spreadsheet looks like Figure 10-22.

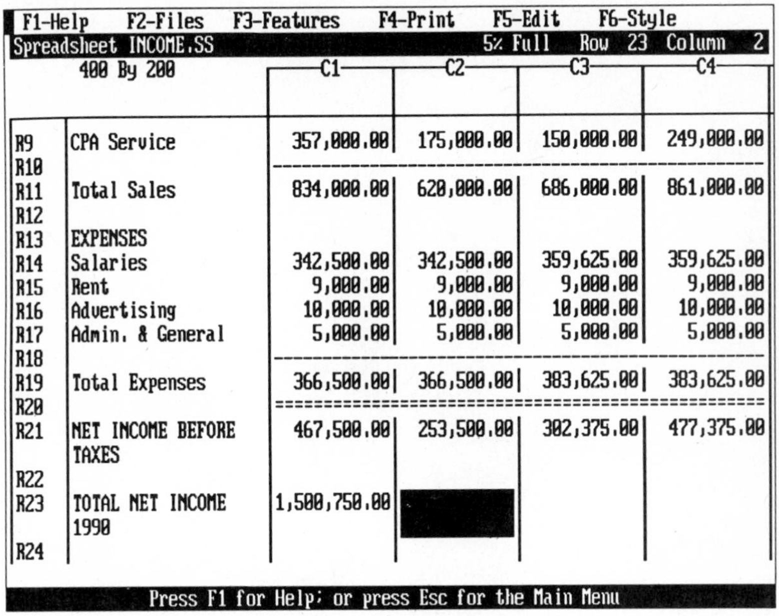

```
 F1-Help    F2-Files   F3-Features    F4-Print    F5-Edit    F6-Style
 Spreadsheet INCOME.SS                      5% Full   Row  23  Column   2
         400 By 200          ─C1─       ─C2─       ─C3─       ─C4─

 R9   CPA Service         357,000.00  175,000.00  150,000.00  249,000.00
 R10                      ──────────────────────────────────────────────
 R11  Total Sales         834,000.00  620,000.00  686,000.00  861,000.00
 R12
 R13  EXPENSES
 R14  Salaries            342,500.00  342,500.00  359,625.00  359,625.00
 R15  Rent                  9,000.00    9,000.00    9,000.00    9,000.00
 R16  Advertising          10,000.00   10,000.00   10,000.00   10,000.00
 R17  Admin. & General      5,000.00    5,000.00    5,000.00    5,000.00
 R18                      ──────────────────────────────────────────────
 R19  Total Expenses      366,500.00  366,500.00  383,625.00  383,625.00
 R20                      ==============================================
 R21  NET INCOME BEFORE   467,500.00  253,500.00  302,375.00  477,375.00
      TAXES
 R22
 R23  TOTAL NET INCOME  1,500,750.00
      1990
 R24
            Press F1 for Help; or press Esc for the Main Menu
```

**Figure 10-22.** Spreadsheet calculating Net Income for 1990.

# Graphing Your Spreadsheet

First Choice lets you graph your spreadsheet data or create graphs independently with the graphics application feature. In this section, we will review the procedures for using existing information from your spreadsheet to prepare a graph. In Chapter 11, you will learn about using graphics as a stand-alone application, the different graph types, and steps for creating graphs.

First Choice provides two different ways to generate graphs using spreadsheet data. The first way is to simply transfer the data from the spreadsheet to the First Choice graphics application with the clipboard (using the cut and paste feature). With this method, the spreadsheet data is *not directly linked* to the graph. You can change the graph information without affecting the original spreadsheet data.

The second method of creating a graph does indeed link the spreadsheet data directly to the graph. This method generates a graph using the same spreadsheet cell references in the **Choose data for graph** form found in the graphics module. The graph information is automatically saved as a part of the spreadsheet when the spreadsheet itself is saved. In other words, the spreadsheet data and the graph are *directly linked* so that each time you make a change to the spreadsheet data, First Choice automatically updates the graph.

The steps for graphing spreadsheet data using the cut and paste method are discussed in Chapter 11. The rest of this chapter discusses the graphing method that links your spreadsheet data to the graph. The beauty of creating graphs with First Choice using this method is that you can generate graphs based on up to eight different sets of information from a single spreadsheet. Because the information is linked, each time you modify your spreadsheet's data, you can create a different graph to show the results (up to eight graphs) of each variation of the spreadsheet. Then, when the spreadsheet is saved, each of the variations of the graph is saved automatically. The steps generally followed for creating a graph linked to the spreadsheet data include:

- choosing the information to show in the graph
- choosing the type of graph (there are nine types)
- drawing the graph
- saving the graph

## Choosing the Graph Information

Once you have either created a new spreadsheet or retrieved an existing spreadsheet file, the next step to creating a graph is to choose the information that the graph will illustrate. You specify this information by using the Choose data for graph form in the graphics module.

To access the Choose data for graph form, you must choose **Use graphics** from the Features menu. The Graphics menu will appear as shown in Figure 10-23. Next, choose **Select or create a graph** from the Graphics menu and assign a name to the graph describing its nature. A name can be up to eight characters, including the usual letters, numbers, and special characters. (For practice, we are going to plot the quarterly net income from the Wikley Company Income Statement. Use QTRLYINC as the name.) Once you have entered the descriptive name, press Enter and the Choose data for graph form is displayed as shown in Figure 10-24.

Once the Choose data for graph form appears on your screen, specify which data from your spreadsheet you want included in your graph. You may graph up to eight different sets of related data, called *series*, from your spreadsheet. The eight series are labeled A through H on the Choose data for graph form. You specify which cells from your spreadsheet are to be included in a particular series by either

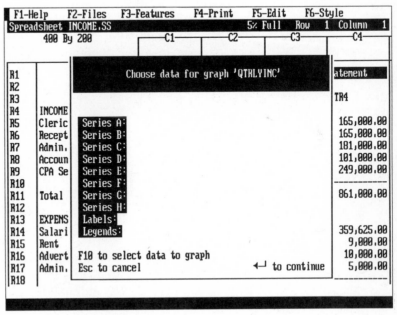

| F1-Help | F2-Files | F3-Features | F4-Print | F5-Edit | F6-Style |

Spreadsheet INCOME.SS      5% Full   Row   1   Column   1

400 By 200     C1     C2     C3     C4

**Graphics Menu**

|  |  |  |  |
|---|---|---|---|
| R1 |  |  | 1990 Income Statement |
| R2 |  |  |  |
| R3 | ▶ 1-Select or create a graph | QTR3 | QTR4 |
| R4 | INCOME | 2-Choose data for graph |  |
| R5 | Clerical Temps | 3-Set graph type | 115,000.00 | 165,000.00 |
| R6 | Receptionist | 4-Enter titles | 201,000.00 | 165,000.00 |
| R7 | Admin.Assist. | 5-Choose options | 142,000.00 | 181,000.00 |
| R8 | Accounting Cle | 6-Draw graph | 78,000.00 | 101,000.00 |
| R9 | CPA Service |  | 150,000.00 | 249,000.00 |
| R10 |  |  |  |
| R11 | Total Sales | 834,000.00 | 620,000.00 | 686,000.00 | 861,000.00 |
| R12 |  |  |  |  |  |
| R13 | EXPENSES |  |  |  |  |
| R14 | Salaries | 342,500.00 | 342,500.00 | 359,625.00 | 359,625.00 |
| R15 | Rent | 9,000.00 | 9,000.00 | 9,000.00 | 9,000.00 |
| R16 | Advertising | 10,000.00 | 10,000.00 | 10,000.00 | 10,000.00 |
| R17 | Admin. & General | 5,000.00 | 5,000.00 | 5,000.00 | 5,000.00 |
| R18 |  |  |  |  |  |

Use ↑ or ↓ to choose a selection, and then press ↵; Or press F1 for Help

**Figure 10-23.** The Graphics menu is accessed from the Features menu.

| F1-Help | F2-Files | F3-Features | F4-Print | F5-Edit | F6-Style |

Spreadsheet INCOME.SS      5% Full   Row   1   Column   1

400 By 200     C1     C2     C3     C4

**Choose data for graph 'QTRLYINC'**

|  |  |  |  |
|---|---|---|---|
| R1 |  |  | atement |
| R2 |  |  |  |
| R3 |  |  | TR4 |
| R4 | INCOME |  |  |
| R5 | Cleric | Series A: | 165,000.00 |
| R6 | Recept | Series B: | 165,000.00 |
| R7 | Admin. | Series C: | 181,000.00 |
| R8 | Accoun | Series D: | 101,000.00 |
| R9 | CPA Se | Series E: | 249,000.00 |
| R10 |  | Series F: |  |
| R11 | Total | Series G: | 861,000.00 |
| R12 |  | Series H: |  |
| R13 | EXPENS | Labels: |  |
| R14 | Salari | Legends: | 359,625.00 |
| R15 | Rent |  | 9,000.00 |
| R16 | Advert | F10 to select data to graph | 10,000.00 |
| R17 | Admin. | Esc to cancel | ↵ to continue | 5,000.00 |
| R18 |  |  |  |

**Figure 10-24.** The Choose Data for Graph form.

typing or selecting the cell references (that is, you type or select the cell coordinates).

*First Choice will ignore any non-numeric data selected in a range of cells. Only numeric information is used to plot a graph.*

If you choose to type the cell coordinates, you simply type the entry as a range. For example, you can type **R1C1..R1C4** to specify the beginning and ending cells in a range. Don't forget to include the (..) symbol to separate the beginning and ending cells in the range. You can specify an entire row (such as R3) or an entire column (C4). You can also specify a group of individual cells where each individual item is separated by a comma (for example, R2C5, R6C4, R8C1..R8C4). Each item the group of cells can be a single cell, a single row or column, or a range of cells. If you use a range of cells as an item, the range can only be one row deep or one column wide.

Another method for specifying the data is to select the cell references by highlighting them. To illustrate this method, let's plot the net income for the four quarters from the Wikley Income Statement example as a bar/line graph. To create this graph, complete the following steps:

1. From the Choose data for graph form, press the F10 key to return to the spreadsheet.

2. Select a range of cells to be included in the current graph (such as the current series). From the example, you want to select the cells containing the net income for the four quarters. Simply position the cursor in the first cell of the range, press Alt-S to turn on the selection mode, and then move the cursor with the cursor keys to highlight the rest of the desired range. Mouse users can also point and drag to select the range.

3. Once the range has been selected, press F10 again to return to the Choose data for graph form. Notice that the selected range will automatically be entered into the form as shown in Figure 10-25.

Once you have typed or selected your data, you have the option of including *labels* and *legends* with your graph. Labels are the values that appear along the vertical axis (the y axis), and legends appear along the bottom of the graph or x axis. Labels and legends are used to help identify the contents of the graph. You can choose not to specify any cells for labels or legends, and First Choice will do it for you. Or, you can select the values for labels and legends by typing in the coordinates of existing cells. Labels can be strings or numeric values. You can use R0 to specify the row of column headings or C0 for the column of row headings. If you're creating a pie graph, you must enter the label references after Pie 1 Labels and Pie 2 Labels. You can't choose legends for pie graphs.

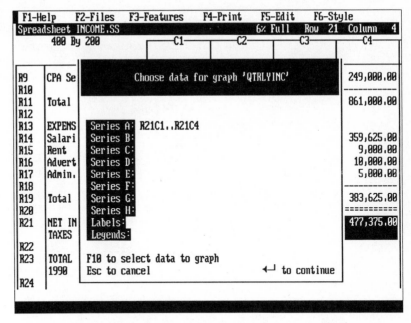

**Figure 10-25.** Selected data is automatically entered.

## Choosing the Graph Type

First Choice provides nine different graph types: pie, line, bar, stacked bar, high/low/close, area, column, linked, and combination. The graph types are divided into four different categories: Bar/Line, Area, High/Low/Close and Pie. In Chapter 11, we will review all of these graph types. For our example, we will use the Bar/Line graph option. To choose a graph type, open the Graphics menu and choose **Set graph type** as shown in Figure 10-26.

## Other Graph Options

Before you draw or print your final graphs, you will probably wish to add some additional modifications that might help the reader better understand the graph contents. You can select from a different set of options depending upon the type of graph selected. However, some simple graphs (such as a basic pie graph) can be completed without the need to add titles and other niceties. In Chapter 11, we will review how to add all the modifications to a graph, using the **Choose**

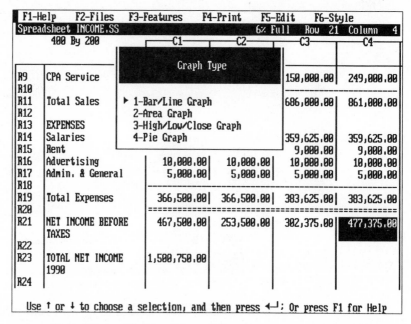

**Figure 10-26.** There are four different categories of graphs.

**options** command from the Graphics menu. For now, you can use labels or legends to add simple explanations to the graphs contents as described earlier in this chapter.

## Drawing the Graph

If you have completed the necessary steps to create a graph, including naming the graph, specifying the data to be graphed (with the Choose data for graph form), and selecting the type of graph, you can choose **Draw graph** from the Graphics menu. Figure 10-27 and Figure 10-28 show the quarterly income from the Wikley Income Statement as a bar graph and pie graph respectively. After the graph appears, pressing any key will return you to the Graphics menu. From the Graphics menu, press Esc to return to the spreadsheet.

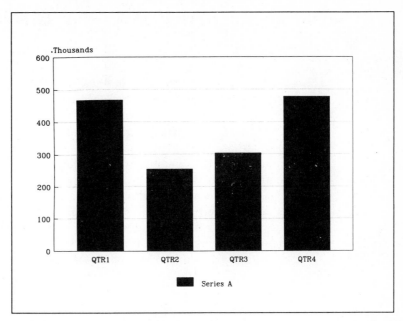

**Figure 10-27.** Bar graph showing The Wikley Company's quarterly income.

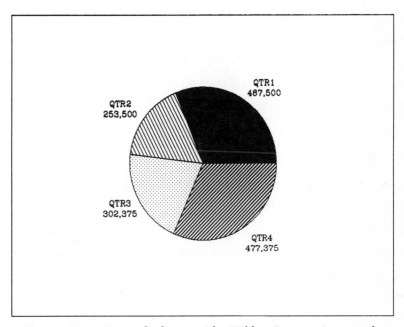

**Figure 10-28.** Pie graph showing The Wikley Company's quarterly income.

## Saving and Retrieving an Existing Graph

Each time you save the spreadsheet, First Choice automatically saves any of the graphs created with the spreadsheet data. In order to retrieve a graph, simply get the spreadsheet file again and then choose **Use graphics** from the Features menu. Then, choose **Select or create a graph** from the Graphics menu. The list of graphs attached to the current spreadsheet file will appear. Then, simply use the cursor to highlight the graph that you want and press Enter (or use the mouse and double-click) to open the Choose data for graph form for that particular graph. To display the graph, choose **Draw graph**.

First Choice also allows you to save a graph in a different format or as a separate file. To do this, open the Files menu and choose **Save the graph as a file**. Choose the format for the file and then press Enter. If you save a graph independently using this method, you can then easily retrieve the existing graph from the Directory Assistant without first retrieving the spreadsheet file it was based on.

# Summary

- You reviewed the built-in library of functions, called keywords.

- You learned that there are two modes for recalculating your spreadsheet: the automatic mode, which is the default, and the manual mode.

- You learned how to change the format or style of a cell's contents (values only), including displaying currency symbols, commas, % signs, numbers in date and/or time format, and the number of decimal places. Further, you learned how to change the style of a single cell, or globally change the style for all cells.

- You learned how to use some basic keys for simple editing of cell contents. For example, you learned how to use the Backspace, Delete and Insert keys. You also learned that Alt-W will erase the contents of a cell.

- More advanced editing techniques were discussed, including how to insert or delete rows and columns in your spreadsheet. You learned how to erase the contents of a single cell or an entire spreadsheet.

- Using the clipboard, you learned how to move (cut) or copy and paste the contents of a cell from one location to another. You also used this method to move data from one file to another.

- You learned how to merge the contents of two spreadsheets and to set the current spreadsheet format as the default.

- Finally, you learned about the steps necessary to create a graph based on the contents of an existing spreadsheet. Specifically, you learned how to name the graph, choose the information for the graph, select the type of graph, draw the graph, and to save and retrieve the graph.

# Creating Graphs and Slides

**In this chapter:**

- The Different Types of Graphs
- Creating A New Graph
- Saving and Retrieving Graph Files
- Printing Graphs
- Creating Slides
- Summary

This chapter shows you how to use the graphics application module to create graphs. You can create graphs based on spreadsheet data, or you can enter data directly into the graphics application module. Specifically, the chapter describes the different types of graphs available and how to create, save, retrieve, and print graphs. In addition, you will learn how to create slides that summarize information. With First Choice, you can either print the slides to make transparencies or display the slides on your computer screen.

## The Different Types of Graphs

One of the neatest features of First Choice is its graphing ability. The old saying, "A picture is worth a thousand words" might be an exaggeration, but it does have merit. You can easily use the graphic module to create a visual aid explaining an important point in a presentation.

Graphs help you convey routine or difficult information at a glance. For example, a letter to the sales staff about monthly quotas has more impact when it includes a bar graph depicting sales levels.

A bar graph is just one type of graph that you can create with First Choice. The following types of graphs are available:

- bar graphs (includes overlapped bars)
- stacked bar graphs
- line graphs, including trend, curve, point or scatter
- combination graphs
- area graphs
- high/low/close graphs
- pie graphs
- column graphs

These graphs are grouped into four different categories: Bar/Line, Area, High/Low/Close and Pie. The type of graph you choose depends on the information you want to present. Your selection can also depend on personal preference. Sections later in the chapter review general suggestions for when to use a particular type of graph. Before you begin, however, there are some general terms used by First Choice in explaining the creation of graphs. These terms are summarized as follows:

*Graph formats*—Many graph types, such as bar and line graphs, use the graph axes as the basic format for the graph. The horizontal axis, called the x-axis, is the line that appears at the bottom of a graph. The x-axis displays the data series (the information you wish to measure), which generally consists of either time (for example, months, quarters, years) or some product (such as gadgets, widgets, goobers). A vertical line, also called the y-axis, appears at the left of the graph. The y-axis provides the graph's unit of measure, such as dollars ($), numbers or percentages. Pie and column graphs do not use an x-axis. Figure 11-1 shows a simple bar chart with products shown by the x-axis and each product's sales level shown by the y-axis.

*Data series*—A data series is a set of information displayed on a graph. Figure 11-1 illustrates the set of data for gadgets, widgets and goobers of the Very Big Corporation. A graph can also show more than one data series at a time, such as the total sales for each product during the first three months of the calendar year, as shown in Figure 11-2. In the figure, the series are distinguished by the different bar patterns.

*Labels and legends*—Labels and legends are used to provide the reader with more information about the graph. *Labels* identify the type of information that is graphed. For example, the name of each product

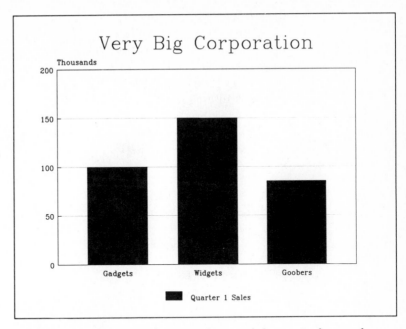

**Figure 11-1.** The x-axis shows products and the y-axis shows sales levels in this bar graph.

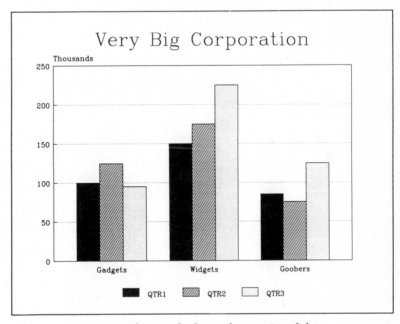

**Figure 11-2.** This graph shows three series of data.

in Figure 11-1 labels the bar with the graphed information. Labels are classified by name, such as months, product names, regions of the country, etc. Think of *legends* as the key to the graph. In other words, the legends tell what the bars in a bar graph mean. Legends are often used when there is more than one data series (set of information) used in a graph, as in Figure 11-2.

## Bar Graphs and Line Graphs

Bar graphs and line graphs should be used when you wish to show the change in data over a period of time. You can also use a bar or line graph to compare two or more series of data. In Figure 11-3, a simple bar chart depicts the revenue of the Wikley Company's clerical temp services for the four quarters of 1989. First Choice offers three kinds of bar graphs: normal, stacked and overlapped. In addition, you can choose between four types of line graphs: line, trend, curve and point.

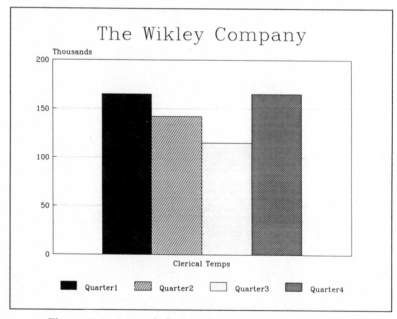

**Figure 11-3.** A simple bar graph comparing data over time.

## Bar-Line Combination Graphs

A bar-line combination graph is a common graph for showing information that varies over time. For example, if you wish to show the budget for revenue against actual revenue for the Wikley Company's temp services, you could show the budget as a second data series as in Figure 11-4.

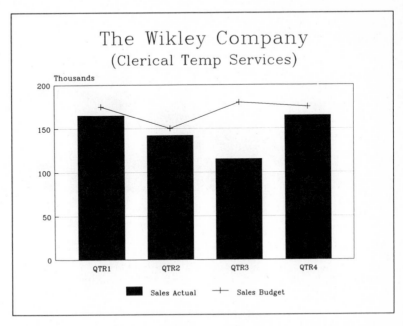

**Figure 11-4.** A bar-line combination graph compares different sets of data over time.

## Area Graphs

You can most effectively represent the data series over many time periods with an area graph. The area graph in Figure 11-5 shows the revenue for two products of the Wikley Company (i.e., clerical and accounting services) over a 12-month period.

## High/Low/Close Graphs

Those of you who work with stock or bond prices might find the high/low/close graph beneficial. In general, you should enter four series of information (A, B, C, and D) in a high/low/close graph to represent the daily high values (A), the daily low values (B), the daily closing values (C) and the daily opening values (D) of a stock or bond. (Entering series C and D is not required). The order for the graph information can't be

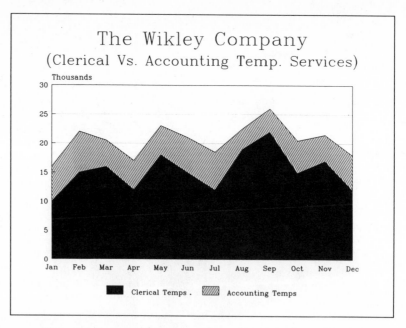

**Figure 11-5.** A simple area graph tracking two data series over
12 months.

changed (series A must always be the high values, and so on). Figure
11-6 is an example of a high/low/close graph. (Notice that the hash
mark on the right of a box represents the closing value of the stock
while the hash mark on the left represents the opening value of the
stock. Naturally, the closing value of one day will be the opening value
of the next day. The top and bottom of the open box represent the high
and low prices for the stock on a particular day.)

## Pie Graphs and Column Graphs

Pie graphs are always fun. Used to show how a part relates to a whole,
pie graphs can also be shown as column graphs. It's easy to understand
percentages when they are depicted as parts of a whole in a pie or column graph. Figure 11-7 includes the pie graph and column graph for a
data series.

# Creating A New Graph

First Choice provides three methods for creating graphs with the
graphics module. As discussed in Chapter 10, two methods involve

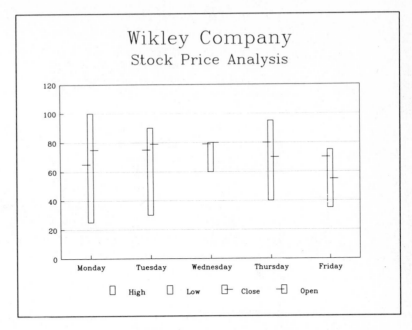

**Figure 11-6.** A high/low/close graph for the Wikley Company.

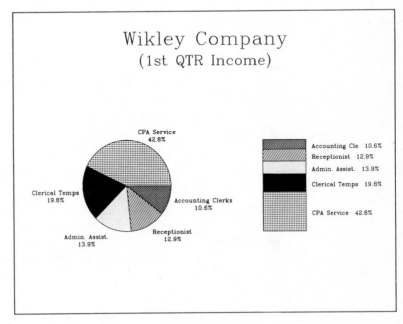

**Figure 11-7.** A pie graph and column graph depicting the same information.

using spreadsheet data. First, you can use the Features menu to access the graph feature directly from the spreadsheet and use the spreadsheet data in order to build your graph. The advantage of this method is that the spreadsheet data and the graph data are directly linked together (see the end of Chapter 10 for more details). Saving the spreadsheet automatically saves the graph generated using this method, as well. To create graphs using the second method discussed in Chapter 10, simply copy the spreadsheet data to the clipboard, close the spreadsheet, open the graph module and then paste the data into your graph as the series data. This approach allows you to change the data before drawing the graph without affecting the content of the existing spreadsheet.

This section reviews the third method for creating a graph—entering new data directly into the graph application module. The first step, of course, is to choose the **Create a graph** command from the Main menu. First Choice displays the opening screen of the graph module as shown in Figure 11-8. You will enter all the data necessary to build your graph into the Graph information form.

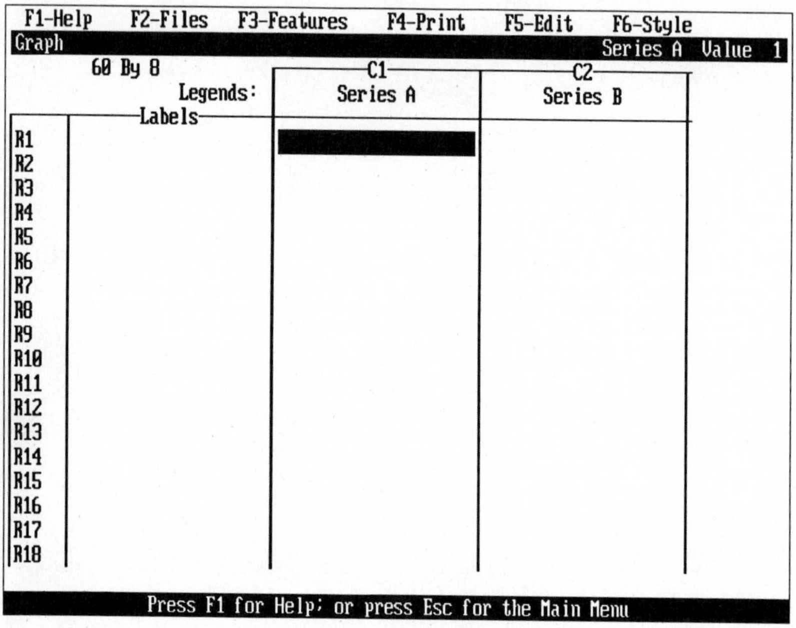

**Figure 11-8.** The Graph Information form resembles a spreadsheet.

Notice that the Graph information form resembles the layout of a spreadsheet. For example, the rows are labeled R1, R2, etc., and the columns are labeled C1, C2, etc. The rows and columns intersect to form a grid with cells identified by coordinates. In order to create a graph, type information directly (or paste data from the clipboard) into the cells of the Graph information form. Depending upon the type of graph you are creating, some optional steps are recommended for completing the Graph information form. In general, the steps necessary to create a graph with the Graph information form include:

- entering labels and legends
- entering the data series information
- setting graph options (such as the type of graph, titles, etc.)
- drawing your graph

The following sections review the steps necessary to create a bar graph the Wikley Company as shown in Figure 11-9. (Printing, saving and retrieving your graph will be described in later sections.)

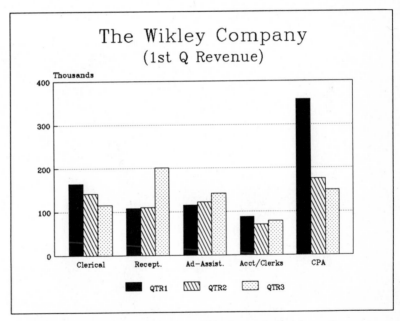

**Figure 11-9.** A bar graph of the Wikley Company's 1st quarter revenue.

## Entering Labels and Legends

Remember that labels describe the information you are graphing. Labels appear along the x-axis of the graph or are applied to each slice of a pie graph. The first step in creating your graph is deciding what information to use as the graph labels. On the left side of the Graph information form, you will find the column named Labels. Enter the labels in the Label column. Generally, a label will be a time period, such as months, quarters or years, or an item, such as a product or expenses.

Legends are generally used when you are comparing more than one data series over a period of time (that is, more than one product over several months, quarters, or years in a bar chart). Legends help you identify the various patterns that appear in a graph.

Enter the labels for your graph in the order that you wish them to appear from left to right across the horizontal axis.

As you enter labels, use the following guidelines:

- Labels can be up to 20 characters in length and may be alphanumeric (for example, Quarter1).

- If you use numbers, the following characters are allowed: numerals 0-9, decimal points, commas and the positive or negative sign. You can also write numbers in scientific notation (1000 is 1.0E3 in scientific notation).

- Use common labels that make sense. Any label that exceeds 20 characters will be truncated. Rows left blank will be ignored.

To illustrate, let's enter the labels for a Wikley Company bar graph. Complete the following steps:

1. In the Graph information form, position the cursor in the first row, R1, under the Labels column. (Use the mouse or press Shift-Tab to move the cursor from R1C1 to R1C0.) Type:

   `Clerical`

   and then press Enter.

2. The cursor drops down to row 2 in the Labels column. Enter the remaining labels for your graph. For our example, enter `Recept.` for row 2, `Ad-Assist.` for row 3, `Acct/Clerks` for row 4, and `CPA` for row 5. When all your labels are entered, the screen should look like Figure 11-10.

   Note: You will notice that the labels in Figure 11-10 are the same as those used in our Wikley spreadsheet introduced at the end of Chapter 10. To make sure the x-axis has enough room for our labels, we abbreviated them further.

3. Move the cursor to the column 1 heading area named Series A. (Use the mouse to click or the arrow keys). This area is called the Legends heading area. If you don't provide legends to your graph, First Choice will add something for you (such as Series A, Series

B, etc.). Legends, like labels, can be 20 characters in length and will be truncated if longer.

4. Press Alt-W to quickly erase the Series A legend information. Then, type the following for the first label:

QTR1

and press Tab. The cursor will move to column 2. Repeat this step and enter QTR2 and QTR3 for the legends in column 2 and column 3 respectively as shown in Figure 11-11.

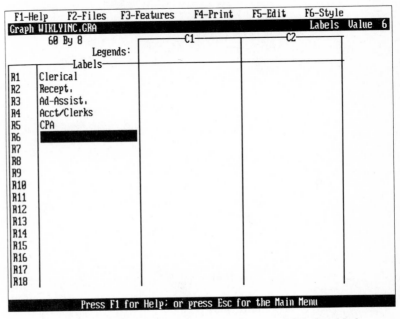

**Figure 11-10.** The Graph Information form with labels added.

Don't forget that you can use the First Choice quick entry feature to enter label or legend information quickly. For example, if you enter the first label as Jan and select it, you can press Alt-Q to activate quick entry and then press Enter to add Feb, Mar, Apr, etc. using the quick entry feature.

## Entering the Data Series Information

Once the labels and any legends are entered into the Graph information form, you are ready to enter the actual data to be graphed.

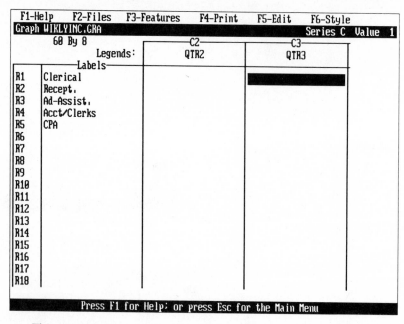

**Figure 11-11.** Legends can be added to the Graph Information form.

The data for the first series is entered into column 1, data for the second series in column 2, and so on. The series data must numerical and follow the same rules for entering numbers in labels as discussed previously. You can enter up to eight different series of data (series A through H), and each series can have up to 20 data points (that is, up to row 20). To illustrate, we will complete the following steps to enter data series for our Wikley Company example:

1. Use the mouse or the arrow keys and type the following number in the first cell, R1C1:

   165000

   and then press Enter. The cursor will drop down to R2 with the number entered. Continue to complete the data series for column 1 by typing the following numbers:

   | For this row: | Type: |
   | --- | --- |
   | R2 | 108000 |
   | R3 | 116000 |
   | R4 | 88000 |
   | R5 | 357000 |

2. Position the cursor in column B, or R1C2. (This step is only necessary if you are including more than one data series in your graph, such as our example). Enter the data series for column 2 as follows: 142000, 110000, 123000, 70000, 175000. Once you complete this step, the Graph information form for the first two data series will look like Figure 11-12.

3. Position the cursor in column C, or R1C3. Repeat the steps necessary to enter the third data series with these values:

   115000, 201000, 142000, 78000, 150000

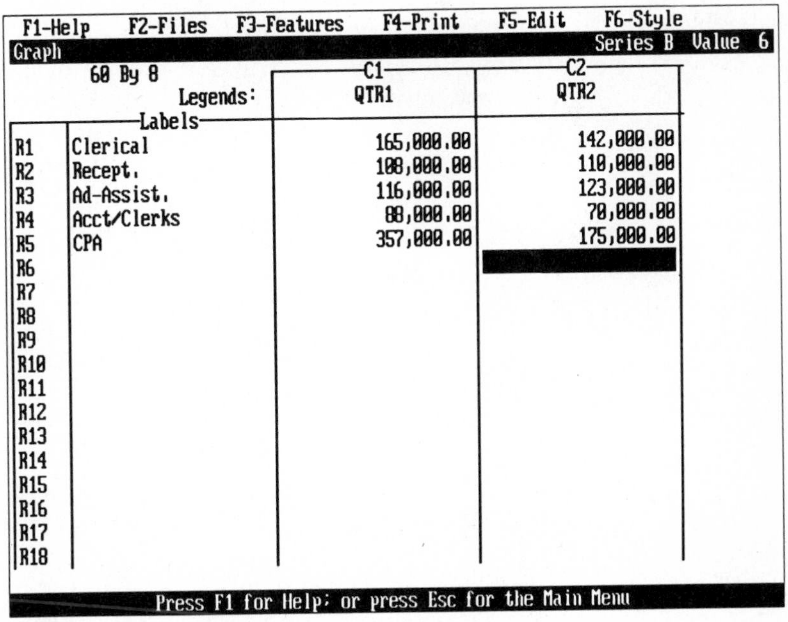

**Figure 11-12.** The data series for columns 1 and 2 entered in the Graph information form.

## Pasting Information from the Spreadsheet

First Choice allows you to enter data directly into the Graph information form as described above, or you can cut and paste data from an existing spreadsheet. To cut and paste, you must first open the spreadsheet file. To illustrate this method using the same information we entered in the previous steps, we can quickly cut and paste the information from the INCOME.SS spreadsheet file we created for the Wikley Company at the end of Chapter 10. Simply complete these steps:

1. Open the spreadsheet file with the data you wish to graph. For this example, open the Wikley spreadsheet file that you created with instructions from Chapter 10.

2. Position the cursor in the first cell of the range that you wish to graph and highlight the entire range. For our example, press Alt-S and then select the data for the first three quarters as shown in Figure 11-13.

3. Press Alt-C to copy the selected data to the clipboard.

4. Press Enter to return to the Main menu and then choose **Create a graph** to open the graph module. (If the graph file already exists, you can use **Get an existing file** to retrieve the file. We will discuss saving graph files shortly).

5. On the open Graph Information form, position the cursor in the first cell of the range where you want to copy the data from the clipboard. For this example, position the cursor in R1C1.

6. Press Alt-P to paste the data from the clipboard to the Graph information form. Since your screen can only show two columns or data series at a time, column C1 will scroll to the left and out of sight. The result will look something like Figure 11-14 to show that all three quarters of data are included in the Graph information form.

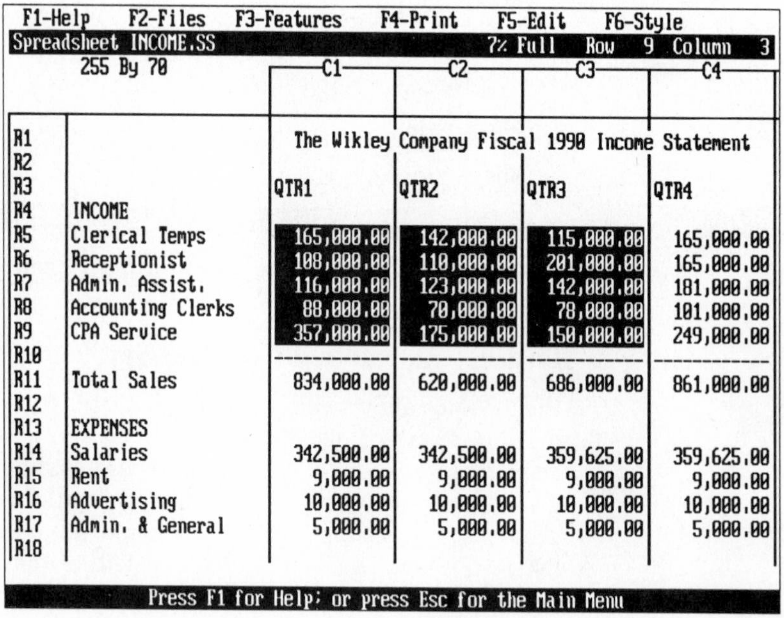

| F1-Help | F2-Files | F3-Features | F4-Print | F5-Edit | F6-Style |
|---|---|---|---|---|---|

Spreadsheet INCOME.SS      7% Full    Row   9   Column   3
255 By 70

|  |  | C1 | C2 | C3 | C4 |
|---|---|---|---|---|---|
| R1 |  | The Wikley Company Fiscal 1990 Income Statement | | | |
| R2 |  |  |  |  |  |
| R3 |  | QTR1 | QTR2 | QTR3 | QTR4 |
| R4 | INCOME |  |  |  |  |
| R5 | Clerical Temps | 165,000.00 | 142,000.00 | 115,000.00 | 165,000.00 |
| R6 | Receptionist | 108,000.00 | 110,000.00 | 201,000.00 | 165,000.00 |
| R7 | Admin. Assist. | 116,000.00 | 123,000.00 | 142,000.00 | 181,000.00 |
| R8 | Accounting Clerks | 88,000.00 | 70,000.00 | 78,000.00 | 101,000.00 |
| R9 | CPA Service | 357,000.00 | 175,000.00 | 150,000.00 | 249,000.00 |
| R10 |  | ---------- | ---------- | ---------- | ---------- |
| R11 | Total Sales | 834,000.00 | 620,000.00 | 686,000.00 | 861,000.00 |
| R12 |  |  |  |  |  |
| R13 | EXPENSES |  |  |  |  |
| R14 | Salaries | 342,500.00 | 342,500.00 | 359,625.00 | 359,625.00 |
| R15 | Rent | 9,000.00 | 9,000.00 | 9,000.00 | 9,000.00 |
| R16 | Advertising | 10,000.00 | 10,000.00 | 10,000.00 | 10,000.00 |
| R17 | Admin. & General | 5,000.00 | 5,000.00 | 5,000.00 | 5,000.00 |
| R18 |  |  |  |  |  |

Press F1 for Help; or press Esc for the Main Menu

**Figure 11-13.** Select the data that you wish to graph.

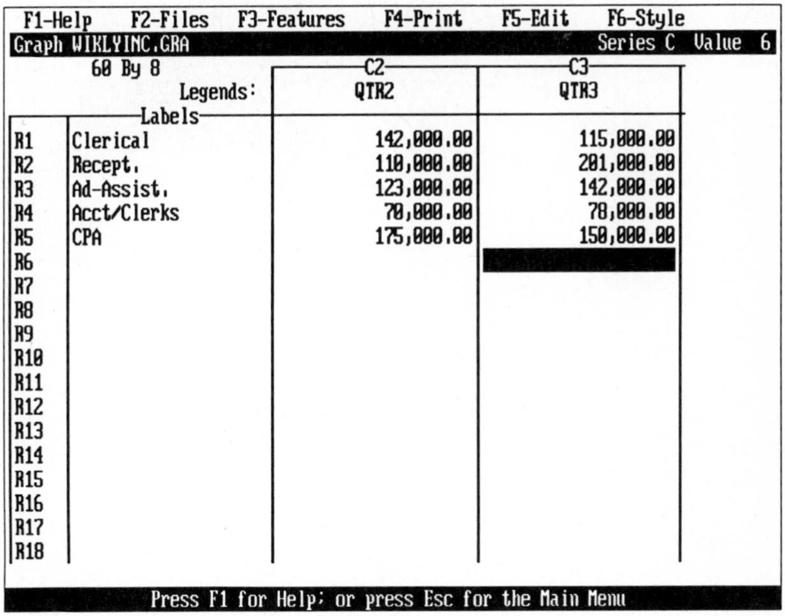

```
 F1-Help    F2-Files   F3-Features    F4-Print    F5-Edit    F6-Style
Graph WIKLYINC.GRA                                    Series C   Value  6
          60 By 8                      C2               C3
                        Legends:       QTR2             QTR3
                    Labels
R1    Clerical                        142,000.00       115,000.00
R2    Recept.                         110,000.00       201,000.00
R3    Ad-Assist.                      123,000.00       142,000.00
R4    Acct/Clerks                      70,000.00        70,000.00
R5    CPA                             175,000.00       150,000.00
R6
R7
R8
R9
R10
R11
R12
R13
R14
R15
R16
R17
R18
            Press F1 for Help; or press Esc for the Main Menu
```

**Figure 11-14.** The entire data series for the Wikley Company Graph.

Cutting and pasting data into the Graph information form is faster than typing the data into the form. Of course, if you wish to link the graph with the spreadsheet data, you must choose the **Use graphics** option from the Features menu within the spreadsheet module.

## Setting Graph Options

You now have entered labels (and legends) and the data series into the Graph information form. Next you need to set the graph options prior to drawing the graph. Specifically, choose **Set graph options** from the Features menu so you can tell First Choice what type of graph to draw and select other options. Soon the Graph Options menu is displayed as shown in Figure 11-15.

### Choosing Graph Types

From the Graph Options menu, choose **Set graph type**. First Choice will provide four different graph types to choose from: Bar/Line, Area, High/Low/Close and Pie.

The default selection is Bar/Line, and for our example, this option will do just fine. Make your selection and then press Enter to return to the Graph Options menu.

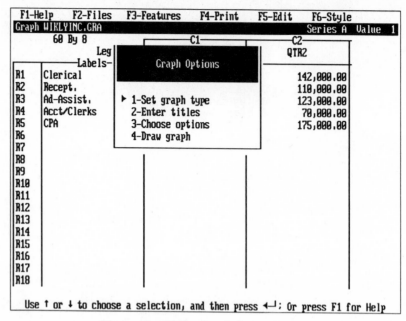

**Figure 11-15.** The Graph Options menu.

## Entering Titles

You can give your graph a title, subtitle and even a footnote to help your reader better understand the origin of the graph. From the Graph Options menu, choose **Enter titles** and the Graph Titles screen will appear as shown in Figure 11-16.

To enter a title for a graph, type something descriptive at the Title: prompt. For our example, type:

`The Wikley Company`

Do not press Enter just yet (if you do, choose **Enter titles** a second time from the Graph Options menu). Press Tab to move to the Subtitle prompt. Type:

`(1st Q Revenue)`

First Choice will center the title and any subtitle at the top of your graph. If you wish to enter a footnote, type it at the Footnote prompt. Footnotes are positioned in the bottom left corner of the graph and are generally used for dates or sources.

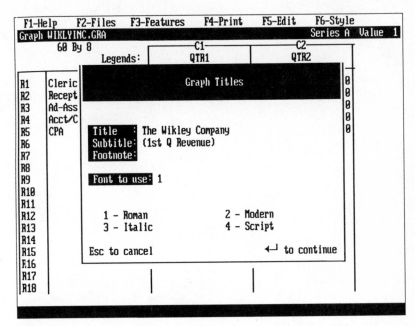

**Figure 11-16.** Entering optional information in the Graph Titles screen.

The last option on the Graph Titles screen is to choose from four different fonts in which to display the title, subtitle and footnote information. You can choose from the Roman (default), Modern, Italic and Script fonts. Of course, your printer must be capable of printing the font you select. Otherwise, use the default Roman selection.

Once all title selections have been made, simply press Enter to return to the Graph Options menu.

## Other Graph Options

Once you have picked your graph type, select **Choose options** from the Graph Options menu, which allows you to specify how the information is to be displayed. The Graph Options screen for the type of graph you've selected appears. Figure 11-17 appears, for example, if you have selected the Bar/Line graph type. At the top of the form, you can specify how to display each data series. For example, the data series in a bar graph can be shown as bars, a line, a trend, a curve, or points. The default setting for Bar/Line graphs is all bars. To change an option in the Graph Options screen, press Tab to move from one item to another and enter the appropriate letter representing the option (i.e., B, L, C, or P). The top portion of the screen also gives you the opportunity to turn a series on and off or to show the data as cumulative data. As shown in Figure 11-17, the Graph Options screen lets you specify these options for up to eight different series (A through H).

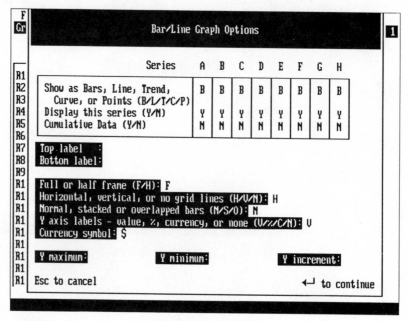

**Figure 11-17.** The Graph Options screen appears when the Bar/Line graph type is selected.

The bottom portion of the Graph options screen (on the Bar/Line Graph Options screen) offers some additional control over how your graph will be displayed. Specifically, you can enhance the appearance of your graphs by:

- adding settings for labels (up to 40 characters long)
- adding either a full or half frame around your graph (half frames are made up of the x-axis and y-axis)
- adding horizontal or vertical grid lines (or specifying no grid lines) for better identifying values
- showing bars as normal, stacked or overlapping
- adding labels to the y-axis (By default First Choice places numbers (values or V) on the y-axis. You can change this selection to % for percentages, C for currency values, or N for no values. If you choose C for currency, you can also change the

default $ symbol to any of the 16 available currency symbols as discussed in Chapter 10.)

- specifying at the bottom of the screen the Y maximum, Y minimum and Y increment of values to be displayed on the y-axis

For our example, the default options selected for the Graph Options screen will do just fine (see Figure 11-17). However, if you choose a different type of graph, the Graph Options screen may offer some other choices. For example, the Pie Graph Options screen appears as shown in Figure 11-18. The Pie Graph Options allow you to display the graph as an ordinary pie or a column pie graph. You can even display the same graph as both a pie and a column on the same graph (see Figure 11-7). If you have more than one data series, you can show two pies, link the pies, and even compare related slices of each pie in a separate pie. You can also sort the slices of a pie.

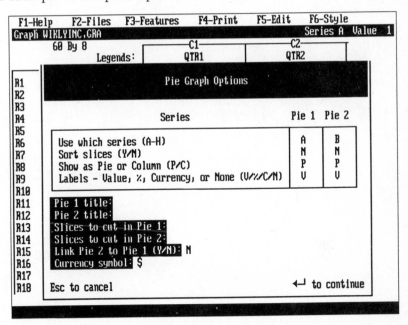

**Figure 11-18.** The Pie Graph Options screen.

## Drawing Your Graph

Now that you have completed the Graph Information form and set all the graph options, the next step is to preview how your graph will look when drawn. To do this, simply choose **Draw graph** from either

You must have a color or monochrome graphics card to display graphs on your screen with the Draw graph command.

the Features menu or the last option on the Graphic Options menu. The Wikley Company bar graph should appear (as shown in Figure 11-9). After your graph appears, you can return to the Graph information form by pressing Esc. Pressing any key will return you to the previous screen (either the Graphic Options menu or the Graph information form).

# Saving and Retrieving Graph Files

Now that you have created your graph, it is a good idea to save it. First Choice allows you to save your graph in a variety of formats. To save the graph, simply open the Files menu and choose **Save a copy of this graph**. First Choice presents several formatting options as shown in Figure 11-19. These options are summarized as follows:

| **Choosing This Option:** | **Does This:** |
|---|---|
| First Choice Graph | Saves the graph as a .GRA file. This file is only compatible with First Choice. |
| *Graph format/ Professional Write | Inserts the graph into either a First Choice or Professional Write document file. |
| Slide Show | Saves the graph to be used only in a First Choice slide show. |
| Harvard Graphics | Saves the graph for use with Harvard Presentation Graphics. |
| normal or small size | Selects the graph size. You can use the graph with PFS: First Publisher in one of two sizes (normal is approximately 4 by 6 inches and small is approximately 2 by 3 inches). |

Note that if you are going to insert your graph into either a First Choice or a Professional Write document, you will choose the *Graph format option. Before the file is saved under this option, you must also select two other options that relate to printing. Choose between draft, standard or high quality printing. You may also choose to print your graph in color (up to six colors plus black). Of course, the color printing option requires that you have a color printer connected to

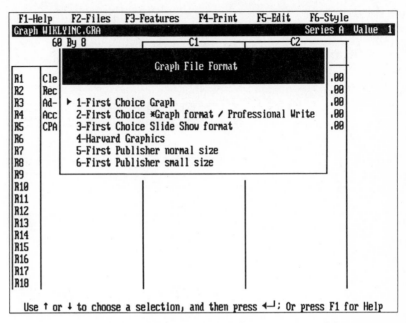

**Figure 11-19.** You can save your graph in a variety of formats.

your system. One last point. All current information for using your printer is saved in the *Graph format file. If you change your printer setup (that is, if you change printers via the Set up equipment option on the Main menu), you will need to go back and save the graph data a second time with *Graph format.

Once you select the graph format, type a name for the graph. You don't need to add the extension since First Choice will do it automatically. (Keep in mind, though, that if you save the graph in a format other than the standard First Choice .GRA format, you can't work on it again with First Choice.) To retrieve the saved graph file, choose **Get an existing file** from the Main menu and select the graph file from the Other column in the Directory Assistant. If you modify your graph, you can save the file again using the same name, or if you wish to retain the old version, save the graph with a new name.

# Printing Graphs

If you have completed the Graph information form and selected the graph type and any graph options, then you are ready for the last step—printing your graph.

*Make sure your printer is ready to go and that paper is properly installed before printing your graph.*

With the Graph information form for the graph that you wish to print currently on the screen, choose **Print graph** from the Print menu. The Print Graph Options screen will appear as shown in Figure 11-20. If your printer cannot support graph printing, First Choice will tell you in a screen message.

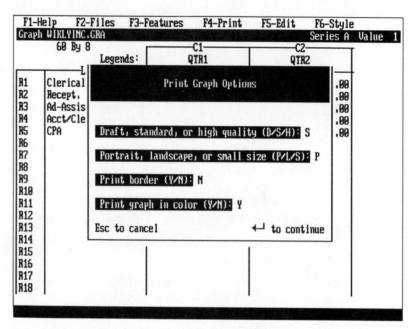

**Figure 11-20.** The Print Graph Options screen.

From the Print Graph Options menu, you can choose the print quality of the graph to be printed. Enter D for draft, S for standard or H for high quality. The higher the quality selected, the longer it will take to print your graph.

You can also specify the size and orientation in which to print your graph. Type S for a small graph. Type P for the default Portrait format, which centers and prints the graph on the top half of the page. Type L for landscape, which will make the graph horizontal and print it as a full page.

You can add a border by choosing Y at the Print border prompt. However, if you chose to frame the graph with the Graph Options menu, you don't need to add a border here.

Finally, you can choose to print your graph in color if you have a color printer (though you can't specify the colors). If you don't have a color printer, different bars in a graph or slices in a pie are printed in black and in different patterns.

# Creating Slides

First Choice provides the opportunity to create presentation graphics in the form of a *slide show*. A *slide* is generally a single page or screen of output that you can use in a presentation. You can either create a series of slides and print them as overhead transparencies or display them on your computer screen. The use of slides in this fashion is often referred to as a slide show. When you use your computer screen to present the slide show, you can control how quickly to move from one slide to another either manually or with a specific timing command to tell First Choice how long to display each slide.

Slides are created with the word processor. You create the text just like any other document, and then you have the option of choosing a different font and the size of the fonts. First Choice provides Roman, Modern, Italic and Script font styles for your text. You can choose sizes from 10 to 444 points (72 points equal one inch) in either proportional or monospaced type.

You can also add graphs, change the spacing or add bullets to spruce up the appearance of your slides. Once the slide is created, you then direct your output to either the printer (for making transparencies) or to the computer's screen.

As you create your slides, keep the information on each slide simple and to the point. Don't use too many type styles or wordy phrases. Each slide has a limited amount of space. You want your readers to be able to pick out the most important point of the slide without marvelling at all the pretty graphics.

## Entering Text for the Slide

Since the word processor is used for creating slides, you don't have many new things to learn. For example, you can use the following steps to create a simple slide for the Wikley Company.

*You can include as many blank lines between text lines or spaces between text and bullets as you wish.*

1. Because you begin with the word processor, choose **Create a document** from the Main menu. An empty screen appears.

2. Move the cursor to the position where you want the first line of text to appear. To keep things simple, if necessary, move the cursor to the beginning of the first line.

3. Type the following text exactly as it appears. Be sure to press Enter after each line in order to insert a blank line between each text line, and tab as necessary. When finished, your screen will look like Figure 11-21.

```
The Wikley Company
New 1990 Services
.Accounting Clerks
.CPA Service
```

Note that the periods in lines 3 and 4 of the preceding steps tell First Choice to precede these two items with bullets. When you show the slide as a display (discussed shortly) or print it out, the periods will be replaced by asterisks or bullets.

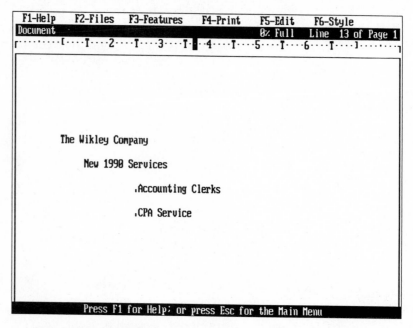

**Figure 11-21.** Text for a slide entered into the word processor.

## Choosing the Font Style and Size

After entering the slide text, choose one of the four different type fonts and select a character size from 10 to 444. You can change the font and size selection using one of the two methods discussed next. To continue with our Wikley Company example, complete the following:

1. Move the cursor to the beginning of the line for which you want to change the font. For this example, move it to the beginning of the first line (The Wikley Company).

2. Choose **Change slide font** from the Style menu. The Change current slide show font screen appears as shown in Figure 11-22. To change the font, size or spacing from the default values, simply move the cursor (use the mouse or press Tab) and type the appropriate letter or value. For our example, type R for Roman, 70 for the character size and P for proportional spacing.

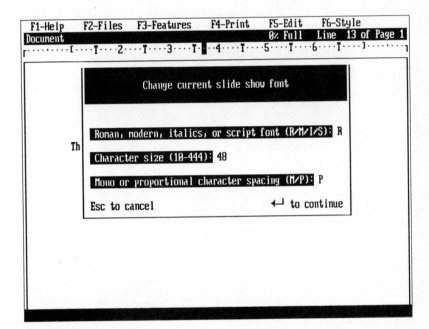

**Figure 11-22.** You can change the character font, size and spacing for your slide.

3. Press Enter. First Choice returns you to the word processor display and inserts the special font command (*font Roman 70 Prop*) into your document at the location of the cursor (see Figure 11-23). The font command simply represents the selections that you made on the Change current slide show font screen.

4. Now, unless you insert another font command, the remaining lines will have the style described by the first font command. Let's add another font command by moving the cursor to the beginning of the second line (New 1990 Services). Select **Change slide font** from the Style menu again. Now, choose R for Roman, 48 for the character size, and P for Proportional spacing. Press Enter when finished.

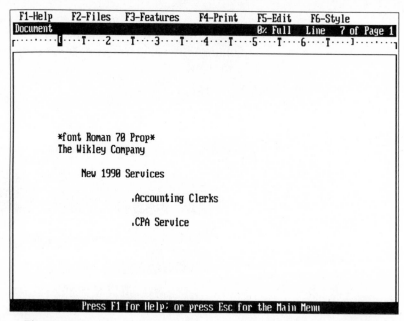

**Figure 11-23.** The font command is inserted into your document.

If you inserted both commands as indicated in the preceding steps, your screen will look like Figure 11-24.

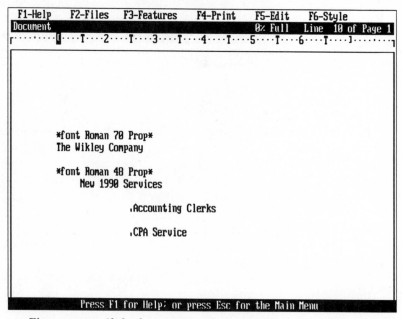

**Figure 11-24.** Slide document with two font commands inserted.

You can use the **Change slide font** option to enter font commands or you can enter the codes directly into your text. Simply position the cursor on a line before the line you want to format and type the font command. For example, if you were to position the cursor on a line before the first line of the slide in our Wikley example, you would type:

★font Roman 70 Prop★

Remember to enter the special character code (★), as well as the spaces between commands. The character code you typed before the first line of the Wikley example tells First Choice to print everything in the Roman font with a character size of 70 and proportional spacing. All text that follows will be printed in this style until First Choice encounters another font command.

## Displaying Your Slide

To see how your slide will look on the screen, choose **Display slides from this document** from the Print menu. The slide appears. To return to the document display, simply press the Esc key.

*To view the contents of successive slides, simply press the Page Down or Page Up keys.*

By displaying your slide on the screen before printing it out or finalizing it for a slide show, you get a sneak peek at how the slides will look. Generally, if you enter too much text on a single line, then it will flow over to the next line. Similarly, if there are too many lines of text to fit on a single page, then the text will automatically flow to the next slide. After identifying such problems when you display the slides, you may wish to go back and adjust the amount of text on the slide in order to make it fit on a single line or page. To make your adjustments, use the editing tools of the word processor just as you would with any document.

## Editing Your Slides

As mentioned, you can use the standard word processor editing tools to change the text in your slides. However, some of the editing tools on the menus are not available. For example, you can show your text in Roman, modern, or script font, but you can only choose the italic style instead of the bold style available on the standard Style menu. If you choose bold for selected text, it will appear bold on the word processor screen, but it won't appear bold when the slide is printed or displayed on the screen.

As previously mentioned, First Choice will automatically overflow text that is too long to fit on a single slide. However, you might not like where First Choice decides to break the text. To override automatic page breaks and provide some control, you can insert a page break at the location of the cursor by choosing **Start new page** from the Features menu. This feature allows you to tell First Choice what text should appear on a slide before moving on to the next slide.

## Saving Your Slides

Once you are satisfied with your slides, you can easily save them just like any other document. To save the text for the slide, simply choose **Save a copy of this document** from the Files menu. As with standard document files, Save a copy of this document will save the entire set of slides created. If you wish to save each slide as a separate document, you would first select the text for the individual slide, and then choose **Save selected text only** from the Features menu. Of course, you would give each slide a different file name in order to retain the original slide document file.

## Printing Your Slides

Before you can print your slides, your printer must be able to print graphics (a message will appear on your screen if your printer can't support graphics). When you're ready to print your slides, choose **Print slides from this document** from the File menu. The Print Graph Options menu will appear, allowing you to choose the appearance of your printed slides. For example, you can choose the print orientation the slides (portrait, landscape, or small). It should be noted that the orientation selection and the size of the printout from the Graph Options menu will have no effect on the display of your slides on the computer screen. Figure 11-25 depicts The Wikley Company slide with a border and in horizontal orientation.

## Adding Graphs to Your Slides

You may decide to add a graph to your slide to provide a little "punch" to your presentation. To add a graph, you must create it using the standard First Choice procedures discussed previously in this chapter and then save that graph file in the slide show format. Graphs saved in the slide show format will have the .SLD extension attached to the graph file name. To illustrate, we will use a simple pie graph created for the Wikley Company and saved in the slide show format. Then, the graph will be added to a simple slide using the following steps:

1. Once you have created a pie graph (and saved it as Expenses), open the word processor and enter the following text:

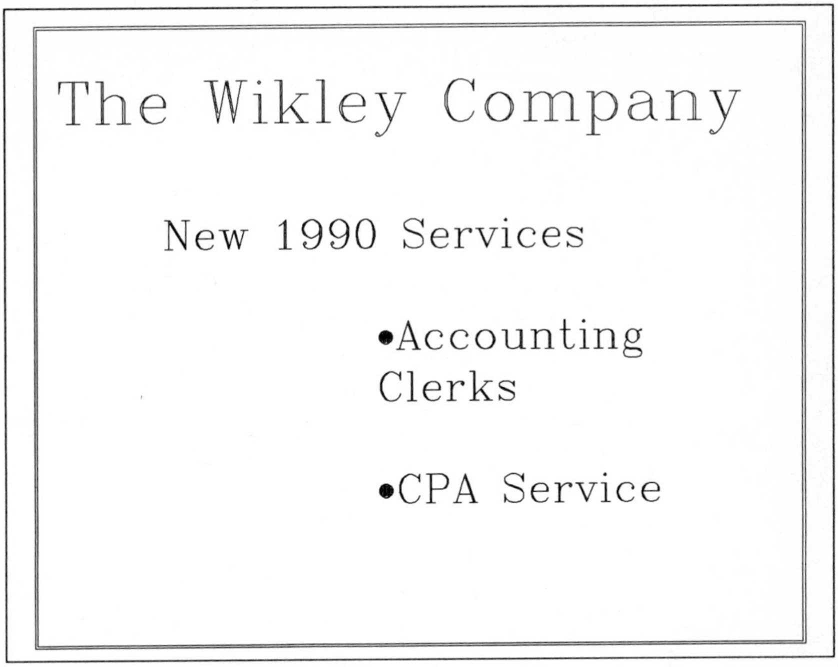

The Wikley Company

New 1990 Services

•Accounting
Clerks

•CPA Service

**Figure 11-25.** Printout of the Wikley Company slide with a border.

The Wikley Company Fiscal 1990 Expenses

2. Position the cursor where you wish to insert the graph. For this example, position the cursor on the second line and then type the screen command as follows:

*SCREEN Expenses*

*When First Choice encounters the *SCREEN graph name* command, it may pause for you to press Enter to move on to the next slide containing the graph itself.*

When First Choice encounters the *SCREEN *graph name** command, it inserts the graph file named *Expenses* at the location of the cursor. If your graph file resides in a specific directory or on a separate disk file, simply include the appropriate path file name. For example, if the file were stored on a disk in drive B, you would enter the command as:

*SCREEN B:Expenses.SLD*

## Creating a Slide Show

After you have created all your slides, you can use the slide show feature of First Choice to display them. To display the slide show, you can either use the keys to manually page through each slide, or you can insert a *timer* command to flip through the slide show for you. Before you begin your slide show, insert a page break between each slide of text in the slide show. To do this, position the cursor at the bottom of the current slide, and then either choose **Start new page** from the Features menu, or simply type:

*new page*

on a line by itself after the text for that slide.

To manually control your slide presentation, choose the **Display slides from this document** command from the Print menu. The first slide from the slide presentation appears on your screen. You can then use the following keystrokes to move manually through the slide presentation:

| **Slide** | **Key** |
|---|---|
| Next slide in presentation | Press Down Arrow, Page Down, +, Enter, Tab, Space Bar or F10, or click the mouse button once. |
| Previous slide in presentation | Press Up Arrow, Page Up, -, Shift-Tab or F9. |
| First slide in presentation | Press Home or Ctrl-Home. |
| Last slide in presentation | Press End or Ctrl-End. |
| Slide the cursor is on in document | Press C. |
| Interrupt slide show and return to word processor | Press Esc. |

In order to automate your slide show, you can insert a timer command that will tell First Choice how long to display each slide in the presentation before moving on to the next slide. To insert a timer command, do the following:

1. At the top of the document for the first slide, type the following command:

*TIMER sec*

where sec is a number from 1 to 255. The number that you enter represents the time delay between slides in seconds. For example, enter *TIMER 15* to delay the time between slides at 15 seconds.

2. Display the first slide of the presentation by choosing **Display slides from this document**. (Remember to first insert the page break command between slides.) The slide presentation will follow with a 15 second delay between slides (or whatever sec value you typed) until First Choice encounters another timer command. You can insert more than one timer command between slides in order to vary the time length between slides.

Once an automatic slide show is underway, you can terminate the slide show by pressing the Esc key. The slide show will continue to cycle from the last slide to the first slide until you press the Esc key to terminate the cycle. You can also press almost any key (except Esc) to override the timer and immediately go onto the next slide in the slide show presentation without terminating the show itself.

# Summary

- In this chapter you learned about the different types of graphs available with First Choice, including: Bar/Line, Area, High/ Low/Close, and Pie and Column graphs.

- You learned how to create a graph. Specifically, you learned how to complete the Graph information form and enter the labels, legends and data series for a graph.

- You learned about all the graph options, including how to choose different graph types, add titles to a graph and draw a graph on your screen to preview it before printing.

- You learned how to save a graph in different formats and to retrieve a graph file from the Directory Assistant.

- You learned how to use the word processor to create slides. Specifically, you learned how to enter text for the slide and change the text's font, the size of the characters and the spacing. You learned how to add bullets and graphs to your slides.

- Finally, you learned how to create either a manual or automatic presentation slide show on your computer screen.

# Utilities

**In this chapter:**

- Calculator
- Bookmarks
- Disk Utilities
- Macros
- Adding to the Main Menu
- Summary

This chapter covers the handy utilities available in First Choice applications. We'll start off by discussing the calculator, a useful utility that can solve fairly complex mathematical expressions and even paste the result into the document, spreadsheet, or database record with which you're currently working. Next we'll cover the bookmark feature, which allows you to jump quickly from one point to another in the same file, a different file, or even a different First Choice application. Then we cover First Choice's disk utilities. These provide easy access to many of the cumbersome disk and file operations normally available only through the DOS C:> (or D:>) prompt (screen message). After exploring the disk utilities you'll learn how to create and use macros. Macros allow you to record an operation's keystrokes so you can "play them back" by pressing a single key. Finally, we'll see how to access your other favorite DOS programs and utilities by adding selections to First Choice's Main menu.

# Calculator

The calculator can be activated by one of several different menu selections depending upon which application you're currently running, as listed here:

| Application | Menu Selection for Calculator |
|---|---|
| Word processor | B |
| Spreadsheet | 9 |
| Database | A |

The calculator's speed key, Alt-A, is the same no matter which First Choice application you're currently running. Therefore, the speed key provides the easiest (and fastest) way to invoke the calculator. The calculator's pop-up window looks the same regardless of which application is active (Figure 12-1).

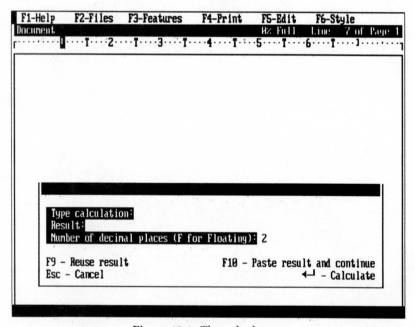

**Figure 12-1.** The calculator.

The calculator window provides space for three different entries: the calculation, the result, and the number of decimal places. The **Type calculation** field is where you type in a calculation. For example, type in the calculation 2+2, as shown in Figure 12-2. After you press Enter, the answer, 4.00, is displayed in the **Result** field (Figure 12-3).

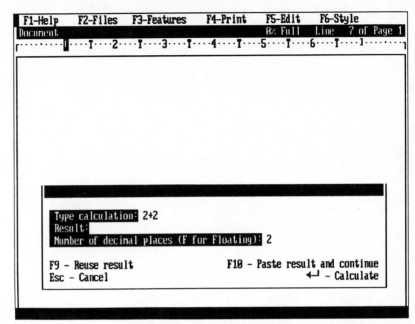

**Figure 12-2.** A simple calculation.

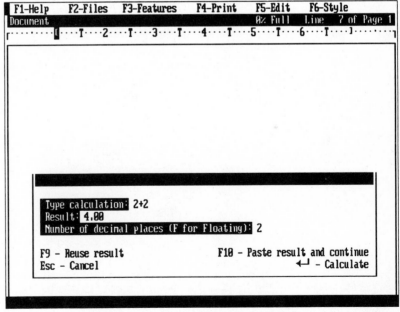

**Figure 12-3.** Result of simple calculation.

You can close the calculator's window at any time by pressing Escape.

## Mathematical Operators

Any of the mathematical operators shown in Table 12-1 may be used in your calculation expressions.

**Table 12-1.** Calculator mathematical operators.

| Symbol | Mathematical Operation |
| --- | --- |
| + | Addition |
| – | Subtraction |
| * | Multiplication |
| / | Division |
| ^ or ** | Exponentiation |

As you might expect, you can specify fairly sophisticated expressions in the **Type calculation** field. Up to 48 characters may be used in a calculation expression. As you may recall from previous discussions (of the spreadsheet and the database), First Choice evaluates mathematical expressions from left to right. Each mathematical operator has a relative *precedence* (order of priority) associated with it, and parentheses may be used to alter the normal order of evaluation. (Refer to the section on precedence of mathematical operators in Chapter 7, *Form Programming,* for a detailed discussion of operator precedence, use of parentheses, etc.) Table 12-2 shows the mathematical operators in order of precedence.

**Table 12-2.** Mathematical operator precedence.

| Operation | Precedence |
| --- | --- |
| ^ or ** | Highest |
| * and / | Middle |
| + and – | Lowest |

The calculation in Figure 12-3 shows the result, 4.00, with 2 digits to the right of the decimal point. This is because you did not modify the default value 2 in the **Number of decimal places** field. Any value from 0 to 9 may be used in this field to designate how many decimal digits you want in the Result value. As the complete field name indicates, you can place an F, for floating point number, in this field. If you do so, one of the two following events will take place:

One decimal digit, 0, will be displayed for all whole number Result values (for example, the Result for $2+2$ is 4.0)

*or*

The minimum number of decimal digits for the Result will be displayed. In other words, all significant digits will be displayed and the trailing zeroes will be stripped off (for example, the Result of $2.12300+3$ will be 5.123).

## Reusing Results

*Press F9 instead of Enter to reuse calculations.*

In Figure 12-3 the answer to our calculation is shown in the **Result** field. Quite often it is desirable to use the result from one calculation in another calculation. For example, I want to add the following numbers:

$$5 + 27 + 12 + 23$$

I could place this expression in the **Type calculation** field and press Enter to find the result, but I would rather add two numbers at a time and watch the running subtotal (Table 12-3).

**Table 12-3.** Subtotal of each individual addition.

| Operation | Subtotal |
| --- | --- |
| 5 + 27 | 32 |
| 32 + 12 | 44 |
| 44 + 23 | 67 |

You can maintain subtotals like those shown in Table 12-3 by entering each addition operation separately and pressing F9 rather than Enter:

1. Set the Number of decimal places to 0.

2. Enter the first addition, **5+27**, and press F9. The result, 32, is shown in both the **Type calculation** and **Result** fields (Figure 12-4).

3. Now we want to add the next number, 12, to this result. Press the Ins (Insert) key to change the cursor to a blinking rectangle, and enter **12+** in the **Type calculation** field. You must press the Ins key

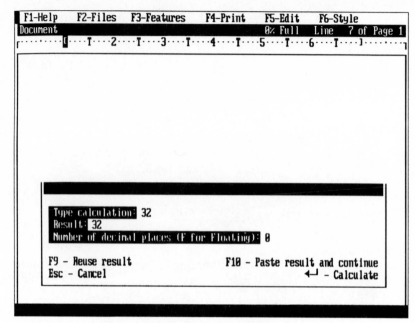

**Figure 12-4.** Reusing a calculation result.

to insert the 12 + in front of the 32; otherwise, you'll overwrite the 32. The **Type calculation** field should now look like this:

    12+32

4. Press F9 and the new subtotal, 44, is displayed in the **Type calculation** and **Result** fields (Figure 12-5).

5. Press Insert; then enter 23+ in front of the 44 in the **Type calculation** field.

6. Press F9 again and the final total, 67, is displayed.

Reusing results via F9 is a handy feature when you have a series of numbers to add, subtract, etc. and you want the calculator utility to function like a hand-held calculator (so that you can see the results step-by-step).

## Pasting Results

*Press F10 to paste the calculator's result in the working copy.*

The calculator also enables you to paste the Result at the cursor's position in the working copy. Suppose you are adding a record for Mary Zale to the Wikley Company Employee database. Rather than specifying a dollar amount for the **Min. Rate** field, the applicant has written that

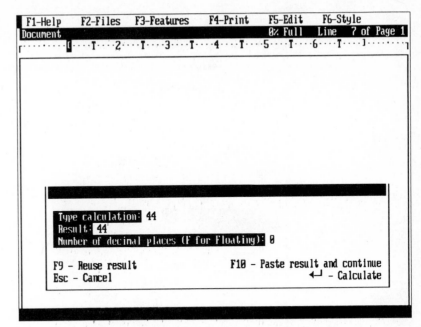

**Figure 12-5.** Reusing another calculation result.

she will "accept any hourly rate which is at least twice the minimum wage." Instead of reaching for a hand-held calculator, you can follow these steps to determine her minimum rate and paste it in the database field:

1. Position the cursor at the **Min. Rate** field in Mary's record, delete any information that appears in the field, and press Alt-A to open the calculator window (Figure 12-6).
2. Now enter Mary's Min. Rate calculation, **3.75\*2**, in the **Type calculation** field and press F10. The result of the calculation, 7.50, is pasted onto Mary's record at the **Min. Rate** field (Figure 12-7).

You can now press Tab to move to the next field on the database form and continue data entry.

## Using Keywords with the Calculator

A list of all of the keywords which may be used in calculator expressions follows. (Refer to Chapter 10, *More on Spreadsheets*, for a complete discussion of First Choice keywords.)

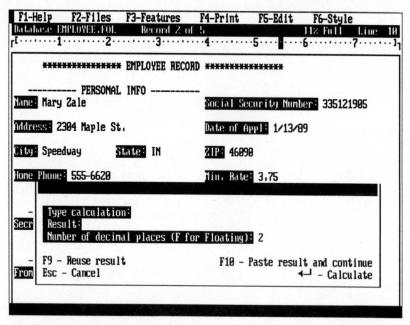

**Figure 12-6.** Opening the calculator window at the **Min. Rate** field.

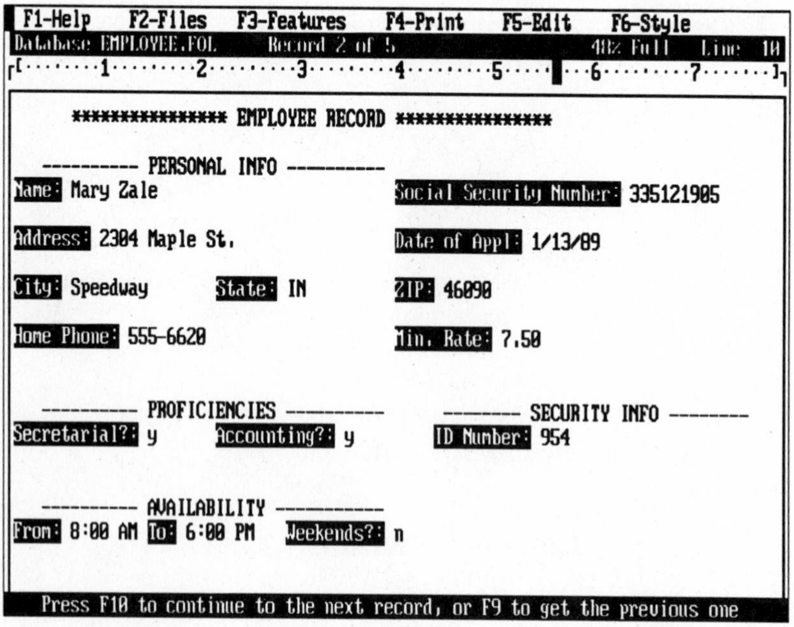

**Figure 12-7.** After pasting the calculator result in the **Min. Rate** field on the database record.

**Keywords available in calculator expressions**

| | |
|---|---|
| ABS | NOW |
| ACOS | PAYMENT ON...AT...OVER |
| ASIN | PV ON...AT...OVER |
| ATAN | PI |
| COS | ROUND...TO |
| DATE | SECOND |
| DATEVAL | SIN |
| DAY | SLN |
| DDB | SQRT |
| FV ON...AT...OVER | SYD |
| HOUR | TAN |
| INTEREST ON...AT...OVER...FOR | TIME |
| LOG | TIMEVAL |
| MINUTE | YEAR |
| MONTH | |

Figure 12-8 shows an example of how to use one of the key-words—the INTEREST ON... expression. This particular expression determines how much interest is paid during the first month of an expensive car loan.

The calculator may be used in any of First Choice's applications. Let's take a look at another utility, bookmarks, which may be used to jump quickly between First Choice files and applications.

# Bookmarks

*You can place bookmarks in all First Choice file types except reports and communications.*

First Choice offers nine bookmarks which may be used to denote specific locations within a file. Follow these steps to set a bookmark in the Wikley Company Employee database:

1. Retrieve the Wikley Company Employee database and press F10 until Kelly Craig's record is displayed (Figure 12-9).

2. Select option 7, **Set bookmark**, from the Features menu. The Set Bookmark dialog box shown in Figure 12-10 is displayed.

3. Select bookmark #1 by entering a 1 at the **Set which bookmark** field and pressing Enter.

F1-Help F2-Files F3-Features F4-Print F5-Edit F6-Style
Document 0% Full Line 7 of Page 1
Type calculation: @INTEREST ON 15000 AT 13%/12 OVER 60 FOR 1
Result: 162.50
Number of decimal places (F for Floating): 2
F9 - Reuse result
Esc - Cancel
F10 - Paste result and continue
- Calculate

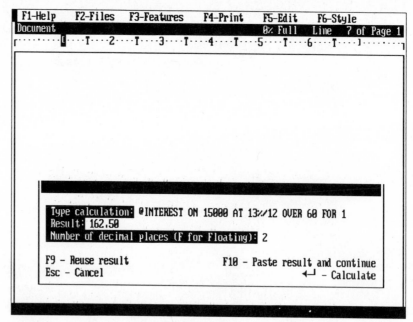

**Figure 12-8.** Using the INTEREST ON... keyword with the calculator.

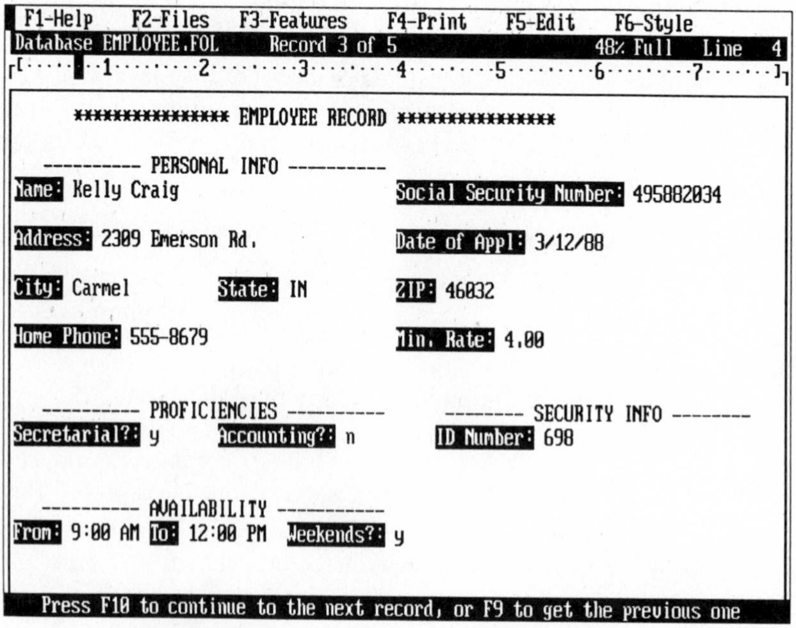

F1-Help F2-Files F3-Features F4-Print F5-Edit F6-Style
Database EMPLOYEE.FOL Record 3 of 5 48% Full Line 4
**************** EMPLOYEE RECORD ****************
---------- PERSONAL INFO ----------
Name: Kelly Craig
Social Security Number: 495882034
Address: 2309 Emerson Rd.
Date of Appl: 3/12/88
City: Carmel
State: IN
ZIP: 46032
Home Phone: 555-8679
Min. Rate: 4.00
---------- PROFICIENCIES ----------
-------- SECURITY INFO --------
Secretarial?: y
Accounting?: n
ID Number: 698
---------- AVAILABILITY ----------
From: 9:00 AM To: 12:00 PM Weekends?: y
Press F10 to continue to the next record, or F9 to get the previous one

**Figure 12-9.** Kelly Craig's record in Employee database.

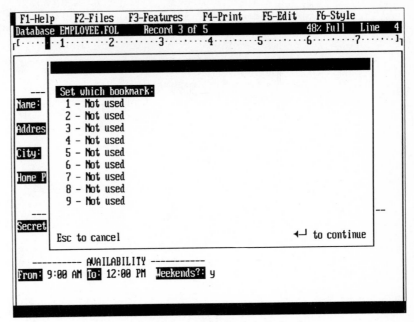

**Figure 12-10.** The Set Bookmark dialog box.

The form screen containing Kelly Craig's record is redisplayed after completing step 3. If you have a color monitor, you'll notice that the K in Kelly Craig's first name is highlighted—this indicates the location of a bookmark.

Now let's step through the database via F10 until John Adams's record is displayed. Follow the previous steps to set a bookmark at John's name, only this time, select bookmark #2. Once you've completed these steps for John's record, the J in his name is highlighted (on color monitors) to indicate this bookmark.

At this point you can quickly jump back to Kelly Craig's bookmark by following these steps:

1. Select option 8, **Find bookmark**, from the Features menu. The Find Bookmark dialog box shown in Figure 12-11 is displayed.

2. Select bookmark #1 by typing 1 and pressing Enter. You are returned to Kelly Craig's record.

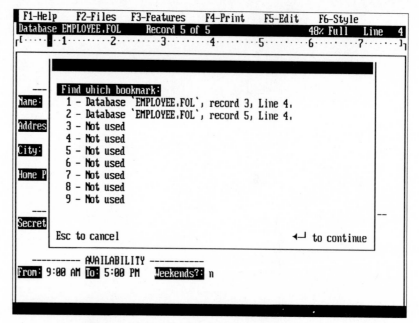

**Figure 12-11.** The Find Bookmark dialog box.

Did you notice the bookmark information provided in the Find Bookmark dialog box? The following details are listed for each bookmark:

- application file type (here, Database)
- file name (here, EMPLOYEE.FOL)
- location (here, record 3, Line 4)

As mentioned previously, bookmarks may be placed in any type of First Choice file except for reports or communications. Let's set one in the INCOME.SS spreadsheet by following these steps:

1. Retrieve the INCOME.SS spreadsheet and select option 7, **Set bookmark**, from the Features menu to display the Set Bookmark dialog box.

2. Select bookmark #3 by entering **3** and pressing Enter.

Now for the real beauty of bookmarks: let's jump from the INCOME.SS spreadsheet to the Employee database by following these steps:

1. Select option 8, **Find bookmark**, from the Features menu to display the Find Bookmark dialog box.
2. Select bookmark #2 by typing 2 and pressing Enter.

A small dialog box with a "Getting..." message is displayed while First Choice switches to the database application. John Adams's record is displayed on the form screen when this application switching process is complete.

The speed keys Alt-1 through Alt-9 may be used to jump quickly to any of the nine possible bookmarks. For example, press Alt-2 to jump to bookmark #2.

*Bookmarks have no effect on the contents of files in which they are set.*

Bookmarks cannot be deleted or erased. All unused bookmarks are shown as "Not used" in the Set/Find Bookmark dialog boxes. I have never been able to restore a bookmark to this "Not used" status once it has been used; this includes deleting the BOOKMARK.IDX file, which apparently contains bookmark information.

A bookmark may be moved to a new position by selecting it from the Set Bookmark dialog box. For example, you could place bookmark #1 in the INCOME.SS spreadsheet, thus moving it from the Employee database.

Finally, these rules must be followed when placing bookmarks:

- Bookmarks may not be placed in a file until that file has been saved to disk.
- A bookmark may be placed on any non-space character.
- No more than one bookmark may be located on a character.

Now let's explore another set of tools accessible throughout First Choice: the disk utilities.

# Disk Utilities

The disk utilities may be accessed by either:

selecting option 9, **Use disk utilities**, from the Main menu

*or*

selecting the **Use disk utilities** option from the Files menu within a First Choice application

The menu shown in Figure 12-12 is displayed when the disk utilities are invoked from the Main menu.

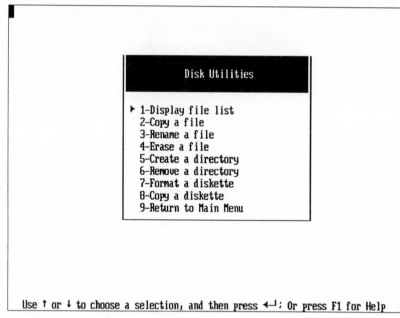

**Figure 12-12.** Disk Utilities menu (invoked from Main menu). Note that there are nine selections.

*Options for diskette copying and formatting are not available in the disk utilities menus displayed from within an application.*

A different menu than the one in Figure 12-12 is displayed when the disk utilities are invoked from within a First Choice application (for example, Figure 12-13 shows the menu displayed when the disk utilities are invoked from within the database application). This second menu (Figure 12-13) contains a subset of the options in Figure 12-12.

This disk utilities discussion covers each option in the full Disk Utilities menu shown in Figure 12-12.

## Displaying File List

Suppose you want to view a listing of files to find out whether a certain file is still on your disk. When you select option 1, **Display file list**, from the Disk Utilities menu, the familiar Directory Assistant screen is displayed (Figure 12-14).

The input request in Figure 12-14 reads "List which files:." Figure 12-14 shows files in all categories (Documents, Databases, etc.). You can list only document files (.DOC) by typing:

    *.DOC

at the **List which files** field and pressing Enter (Figure 12-15).

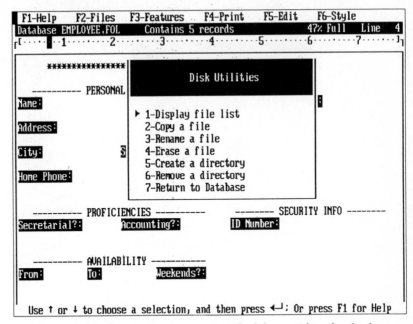

**Figure 12-13.** Disk Utilities menu (invoked from within the database application). Note that there are seven selections.

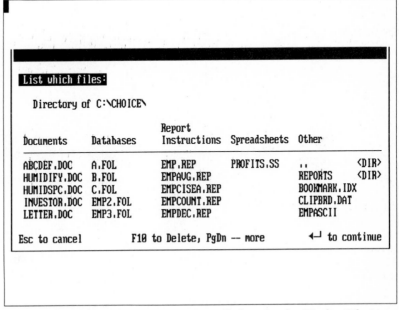

**Figure 12-14.** The Directory Assistant called up by the Display File List option.

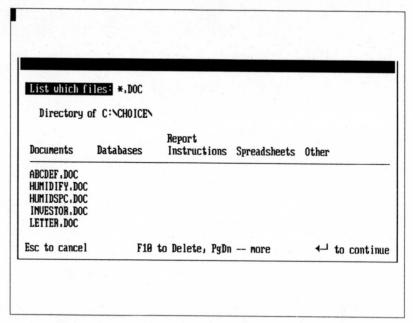

**Figure 12-15.** Screen requesting a listing of .DOC files only.

By the way, you can also delete files via this screen by selecting the file, pressing F10, and then Enter to acknowledge the deletion warning. However, I don't find this disk utility option very useful since it doesn't provide any important feature that's not available in other Directory Assistant screens.

## Copying a File

The Directory Assistant screen shown in Figure 12-16 is displayed when you select option 2, **Copy a file**, from the Disk Utilities menu.

Follow these steps to copy a file:

1. Select or enter the name of the file you wish to copy (also called the *source file*) in the **File to copy** field of the screen shown in Figure 12-16 and press Enter. The Directory Assistant screen that appears in Figure 12-17 is then displayed.

2. Select or enter the name of the new file copy, also called the *destination file*, in the **File to copy to** field and press Enter. A warning message is displayed (Figure 12-18) if the file name entered on screen Figure 12-17 already exists.

```
┌─────────────────────────────────────────────────────────────┐
│ ■                                                           │
│                                                             │
│ ████████████████████████████████████████████████████████   │
│                                                             │
│ ┌────────────┐                                              │
│ │File to copy:│                                             │
│ └────────────┘                                              │
│     Directory of C:\CHOICE\                                 │
│                                                             │
│                         Report                              │
│    Documents    Databases  Instructions  Spreadsheets  Other│
│                                                             │
│    ABCDEF.DOC   A.FOL     EMP.REP       PROFITS.SS   ..      <DIR> │
│    HUMIDIFY.DOC B.FOL     EMPAVG.REP                 REPORTS <DIR> │
│    HUMIDSPC.DOC C.FOL     EMPCISEA.REP               BOOKMARK.IDX │
│    INVESTOR.DOC EMP2.FOL  EMPCOUNT.REP               CLIPBRD.DAT │
│    LETTER.DOC   EMP3.FOL  EMPDEC.REP                 EMPASCII │
│                                                             │
│    Esc to cancel      F10 to Delete, PgDn -- more    ↵ to continue │
│                                                             │
└─────────────────────────────────────────────────────────────┘
```

**Figure 12-16.** First Directory Assistant screen for Copy, requesting the source file.

```
┌─────────────────────────────────────────────────────────────┐
│ ■                                                           │
│                                                             │
│                                                             │
│ ████████████████████████████████████████████████████████   │
│                                                             │
│ ┌───────────────┐                                           │
│ │File to copy to:│                                          │
│ └───────────────┘                                           │
│     Directory of C:\CHOICE\                                 │
│                                                             │
│                         Report                              │
│    Documents    Databases  Instructions  Spreadsheets  Other│
│                                                             │
│    ABCDEF.DOC   A.FOL     EMP.REP       PROFITS.SS   ..      <DIR> │
│    HUMIDIFY.DOC B.FOL     EMPAVG.REP                 REPORTS <DIR> │
│    HUMIDSPC.DOC C.FOL     EMPCISEA.REP               BOOKMARK.IDX │
│    INVESTOR.DOC EMP2.FOL  EMPCOUNT.REP               CLIPBRD.DAT │
│    LETTER.DOC   EMP3.FOL  EMPDEC.REP                 EMPASCII │
│                                                             │
│    Esc to cancel      F10 to Delete, PgDn -- more    ↵ to continue │
│                                                             │
└─────────────────────────────────────────────────────────────┘
```

**Figure 12-17.** Second Directory Assistant screen for Copy, requesting the destination file.

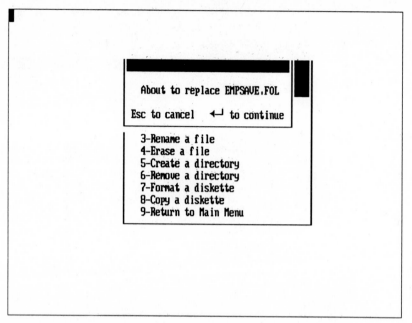

**Figure 12-18.** Copy Overwrite warning message.

3. You can acknowledge the warning in Figure 12-18 and overwrite the existing file by pressing Enter; press Escape if you don't want to overwrite the existing file.

## Renaming a File

The Directory Assistant screen shown in Figure 12-19 is displayed when you select option 3, **Rename a file**, from the Disk Utilities menu.

Follow these steps to rename a file:

1. Select or enter the name of the file you wish to rename in the **File to Rename** field of Figure 12-19 and press Enter. The Directory Assistant screen shown in Figure 12-20 is then displayed.

2. Enter the new name of the file in the **Rename file as** field and press Enter.

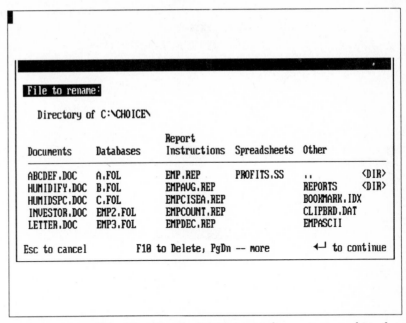

**Figure 12-19.** First Directory Assistant screen for a rename, asking for the file's current name.

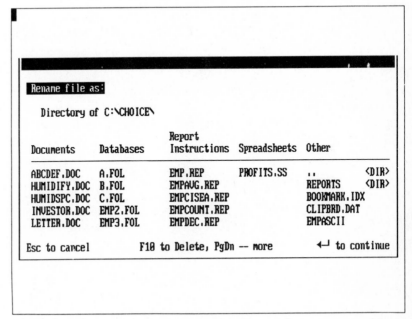

**Figure 12-20.** Second Directory Assistant screen for a rename, asking for the new name.

The name entered in the **Rename file as** field cannot be the name of an existing file. For example, if A.DOC and B.DOC already exist, you cannot rename A.DOC to B.DOC thereby overwriting B.DOC.

## Erasing a File

*Use F10 as a shortcut for erasing files.* The Directory Assistant screen shown in Figure 12-21 is displayed when you choose option 4, **Erase a file**, from the Disk Utilities menu.

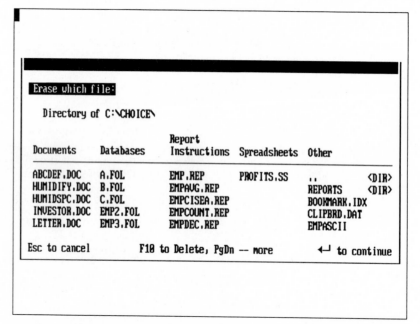

**Figure 12-21.** Directory Assistant screen for Erase.

Follow these steps to erase a file:

1. Enter the name of the file to erase in the **Erase which file** field and press Enter. The warning message shown in Figure 12-22 is displayed as a safeguard to make certain you want to delete the file.

2. You can acknowledge the warning in Figure 12-22 and erase the file by pressing Enter; press Escape if you don't want to erase the file.

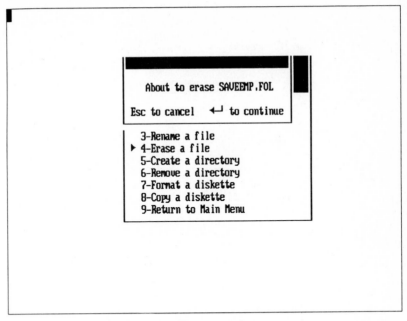

**Figure 12-22.** Erase warning message.

*Note:* There's no need to go through the Disk Utilities menus when you want to erase a file. Remember that you can delete a file at any Directory Assistant screen by selecting it and pressing F10.

## Creating a Directory

The Directory Assistant screen shown in Figure 12-23 is displayed when you choose option 5, **Create a directory**, from the Disk Utilities menu.

Follow these steps to create a directory:

1. Enter the new directory name (e.g., C:\CHOICE\WIKLEY) in the **Directory to create** field and press Enter.
2. You will then be asked, "Okay to create the directory (Y/N)?" Press Y to create the directory or N to back out of the selection.

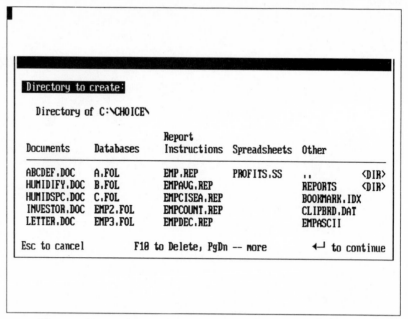

**Figure 12-23.** Directory Assistant screen for Create Directory.

## Removing a Directory

The Directory Assistant screen shown in Figure 12-24 is displayed when you select option 6, **Remove a directory**, from the Disk Utilities menu.

Follow these steps to remove a directory:

1. Enter the directory name you want to delete (e.g., C:\CHOICE\WIKLEY) in the **Directory to delete** field and press F10, not Enter.

2. You will then be asked, "Okay to remove the directory (Y/N) ?" Press **Y** to remove the directory or **N** to back out of the selection.

Unlike most of the other disk utilities, First Choice does not return to the Disk Utilities menu after creating or removing a directory. Therefore, you can create or remove several directories without having to proceed through the Disk Utilities menu each time.

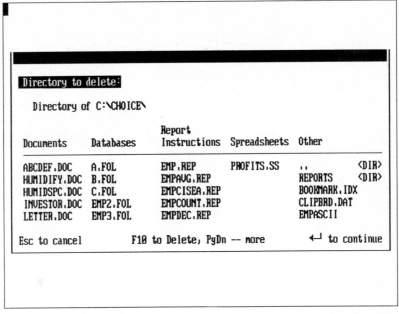

**Figure 12-24.** Directory Assistant screen for removing a directory.

## Formatting a Diskette

*This selection is available only when running the Disk Utilities from the Main menu.*

The diskette format selection box in Figure 12-25 is displayed when you select option 7, **Format a diskette**, from the Disk Utilities menu.

Follow these steps to format a diskette:

1. Enter the drive letter (**A** or **B**) where the diskette will be formatted in the **Drive to format** field and press Enter.

2. First Choice then starts up the DOS FORMAT.COM program and, from this point on, your screen looks as it would if you'd run FORMAT from the DOS prompt. When the formatting is complete, the Main menu, rather than the disk utilities menu, is displayed.

This is truly a no-frills disk utility that allows you to format diskettes only (that is, you can't format your hard disk with this utility). The DOS FORMAT command allows you to format low-density diskettes in a high-density drive. First Choice's diskette format utility uses the drive's default density when formatting a diskette. In other words, you can't format a low-density diskette in a high-density drive via this utility; if you need to perform this advanced type of formatting, you should do it directly through DOS (by leaving First Choice).

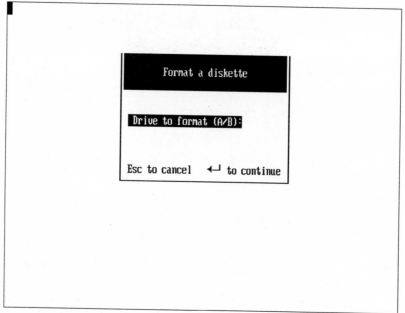

**Figure 12-25.** Diskette Format selection box.


## Copying a Diskette

*This selection is available only when running the Disk Utilities from the Main menu.*

The diskette copy selection box in Figure 12-26 is displayed when you select option 8, **Copy a diskette**, from the Disk Utilities menu. Follow these steps to copy a diskette:

1. Enter the drive letter (**A** or **B**) for the source and destination drives in the **Drive to copy from** and **Drive to copy to** fields, respectively; then press Enter.

2. First Choice then starts up the DOS DISKCOPY.COM program and, from this point on, your screen looks as it would if you'd run DISKCOPY from the DOS prompt. When the disk copy process is complete, the Main menu, rather than the disk utilities menu, is displayed.

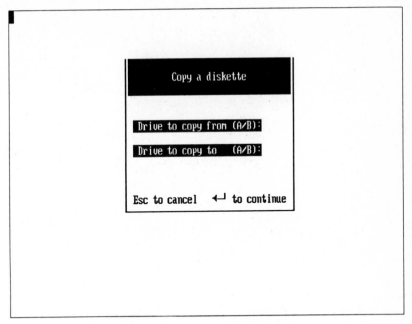

**Figure 12-26.** Diskette Copy selection box.

Note that you can use the same drive letter for both the source and destination. You should expect to do some disk swapping if the source and destination refer to the same drive. Because disk swapping is a cumbersome process, you should avoid using the same drive for the source and destination whenever possible.

## Summing Up the Disk Utilities

First Choice's disk utilities provide you with several tools which otherwise would be available only at the DOS prompt. You may not need to do any more sophisticated disk operations than those discussed above. However, if you do need regular access to more complex disk operations or other DOS functions, I suggest you employ my DOS Shell add-on feature, which we'll look at later in the section on adding to the Main menu. Now let's take a look at a real time-saving utility provided by First Choice: macros.

# Macros

In Chapter 7 you learned how to write database form programs. Remember how cumbersome it was to actually get to the form program screen? First you had to select option 5, **Change form design**, from the Features menu. Then you had to press Enter to acknowledge the warning message which is displayed each time this menu option is selected. Next you had to select option 7, **Program form**, from the Change Form Design menu. Finally the Form Program screen was displayed and you could start entering form program instructions.

Wouldn't it be nice to automate this sequence so that you had to press only one key to go from the form screen to the Form Program screen? Fortunately, First Choice provides you with just that capability, via macros.

A macro is a collection of one or more keystrokes which may be recorded and replayed later by pressing a control key combination. Let's create a macro which will allow us to automate the process of going from the form screen to the Form Program screen.

## Creating a Simple Macro—Form Program

Follow these steps to record the keystrokes for the form program macro:

1. Retrieve the Employee database and at the form screen, shown in Figure 12-27, press Alt-0 (that's Alt with zero) to display the Macro menu (Figure 12-28).

2. Select option 1, **Record a new macro**, from the Macro menu. The Macro Specifications dialog box in Figure 12-29 is displayed.

3. Enter f or F in the **Key to be used to start macro CTRL** field and press Tab to move to the **Macro description** field. (Macros are not case-sensitive, so you can use either uppercase or lowercase F.)

4. Enter the description Edit Form Program in the **Macro description** field, as shown in Figure 12-30, and press Enter.

5. The employee form is redisplayed and macro recording mode is indicated by the "Recording" message in the top left corner of your screen (Figure 12-31).

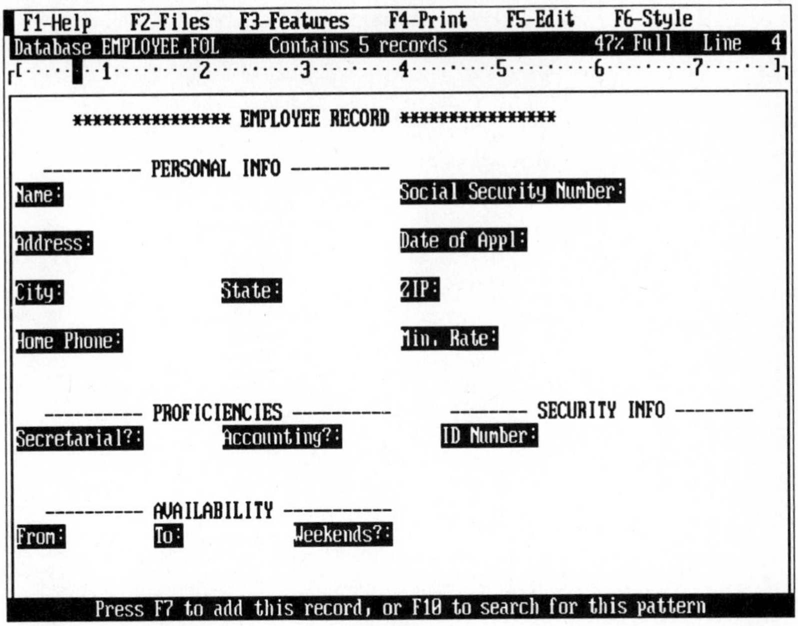

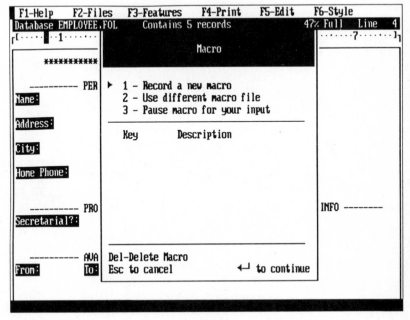

**Figure 12-27.** Blank Form screen for the Wikley Company Employee database.

**Figure 12-28.** Macro menu.

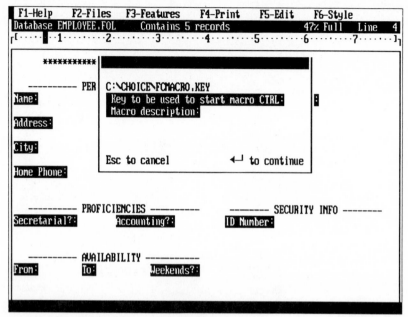

**Figure 12-29.** Macro Specifications dialog box not yet filled in.

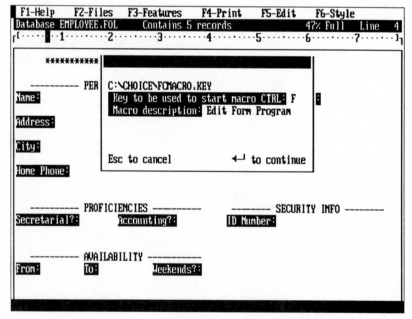

**Figure 12-30.** Macro Specifications dialog box with values.

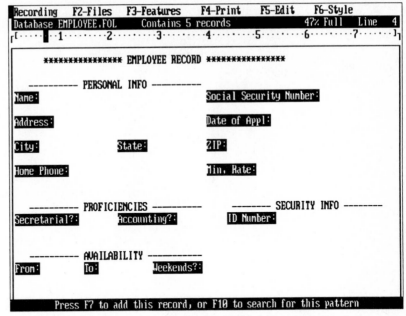

**Figure 12-31.** Form screen for the Wikley Company Employee database (in macro recording mode).

6. Now start recording the keystrokes required to get to the form program screen. First, press F3. This selects the Features menu.

7. Next, press **5** to select option 5 from the Features menu selected in Step 6 above.

8. Press Enter to acknowledge the "Form Design Modification" warning message.

9. Press 7 to select option 7, **Program form**, from the Change Form Design menu. Now the form program screen is displayed (Figure 12-32).

Now you should stop recording keystrokes by following these steps:

1. Press Alt-0 (again, that's Alt with zero) to display the Macro menu shown in Figure 12-33.

2. Select option 1, **End and save recorded keystrokes**, from the Macro menu.

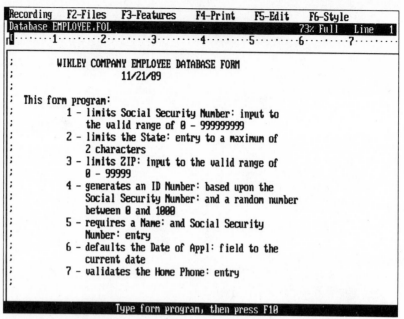

**Figure 12-32.** Form Program screen (in macro recording mode).

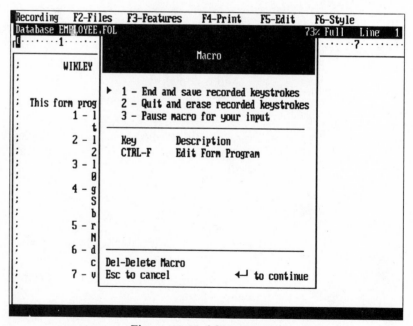

**Figure 12-33.** Macro menu.

The form program screen is redisplayed without the "Recording" indicator in the top left corner. Notice the entry for our new macro in Figure 12-33:

```
Key          Description
CTRL-F       Edit Form Program
```

Now let's verify that this macro really works!

## Executing a Macro

Press Escape to return to the form screen (Figure 12-27), press Ctrl-F (or Ctrl-f), and watch closely as First Choice magically progresses through each of the selections necessary to get to the form program screen. You can tell that First Choice is in macro playback mode by the "Play Back" message in the top left corner of each screen. That's all there is to executing a macro; simply press Control in conjunction with the key assigned to the macro in Figure 12-30.

*Most macros you'll create will only be useful when executed at one particular screen.*

Although Ctrl-F could be pressed at any screen in First Choice, it's probably useful only when it's pressed at the form screen. To prove this point, press Ctrl-F while the Form Program screen is displayed. What happens? Pressing Ctrl-F causes these keystrokes to be replayed:

F3

5

Enter

7

Therefore, when Ctrl-F is pressed at the Form Program screen, the Features menu (because of the F3) is pulled down and option 5 is selected. Wait a minute! The Features menu on the form program screen has only three selections. As a result, the recorded keystroke 5 doesn't do anything. Next, the Enter keystroke is processed, causing option 1, **Find and replace**, to be selected from the Features menu. Finally, the 7 keystroke is processed and placed in the **Find what** field of the Find and Replace dialog box (Figure 12-34). So pressing Ctrl-F at the Form Program screen doesn't provide us with any useful results.

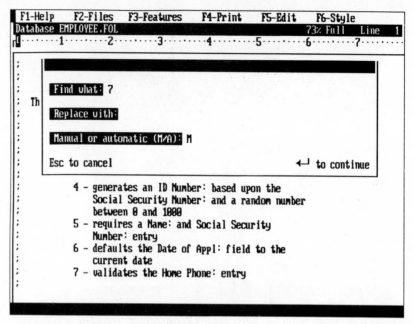

**Figure 12-34.** Find and Replace dialog box.

Later we'll see a few macros that can be used on different screens and in different applications.

### Running a Macro from the Macro Menu

Although it's not as convenient as pressing Ctrl and the macro key, you can execute a macro directly from the Macro menu. With the Macro menu displayed, run a macro by highlighting its entry (with the Down Arrow or the mouse) and pressing Enter or the mouse button.

## Halting Macro Execution

Now that you know how to execute a macro, how can you halt execution if you accidentally press the wrong macro key? For example, rather than letting our Ctrl-F macro continue to run from the Form Program screen, we'd like to stop it before it performs any more nonsense selections. Press Escape at any point during macro playback to halt execution. Macro playback terminates once Escape is pressed—then it's up to you to back out of any menu selections, etc. that the macro already made.

# Pausing for Input Within a Macro

The previous macro performs the steps necessary to go from the form screen to the Form Program screen with no intervention from the user. Sometimes, however, you may want to create a macro for a process which includes a user selection. For example, you may want to write a macro which, when executed at the Main menu, causes a file to be printed. The macro must allow the user to specify which file to print.

*You can place a pause at any point in the macro.*

Fortunately, it is possible to create macros that pause for input at one or more points during playback. Follow these steps to create a quick print macro which may be executed from the Main menu:

1. Return to the Main menu and press Alt-0 (Alt-zero) to display the Macro menu.

2. Select option 1, **Record a new macro**, from the Macro menu; the Macro Specifications dialog box is displayed.

3. Enter Q (or q) in the **Key to be used to start macro CTRL** field and press Tab to move to the **Macro description** field.

4. Enter the description Quick Print in the **Macro description** field and press Enter.

5. The Main menu is redisplayed and macro recording mode is indicated by the "Recording" message in the top left corner.

6. Press 6 to select option 6, **Get an existing file**, from the Main menu, to display the Directory Assistant.

7. Now press Alt-0 to display the Macro menu and select option 3, **Pause macro for your input**. Notice the "Pause" message in the top left corner of the Directory Assistant screen (Figure 12-35) after this option is selected.

8. Select a word processing document (e.g. WIKLEYLT.DOC) on the Directory Assistant screen and press Enter. Notice that the "Recording" message is redisplayed in the top left corner of the word processing screen (Figure 12-36).

9. Now press F4 to pull down the Print menu.

10. Press 1 to select option 1, **Print this document**, from the Print menu.

11. Press Enter to accept the default values in the Print Options dialog box.

12. Press Alt-0 to display the Macro menu.

13. Select option 1, **End and save recorded keystrokes**, from the Macro menu.

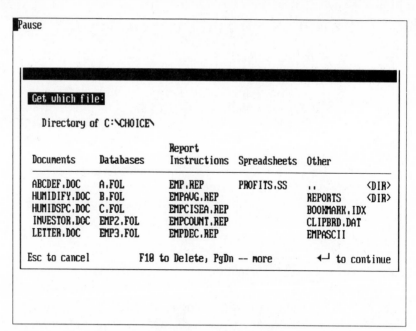

**Figure 12-35.** The macro pausing at the Directory Assistant screen for the user to type in the file to be printed.

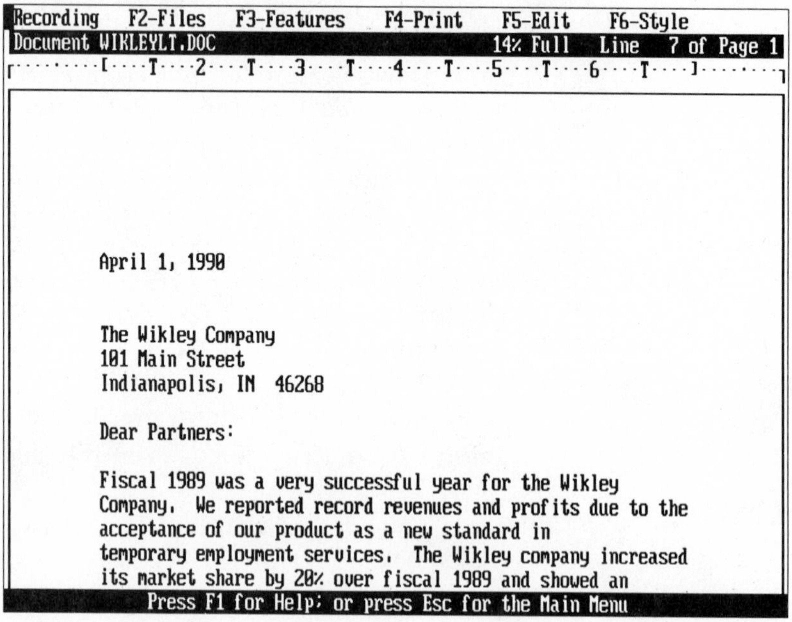

```
Recording    F2-Files    F3-Features    F4-Print    F5-Edit    F6-Style
Document WIKLEYLT.DOC                          14% Full    Line    7 of Page 1
┌·····[···T···2···T···3···T···4···T···5···T···6···T···]·····┐




     April 1, 1990


     The Wikley Company
     101 Main Street
     Indianapolis, IN  46268


     Dear Partners:

     Fiscal 1989 was a very successful year for the Wikley
     Company.  We reported record revenues and profits due to the
     acceptance of our product as a new standard in
     temporary employment services.  The Wikley company increased
     its market share by 20% over fiscal 1989 and showed an
              Press F1 for Help; or press Esc for the Main Menu
```

**Figure 12-36.** Macro keystroke recording resumes and the letter you want to print is on-screen.

Now return to the Main menu and press Ctrl-Q. Select a word processing document to print when the Directory Assistant is displayed (notice the "Pause" message in the top left corner of the Directory Assistant screen during playback). After you select a file and press Enter, the macro resumes playback mode and performs all the steps necessary to print the document. When a pause is encountered during playback, First Choice suspends macro execution until Enter is pressed.

You've seen how this quick print macro can be used to print document files. It can also be used to print a spreadsheet or a database record. This is because the keystrokes for printing spreadsheets and database records are identical to the ones for printing a document (F4, 1, and Enter).

# Rules of the Road for Macro Construction

Now that you've seen how to record and play back a couple of macros, let's discuss a few issues you should keep in mind when building your own macros.

### Definable Macro Keys

You used the F and Q keys in conjunction with Control to execute each of the two previous macros. With the exception of *h*, *i*, *j*, and *m*, any of the letters *a* through *z* may be used to define the macro key in Figure 12-29. In addition, any of the function keys (F1 through F10) may be coupled with Control and used as macro keys.

### The FCMACRO.KEY File

The macro keystrokes you have recorded up to now are held in a macro file named FCMACRO.KEY (a macro file is identified by the .KEY extension). Up to 1,024 keystrokes can be stored in a macro file. Unless you have many lengthy macros, this 1,024-keystroke maximum should be plenty. However, you're not limited to using just one macro file. In the next section, Using Different Macro Files, we'll see how to create and use other macro files.

# Using Different Macro Files

Although it's unlikely that you'll need to store more than 1,024 macro keystrokes, there are other reasons why you may want to have more than one macro file. Our Ctrl-F macro (to get to the Form Program screen) is very handy in the database application. However, now that we've defined Ctrl-F as a database macro, we can't use F as another application's macro key. First Choice lets you have separate macro files because people often want to use one macro key (e.g., Ctrl-F) to perform different operations in different situations.

Follow these steps to use a different macro file:

1. Press Alt-0 to display the Macro menu and select option 2, **Use different macro file**.

2. Enter the name of the new macro file in the **Macro file to be used** field of Figure 12-37 (remember, a macro file must have a .KEY extension) and press Enter.

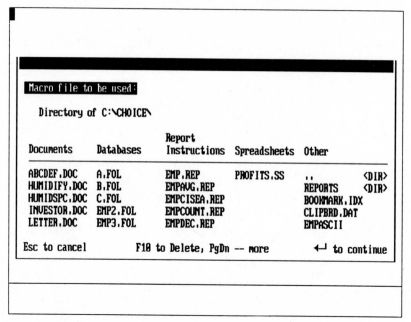

**Figure 12-37.** New Macro File Directory Assistant screen.

*The default macro file, FCMACRO.KEY, is used each time the First Choice program (FIRST.COM) is executed.*

If the macro file specified in step 2 doesn't exist, First Choice will create it for you. After you perform these steps, any macros built (or executed) will be recorded (or played back) to (or from) the new macro file. This new macro file will be used until you either

select a new macro file via option 2, **Use different macro file**, in the Macro menu

*or*

leave First Choice.

## Changing a Macro

There's no easy way to make modifications to a macro recording. It would be nice if First Choice would offer some sort of macro editor allowing you to add an F3 selection here or remove an Enter keystroke there.... Instead, if you want to make even the simplest modification to an existing macro you must completely re-record it. Follow the steps outlined earlier for macro creation and specify the key of the macro to change in the Macro Specifications dialog box (Figure 12-29). Then press Enter to acknowledge the "Macro Replacement" warning message, shown in Figure 12-38, and start recording the new keystrokes.

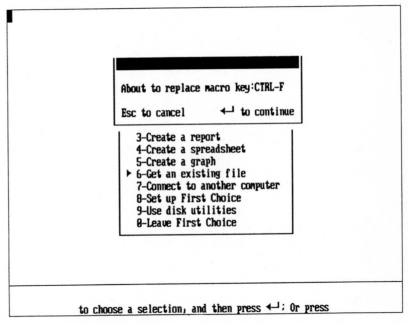

**Figure 12-38.** Macro Replacement warning message.

## Deleting a Macro

Deleting a macro from the macro file is accomplished rather easily:

1. Press Alt-0 to display the Macro menu and highlight the macro entry.
2. Press the Delete key.
3. Press Enter to acknowledge the "Macro Deletion" warning message shown in Figure 12-39.

427

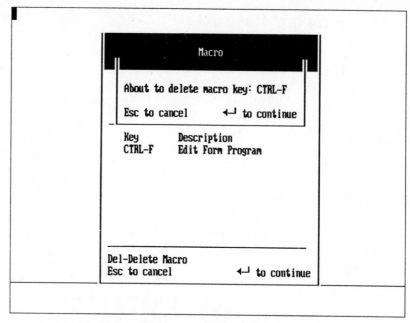

**Figure 12-39.** Macro Deletion warning message.

Now let's see how to add other program selections to First Choice's Main menu.

# Adding to the Main Menu

As many as five alternate selections can be added to First Choice's Main menu. These selections can be used to:

1. Start other programs (for example, WordPerfect).
2. Run DOS batch files (refer to *The Waite Group's Using PC DOS* from Howard W. Sams & Co. for a thorough coverage of DOS batch files).
3. Execute macros.

Let's take a look at how to add each of these selection types to the Main menu.

# Adding a Program

Follow these steps to add a program to the Main menu. We'll use WordPerfect 5.1 as an example, but you can substitute the data for another program if you don't have WordPerfect 5.1.

1. Select option 8, **Set up First Choice**, from the Main menu; the Setup menu (Figure 12-40) is displayed.

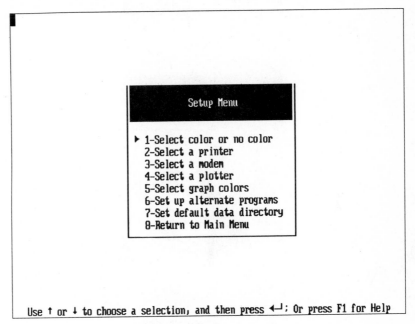

**Figure 12-40.** Setup menu.

2. Select option 6, **Set up alternate programs**, from the Setup menu. This step displays the Set Up Alternate Program dialog box (Figure 12-41).

3. The Set Up Alternate Program dialog box is separated into five areas, A through E, one for each of the possible alternate programs. Enter the values WordPerfect 5.1 and C:\WP51\WP.EXE in the **Program name** and **Path** fields as shown in Figure 12-42, press Enter, and the Setup menu is redisplayed. (Of course, if you're using D or another drive, you'll substitute that letter for the C.)

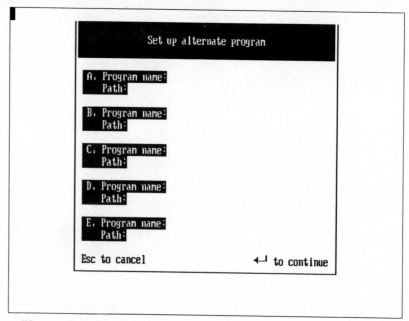

**Figure 12-41.** Set Up Alternate Program dialog box not yet filled in.

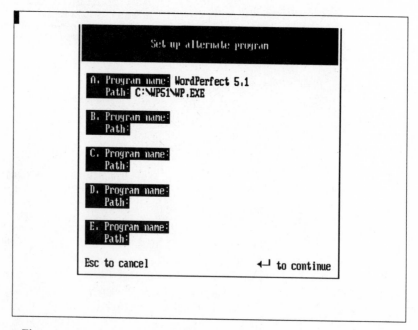

**Figure 12-42.** Set Up Alternate Program dialog box with WordPerfect 5.1 entries.

4. Now press Escape at the Setup menu. The Main menu is displayed with the new selection: **A-WordPerfect 5.1** (Figure 12-43).

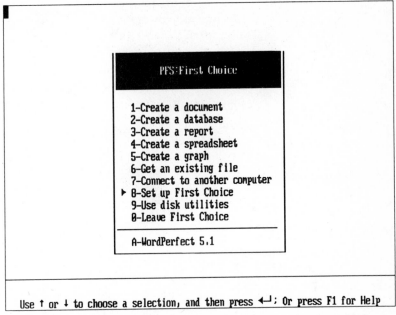

**Figure 12-43.** Main menu with WordPerfect 5.1 selection added.

As you may have guessed, the **Program name** field in Figure 12-42 represents the name of the alternate program as it will appear in the Main menu (here, WordPerfect 5.1). The entry placed in the **Path** field should match the command you would type in at the DOS prompt (`C:\>`) to start the program (here, `C:\WP51\WP.EXE`).

When you finish your WordPerfect session, First Choice will automatically reload itself and return you to the Main menu. If you select option A, **WordPerfect 5.1**, from the new Main menu, First Choice will stop running and start the WordPerfect program (WP.EXE).

## Adding a Macro

Follow these steps to add the quick print macro (Ctrl-Q) to the Main menu:

1. Select option 8, **Set up First Choice**, from the Main menu; the Setup menu (Figure 12-40) is displayed.

2. Select option 6, **Set up alternate programs**, from the Setup menu to display the Set Up Alternate Program dialog box (Figure 12-41).

3. Press Tab four times to move the cursor to the entries for alternate program B. Enter the values `Quick Print` and Ctrl-Q in the **Program name** and **Path** fields, press Enter, and the Setup menu is redisplayed. Notice that what you typed is not a directory path, but a keystroke sequence.

4. Now press Escape at the Setup menu. The Main menu is displayed with the new selection: **B-Quick Print** (Figure 12-44).

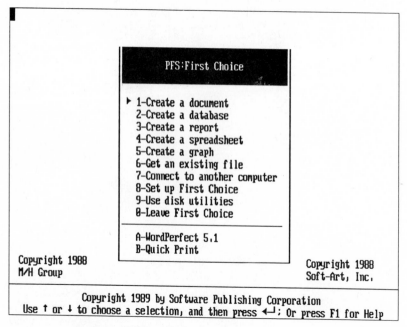

**Figure 12-44.** Main menu with Quick Print selection.

Now you can run the quick print macro by either pressing Ctrl-Q or selecting option B from the Main menu. First Choice knows to execute the quick print macro when option B is selected because we specified Ctrl-Q in the **Path** field of the Set Up Alternate Program dialog box (step 3).

# Summary

- The calculator is a useful utility that can solve fairly complex mathematical expressions and even paste the result into the document, spreadsheet, or database record with which you're currently working.

- The calculator's speed key, Alt-A, is the same, no matter which First Choice application you're currently running. Therefore, the speed key provides the easiest (and fastest) way to invoke the calculator.

- Up to 48 characters may be used in a calculation expression.

- The F9 key may be pressed to calculate and reuse the result in the next calculation. The F10 key may be pressed to paste the result of a calculation at the cursor's position in the working copy.

- Many of First Choice's keywords can be used in calculation expressions (refer to Chapter 10, *More on Spreadsheets*, for a complete discussion of First Choice keywords).

- First Choice offers nine bookmarks that may be used to denote specific locations within a file. Bookmarks may be placed in all First Choice application file types except reports and communications.

- Bookmarks have no effect on the contents of files in which they are set.

- Bookmarks may not be placed in a file until that file has been saved to disk. A bookmark may be placed on any non-space character. No more than one bookmark may be located on a character.

- The disk utilities allow you to perform the following operations from within First Choice: display file lists, copy files, rename files, erase files, create directories, remove directories, format diskettes, and copy diskettes.

- The options for formatting and copying diskettes are not available when you call up the Disk Utilities menus from within applications. In other words, the only Disk Utilities menu that offers these two options is the one displayed after selecting option 9, **Use disk utilities**, from the Main menu.

- A macro is a collection of one or more keystrokes which may be recorded and replayed later by pressing a Control key combination for speedy execution of a given task.

- Press Control in conjunction with the key assigned to the macro to play it back. Macros can be played back via the Macro menu as well.

- Press Escape to halt macro playback.

- Pauses for user input can be incorporated into First Choice macros.

- With the exception of *h, i, j,* and *m,* any of the letters *a* through *z* may be used to define the macro's key. In addition, any of the function keys (F1 through F10) may be coupled with Ctrl and used as macro keys.

- By default, macro keystrokes are recorded in a macro file named FCMACRO.KEY; a macro file is identified by the .KEY extension. Up to 1,024 keystrokes can be stored in a macro file.

- Additional macro files can be created and used if needed.

- If a macro needs to be modified, it must be completely re-recorded. First Choice does not offer an editor to enable you to make minor modifications to macro recordings.

- As many as five alternate selections can be added to First Choice's Main menu. These selections may be used to execute programs or macros.

# Communications

**In this chapter:**

- Communications Concepts
- Setup Menu
- Service Menu
- Service Information Dialog Box
- Connecting to Another Computer
- Exchanging Files
- Customizing the Services List
- Automating the Sign-On Process
- Answering an Incoming Call
- Summary

This chapter covers the communications feature of First Choice, which allows your computer to "talk to" other computers. We'll start off by discussing some communications lingo and concepts. Then, after configuring First Choice for your communications hardware, we'll walk through the various communications menus and dialog boxes. Next you'll see how to connect to another computer, exchange files, and terminate a communication session. Finally, we'll see how to automate part of the dial-up process and answer incoming calls from other computers.

# Communications Concepts

In order to use First Choice's communications application, you'll need to properly connect a *modem* to both your computer and telephone line. A modem is a device that translates computer data so that it may be sent through a communications line (for example, a telephone line) to a remote modem (a modem in another location); this remote modem then translates the data for processing by a computer connected to it. This configuration is illustrated in Figure 13-1.

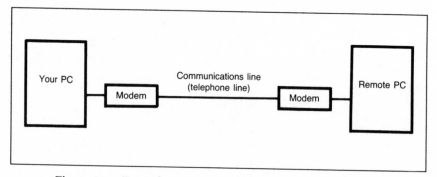

**Figure 13-1.** Typical computer communications configuration.

*The terms baud rate, bits per second, and bps are interchangeable.*

Modem prices range from approximately $50 to well over $1,000. One of the major reasons modems differ so much in price is due to differences in *baud rate*, which indicates the speed at which the modem exchanges data with other modems. You'll often see baud rates expressed as bits per second, or, bps. Typical modem baud rates include 300bps, 1200bps, 2400bps, and 9600bps. In general, modems with higher baud rates are more expensive than those with lower ones.

With First Choice and a modem, your PC can communicate with other remote, or host, computers. These remote computers may be as simple as your neighbor's PC or as sophisticated as CompuServe, a large on-line computer information service. If you check around you'll undoubtedly discover many local electronic bulletin board systems (BBS) in your local area. For a small fee (if any), these BBS's offer many useful features, including public domain software which you can *download* to your PC.

*Follow the directions accompanying your modem for proper installation procedures.*

After installing your modem, you need to provide First Choice with some information about both it and your telephone line before you can begin communicating with other computers.

# The Setup Menu

Follow these steps to provide First Choice with information about your modem:

1. Select option 8, **Set up First Choice**, from the Main menu to display the Setup menu shown in Figure 13-2.

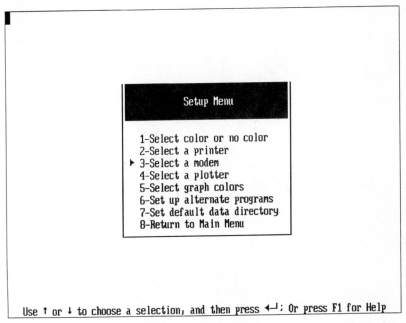

**Figure 13-2.** Setup menu.

2. Select option 3, **Select a modem**, from the Setup menu. You will see the Modem Information dialog box (Figure 13-3).

3. Use the Page Up (PgUp) and Page Down (PgDn) keys to step through the list of modems supported by First Choice. Enter the numeric selection for your modem in the **Modem** field and press Tab to move to the **Modem connects to** field. If you don't find your modem listed, and it is not an *acoustic* modem (that is, the older kind of modem which has cups fitting over the earpiece and mouthpiece of the receiver), consult its literature to see whether it is compatible with one that is listed, and select the latter. If you still don't find a modem to select, type 1. If your modem is the

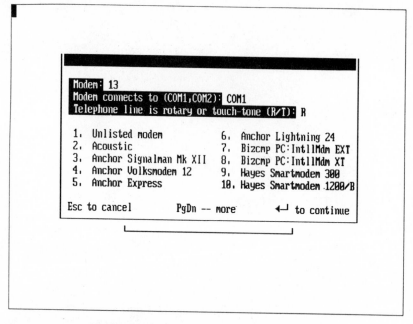

**Figure 13-3.** Modem Information dialog box.

acoustic type, type 2. (These two kinds of modems are generic, meaning they won't dial numbers automatically for you.)

4. Enter COM1 in the **Modem connects to** field unless your modem is connected to the secondary communications port (COM2). Press Tab to move to the **Telephone line is rotary or touch-tone** field.

5. Type R if your telephone has a rotary (clicking) dial; type T if your telephone has a touch-tone (beeping) numeric keypad.

6. When you are satisfied with your entries in the Modem Information dialog box, press Enter. The Setup menu is redisplayed. Press Escape to return to the Main menu.

Now that your modem is installed and configured within First Choice, select option 7, **Connect to another computer**, from the Main menu to display the Service menu (Figure 13-4).

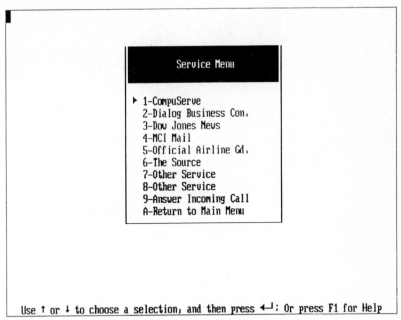

**Figure 13-4.** Service menu.

# The Service Menu

The first six selections in the Service menu list several commercially available information and bulletin board systems. Follow these steps to obtain detailed information about any of these systems:

1. Move the cursor to highlight a service and press the Help key, F1. Figure 13-5 shows the Help window displayed for CompuServe.

2. Make a regular telephone call to the toll-free number shown in the Help window for service-specific information.

The seventh and eighth selections in the Service menu are generically listed as "Other Service." These two selections are provided so that you can add your own local bulletin board systems, your friends' PCs, etc. to the Services menu. Later on, in the section customizing the Services List, you'll learn how to customize these and other selections in the Service menu.

The next selection, **Answer Incoming Call**, should be used when you want First Choice to answer a call initiated by a remote PC. This selection is discussed later in this chapter.

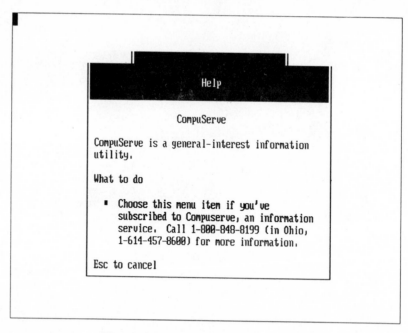

**Figure 13-5.** CompuServe Help information.

# The Service Information Dialog Box

Let's take a closer look at the information you must provide to connect to a service. Although I will be using CompuServe in many of the following communications examples, the steps described are fairly generic so only minor modifications are needed to use them for other services. Perform the following steps to prepare for connection to a service.

## Step 1—Select the Service

Select option 1, for CompuServe; the Service Information dialog box shown in Figure 13-6 is displayed. The first field in this dialog box, **Service name**, contains the name of the communications service. This is the field to modify if you wish to change the service names appearing in the Service menu (Figure 13-4).

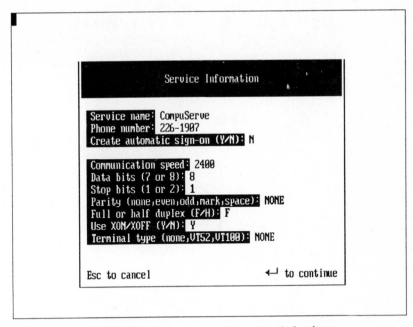

**Figure 13-6.** Service Information dialog box.

## Step 2—Type the Phone Number

*You can put parentheses, spaces and/or a hyphen in the phone number to make it more readable.*

Place the phone number of the communications service in the **Phone number** field. First Choice lets you use parentheses, spaces, and/or a hyphen to make the phone number easier to read. An example is (555) 555-5555. This phone number will be dialed automatically when you press Enter at this dialog box—unless you chose item 1 (Unlisted modem) or 2 (Acoustic) at the Modem Information dialog box (Figure 13-3), Later you'll see how to dial phone numbers manually for these generic modems.

Many corporate phone systems require that you dial a number (9 is common) just to get a dial tone for an outside line. Usually you must wait a second or two after dialing this outside line access number before dialing the actual phone number. If your phone system is like this, place a comma in the phone number entry to force the modem to pause before dialing the remainder of the number. For example, suppose I must dial a 9 to get an outside line. If I want to call 555-5555 I would enter this in the **Phone number** field:

9,555-5555

The comma represents a pause of approximately two seconds. More than one comma may be specified in a number. Thus, if I need to pause for four seconds after dialing 9 and before dialing the 555-5555, I could specify:

9,,555-5555

Most large services (CompuServe, The Source, etc.) provide local access telephone numbers so you don't have to pay hefty long distance telephone rates while communicating with their computers. (For example, at the time of this writing I lived in Dayton, OH, where the local number for CompuServe is 226-1907.) Be sure to inquire about this feature to avoid wasting money on your phone bills.

## Step 3—Supply the Remaining Values

The next field in the Service Information dialog box, **Create automatic sign-on**, is thoroughly discussed later in the section on automating the sign-on process. Until you create a macro-like file for automatic sign-on, press N here.

*Refer to your service's specifications for the values you should place in these fields.*

The rest of the fields in the Service Information dialog box refer to values for communications *protocol* (a set of rules used by telecommunicating computers) which must be properly set to enable communication between your PC and the remote computer. Because I have a 2400bps modem and CompuServe can communicate at 2400bps as well, I use these settings for CompuServe:

Communication Speed: 2400

Data bits (7 or 8): 8

Stop bits (1 or 2): 1

Parity (none,even,odd,mark,space): NONE

Full or half duplex (F/H): F

Use XON/XOFF (Y/N): Y

Terminal type (none,VT52,VT100): NONE

Use the highest communication speed common to both your system and the remote system to save time and money. For example, if your modem is capable of 1200bps or 2400bps and the remote system can handle either 1200bps, 2400bps or 4800bps, you should use 2400bps.

# Connecting to Another Computer

Now that you know how to set up your computer for your equipment, let's learn how to make it actually "talk to" another computer.

## Using an Auto-Dial Modem

If you selected an auto-dialing modem—that is, a selection *other than* "Unlisted modem" or "Acoustic"—in the Modem Information dialog box (Figure 13-3), First Choice will start dialing the phone number specified when you press Enter at the Service Information dialog box (Figure 13-6). A small "Dialing xxx-xxxx" (where xxx-xxxx is the phone number) message is displayed while First Choice is dialing the phone number.

### The Line Is Busy!

If the phone number dialed is busy, First Choice will display a message indicating an unsuccessful dial attempt. First Choice then waits several seconds and tries dialing the number again. You can press Esc at any point during the dialing process to cancel the call.

### A Successful Connection

The Communications Dialog screen in Figure 13-7 is displayed after successful connection to the service. It is a blank screen except for a message at the top left of the screen, which, by the way, is somewhat misleading because you really won't yet be actually connected to the service.

At this point you should refer to the service's documentation to determine what you must do next to sign on and/or initiate a dialog with the service system. For example, the CompuServe system requests Host, User ID, and Password entries before permitting access to its services.

## Using a Manual Dial Modem

If you selected either "Unlisted modem" or "Acoustic" in the Modem Information dialog box (Figure 13-3), you'll have to dial the service's phone number manually. As you remember, when you've finished entering the values for the Service Information dialog box (Figure 13-6), you press Enter to confirm your selections. When the Communications

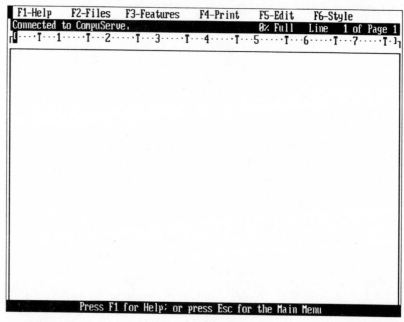

**Figure 13-7.** Communications dialog screen. Notice its resemblance to the word processing Edit screen.

Dialog screen (Figure 13-7) is displayed, type the necessary modem dial command along with the service phone number. Your modem's documentation should list the dial command. The dial command for my Hayes modem is ATD. Therefore, to dial the number 555-5555, I would type ATD 555-5555 and press Enter.

*The transmission line is a line on the screen, not a telephone line.*

First Choice won't display the characters you type in because when you're performing it, the cursor is placed on what is called the *transmission line* of the screen. Earlier I referred to the message "Connected to CompuServe" in the top left corner, or status line, of Figure 13-7. You might think that this message means that your PC has established a communications line with the service (CompuServe). However, what it really means is that the cursor is on the transmission line and First Choice is waiting for you to dial a phone number manually. If the status line reads "Connected to CompuServe, but off last line" First Choice is telling you that the cursor is not on the transmission line.

The cursor must be on the transmission line in order for you to send a message (such as a dial command) to your modem. If for some reason the cursor has been moved off the transmission line, press Ctrl-Enter to move it back.

As with auto-dialing, once your modem is connected to the service, you should refer to the service's documentation to determine what you must do next to sign on and/or initiate a dialog with the service system.

## The Dialog Process

*The Communications Dialog screen closely resembles the word processing Edit screen.*

You probably know that the way you communicate with a service is by typing. The Communications Dialog screen looks very much like the Edit screen of the word processing application; this is no accident, because the telecommunications feature is designed to make it easy to treat your "conversations" like documents. As you electronically converse with a service the dialog is displayed on the screen and eventually starts to scroll off the top. Just like a word processing document that you are first creating, the entire dialog is held in RAM, is called the working copy, and can be saved to a .DOC file at any point. This is very handy if you want to communicate quickly with a service, save the dialog, and then look more closely at the dialog after disconnecting. (Remember, most services charge you for every minute you're on-line, so it pays to keep your dialogs brief and to the point.)

Keep an eye on the percentage in the "% Full" indicator on the status line of the Communications Dialog screen. This number indicates how much space the dialog occupies in the working copy; you'll see the percentage gradually increase as the dialog continues. When it reaches approximately 98% full, First Choice will start to overwrite some of the previous dialog in the working copy. For example, in one dialog I had with CompuServe the working copy was 98% full; then it dropped down to 94% full. First Choice removed some of the earlier dialog to increase the available space from 2% to 6%. If you want to save a dialog to a .DOC file you should do so before the percentage full indicator reaches 90%. Follow these steps to save your dialog:

1. Select option 1, **Save this session**, from the Files menu (or press its speed key, Alt-Q). The Directory Assistant is displayed.
2. Specify a file name for the dialog (with or without the .DOC extension) and press Enter.

After the file has been saved to disk you may resume your dialog with the connected service. Then after you've disconnected, you can retrieve the .DOC file in the word processor and browse through it at your leisure.

## Disconnecting

To disconnect quickly, press Esc.

Most services offer a logoff command (off and bye are examples) which you should issue when you are finished with the communication session. Once you've logged off the service computer, you can hang up, or disconnect, by pressing the Esc key or selecting option 4, **Disconnect**, from the Features menu. Alternatively, you can press Esc at almost any point in a communication session to quickly disconnect from the service.

# Exchanging Files

*One of the most popular reasons for communicating with bulletin board and information systems is to exchange files.*

Many bulletin board systems offer software and/or data files to their subscribers. This is called *freeware*, or *shareware*, and is usually available for little or no charge, respectively. Downloading is the term used to describe the process of receiving files from a host computer; uploading means sending files to a host computer. When your computer is the one initiating the process, the remote computer must be ready to download or upload the files before you can actually start the process in First Choice. This "readying" stage differs between services, so refer to your service's documentation to determine what steps are necessary.

*Note:* The only protocol that First Choice supports for downloading and uploading files is the XMODEM protocol. If you intend to exchange files with another PC or service, you must make sure the remote system supports XMODEM. This is not much of a concern, however, because of XMODEM's popularity. Now let's see how to download files from a host system.

## Downloading Files

Let's assume that you've successfully connected to a remote system and are ready to download a file to your PC. Further, you have informed this host system that you want to retrieve a file using XMODEM protocol. The host is waiting for a message from you telling it to start sending data. Follow these steps to download the file:

1. Select option 7, **Receive a file (using XModem)**, from the Features menu. The Directory Assistant screen is displayed.

2. Enter the directory and name of the file as you want it to be stored on your disk and press Enter. Note that this directory and name

specification does not have to match that of the host system. That is, if the file is C:\TEMP\MEMO.DOC on the host, you can download it to your PC as C:\CHOICE\MYMEMO.DOC by typing `C:\CHOICE\MYMEMO.DOC` in the **Receive which file** field.

3. Then press Enter.

*You can press Escape at any time to abort the download process.*

File transmission from the host begins after you press Enter. Files are transmitted one piece, or block, at a time. A block processing message is displayed as the file is received (for example, "Receiving block #29"). The Communications Dialog screen (Figure 13-7) is redisplayed when the transmission is complete.

To get an idea of how fast files are transmitted, look at the previous paragraph. It contains 298 characters. At 1200 baud, approximately 120 characters are transmitted per second. Therefore, it would take a little more than two seconds to transmit the paragraph. Now let's look at the flip side of file exchange: uploading files.

## Uploading Files

Like downloading files, the file upload process generally requires a bit of synchronization between your PC and the remote system. For example, if you are uploading to a bulletin board system, you must take the necessary actions to ready the BBS for your transmission. Follow these steps to upload a file once the remote system is ready to receive it:

1. Select option 6, **Transmit a file (using XModem)**, from the Features menu to display the Directory Assistant screen.
2. Enter the name of the file to transmit in the **Transmit which file (using XMODEM)** field.
3. Press Enter.

*Press Esc to stop transmission.*

A block processing message is displayed as the file is transmitted (for example, "Transmitting block # 29"). You can press Esc at any time to abort the file transmission. The Communications Dialog screen (Figure 13-7) is redisplayed when the transmission is complete.

## Exchanging Files with Other First Choice Users

*These messages remain on the screen until the remote system is ready to send or receive the file.*

If you're exchanging files with another PC running First Choice, there's no need to worry about readying the remote system for uploading or downloading. If you try to receive a file before the remote system is ready to send it, First Choice displays the message "Waiting to receive the file." Similarly, if you try to send a file before the remote system is ready to receive it, First Choice displays the message "Waiting to transmit the file." Press Esc when these messages are displayed if you wish to abort the transmission process.

There is an awkward feature I've encountered when exchanging files between two PCs via First Choice. The host PC always displays the entire dialog between itself and the calling PC. However, the calling PC displays only the dialog entries made at the host; the calling PC does not display any dialog entered via its own keyboard. Since you can't see what you're typing, this fact makes it difficult to check your spelling as you send messages to the host.

## Customizing the Services List

*Any of the pre-defined services can be redefined as other services.*

You probably won't be using all the pre-defined services listed on the Service menu. Two "Other Service" selections are provided in the Service menu for adding unlisted services. However, you may need further personalization. You may need to add more than two unlisted services or, you may simply want to remove some of the predefined ones if you don't have a subscription to them. For example, if you don't have a subscription to Dow Jones News, you could follow these steps to redefine that selection (item 3 on the Service menu) so it refers to a friend's PC:

1. Select option 3, **Dow Jones News**, from the Service menu.
2. Enter the values shown in the Service Information dialog box, as shown in Figure 13-8, for Bill's PC. Now when the Service menu appears on your screen, it will list your friend's PC instead of the Dow Jones News, as Figure 13-9 shows.

## Automating the Sign-On Process

As noted earlier, most services require entry of an ID and/or password before granting access to the system. These items must be entered each time you connect to the service. First Choice offers a feature, similar to the macro feature discussed in Chapter 12, which allows you to "record" the keystrokes for a service's sign-on process. The next time you call the service, you can play back this "recording."

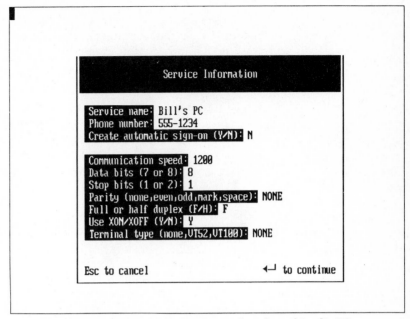

**Figure 13-8.** Service information data for a friend's PC.

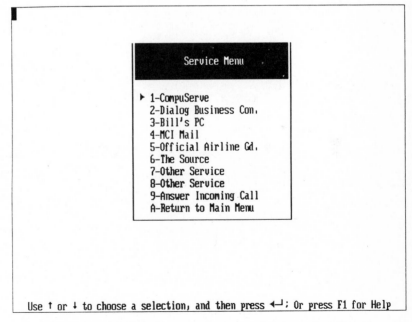

**Figure 13-9.** Modified Service menu with option for Bill's PC.

Follow these steps to record a service's sign-on process:

1. Select the service from the Service menu (Figure 13-4) to display the Service Information dialog box (Figure 13-6).

2. Enter the phone number and the appropriate protocol values, type Y in the **Create automatic sign-on** field, and press Enter.

3. Once a connection is made, the Communications Dialog screen in Figure 13-10 is displayed. The message at the bottom of the screen in Figure 13-10, "Press F10 to stop recording the automatic sign-on," indicates that First Choice is recording your sign-on keystrokes.

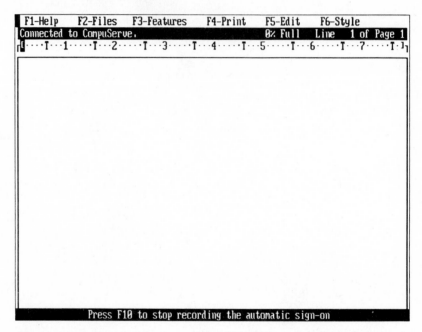

**Figure 13-10.** Communications dialog box during recording of sign-on.

4. Perform the necessary keystrokes to sign onto the system (for example, enter the host ID, your account ID, and then your password).

5. Then press F10 to halt the recording process.

The next time the Service Information dialog box is displayed for that service, it includes a message about pressing F10 to sign on manually (see Figure 13-11). This is one way in which you can remember whether you've automated the sign-on procedures for a particular service.

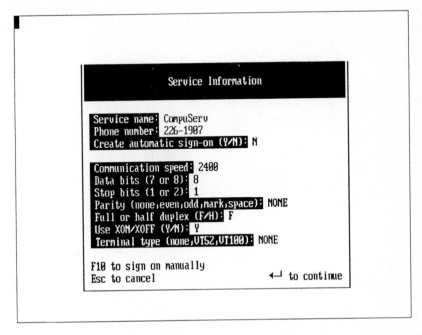

**Figure 13-11.** Service Information dialog box for a service that has automatic sign-on defined.

If you press Enter while the screen in Figure 13-11 is displayed, the sign-on process will be replayed automatically; press F10 if you want to call the service and manually sign on.

## An Anomaly with Automatic Sign-On

*Be careful when trying to record Control key combinations in an automatic sign-on process.*

Some services require you to press a Control key combination (for example, CompuServe uses Ctrl-C) to make the sign-on prompt appear. I included this Ctrl-C depression in an automatic sign-on recording for CompuServe. When the sign-on process was played back it appeared that the Ctrl-C caused the communication session to lock up.

## Halting Automatic Sign-On Playback

If something goes awry during automatic sign-on playback, you can press Esc to abort the process. First Choice immediately stops playback and you can continue the sign-on process manually.

## Changing the Automatic Sign-On Process

Once you've recorded a sign-on process for a service, you must completely re-record it if you want to make modifications. Follow the previous steps for sign-on recording, press Enter to acknowledge the Sign-On File Replacement warning message in Figure 13-12, and then continue recording the new sign-on process.

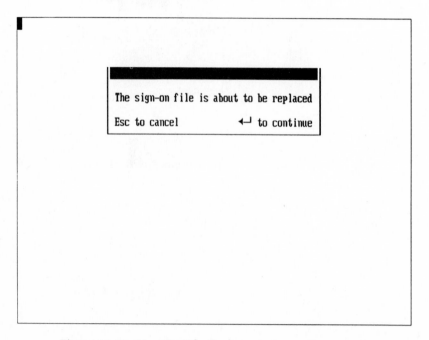

The sign-on file is about to be replaced

Esc to cancel          ↵ to continue

**Figure 13-12.** Sign-On File Replacement warning message.

## Removing Automatic Sign-On

If you have more than one membership to a service, you may want to use different user IDs and passwords at sign-on. Follow these steps to erase the automatic sign-on process from a service:

1. Enter Y in the **Create automatic sign-on** field of the Service Information dialog box and press Enter.
2. Press Enter to acknowledge the sign-on file replacement warning message shown in Figure 13-12.
3. Press F10 immediately when the Communications Dialog screen is displayed.

Any subsequent communication sessions with that service will require manual sign-on.

# Answering an Incoming Call

Select option 9, **Answer Incoming Call**, from the Service menu to prepare your PC as a host for a communication session. After this option is selected, the screen in Figure 13-13 is displayed until an incoming call is received.

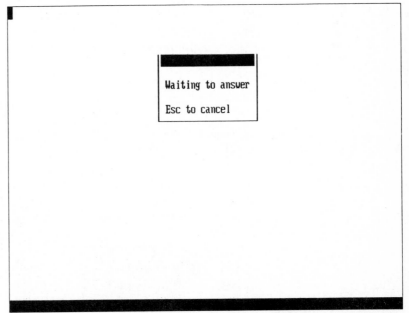

```
Waiting to answer

Esc to cancel
```

**Figure 13-13.** Waiting to Answer message.

First Choice then answers the next incoming call and the displays the Communications Dialog screen with the message "Connected to Answer Incoming Call" on the status line.

# Summary

- A modem is a device that translates computer data so that it may be sent through a communications line (that is, a telephone line) to another modem; this remote modem then translates the data for processing by a remote computer.

- One of the major reasons for the price differences between modems is baud rate, which is the speed at which the modem exchanges data with other modems.

- Before communicating, you must provide First Choice with some information about your modem, phone line, etc. Use the Setup menu to configure First Choice for your communications setup.

- When setting up your system to dial a service automatically, you can place parentheses, spaces and/or a hyphen in the service's phone number to make it more readable. If you need to dial a certain number before obtaining an outside line and pause a few seconds before dialing the actual number, place one or more commas in the phone number entry.

- Most large services (CompuServe, The Source, etc.) provide local access telephone numbers so you don't have to pay hefty long distance telephone rates while communicating with their computers.

- You should use the highest communication speed common to your system and the remote system to save time and money.

- The cursor must be on the line of the screen called the transmission line in order for you to send a message (such as a dial command) to your modem. If for some reason the cursor has been moved off the transmission line, you can press Ctrl-Enter to move it back.

- First Choice saves your entire conversation in a *working copy* very much like a word processing file. The ability to save the working copy in a .DOC file is handy for taking a closer look at the dialog after disconnecting.

- When the working copy becomes approximately 98% full, First Choice will start to overwrite some of the previous dialog.

- You can press Esc at almost any point in a communication session to disconnect from the service quickly.

- First Choice supports only the XMODEM protocol for downloading and uploading files.

- Files are transmitted one piece, or block, at a time.
- If you're exchanging files with another PC running First Choice, there's no need to worry about readying the remote system for uploading or downloading.
- You can customize the list of who you communicate with.
- First Choice offers a feature similar to the macro feature that allows you to "record" the keystrokes for a service's sign-on process.
- First Choice can answer incoming phone calls, allowing your PC to act as the host in a communication session.

# Program Integration

**In this chapter:**

- Using the Clipboard
- Moving Spreadsheet Data into a Document
- Placing a Database Report in a Document
- Placing a Graph in a Document
- Creating and Printing Form Letters
- Generating Mailing Labels
- Summary

This chapter on program integration shows you how to unite many of the First Choice features covered in earlier chapters. The chapter begins with a look at the clipboard, that convenient data transfer tool accessible throughout First Choice. Then we'll start assembling the annual report for Wikley Company. During this discussion you'll see how to place a spreadsheet, database report, and graph in a document file. The chapter concludes with coverage of how to generate form letters and mailing labels.

## Using the Clipboard

The clipboard provides perhaps the easiest method of moving data from one First Choice application to another and is accessible through F5, the Edit menu. In the following discussion, the word "text" also refers to spreadsheet cells. For example, the more general "Select text" option is called "Select cells" in the spreadsheet application. Let's take a close look at the four clipboard-related selections in the Edit menu.

## Select Text (Alt-S)

*First Choice's response to mouse movement during text selection is often sluggish at best.*

When the Edit menu's first option, **Select text**, is chosen, the cursor may be moved about the screen (via the cursor keys) to highlight a block of the working copy, as shown in Figure 14-1. Text may also be selected by dragging the mouse from the beginning to the end of the block. However, I think you'll find that the mouse method of selecting text is a bit more awkward than the keyboard method. Once the text is selected, the block can be moved to the clipboard with the Edit menu's option 2, **Move selected text to clipboard**.

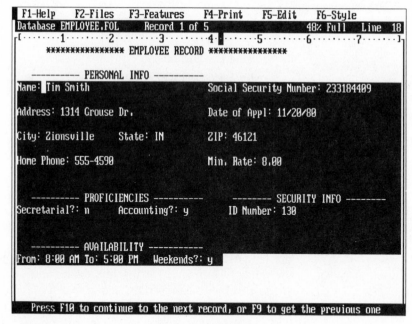

**Figure 14-1.** Highlighted block in the working copy of a record in the database application.

## Move Selected Text to Clipboard (Alt-M)

When you choose this option, the selected text is removed from the working copy and placed in the clipboard. If you want to place the selected text in the clipboard without simultaneously removing it from the working copy, select the Edit menu's option 3, **Copy selected text to clipboard**.

## Copy Selected Text to Clipboard

Like **Move selected text to clipboard**, this operation places the selected text in the clipboard. The selected text is not removed from the working copy as a result, however. Both selections (move and copy) overwrite the previous contents of the clipboard. In other words, it is impossible to append to the contents of the clipboard; once you move or copy anything to it, you destroy what was there before.

Once you've placed a block of text in the clipboard, you can use the next option, the last clipboard-related option on the Edit menu, **Paste from clipboard**, to locate the block elsewhere.

## Paste from Clipboard (Alt-P)

To perform this operation, move the cursor to where the clipboard's contents should be placed; then select the Edit menu's option 4, **Paste from clipboard**. The paste operation does not affect the contents of the clipboard. You can paste the same block again and again without having to repeat the select and move (or copy) to clipboard steps. Because clipboard data is stored in a file (CLIPBRD.DAT), its contents are not lost when you leave First Choice or turn off your computer. The next time you run First Choice you can paste whatever was last placed in the clipboard.

## Cutting and Pasting Between Applications

It's no surprise that the clipboard may be used to cut and paste blocks within a document, spreadsheet, database, etc. But the clipboard can be used to cut and paste between applications as well. As an example, let's discuss the steps involved in pasting spreadsheet data into a document.

# Moving Spreadsheet Data into a Document

*The steps required for inter-application cut-and-paste are almost identical regardless of the applications involved.*

Follow these steps to paste the Wikley Company annual report spreadsheet (INCOME.SS in Chapter 10) into the Wikley partnership letter (WIKLEYLT.DOC) from Chapter 2:

1. Choose option 6, **Get an existing file**, from the Main menu and select the INCOME.SS file from the Directory Assistant.

2. Select the entire spreadsheet (except for the title) by either method discussed in the previous Select Text section, as illustrated in Figure 14-2.

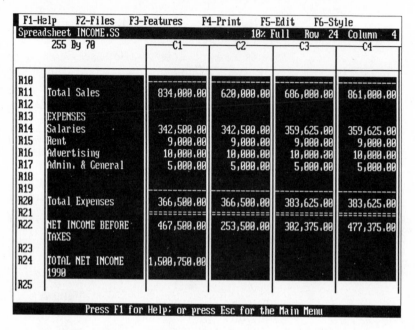

**Figure 14-2.** Entire spreadsheet in INCOME.SS selected.

3. Select option 3, **Copy selected cells to the clipboard**, from the Edit menu to place the spreadsheet in the clipboard.

4. Choose option 4, **Get an existing file**, from the Files menu and select the WIKLEYLT.DOC file from the Directory Assistant.

5. Select option 8, **Change current ruler (margins/tabs)**, from the Features menu and set the left margin 10 spaces to the left and the right margin five spaces to the right (to accomodate the width of the INCOME.SS spreadsheet).

6. Insert a couple of blank lines between the first and second paragraphs in WIKLEYLT.DOC.

7. Position the cursor between the first two paragraphs as shown in Figure 14-3 and select option 4, **Paste from clipboard**, from the Edit menu. The spreadsheet is pasted into WIKLEYLT.DOC, as Figure 14-4 shows.

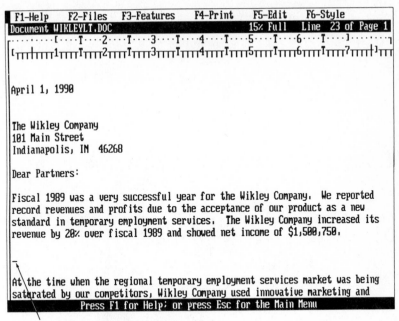

---

```
 F1-Help    F2-Files   F3-Features   F4-Print   F5-Edit   F6-Style
Document WIKLEYLT.DOC                       15% Full   Line  23 of Page 1
```

April 1, 1990


The Wikley Company
101 Main Street
Indianapolis, IN  46268

Dear Partners:

Fiscal 1989 was a very successful year for the Wikley Company.  We reported
record revenues and profits due to the acceptance of our product as a new
standard in temporary employment services.  The Wikley Company increased its
revenue by 20% over fiscal 1989 and showed net income of $1,500,750.



At the time when the regional temporary employment services market was being
saturated by our competitors, Wikley Company used innovative marketing and

```
          Press F1 for Help; or press Esc for the Main Menu
```

Position cursor where spreadsheet will be pasted

**Figure 14-3.** Cursor position in WIKLEYLT.DOC.

---

```
 F1-Help    F2-Files   F3-Features   F4-Print   F5-Edit   F6-Style
Document WIKLEYLT.DOC                       20% Full   Line  30 of Page 1
```

The Wikley Company
101 Main Street
Indianapolis, IN  46268

Dear Partners:

Fiscal 1989 was a very successful year for the Wikley Company.  We reported
record revenues and profits due to the acceptance of our product as a new
standard in temporary employment services.  The Wikley Company increased its
revenue by 20% over fiscal 1989 and showed net income of $1,500,750.

|                   | QTR1       | QTR2       | QTR3       | QTR4       |
|-------------------|-----------:|-----------:|-----------:|-----------:|
| INCOME            |            |            |            |            |
| Clerical Temps    | 165,000.00 | 142,000.00 | 115,000.00 | 165,000.00 |
| Receptionist      | 108,000.00 | 110,000.00 | 201,000.00 | 165,000.00 |
| Admin. Assist.    | 116,000.00 | 123,000.00 | 142,000.00 | 181,000.00 |
| Accounting Clerks |  88,000.00 |  70,000.00 |  78,000.00 | 101,000.00 |
| CPA Service       | 357,000.00 | 175,000.00 | 150,000.00 | 249,000.00 |
|                   | ---------- | ---------- | ---------- | ---------- |
| Total Sales       | 834,000.00 | 620,000.00 | 686,000.00 | 861,000.00 |

```
          Press F1 for Help; or press Esc for the Main Menu
```

**Figure 14-4.** Result of pasting INCOME.SS spreadsheet in
WIKLEYLT.DOC document.

The results shown in Figure 14-4 illustrate one of the niceties of working with an integrated package like First Choice: In general, data can easily be moved from one type of file to another (for example, from an .SS file to a .DOC file).

Go ahead and save the WIKLEYLT.DOC file as it appears in Figure 14-4 by pressing Alt-Q. Then press Esc to return to the Main menu. Now let's see how easy it is to insert a database report into a document.

# Placing a Database Report in a Document

*A database report cannot be directly inserted into a document.*

A report must first be saved as a document (.DOC) so that it may be placed in another document file. Follow the directions in Chapter 8 to create the desired database report instructions. When you're creating the report instructions, place a .DOC file name in the **Print to** field of the Print Options dialog box (Figure 14-5) to write the database report to a document file.

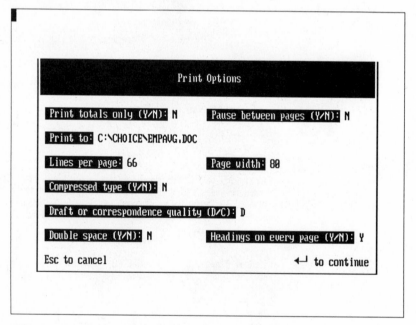

**Figure 14-5.** Database Report Print Options dialog box, saving a database report as a document file.

Once the database report has been written to a .DOC file, it can be inserted in another document via option 3, **Merge another file**, in the word processing Files menu. Then you can use the Style menu selections to massage the report into an eye-appealing format. That's all there is to it!

# Placing a Graph in a Document

Now let's see how to enhance the Wikley Company annual report by adding a graph. In order to place a First Choice graph in a document, the graph must first be saved in *Graph format (that is, to a file with a .PF extension). In this discussion we'll be placing a graph of the INCOME.SS spreadsheet into the Wikley Company annual report. Follow these steps to save a graph in *Graph format:

1.  Choose option 6, **Get an existing file**, from the Main menu and select the INCOME.SS file from the Directory Assistant.

2.  Select option 3, **Save the graph as a file**, from the Files menu to display the Graph File Format dialog box (Figure 14-6).

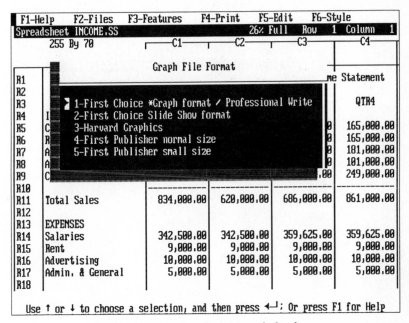

**Figure 14-6.** Graph File Format dialog box.

3.  Select option 1, **First Choice *Graph format/Professional Write**; the Directory Assistant screen is displayed.

4. Specify the *Graph file name INCOME.PF (with or without the .PF extension) in the **Save as** field on the Directory Assistant screen, and press Enter. The *Graph format options dialog box is displayed (Figure 14-7).

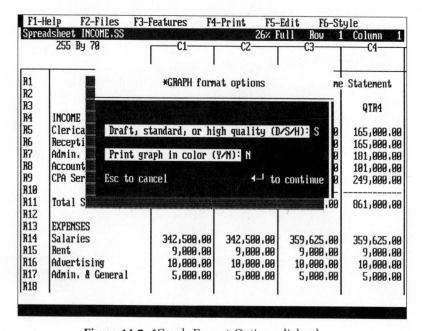

**Figure 14-7.** *Graph Format Options dialog box.

5. Select the appropriate quality level (Draft, Standard, or High), place an N (No) in the **Print graph in color** field, and press Enter.

6. When the *Graph file save process is complete press Esc to return to the Main menu.

Now that the INCOME.SS graph is in *Graph format, you can include it in the Wikley Company annual report with the *GRAPH* statement whose syntax is

`*GRAPH filename*`

where *filename* is the full name of the .PF file. Notice I say "full" file name—you must specify the *Graph file's .PF extension in the *GRAPH* statement. Therefore, to include the INCOME.PF graph in a document, you would use the following *GRAPH* statement:

*GRAPH INCOME.PF*

Follow these steps to place the INCOME.PF graph in the Wikley Company annual report:

1. Choose option 6, **Get an existing file**, from the Main menu and select the WIKLEYLT.DOC file from the Directory Assistant.

2. Insert the *GRAPH* statement *GRAPH INCOME.PF* in WIKLEY-LT.DOC, as shown near the bottom of Figure 14-8.

```
 F1-Help    F2-Files   F3-Features   F4-Print    F5-Edit    F6-Style
Document WIKLEYLT.DOC                          28% Full   Line  47 of Page 1
[·······1···T···2···T···3···T···4···T···5···T···6···T···7····]···
               _____  _____  _____  _____

Total Sales      834,000.00    620,000.00    686,000.00    861,000.00

EXPENSES
Salaries         342,500.00    342,500.00    359,625.00    359,625.00
Rent               9,000.00      9,000.00      9,000.00      9,000.00
Advertising       10,000.00     10,000.00     10,000.00     10,000.00
Admin. & General   5,000.00      5,000.00      5,000.00      5,000.00


               _____  _____  _____  _____
Total Expenses   366,500.00    366,500.00    383,625.00    383,625.00
               =============  ============  =============  ============
NET INCOME BEFORE 467,500.00    253,500.00    302,375.00    477,375.00

TOTAL NET INCOME 1,500,750.00


            *GRAPH INCOME.PF*

At the time when the regional temporary employment services market was being
saturated by our competitors, Wikley Company used innovative marketing and
            Press F1 for Help; or press Esc for the Main Menu
```

**Figure 14-8.** Wikley Company Annual Report with *GRAPH* statement.

3. Press Alt-Q to save the modified version of the WIKLEYLT.DOC file.

If your printer supports graphics characters, you can use these steps to print the WIKLEYLT.DOC file with the INCOME.PF graph:

1. Select option 1, **Print this document**, from the Print menu to display the Print Options dialog box.

2. Make any necessary changes to the selections in the Print Options dialog box and press Enter to print the annual report with the INCOME.PF graph.

*\*G INCOME.PF\* is short
for \*GRAPH INCOME.PF\**

The \*GRAPH\* statement tells First Choice to insert the specified
.PF \*Graph file at that location when the document is printed. If First
Choice cannot find the specified .PF file, or if you omit the .PF extension, the erroneous \*GRAPH\* statement is printed with the document
and no graph is printed.

First Choice also offers an abbreviated form of the \*GRAPH\* statement which looks like this:

`*G filename*`

where "GRAPH" is shortened to "G." Since both

`*GRAPH INCOME.PF*`

and

`*G INCOME.PF*`

generate the same results, you could have used either statement in the
Wikley Company annual report.

As you can see, it's not very difficult to incorporate a graph in a
document: just save the graph in \*Graph format and place a \*GRAPH\*
statement at the desired location in the document.

The Wikley Company annual report is almost complete. But what
about the letter heading? Your WIKLEYLT.DOC letter is addressed to
"Dear Partners:." You need to send a copy of this letter to each individual in the Wikley Company partnership database (see the PART-
NER.FOL database in Chapter 4). First Choice makes it easy to turn the
WIKLEYLT.DOC document into a form letter that may be custom-
printed for each partner in the PARTNER.FOL database. The next section discusses this simple yet valuable feature.

# Creating and Printing Form Letters

You've undoubtedly received a form letter or two in the mail. You know
the same letter was sent to thousands of other people and yet it doesn't
start with a generic salutation like "Dear Sir" or "Dear Madam." Some-
how the sender was able to individually greet each addressee with
"Dear Joe" or "Dear Kelly" or whatever your name is. A form letter is a
"plain vanilla," or generic, document that uses specific fields in a
database to customize each printed copy.

Recall that the PARTNER.FOL database contains fields for Name, Address, City, State, ZIP, etc. Because of this, you can use data from PARTNER.FOL to customize the generic version of WIKLEYLT.DOC. Figure 14-9 shows the WIKLEYLT.DOC file with your form letter modifications.

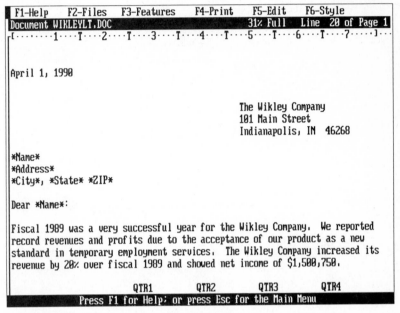

**Figure 14-9.** WIKLEYLT.DOC with form letter modifications.

Notice that the letter heading in Figure 14-9 has been modified to read:

```
*Name*
*Address*
*City*, *State* *ZIP*

Dear *Name*:
```

The items within asterisks (such as Name) tell First Choice to insert a specific database field value at that location when the form letters are printed.

In this heading we are referring to five separate database fields:

Name
Address
City
State
ZIP

Notice that the **Name** field is referenced in both the address block and the salutation. You can reference a database field as many times as necessary within a form letter.

*For readability and consistency, use the same type case in both the form letter and the database.*

Field name specifications within a form letter are not case sensitive. That is, the field reference's case in the form letter does not necessarily have to match the field name's case in the database. However, for the sake of consistency and ease in reading, it is a good idea to use the same case of letter in both places. Further, although field names are identified by a terminating colon (:) in the database form, this colon should not be included in the form letter field reference.

Now that you've indicated which fields to insert in the form letter, follow these steps to print the form letters using the PARTNER.FOL database:

1. Select option 3, **Print form letters**, from the Print menu; the Print Options dialog box in Figure 14-10 is displayed.

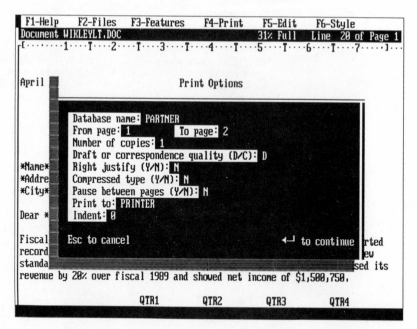

**Figure 14-10.** Print Options dialog box (for a form letter).

2. Type PARTNER in the **Database name** field of the Print Options dialog box, and press Enter. The Search Instructions screen (Figure 14-11) is displayed.

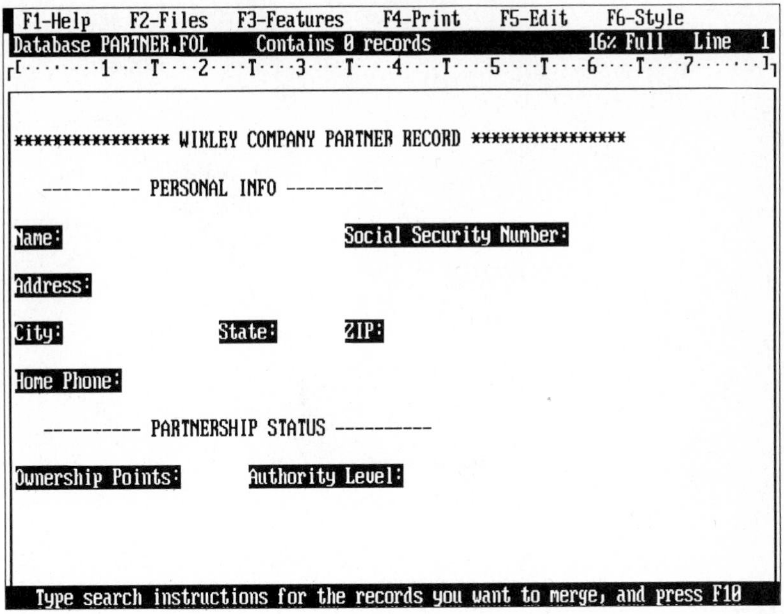

```
F1-Help    F2-Files   F3-Features   F4-Print   F5-Edit   F6-Style
Database PARTNER.FOL      Contains 0 records          16% Full   Line   1
r[·····1···T···2···T···3···T···4···T···5···T···6···T···7·····]ㄱ


*************** WIKLEY COMPANY PARTNER RECORD ***************

    ---------- PERSONAL INFO ----------

Name:                          Social Security Number:

Address:

City:              State:      ZIP:

Home Phone:

    ---------- PARTNERSHIP STATUS ----------

Ownership Points:       Authority Level:




Type search instructions for the records you want to merge, and press F10
```

**Figure 14-11.** Search Instructions screen.

3. Press F10 to select all records in the PARTNER.FOL database. The first form letter is printed.

When printing is complete, the message in Figure 14-12 is displayed. This message shows the number of form letters printed. Press Enter to acknowledge this message and return to the document screen (Figure 14-9).

As you may have guessed, you can use any of the search specifications discussed in Chapter 5 to print form letters for specific database records. For example, to print form letters for Indianapolis-based partners only, you would have placed the value Indianapolis in the **City** field in the screen that appears in Figure 14-11.

*Colons in form letter field names are treated as errors.*

Any form letter field names that don't exist in the selected database are printed on the form letters. For example, if you accidentally type *Vity* instead of *City*, the literal value *Vity* would be printed on all form letters. And finally, an important warning: *City:* is not the same as *City*.

The Wikley Company annual report is now complete and you've printed copies of it for each of the partners. Press Alt-Q to save the form letter modifications. Now let's see how to print mailing labels for the annual report envelopes.

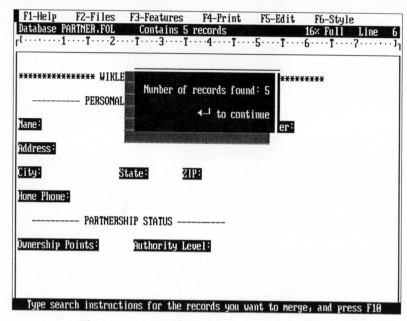

**Figure 14-12.** Number of Form Letters message.

# Generating Mailing Labels

Mailing labels can be printed by using many of the concepts discussed above for form letters. Follow these steps to create mailing labels for the Wikley Company annual report:

1. Create a new document containing database field names like the one shown in Figure 14-13.

2. Select option 4, **Set page size, headers, and footers**, from the Features menu. The dialog box in Figure 14-14 is displayed.

3. Enter the values shown in Figure 14-14:

   Page length (in lines): 6
   Left margin: 1
   Right margin: 33
   Top margin: 0
   Bottom margin: 0

4. Press Enter.

5. Select option 4, **Print labels**, from the Print menu to display the Print Options dialog box in Figure 14-15.

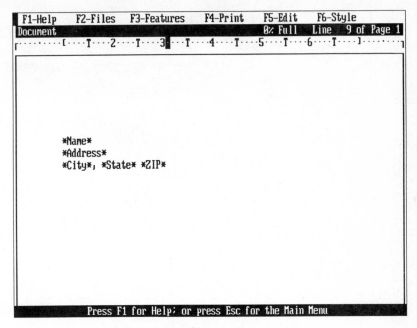

**Figure 14-13.** Mailing label document.

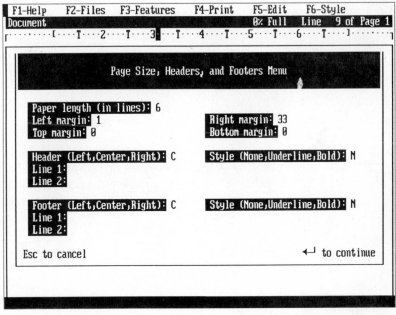

**Figure 14-14.** Page Size, Headers, and Footers dialog box.

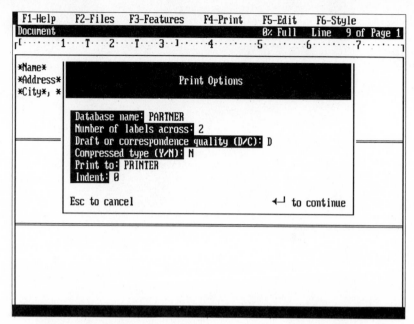

**Figure 14-15.** Print Options dialog box (for mailing labels).

6. Enter PARTNER in the **Database name** field.

7. Type the number of labels in a row on your label sheets (my label sheets have two labels in each row) in the **Number of labels across** field and press Enter. The Search Instructions screen is displayed (Figure 14-11).

8. Press F10 to select all records in the PARTNER.FOL database. The mailing labels are printed.

As mentioned, my mailing label sheets contain two labels across each row. First Choice can print from one to five labels across. If your label sheets contain a different number, enter that value in the **Number of labels across** field in step 6. Also, you may need to tweak some of the values listed in step 3 for your particular mailing labels and printer—try different values to see which ones work best with your setup.

Congratulations! You've completed the last chapter of this book and you now know how to use each of First Choice's applications both individually and in concert with each other. Even though you're now a First Choice expert, be sure to keep *The Best Book of PFS: First Choice* within reach as a handy reference.

# Summary

- The clipboard provides perhaps the easiest method of moving data from one First Choice application to another and is accessible through F5, the Edit menu.

- When you choose the Edit menu's **Move selected text to clipboard** option, the selected text is removed from the working copy and placed in the clipboard.

- The Edit menu's **Copy selected text to clipboard** option places the selected text in the clipboard but does not remove it from the working copy.

- Use the Edit menu's **Paste from clipboard** selection to insert the clipboard's contents into the working copy. The paste operation does not affect the contents of the clipboard.

- Because clipboard data is stored in a file (CLIPBRD.DAT), its contents are not lost when you leave First Choice or turn off your computer.

- A database report cannot be directly inserted into a document— the report must first be saved as a document (.DOC) so that it may be placed in another document file.

- In order to place a First Choice graph in a document, the graph must first be saved in *Graph format (to a file with a .PF extension).

- The *GRAPH* statement tells First Choice to insert the specified .PF *Graph file at that location when the document is printed.

- A form letter is a generic document that uses specific fields in a database to customize each printed copy.

- Reference a database field within a form letter by placing the field name within asterisks. You can reference a database field as many times as necessary within a form letter. Field name specifications within a form letter are not case sensitive.

- Any form letter field names that don't exist in the selected database are printed on the form letters.

- Mailing labels can be printed by using many of the concepts used for form letter generation. First Choice can print from one to five labels across on a sheet.

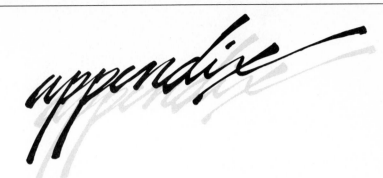

# Setting Up First Choice

Before you can use First Choice, you must complete a few preparations. This section discusses how to make these preparations—whether on a hard disk or floppy disk system. Before you can start up First Choice, the First Choice program files must exist on your hard disk (or, if you do not have a hard disk, on some diskettes, or floppies) and these files must include certain facts about your equipment. Setting up, or installing, First Choice consists of copying the program files onto the disk(s) and telling the program these facts.

Some background may help here. In order for your computer to use First Choice, your system must load the First Choice files into the Random Access Memory (RAM) of your computer (RAM is memory that is volatile and is erased whenever your computer is turned off). If you don't have a hard disk, each time you use the program you need to insert the First Choice disk into your disk drive—either the 5-1/4 inch floppy PROGRAM DISK 1 in Drive A (generally the left hand drive or the top floppy drive), or the 3-1/2 inch disk labeled PROGRAM DISK 1 and DICTIONARY DISK in Drive B—so that the computer can access the files stored on the disk and load them into RAM as needed. After you insert the disk, to start First Choice, type FIRST, as explained in Chapter 1, and press Enter.

In contrast, if you have a hard disk, then you don't need to insert any disks when you want to to use First Choice. You copy the files stored on your First Choice disks to the hard disk once. Once those files are stored on your hard disk, use the Change Directory command (that is, type CD\CHOICE at the DOS prompt and press Enter). This command accesses the directory where the First Choice files are located. Then start First Choice by typing FIRST and pressing Enter.

Diskettes of both sizes are
called floppies.

*Note:* if the First Choice files have already been copied to your hard disk and the setup has been performed, proceed to the section entitled "Quick Start to First Choice" in Chapter 1. If you are preparing your system for First Choice and you have a hard disk, read all of the appendix. If you are preparing your system for First Choice and you have a a a floppy disk system, read all the sections except the ones about hard disks.

The installation procedure itself is straightforward and simple. However, before you begin, you should make a backup copy of all the disks in the size appropriate for your computer.

# Making Backups

It makes good sense to
make backup copies of
your original disks.

When you purchase First Choice, you should immediately make copies, or "backups." Accidental erasures can occur during setup, so making a backup reduces the chance that you will lose a valuable program. Once you've made the duplicates, I suggest you use them to perform the setup operation and put the originals in a safe place in case you need to make another copy.

Do you need to make backups if you have a hard disk? In a word, yes, for the reasons just given. Also, you really shouldn't consider the hard disk itself to be a backup. Age and accidents can affect a hard disk as well, and then you're back to square one. Why not make an extra copy of your software to play it safe? The cost of a set of blank disks is less expensive than the cost of another original set of First Choice disks.

The first step in making backup copies of First Choice is to check to see that you have the same number (and type) of blank diskettes as original diskettes that you wish to copy. Then, determine the configuration of your computer. In other words, does your computer have two disk drives of the same type (that is, two 5-1/4 inch or two 3-1/2 inch drives) or does it have one 5-1/4 inch drive and one 3-1/2 inch drive? Your system may simply have one floppy disk drive (either a 5-1/4 inch or a 3-1/2 inch) and a hard drive. The setup of your system is important because you can't make a copy of a disk inserted into a 5-1/4 inch drive onto a disk inserted into a 3-1/2 inch drive (the configuration of the disks themselves are different).

Next, if you have a hard disk, be sure that you are at the *root* level of your disk. The root level is where your DOS files are stored. In other words, if your system prompt reads D> instead of C>, you may need to change to the root drive by typing C: and pressing Enter at the system prompt.

*Note:* Before you make backups of your original diskettes, cover the write-protect notch on the originals so they can't be written to or erased.

*DISKCOPY formats as well as copies a disk.*

If you have one floppy drive or a system with two different floppy drives, type the following DOS system command from DOS, whether you're in A or C:

```
DISKCOPY A: A:
```

where the DOS command (DISKCOPY) is followed by a space, the source drive (A), a colon, a space, the destination drive (A again), and another colon. (If you're using drive B, just substitute B for both As in the command and in the directions that follow.) You will then see a message telling you to place the source diskette into drive A and press any key. Place any of the original First Choice disks into drive A. You will be told to swap the source disk (the First Choice disk) and the target (a blank disk) several times (the exact number varies with the size of your computer's RAM) until the copy is complete.

*Keep source disks grouped together and physically apart from target disks.*

You will then be asked if you wish to copy another. Press Y. Insert a fresh source disk and label the target disk carefully, adding the word "Backup." Keep using DISKCOPY until you have copied all the First Choice disks. (DISKCOPY makes an exact duplicate of a diskette. If the target disk is not already formatted, DISKCOPY formats the disk automatically.)

If you have two identical drives named A and B, you can type the following command instead (with your DOS disk in drive A if necessary):

```
DISKCOPY A: B:
```

In this case, pressing Enter will tell you to place the source disk (one of the First Choice disks) into drive A and the target disk (one of the blank disks) into drive B, and then to press any key. As before, when the copy is complete, a message will appear asking if you wish to copy another disk. Press Y, insert a fresh source disk, and then press Enter to repeat the procedure until all disks have been successfully copied.

*Warning:* Don't mix the source and target disks during the copy procedure. If you do, you may accidentally erase an original disk.

Don't forget to label your backup disks and put the originals in a safe cool place.

# Making Working Copies for a Floppy System

If you do not have a hard disk, copy the First Choice disks *again*—from your backup set, of course. Then label the new set "working copy," and put the backup set in a safe place. Now you are ready to go on to the section entitled "Customizing First Choice for Your System."

# Your Hard Disk

A hard disk has a tremendous amount of room for storing your files. Using DOS (DOS is short for the Disk Operating System that is used to operate your computer and give it instructions), you divide your hard disk into *directories*, each containing its own set of related files. You can liken the hard disk to a standard filing cabinet, where each drawer represents a different directory. Each directory has a set of its own files, much like the manila folder variety stored in those dusty filing cabinets (see Figure A-1). If you have more than one filing cabinet, you can actually have more than one hard drive designation. It is common for many large hard disks to be partitioned into more than one designated drive, such as the C drive and the D drive. Within each drive is a set of directories and related files.

Directories can be further divided into *subdirectories*; the structure of same is called a *directory tree*. Using our metal filing cabinet analogy, the subdirectories would be the manila folders contained within each metal drawer. The individual pieces of paper within each folder represent individual files (for example, document files or spreadsheet files). Thus, a directory in a tree structure is simply a directory containing subordinate directories.

*Chapter 2 discusses conventions for naming files in First Choice.*

At the top of the directory tree, you will find the initial directory, or *root directory* (see Figure A-2). Sometimes called the main directory, the root directory always has the name of the active drive followed by the backslash character (\). Like file names, directory or subdirectory names can contain only eight characters. Although you can add the optional file name extension (of up to three characters) as well, most people do not. When a directory is displayed from DOS (using the DIR command), you will see the directory name followed by the familiar <DIR> symbol.

(For a more complete review of DOS commands and directories, refer to your DOS manual or pick up a book like *The Best Book of DOS* by Alan Simpson and available from Howard W. Sams & Company.)

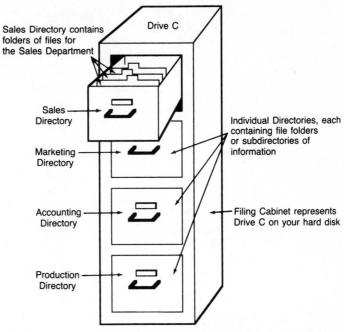

Sales Directory contains folders of files for the Sales Department

Drive C

Sales Directory

Marketing Directory

Individual Directories, each containing file folders or subdirectories of information

Accounting Directory

Filing Cabinet represents Drive C on your hard disk

Production Directory

**Figure A-1.** Storing files on a hard disk is similar to storing files in a standard filing cabinet.

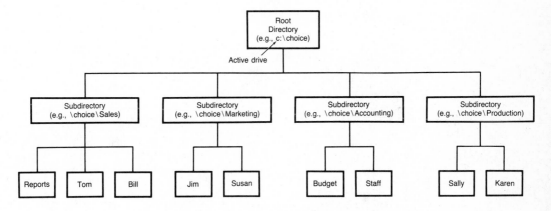

**Figure A-2.** A directory tree may further divide the hard disk into subdirectories.

As you begin to master working with your hard disk, you will find that getting around in it is not a very complicated process. You navigate your hard disk by taking certain simple steps. First, you activate the correct disk drive (select the correct filing cabinet). Next, you open the appropriate directory (the correct cabinet drawer). If necessary, you select the correct subdirectory (the manila folder). And finally, you choose from the available files (the pieces of paper from within the manila folders). On the surface, these steps might seem a little complicated considering the near limitless number of directories and subdirectories that you can create. However, as Chapter 1 points out, the Directory Assistant, a file listing available from within First Choice, has the job of helping you locate and retrieve all the First Choice files stored on your hard disk.

Now that you have an idea of the structure of a hard disk, you are ready to install or copy your First Choice files into a directory on your hard disk.

# Installing First Choice to Your Hard Disk

Assuming that you have made the appropriate backups of your First Choice disks to use in installation (see the earlier section), it's a simple procedure to install First Choice on your hard drive. To do this, complete the following steps:

1. If your computer is not yet turned on, do so now. Respond to the date and time prompts as necessary. (See Chapter 1 for details.) Your computer screen should show a DOS prompt, something like

    `C:\>`

    At this point, your computer is located at the root directory of your hard disk (The root directory is the highest level of your hard disk, as shown in Figure A-2). If your computer is already on, you should return to the root directory by typing

    `cd\`

    (meaning Change Directory—to the root directory) and pressing Enter.

2. The next step is to make a directory to store your First Choice files. To do this, use the Make Directory command by typing

    `md\CHOICE`

3. Press Enter. The backslash (\) in step 2 indicates that CHOICE is the name of the directory one level below the root directory. You can actually use any appropriate name for the directory to store your First Choice files.

4. Now that you have created the new CHOICE directory, you should change to that directory with the change directory command. Type

    `cd\CHOICE`

5. Then press Enter. You are now "in" the new directory.

6. Let's now copy the First Choice files into the CHOICE directory. To do this, insert the 5-1/4 inch floppy disk labeled PROGRAM DISK 1 into drive A. (If you have a 3-1/2 inch diskette, it's labeled PROGRAM DISK 1 and DICTIONARY DISK.)

7. To copy the files from your First Choice disk to your hard disk, type

   `copy a:*.*`

8. Then press Enter. (If you are using drive B, you would type `copy b:*.*` instead.) The files on the program disk will be copied into the current directory.

9. Repeat steps 6, 7, and 8 for each of the First Choice disks. Remember, you should be using backups of your First Choice disks, not the originals. When you have copied all the First Choice disks (there are either three 5-1/4 inch disks or two 3-1/2 inch disks) to the CHOICE directory on your hard disk, you are ready to start First Choice. The First Choice files are permanently stored on your hard disk until you remove or erase them.

# Customizing First Choice for Your System

Now that you have installed First Choice to your hard disk (or copied the program files onto floppies), you need to tell First Choice what type of monitor, printer, modem, etc. that you are using with your computer. Once you have given First Choice this information, the program remembers the information so it can work with your specific hardware. You only need to specify new information when you wish to make some hardware changes, such as using a different printer or monitor.

First Choice comes automatically configured to work with the following setup. If your computer's configuration (hardware setup) is different, then you need to go through all the setup options that will be discussed shortly. The standard setup is

- a monochrome or color monitor
- a parallel printer (such as a dot-matrix Epson printer) connected to the parallel port on your computer. The parallel port is generally called PRN or LPT1. (*Note:* even if you are using a parallel printer, you should tell First Choice which printer you have in order to use all of your printer's features.)

● an unlisted modem connected to the serial port named COM1. The term "unlisted modem" means a modem not listed on the Modem screen, as you will learn later.

● a touch-tone phone

*You can change your mind about any setup option and return to the Setup menu by pressing Esc.*

The first step to configuring First Choice to work with your system, is to start First Choice (type FIRST) and then choose the **Set up First Choice** command, item 8, from the Main menu. (If necessary, see the section entitled "Quick Start to First Choice" in Chapter 1.) The Setup menu of First Choice appears, as shown in Figure A-3. In the sections that follow, we will briefly review all of the setup options. If you wish to back out of any decision and return to the Setup menu at any time, simply press the Esc key or choose item 8, **Return to Main Menu**.

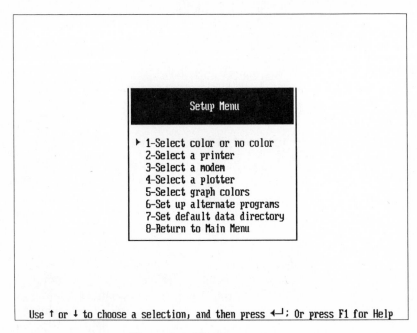

**Figure A-3.** The Setup menu.

## Choosing Your Monitor

For those of you with a color monitor, you can choose a specific color scheme by choosing the **Select color or no color** option from the Setup menu. Choosing this option provides three choices, as shown in Figure A-4.

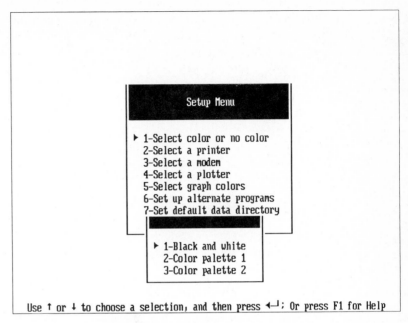

**Figure A-4.** Making the color selection.

For most monochrome or color monitors, you probably won't need to change any settings on the color selection screen in order to use First Choice. For example, if you have a monochrome monitor with a color graphics card (CGA), the background of your screen will probably appear very bright. In this case, you should accept the default **Black and White** option so that First Choice can display correctly. If your system does indeed have a color monitor, you can choose from two different sets of colors. In other words, you can choose either the **Color palette 1** or **Color palette 2** color scheme. These color schemes are preassigned by First Choice and cannot be mixed or altered. You can try one selection, view the results, and then change your mind by returning to the color selection screen and choosing a different color option. The selections are strictly a matter of personal preference.

To choose any of the color scheme options, simply select the option and press Enter, or type the number to the left of the color option.

## Choosing Your Printer

One of the most important setup options is the printer. First Choice requires two key pieces of information. First, it must know what type of

*Become familiar with your printer type before setting up your printer. If necessary, ask your dealer for information.*

printer you are using, and second, it must know where the printer is connected to your computer system (that is, to which port it is connected). The following steps are used to specify the printer options to First Choice. Even if you have the configuration assumed by First Choice—that is, a parallel printer connected to the LPT1 port, it's a good idea to follow these steps so that First Choice can take advantage of all of your printer's features.

1. If necessary, choose **Select a printer** from the Setup menu to display the Printer Selection screen. The screen will look like Figure A-5.

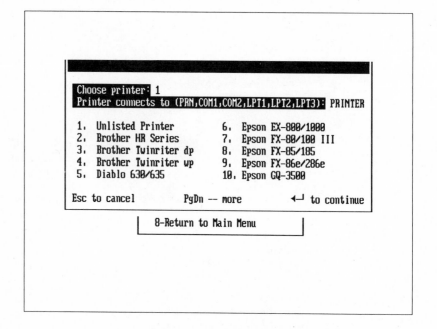

**Figure A-5.** Setting up your printer.

2. From the list of printers, find your particular printer. Use the PgDn key to scroll the list of printers. When you find your printer, type the corresponding number next to the **Choose printer** prompt and press Enter. If your printer doesn't appear in the list, try choosing item 1, **Unlisted printer**. When this option is selected, First Choice can fulfill some of the minimum printing requirements, such as boldface and underline. However, you won't be able to obtain other options, such as italic, superscript or subscript, compressed type, or correspondence quality for documents. Further, you won't be able to print graphs or slides.

3. The next step is to specify the port where your printer is connected to your computer system. If your printer is connected to LPT1, then you can simply press Enter to return to the Setup menu (and skip steps 4 and 5). If your printer is connected to a different port, press Tab to position the cursor on the **Printer connects to...** line.

4. Type in the name of the correct port. If you have a parallel printer (such as an Epson printer or HP Laserwriter), it will be connected to either PRN, LPT1, LPT2, or LPT3. If you have a serial printer, type either COM1 or COM2. Choosing COM1 or COM2 will prompt First Choice to ask for some additional information about your printer. If you don't know the answers (I suggest you read your printer's manual), then you can try and accept the default selections that First Choice will place on your screen. Again, you should always read your printer's manual or ask your dealer to determine the type of printer that you are using and any special settings that are required.

5. After you have made your selections, press Enter to return to the Setup menu.

If you can't find out which type of printer you have, then skip the printer selection process. By doing this, you accept the default options automatically set by First Choice.

## Choosing Your Modem

If you are planning to use First Choice to communicate with another computer, then you must have a modem connected to your computer. In order to use the modem, you must tell First Choice what type of modem you are using and which port it is connected to. You must also tell First Choice whether you are using a rotary or touchtone telephone line. To give this information to First Choice, complete the following steps:

1. From the Setup menu, choose **Select a modem**. The modem selection screen appears, as shown in Figure A-6.

2. At the **Modem** prompt, type the number corresponding to the type of modem that you are using. If you don't see your modem type, press PgDn to see more types. Once you have selected your modem type, press Enter. If you can't find your modem type, simply type 1 for **Unlisted modem**. Keep in mind, if you choose this option, you will be required to type commands manually rather than have First Choice (the modem) dial for you. *Note:* The

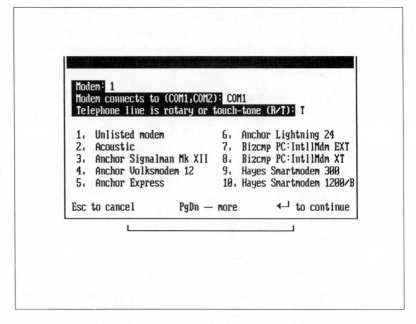

**Figure A-6.** The Modem Selection screen.

literature of some modem types says they are 100% compatible with another type of modem. In this case, find the compatible type of modem and select it.

3. Next, tell First Choice which port your modem is connected to—either COM1 or COM2. Press Tab to move to the **Modem connects to** prompt and type the appropriate port name. (Ask your dealer if you don't know which port is which.) In addition, if you have only one COM1 port on your computer, and you plan on using a mouse or printer connected to this port, you must still specify COM1 as your port selection. Then, when you are ready to use the modem, you must disconnect your mouse or printer before you can use it.

4. Press Tab to move to the **Telephone line is rotary or touchtone** prompt. Type R if you are using a rotary phone and T if your phone is a touch-tone type.

5. Press Enter when you have finished with all the modem selections. You will be returned to the Setup menu.

# Choosing Your Plotter

As with printers and modems, if you plan on using a plotter (a sophisticated printer that draws with pens), you must tell First Choice what type of plotter you have and where it is connected to your computer. To do this, complete these steps:

1. From the Setup menu, choose **Select a plotter**. The plotter selection screen appears, as Figure A-7 shows.

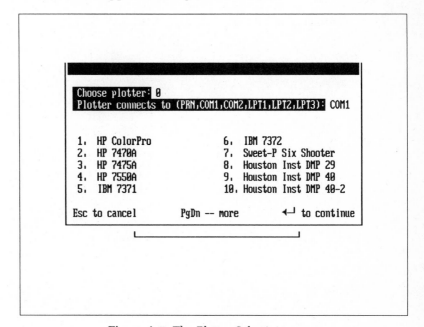

**Figure A-7.** The Plotter Selection screen.

2. From the list of available plotters, locate your plotter and type the corresponding number at the **Choose plotter** prompt. Use the PgDn key to see a second screen of plotter types.

3. Press Enter to return to the Setup menu. *Note:* If you selected COM1 or COM2 for a serial plotter type, then First Choice will request some additional technical details about your plotter. You can either enter the new information, or accept the default values supplied by First Choice. Always refer to your plotter's manual for the correct setting information.

## Choosing Graph Colors

If you have a color monitor, you can choose from three different sets of colors for graph displays. To do this, choose **Select graph colors** from the Setup menu. First Choice will offer the color scheme selections as shown in Figure A-8. Unfortunately, you won't know what the color scheme looks like until you actually try it out. Experiment with each of the color schemes by alternating between this menu and First Choice.

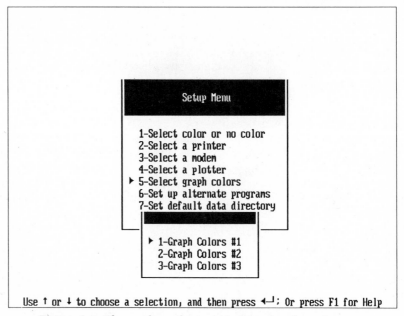

**Figure A-8.** Choose from three sets of graph color schemes.

## Adding Alternate Programs

First Choice provides a nifty feature to access other programs directly from the First Choice Main menu. Using the **Set up alternate programs** option from the Setup menu, you can add additional programs or even macros to the Main menu in order to save time by doing away with the need to leave First Choice before you can start up another program. For more information on using this option, refer to the section entitled "Adding to the Main Menu" in Chapter 12, *Utilities*.

# Setting the Default Data Directory

When you first begin working with First Choice, all of the files are saved by default in the same directory as the First Choice program files (for example, on a hard disk, the CHOICE directory). However, as you begin to create more and more files, and different kinds of them, such as document files, spreadsheet files, graph files, and so on, you may decide that they require some additional organization. For instance, suppose that it is common for you to work on one kind of file—say, word processing—for a certain period of time, perhaps a week, and then work on another kind of file—say, spreadsheets—the next week. Wouldn't it be convenient if all files of the same type were kept together in a place separate from other file types, and if First Choice automatically placed your files in the appropriate group when you saved them?

As a matter of fact, First Choice gives you this option. You can create a specific "data" directory (as a new directory or subdirectory) for saving files and specify it as the new default directory. For example, you can specify one directory for sales letters (created with the word processor) as LETTERS, and one directory for daily sales reports (created with the spreadsheet) as REPORTS (but remember that these are different from the printed summaries of database files described in Chapter 8, which are also called reports). The advantage is that the new data directory will automatically receive all the files that you create, modify and access most often. Thus, when you save and retrieve files and the Directory Assistant appears, it will automatically have the drive and directory (or subdirectory) that you specified as a default. If you work mainly on spreadsheet files during week one, then perhaps the REPORTS (or the name you specify) directory should be made the default directory for that week. If you work with the word processor most often the next week, you can make that specific directory the default directory for week two, and so on. The key is to set the one that you will work with the most often as the default directory.

Keep in mind though, that making a specific directory the default directory doesn't prevent you from moving from one directory to another within the Directory Assistant. In order to look into another directory, simply type the directory path when you enter the file name on the Directory Assistant screen. In other words, to look for a file in a subdirectory named LETTERS, type

    C:\CHOICE\LETTERS

at the file prompt and then press Enter.

To specify a new default data directory, select **Set default data directory** from the Setup menu. The screen shown in Figure A-9 appears.

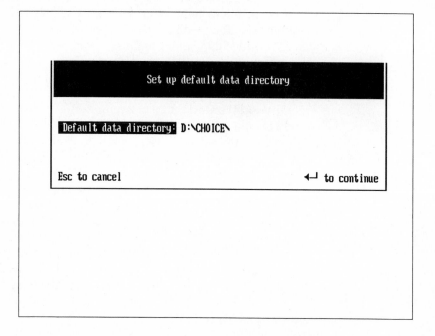

**Figure A-9.** The Default Directory screen.

Type the name of the new default data directory, including the directory path. For example, you might type

`C:\CHOICE\REPORTS`

to tell First Choice that the new default data subdirectory is REPORTS (within the directory named CHOICE). After you have specified the new subdirectory path, press Enter. First Choice will return to the Setup menu.

*Note:* Before you can specify a new directory as the default directory, that directory must exist in the first place. To create a new directory, you can use either the **Disk utilities** option from the Main menu (see Chapter 12 for more information) or use the DOS Make Directory command, **MD**, at the DOS prompt before you start First

Choice. For example, to create a directory called DATA under the root directory, you would type

    MD\DATA

If you're unsure at this time whether you'll need subdirectories, or whether you'll need to specify a default directory, no problem. You can access the Setup menu at any time in the future and make these adjustments.

## Exiting the Setup Menu

After you have made all your equipment specifications, if you haven't returned to the Setup menu yet, return to the Setup menu by pressing Esc repeatedly. When you are at the Setup menu, simply choose **Return to Main Menu**. The Main menu will soon appear on your screen.

# INDEX

@VLOOKUP spreadsheet
function, 319
@YEAR spreadsheet function,
317
FV ON...AT...OVER calculator
keyword, 399

# G

generating mailing labels, 470-472
Get an existing file command, 4-6,
8, 44, 113-114, 153-160, 162-163,
197, 292, 310-311, 460, 463-466
Get ASCII data command, 192-193,
197
GOTO form program statements,
215-219
GRA file extension, 5-6, 378-379
graph
colors, selecting, 488
formats, 360
options, 375-378
Graph File Format dialog box,
463-464
Graph information form, 366-373,
377-378
pasting spreadsheet data,
371-373
Graph options menu
Choose options, 375-378
Draw graph, 377-378
Enter titles, 374-375
Set graph type, 373
Graph titles screen, 375
graph types
area, 353, 360, 363
bar, 353, 360, 362
column, 353, 360, 364-365
combination, 353, 360, 362-363
high/low/close, 353, 360,
363-365
line, 353, 360, 362
linked, 353, 360
pie, 353, 360, 364-365
stacked bar, 353, 360
graphics, work area, 10
Graphics menu

Choose options, 354-355
Draw graph, 354-356
Select or create a graph,
349-351, 356
Set graph type, 353
graphing spreadsheet data, 349-356
graphs, 359-389
adding to slides, 386-387
creating, 364-378
data series, 360
graph formats, 360
labels, 360, 362, 367-369
legends, 360, 362, 367-369
moving into word processor
document, 463-466
pasting spreadsheet data,
371-373
printing, 379-380
retrieving, 378-379
saving, 379
setting options, 373

# H

@HLOOKUP spreadsheet function,
319
@HOUR spreadsheet function, 317
halting macro execution, 422
hard disk
backing up, 476-480
installing First Choice, 480-481
starting First Choice, 2-3
hard disks, 38
hard returns, 33
headers, creating, 71-74
headings
database, reports, 261-262
spreadsheet, 295-297
Headings on every page option,
262
Help, 22, 27
command, 10
menu, 8
Hide rulers command, 66
hiding ruler line, 66
high/low/close graph, 353, 360,
363-365

# First Choice Keywords

| KEYWORD | OPERATION | KEYWORD | OPERATION |
|---|---|---|---|
| **Date and Time** | | **Mathematical** | |
| @DATE | Converts numbers to a First Choice date | @ROUND..TO | Rounds a value to the number of places specified |
| @DATEVAL | Converts a text date to a First Choice date value | @SIN | Isolates the sine of an angle, given in radians |
| @DAY | Isolates the day of month from a date value | @SQRT | Determines the square root of a value |
| @HOUR | Isolates the hour from a time number value | @TAN | Isolates the tangent of an angle, given in radians |
| @MINUTE | Isolates the minute from a time number value | **Statistical** | |
| @MONTH | Isolates the month from a date value | @AVERAGE or AVG | Computes the average mean of a range of cells |
| @NOW | Determines the current date and time | @COUNT | Computes how many non-blank cells in a range of cells |
| @SECOND or SEC | Isolates the second from a time number value | @MAX | Computes the largest value in a range of cells |
| @TIME | Determines the time number from a First Choice time number value | @MIN | Computes the smallest value in a range of cells |
| @TIMEVAL | Converts the text time value to a First Choice time number value | @RANDOM or RAND | Generates a random number between 0.0 and 1.0 |
| @YEAR | Isolates a year from a date number value | @STDEV or STD | Computes the standard deviation |
| **Mathematical** | | @TOTAL or TOT | Computes the sum or total within a range of cells |
| @ABS | Converts any number to a positive value | @VARIANCE or VAR | Computes the variance of the values in a range |
| @ACOS(value) | Isolates a value equal to an angle in radians whose cosine is value | **Financial** | |
| @ASIN(value) | Isolates a value equal to an angle in radians whose sine is value | @CTERM | Computes the number of compounding periods required for an initial sum to grow to a particular future value |
| @ATAN(value) | Isolates a value equal to an angle in radians whose tangent is value | @DDB | Computes depreciation using the double-declining balance method |
| @COS | Isolates the cosine of an angle, given in radians | @FV | Computes the future value of regular payments |
| @EXP | Determines the natural exponential or power of e. | @INTEREST | Computes the interest paid on an amount given a time period of regular payments |
| @FRACT | Isolates the decimal value only of a fraction | @NPV | Computes the net present value of an investment |
| @INTEGER or INT | Isolates the whole number value only of a fraction | @PAYMENT or PMT | Computes the payment on a loan |
| @LN | Determines the natural logarithm or base e | @PV | Computes the present value of a regular annuity |
| @LOG | Determines the common logarithm or base 10 | @RATE | Calculates the interest rate required to accumulate a specific amount |
| @MOD | Isolates the modulus or remainder only of one value divided by another | @SLN | Computes depreciation using the straight-line method |
| @PI | First Choice uses the value: 3.141592653589793 as PI | | |